CONTENTS 1990

CONTENTS 1991–1992

THE

BEST

AMERICAN

SHORT

PLAYS

1990

To Marianne
who is playful

INTRODUCTION

The short play in modern literature has made a significant impact on the international scene. *Riders to the Sea* in 1902 seemed to firmly establish the form's durability when W.B. Yeats declared at the first reading of Synge's script: "Sophocles! No, Aeschylus!" Yeat's proclamation and others like it began to etch the short play into our dramatic repertoire. James M. Barrie's domestic melodrama, *The Twelve Pound Look* conjured up all the familiar turn-of-the-century elements of the well-made play but in the iconoclastic one-act form. Barrie's short piece was to become a model of structure and theatricality for decades to come. The commercial viability of the form was proven by Noel Coward. Coward charmed Broadway and the West End with his series of one-acts, *Tonight at Eight-Thirty,* which made history as well as Gertrude Lawrence.

A few decades later, the European theatrical revolution of the 50s was led by the short plays of Jean Genet, Eugene Ionesco, and Samuel Beckett. These works—*Deathwatch, The Bald Soprano, Krapps Last Tape*—marked the beginning of what Martin Esslin has called The Theatre of the Absurd, a movement for which the short play was a seminal construct. These plays dramatized a vision of a world no longer informed by the traditional logic of cause and effect. In the conventional world that stated, "If this happens, then this results," the dramatist naturally wrote with a beginning, a middle and an end . . . in that order. Such a causal construct determined a neat three-act format where even the most tragic, chaotic action was secured with the latent comfort of cause and effect: If this happens, then this follows, and then this results."

But the Absurd world posited chance rather than logic or predictable intelligence as its informing principle. Instead of giving us a logical episodic story, dramatic action now unfurled in a series of disjointed experiences which illustrated in form and content the absurdity of existence. The tight, immediate absorbing, and captivating structure of the short play accurately reflected the purpose and vision of the absurd sensibility. Esslin, quoting the words of Albert Camus, describes the world view from this absurdist perspective: "Out of harmony . . . devoid of purpose . . . cut off from his religious, metaphysical and transcendental roots . . . man is lost; all his actions become senseless, absurd, useless."

A play became a forty-five minute inventive, imaginative treatment of the vision of an absurd universe. This radical vision which first took dramatic shape in the short plays of Beckett and others would become the informing vision of modern plays, long and short.

The short play in America has played a major role in the evolution of twentieth-century American theater. In the summer of 1915, George Cram Cook and the Provincetown Players made their historic discovery of Eugene O'Neill with his one-act play, *Bound For Cardiff.* In October of 1917, the Washington Square Players introduced O'Neill to New York with their production of his one-act play, *In The Zone.* Tennessee Williams was published in *Best One Acts of 1944,* then edited by Margaret Mayorga, before he became the celebrated writer of *The Glass Menagerie* and *Streetcar Named Desire.* Years after his first appearance in this series, he returned to his short plays (such as Lady of *Larkspur Lotion* and *Ten Blocks on the Camino Real*) for much of his material, stamina and muscle.

The play from which *Fiddler on the Roof* was fashioned premiered first as a short play in the 1959–60 edition under the title of *Tevya and the First Daughter.* Edward Albee came on the theater scene with the production of his short play, *The Zoo Story,* in 1960, but he had already debuted in *Best Short Plays 1959–1960,* with his play *The Sandbox.* Albee has returned to the short play form many times, and unlike the other playwrights mentioned, he has never really abandoned the form.

Albee has never tried extending one of his short pieces into a longer work, the way Miller extended *View from the Bridge* or the way Williams extended *Ten Blocks on the Camino Real* to *Sixteen Blocks on the Camino Real.* Some recent playwrights have followed the Miller-Williams impulse but to less salubrious results. *Open Admissions,* Shirley Lauro's tightly wrought short play published in *Best Short Plays of 1984,* lost much of its vigor in an attenuated Broadway version. Aaron Sorkin's wonderful one-act, *Hidden in This Picture,* published here for the first time, was extended to a "full evening" in the theatre under the title, *Making Movies.* The potency of the original had become somewhat diluted and diffuse; the result was not a fuller experience, but a strangely bloated one.

The short play is not easily tampered with. The form is complete unto itself, but many of us like tinkering with it, behaving as if the child should be allowed to develop into an adult. The fact is, as Albee insists, that a play must be as long as it has to be. A sonnet does not become a better or fuller poem when a fifteenth line is added. It becomes a different poem in a different form. We have attempted to collect here scripts that fulfill their own sense of mission; no more, no less. If any one of these fragile organisms is to be pumped up or transformed into another larger creature, let that maker beware.

For many theatre people, the short play remains insufficient. It offers merely a condition, a situation, a moment, a circumstance of fixed and limited insight, an event without resonance or sustained mystery. For James Joyce such was his judgment of *Riders to the Sea*. Padraic Colum once told me that Joyce refused to confer on Synge's play any tragic stature because it fell short "of a certain magnitude." When Colum challenged him, claiming that the keening scene in which the mourners fill the stage with their red petticoats was so overwhelmingly painful that it was the equal of any tragic dimension, Joyce dismissed Colum with a shaking of the head and a flipping of the hand. Aristotle's maxim required the kind of length, substance and resonance which could not be fulfilled within the forty minutes which Synge allowed himself.

Such a grudging attitude remains, and perhaps with some justification. But another attitude should be welcomed. Just as one might catch a glimpse of the truth from the corner of one's eye (as Berenice claims in *Member of the Wedding),* so one is apt to catch a significant moment of truth through the narrow aperture of the short play. Such an experience may not have Aristototelian magnitude but it may penetrate nonetheless with the insight of that epiphanic moment—as potent, one might suggest, as any of Joyce's short stories in the *Dubliners.*

Just as Yeat's Irish Airman foresees his death after acting on a lonely impulse of delight, so we gain an awareness and richness as a result of a similar lonely impulse of invention which informs and nurtures a short play. What we miss, of course, is the tapestry of reverberation, the Gloucester plot which compounds and embroiders Lear's own story; the Laertes and Fortinbras' stories which extend the credence and profundity of Hamlet's own tale. These enriching dimensions are not usually available in the short play. But the absence of that intricate echo in the short play does not mute its own piercing laser-like siren.

Our experimental life is made up of an endless variety of confrontations, observations, and encounters. The short play delivers a fulcrum into that experimental life. It vouchsafes us a brief super-charged dramatic encounter which may reverberate beyond its longevity on stage. It has a habit of teasing, of arousing a desire for more, a yearning to continue when it suddenly stops in its tracks and allows the audience to imaginatively extend the action.

My first experience with *Best Short Plays* came in the late '40s when the series was called *The Best One-Act Plays*, under the editorship of Margaret Mayorga. My playwriting teacher at Columbia, Theodore Apstein, was a contributor to the volume almost annually. He, in turn, had been introduced to the series by his teacher at the University of Texas, E.P. Conkle, whose first play in the 1938 series, *Hawk A'-Flyin'*, was in 1939. My first play in the series, *In Darkness*, appeared in the '51–'52 season, my second play, *Sight for Sore Thoughts*, in the '59–'60 edition. Here, in *The Best Short Plays of 1990*, three of my former students (Christopher Durang, Alan Knee, and Wendy Wasserstein) continue that tradition started by E.P. Conkle. The thread of the narrative is the thread of humanity.

Glenn Young and I are proud to continue the masterful stewardship of Ramon Delgado whose insight and dedication propelled the series through the 1980s. May we equal the eloquence of his selections in the decades to come.

HOWARD STEIN
Columbia University
April, 1991

SALAAM, HUEY NEWTON, SALAAM

(taken from the autobiography of Marvin X, a work in progress)

Ed Bullins

Ed Bullins

Mr. Bullins is Producing Playwright of The BMT Theatre of Emeryville, California. He teaches African American Humanities and Theatre (literature, history and critical ideology) at Contra Costa College in San Pablo, California. He recently co-wrote with Idris Ackamoor the musical drama, *I Think It's Gonna Turn Out Fine,* which was done last year at Manhattan's La Mama E.T.C. and in Japan, and is being done in Vienna, Austria, this year. Bullins also wrote with Ackamoor the autobiographical play, *American Griot,* which premiered at La Mama last winter.

Mr. Bullins has written many plays, many of them produced throughout the United States and abroad. Among his better-known works is *The Taking of Miss Janie (Best American Play/1974–75/*New York Drama Critics), *The Duplex, The Electronic Nigger* (Obie, Drama Desk Award) and *A Son, Come Home* (Obie Award). He is the author of collections of his own plays, a novel and a book of short prose—*The Hungered One, The Duplex, Four Dynamite Plays, The Theme is Blackness* (all Morrow), *The Reluctant Rapist* (Harper & Row) and *Five Plays by Ed Bullins* (Bobbs-Merrill). He has edited two anthologies of plays: *New Plays From the Black Theatre* (Bantam) and *The New Lafayette Theatre Presents* (Doubleday/Anchor).

Characters

MARVIN X (a.k.a. Marvin Jackmon)
YOUNG BROTHER
HUEY P. NEWTON

Setting:

West Oakland, a street corner beside the now fallen Cypress Expressway.

(A FIGURE *sits upon a garbage can, in shadows from the project homes on the street. The time is now. The* FIGURE *lights a butane lighter and applies it to a crack pipe. As the stage lights rise, he sucks at the pipe and speaks)*

MARVIN: *(Smokes)* Yeah . . . I tried to help him . . . but I couldn't . . . I couldn't help Huey because I was sick myself . . . The Bible says when the blind lead the blind, they both fall in the ditch together . . . The last time I saw Huey alive was in front of this same crack house here in West Oakland's infamous Acorn housing project, right next to the Cypress freeway that was devastated during the October 17, 1990 earthquake.

In 1984 I became addicted to crack cocaine . . . Many people, especially members of my family, found my addiction difficult to understand. "You're so strong," they would say. "How could you become a weak, pitiful dope fiend?" But I did . . . My addiction came in my fortieth year, for many people, a time of disillusionment with life, and certainly it was for me . . . I was burnt out . . . Tired of revolution, tired of family life, sex and women, tired of working in the educational system, tired of the black middle class and the grass roots, tired of religious sectarianism, Christian and Muslim alike, tired . . .

Maybe this is what happens when one lives too fast. You not only get burned out, but you run out of ideas . . . What mountain shall I conquer next? . . . And a voice came to me and said: "You shall become Sisyphus. You shall roll a rock up a mountain and it shall fall to earth, and you shall begin again each day for eternity, since you can't figure out anything else to do, you big dummy!"

So I was a sitting duck for an addiction, that is, a new addiction, especially when I became an entrepreneur and had large sums of cash on a daily basis. Yeah, I sold incense and perfume oils and lots of stuff on the street at Market and Powell in San Francisco. I made a lot of quick, easy money . . . And money added to my problems because I hated making money. I actually felt guilty about it and had to do something with all that money I had . . . So my friends, including my so-called Muslim brothers, introduced me to crack . . . I didn't like sniffing cocaine. For one reason, my mind is naturally speedy, so I did not want anything to speed it up more. I wanted to slow down, relax. My thing was weed. I admit, I abused weed because I smoked it from morning 'til night for over twenty years . . . My thing was weed, wine and women. I always said I wanted to die from an overdose of weed, wine and women, but along came crack and soon I had no desire for wine, weed or women. With all my knowledge, I had forgotten the simple rules of life: for every blues, there is a happy song—sing a happy song—it takes the same energy as the blues . . . Even before my addiction to crack, why couldn't I think of all the good in my life? Why couldn't I sing songs of praise to Allah, my God, for the beautiful parents He had blessed me with, for my beautiful brothers and sisters, for the beautiful, intelligent women I had had, for the most beautiful children any man could imagine? Why? Why? Why? . . . Yes, I know now . . . because I thought I was self-sufficient.

I had sat and watched my friends smoking crack, but at first it didn't interest me. I did not like the way they behaved . . . I'd come into the room and they wouldn't even look up and acknowledge my presence. They were all staring at whoever had the pipe . . . But finally, the devil caught me, only because I forgot Allah.

(He chants)

> I lost my wife behind the pipe
> I lost my children
> behind the pipe
> I lost my money
> behind the pipe
> I lost my house
> behind the pipe
> I lost my mind
> behind the pipe
> I lost my life
> behind the pipe . . .

Yes, crack sent me to the mental hospital four times . . . Many times I put crack on my pipe and took that big 747 hit, and I could feel death coming, could feel my body surrounded by the strangest sensation. I would run to the window for air, or run outside for air. But after the moment of death had passed, I returned to my room and continued smoking . . . Once I accidentally cut my wrist, cut an artery. I dropped one of my pipes and grabbed at the broken pieces, cutting me critically, but I was unaware. I thought the bleeding would stop, but it didn't. I found my backup pipe and fired up . . . A friend tried to get me to go to the hospital, but I thought the blood would stop dripping from my wrist. It didn't. My new pipe became covered with blood. My dope had turned the color of blood. My clothes, the rug, the bed, the curtain, were all covered with blood. But I didn't stop. I kept on smoking . . . Finally, my friend got the hotel manager and he came in with a baseball bat and forced me out of the room . . . The paramedics came and took me to the hospital . . . Ha ha ha . . . after the emergency room crew stitched my wound, I got on the bus and returned to my room to finish smoking . . . Hell, I still had sixty bucks . . . fuck it!

(Lights change. MARVIN *pockets his pipe)*

The last time I saw Huey, I had gone to Acorn projects to buy drugs. My dope friend had told me Huey was there almost every day. "Oh, yeah?" I said, eager to see my friend. And my dope friend said, "Yeah, dude, he's usually over by the basketball courts."

(Lights change. YOUNG BROTHER *enters)*

(To YOUNG BROTHER) Hey, man, I'm finished with this little bit of crack. You come over here to Oakland from Frisco. I know you got some money. Let's go get some more shit.

YOUNG BROTHER: I'm ready for it, Marvin, man.

MARVIN: Hey, maybe we'll run into Huey.

(They start off)

MARVIN: *(Continues/narrating)* We walked toward the basketball court . . . A brother passed us looking like the bum of the week . . .

(A FIGURE *enters, passing* MARVIN *and* YOUNG BROTHER)

(MARVIN *continues narrating)* . . . Now I don't recall if I was looking a hell of a lot better . . . maybe a little better, since I was in a drug program at Glide Church in San Francisco. Reverend Cecil Williams was doing everything he could to help me regain my sanity . . . *(Calls to* FIGURE*)* Say, brother . . . don't I know you?

(The FIGURE *half-turns and looks at* MARVIN *and* YOUNG BROTHER*)*

(Narrates) But the bum needed a shave and a haircut. Something told me this bum was my old friend . . . so I called him. Hey, Huey!

(The FIGURE *walks toward* MARVIN*)*

HUEY NEWTON: Hey, Jackmon . . . what's happening?

*(*HUEY *and* MARVIN *embrace. Then* MARVIN, *hands upon each of* HUEY'S *shoulders, looks at him closely)*

MARVIN: *(Proudly)* Dr. Huey P. Newton.

HUEY: *(Matter-of-fact)* Yeah, man . . . So what's happening?

MARVIN: Ain't much, just trying to get some D. You want to get loaded?

HUEY: Yeah, Jackmon, why not?

MARVIN: Well, hold on a minute, let me go cop. *(To* YOUNG BROTHER*)* Hey, man, let me hold some of that money.

*(*YOUNG BROTHER *gives* MARVIN *a bill)*

YOUNG BROTHER: *(To* MARVIN*)* Get a small one, man.

MARVIN: *(To* YOUNG BROTHER*)* Okay, man. Just stay here with Huey.

(Lights change. Music rises softly. HUEY *and* YOUNG BROTHER *pantomime a conversation. Lights change again, as* MARVIN *returns)*

YOUNG BROTHER: I really respect you, Huey.

MARVIN: Got a spot we can go to, Huey?

HUEY: Yeah, man, let's go to my friend's house on Filbert. He'll be going to work in a minute. He gave me a key to hold, so I'll have someplace to go whenever I need one, so we won't be bothered.

(They stand half in shadows, half under the street light)

MARVIN: So how you been, Huey? People told me you be down here.

YOUNG BROTHER: Yeah, Huey, I really respect you.

HUEY: Look, Dude, I hear ya . . . I been all right, Marvin. *(To* YOUNG BROTHER) This brother was my teacher, young blood. Many of our comrades came through his black theatre.

MARVIN: Well, you taught me a few things too, Huey. Remember all them books you turned me on to: *Facing Mount Kenya, Black Bourgeoisie, Myth of the Negro Past* . . .

HUEY: *(Laughs)* Okay, Jackmon. We taught each other . . . how's that?

(MARVIN *and* HUEY *slap five)*

MARVIN: Yeah, that'll work.

(They enter a run-down Victorian)

HUEY: This is where I'm at for now . . . Yeah, I know what you're thinking. It's a long way from the penthouse I used to live in on Lakeshore Drive.

MARVIN: *(Smiles)* Well, brother, I wasn't trying to make any judgements, you understand?

(HUEY *pulls out his pipe.* MARVIN *takes a small plastic bag from his pocket, extracts a small pebble-like thing and puts it on* HUEY's *pipe)*

YOUNG BROTHER: *(To* HUEY) Yeah, I respect you.

HUEY: *(Irritated)* Hey, brother, don't tell me that again, please. When you keep saying you respect me, it's obvious that you are disrespecting me. Now, me and Jackmon are talking. He's my old friend. We go all the way back to Oakland City College. 1962 . . . And I wish you wouldn't interrupt our conversation again.

MARVIN: *(To* YOUNG BROTHER) Yeah, just cool it . . . Here, get you a hit. *(He gives* YOUNG BROTHER *some drugs)* If you just sit back and chill, you might learn something, young blood.

YOUNG BROTHER: Well, man, I'm not trying to disrespect anybody, but I got a right to say what I want to say. I don't care who he is, man.

MARVIN: *(Narrates)* I waved my hand to tell my young friend to chill. After all, Huey was one of the craziest black men in the hells of North America, but young blood was determined . . . Maybe he was tweaking.

YOUNG BROTHER: *(To* HUEY) Man, you want to throw down . . . we can throw down.

MARVIN: *(Narrates)* Huey was really getting pissed. I think for my sake, he was trying hard to be cool. But I could see him beginning to move nervously in the style of the panther . . . ready to attack.

HUEY: *(To* YOUNG BROTHER) Look, dude, I'm not talking to you. Don't get in our conversation again. 'Cause we can throw down . . . You buff and everything, but you gonna have to kill me, 'cause I'm going to try to kill you. And if you don't kill me, I'm going to search for you to the ends of the earth to kill you . . . Am I telling him right, Jackmon?

MARVIN: *(Narrates)* This crack thing is something else . . . It always involves violence. I once asked everybody I knew who was doing crack about violence . . . and everybody knew what I meant. In rehab sessions . . . in jail . . . I would ask the same questions . . . and the answer was the same . . . there is always violence with crack smoking. *(To* YOUNG BROTHER) There it is, man. *(Embarrassed)* Just let us talk, dude. What the fuck wrong with you? Stop tweakin', nigguh!

YOUNG BROTHER: Yeah, okay, but you think I'm scared of him just because he was the leader of the Black Panther Party?

MARVIN: *(Ignoring* YOUNG BROTHER) Huey, how long you been fucking with this pipe, man?

HUEY: Aw, Jackmon, I don't know . . . two or three years. You know me, I like to do it all: crack, smack, alcohol, weed . . . see what I'm saying?

MARVIN: Yeah, you're what they call a poly-abuser.

HUEY: Is that right?

(They smoke)

Go on, take you a big blast, Jackmon.

MARVIN: *(Takes a hit)* Sho, you right.

HUEY: *(Gesturing)* This youngster here must think I'm a chump . . . I been on death row three times . . . now what have you done?

YOUNG BROTHER: *(High)* I been to jail, man, and that ain't nothin'. My daddy tells me that all the really bad mathafukkers are dead, man . . . Say, I done took mathafukkers out the box too, parna.

MARVIN: *(To* YOUNG BROTHER) Just shut up.

HUEY: What we gonna do about the present situation, Jackmon?

MARVIN: Well, it's a pretty bad situation. The Black army's on crack. And the General's on crack.

HUEY: We can come out of this, man. We came out of slavery . . . see what I'm saying?

MARVIN: Yeah, we're going to come out of it . . . or die as a race . . . as a nation. It's been five years for me, Huey, five years in the prison of my mind. I caused my family great pain and suffering, brother. I'm sure you have too, right?

HUEY: Right.

MARVIN: Caused my woman great pain, my mother and father, my children. For what? Some hot air? . . . You know we made great sacrifices during the revolution, but this ain't about nothing. What we doing now? . . . You look bad, Huey, you look terrible. We got to recover, brother.

HUEY: *(Sucks at pipe)* In time, Jackmon, in time . . . got another hit?

MARVIN: Sure, here. We both need to be hit upside the head with a baseball bat, so we can come back to reality and get back on the battlefield.

HUEY: We had to experience this, Jackmon.

MARVIN: Yeah, I know we did. And on one level, I'm thankful for the experience because I've learned so much about the human soul and the human mind, what the mind will do under certain circumstances . . . I'm sure you'll agree we've both learned some things no college in the world could teach us.

HUEY: You right. People do some pretty scandalous stuff on this crack. I've done some scandalous stuff myself . . . What about you, young blood?

YOUNG BROTHER: Yeah, I have too.

MARVIN: *(Narrating)* I used the parable of the man who was crucified, put into a tomb, but mysteriously, the rock was removed and the man came out, came back to life. And not only was he resurrected, but he ascended.

(To HUEY *and* YOUNG BROTHER*)* He ascended.

HUEY: Teach, Brother Jackmon.

MARVIN: Aw, man . . . I see this crack as the last weapon in the devil's arsenal for the Black nation . . . When we overcome this, he'll never be able to come at us again, not in this world or the next.

HUEY: On a lighter note, have you seen you-know-who lately?

MARVIN: *(Smiles)* Your buddy?

HUEY: *(Playing)* Naw, Jackmon, your buddy.

MARVIN: Don't see him much anymore. He tweaks too hard for me, gets real paranoid, thinks the FBI is following him . . . He be down here in Acorn buying dope. You'll run into him.

HUEY: I don't want to run into that cat. Eldridge Cleaver is out to lunch.

MARVIN: Huey, I have to tell you this. I was riding with him one day . . . you know he drives with dope in one hand and his pipe in the other. He said, "Man, you think the police is following us?" . . . Nigguh, hell naw, I said . . . ain't no police following you. For what? They want you to keep smoking. If they following you, they doing it to bring you some more dope . . . Eldridge said, "Man, if somebody else had told me that, I wouldn't have believed it." . . . The boy is sick, Huey, he's illing, and he's skinny as an Ethiopian. I can't deal with him . . . I wouldn't care if he had a house full of cocaine, I wouldn't want one hit from him . . . Think you and him will ever get together?

HUEY: Not in this life, Jackmon.

MARVIN: Why not?

HUEY: *(Serious)* It's like this, man . . . *(Pauses, takes deep breath)* Too many people lost their lives behind Eldridge. There's too much blood on the path between us, man. Too much blood. So even though I might want to get together with him . . . out of respect to the loved ones of those comrades who went down, I cannot deal with him. I will not deal with him.

MARVIN: Why not, Huey? . . . Hell, Arabs kill each other in Lebanon and Jordan, but the next day they're in the mosque praying together. King Hussein of Jordan massacred Palestinians, but Yassir Arafat is still talking with him. Why can't Black men come together in spite of the past?

HUEY: Not in this life, Jackmon, not in this life . . .

MARVIN: Change the channel, brother. You know our community needs signs and symbols of unity. You see what condition our youths are in. *(Points to* YOUNG BROTHER) Look at this fool sitting over there.

HUEY: Yeah, I know they disrespect us, Jackmon.

MARVIN: You're the general, get on your post, soldier. And I got to do the same thing or we're going to suffer a severe chastisement . . . we're suffering one right now.

HUEY: Right. The army is here, but with no discipline, no ideology, no program. We got to get back on the battlefield . . .

MARVIN: Yeah, before the battle is over. *(He stands to leave)* Well, Huey, we got to get back to the City.

HUEY: You staying in Frisco?

MARVIN: Yeah, for a minute. I'm in a drug program at Glide Church.

HUEY: Reverend Cecil Williams?

MARVIN: Yeah. Trying to get off crack. I blew it today.

HUEY: You know what they say, "one day at a time." But how's Cecil doing?

MARVIN: Man, the brother is trying to deal with us crack heads.

HUEY: He's got a hellava job.

MARVIN: Think he ain't? But he's trying his best, if we don't give him a nervous breakdown. He's a good brother, man, a real good brother. He loves me, man, gives me anything I ask him for, but he don't want to be no co-dependent . . . So we outta here, Huey.

(They all shake hands)

HUEY: *(To* YOUNG BROTHER*)* Take it easy, youngster. If you can be on death row three times and come out, you'll be a bad mathafukker like me.

YOUNG BROTHER: Sho, you right.

MARVIN: I'll run into you again, Huey.

HUEY: Yeah, get back with me, Jackmon.

MARVIN: As-Salaam-Alaikum.

HUEY: Wa alaikum-salaam.

(MARVIN *and* YOUNG BROTHER *turn and exit the space. Light off of* HUEY, *looking after them)*

(Light on MARVIN*)*

MARVIN: *(Narrates)* We made our way through Acorn projects, crossing the Cypress freeway that would soon come tumbling down, and entered the West Oakland BART station for the ride back to Frisco, ass out again, with barely enough money to get on the train. While we waited on the platform, I jammed the youth.

(Light on YOUNG BROTHER*)*

MARVIN: *(To* YOUNG BROTHER*)* Man, why you want to upset Huey? Don't you know he one of the craziest nigguhs in the world . . . and one of the most violent?

YOUNG BROTHER: Man, I don't care. I'm a man just like he is. He can end up in a box like anybody else.

MARVIN: You should have just sat there and listened.

YOUNG BROTHER: That nigguh can't stop me from talking. I ain't no chump.

MARVIN: That ain't the point. The point is to learn something from someone who took things to the bus stop and changed the course of history for Black people, white people and the world. He armed African Americans for self-defense against the police, the police who were murdering us in cold blood.

YOUNG BROTHER: Man, that's history. Now he ain't nothing but a dope fiend. So he can't tell me nothing.

MARVIN: Okay, man, change the channel.

(Lights down on YOUNG BROTHER. MARVIN *stands in his light and narrates)*

MARVIN: *(Continuing)* When we sat on the train, I thought about my friend, Huey P. Newton . . . Little did I know that this would be the last time I would see him alive . . . He was found murdered near the Cypress freeway on August 22, 1989.

For those of us still addicted to crack cocaine, we should feel blessed that we're still alive and have the chance to save our souls, for the sake of ourselves, our families and our community . . . I have no doubt that I will fully recover from crack. Each day I get stronger and stronger. I shall return to the battlefield. I have no choice except to fight or die. For sure, the Black Nation is at war with America. America is using chemical and germ warfare against us—crack, AIDS—along with an infinite supply of guns for our self-destruction.

The main weapon we have is our spirit. We must reclaim our spirit, which is the spirit of God. We are in Him and He is in us. When we forget this, we fall victim to the great lie that all is lost. Yeah, it's raining now, but look, see the sun coming through the clouds. See the rainbow?

Rise, my people. Rise from the projects, rise from the hills, rise and reclaim our souls. A warrior has fallen. But we must continue until victory. But the greatest battle is to win our own souls. And for that reminder, I thank you, Huey. Salaam, Huey, salaam . . .

(Lights down)

NAOMI IN THE LIVING ROOM

Christopher Durang

Christopher Durang

Born in Montclair, New Jersey, in 1949. BA, Harvard, 1971; MFA, Yale School of Drama, 1974. Author of *The Nature and the Purpose of the Universe, The Idiots Karamazov,* (co-authored by Albert Innaurato), *Titanic, The Vietnamization of New Jersey, A History of American Film* (begun at O'Neill National Playwrights Conference, regional theatres 1977, Broadway briefly 1978, Tony award nominee), *Das Lusitania Songspiel* (musical cabaret co-authored and performed with Sigourney Weaver off-Broadway 1980, for which Mr. Durang won a Drama Desk Award), *Sister Mary Ignatius Explains It All To You* (Obie Award 1980; off-Broadway run 1981–1983), *The Actor's Nightmare* (on the bill with *Sister Mary . .*), *Beyond Therapy,* (off-Broadway 1981; Broadway 1982), *Baby with the Bathwater* (Playwrights Horizons 1983), *The Marriage of Bette and Boo* (Public Theatre 1985; Obie Award 1985) and *Laughing Wild* (Playwrights Horizons 1987). All of his plays have had many productions in the United States and abroad.

Mr. Durang has completed four screenplays: for the Ladd Company (co-authored with Wendy Wasserstein), Warner Brothers, the Swann Group (a screenplay of *Sister Mary . .*), and a new screenplay for Herbert Ross. For television he has written *Carol and Carl and Whoopie and Robin* (for Carol Burnett) and for PBS' *Trying Times,* a teleplay called *The Visit* directed by Alan Arkin. He is presently creating a sitcom for the Fox network. Along with having acted on stage in plays of his own and others, he acted in the films *The Secret of My Success, Mr. North,* and the forthcoming *The Butcher's Wife.*

Mr. Durang is a member of the Dramatists Guild Council, a member of the Artistic board of Playwrights Horizons and a member of the Play Selection Committee for the Young Playwrights Festival from 1984 to the present. He has directed readings of new playwrights at the Young Playwrights Festival, Playwrights Horizons and NYU. From 1981 to 1982 he served as King of France. Awards and honors include: CBS Playwriting Fellowship (in residence at Yale Repertory Theatre); Rockefeller Foundation grant (in residence at Arena Stage, Washington, D.C); Guggenheim grant; Lecomte du Nouy Foundation grant; and the Kenyon Festival Theatre Playwriting Prize.

A collection of his work, *Christopher Durang Explains It All For You*, originally published by Avon, has been re-published by Grove Press. Grove Press has also published *Bette and Boo* and *Laughing Wild*.
He is also one-third of the cabaret act, *Chris Durang and Dawne*.

Scene:

A living room. Enter NAOMI, *followed by* JOHN *and* JOHNNA, *an attractive young couple.* JOHN *has a moustache and is dressed in a suit and tie.* JOHNNA *is wearing a dress with a string of pearls.* NAOMI, *though, looks odd.* NAOMI *plants herself somewhere definitive—by the mantlepiece, for instance—and gestures out toward the room.*

NAOMI: And this is the living room. And you've seen the dining room, and the bedroom, and the bathroom.

JOHN: Yes, I know. I used to live here.

NAOMI: The dining room is where we dine. The bedroom is where we go to bed. The bathroom is where we take a bath. The kitchen is where we . . . cook. That doesn't sound right. The kitchen is where we . . . collect kitsch. Hummel figurines, Statue of Liberty salt and pepper shakers, underpants that say Home of the Whopper, and so on. Kitsch. The kitchen is where we look at kitsch. The laundry room is where we do laundry. And the living room is where Hubert and I do all of our living. Our major living. So that's the living room.

JOHNNA: What do you use the cellar for?

NAOMI: *(Suspicious)* What?

JOHNNA: What do you use the cellar for?

NAOMI: We use the cellar to . . . we go to the cellar to . . . replenish our cells. We go to the attic to . . . practice our tics, our facial tics. *(Her face contorts variously)* And we go to the carport, to port the car. Whew! Please don't ask me any more questions, I'm afraid I may not have the strength to find the answers. *(Laughs uproariously)* Please, sit down, don't let my manner make you uncomfortable. Sit on one of the sitting devices, we use them for sitting in the living room.

(There is a couch and one chair to choose from. JOHN *and* JOHNNA *go to sit on the couch)*

NAOMI: *(Screams at them)* DON'T SIT THERE, I WANT TO SIT THERE!!!

*(*JOHN *and* JOHNNA *stand and look frightened.* NAOMI *charges over to the couch, and* JOHN *and* JOHNNA *almost have to run to avoid being sat on by her)*

Shits! Ingrates! It's my house, it's my living room. I didn't ask you, I
can ask you to leave.

*(JOHN and JOHNNA are still standing, and start to maybe edge out of the
room)*

No, no, sit down. Please, make yourselves at home, this is the living
room, it's where Rupert and I do all our living.

*(There's only one chair, so with some hesitation JOHNNA sits in the chair,
and JOHN stands behind her)*

(NAOMI stretches her arms out on the couch) Wow. Boy oh boy. I need a
big couch to sit on because I'M A BIG PERSONALITY!!!! *(Laughs
uproariously)* Tell me, are you two ever going to speak, or do I just have
to go on and on by myself, or WHAT!!!!!!

(NAOMI stares at JOHN and JOHNNA intensely. They hesitate but then speak)

JOHNNA: This is a very comfortable chair. I love it.

JOHN: Yes, thank you.

NAOMI: Go on.

JOHNNA: Ummmm, this morning I washed my hair, and then I dried it.
And we had coffee in the kitchen, didn't we, John?

JOHN: Yes, Johnna, we did.

JOHNNA: *(Pause, doesn't know what else to say)* And I love sitting in this
chair.

NAOMI: I think I want to sit in it, get up, get up.

*(NAOMI charges over, and JOHN and JOHNNA move away from it, standing
uncomfortable. NAOMI sits and moves around in the chair, luxuriating in
it)* Hmmmm, yes. Chair, chair. Chair in the living room. Hmmm, yes.
(Looks at JOHN and JOHNNA, shouts at them) Well, go sit down on the
fucking couch, you morons!

(JOHN and JOHNNA look startled, and sit on the couch)

(Screams off-stage) Leonard! Oh, Leonard! Come on in here in the
living room and have some conversation with us. You don't want me to
soak up everything our son says all by myself, do you? *(NAOMI stands*

and walks over to JOHN *and* JOHNNA *on the couch. She smiles at* JOHNNA)
You probably didn't know John was Herbert's and my son, did you?

JOHNNA: Yes, he told me. I've met you before, you know.

NAOMI: Shut up! *(Calls out)* Hubert! Rupert! Leonard! *(To them)* I hope
he's not dead. I wouldn't know what room to put him in.
We   don't   have   a   dead   room.   *(Smiles;   screams)*
AAAAAAAAAAAAAAAAAAAHHHHHHHHH! *(Looks   at   them)*
Goodness, my moods switch quickly. (NAOMI *sees a tiny stuffed pig in a
Santa Claus suit perched on the mantlepiece. With momentary interest,
she picks it up and looks at it, then puts it down again. Focusing on* JOHN
and JOHNNA *again; a good hostess)* Tell me all about yourselves, do you
have children? *(Sits, listens attentively)*

JOHNNA: We had five children but they all died in a car accident. The
baby sitter was taking them for a ride, and she was drunk. We were
very upset.

NAOMI: Uh huh. Do you like sitting on the couch?

JOHN: Mother, Johnna was telling you something sad.

NAOMI: Was she? I'm sorry, Johnna, tell it to me again.

JOHNNA: We had five children . . .

NAOMI: *(Tries to concentrate, but something impinges on her consciousness)*
Wait a minute, something's bothering me!!!! *(She rushes over to the
little stuffed Santa pig, snatches it up and throws it against the wall in a
fury)* This belongs in the kitchen, *not* in the living room. The living
room is for living, it is not meant for sincerely designed but ludicrously
corny artifacts! Kitsch! *(She sits down again)* Do you like Hummel
figurines?

JOHN: Very much. Now that the children are dead, Johnna and I have
begun to collect Hummel figurines, especially little boy shepherds and
little girl shepherdesses.

NAOMI: Uh, huh, isn't that interesting? Excuse me if I fall asleep. I'm not
tired yet, but I just want to apologize in advance in case your boring
talk puts me to sleep. I don't want to offend you. *(Screams)*
AAAAAAAAAAAAAAAAAAHHHHHHHHH! I'm   just   so   bored
I   could   scream.   Did   you   ever   hear   that   expression?
AAAAAAAAAAAAAAAAAAHHHHHHHHHHH!

JOHN: Excuse me, I want to change my clothes. I'm tired of my color scheme. Do you have a clothes changing room?

NAOMI: No, I don't have a clothes changing room, you certainly are an idiot. Use the bedroom or the bathroom. Really, children these days have no sense. In my day we killed them.

JOHN: *(To* JOHNNA*)* Excuse me, I'll be right back.

JOHNNA: Must you go?

JOHN: Darling, I don't feel comfortable in these colors. They're hurting my eyes.

JOHNNA: Well, bring it back.

JOHN: What?

JOHNNA: *(Sincere, confused)* I'm sorry, I don't know what I mean.

(JOHN *exits*)

He's constantly talking about his color scheme. It's my cross to bear, I guess. That and the death of the children.

NAOMI: So who the fuck are you, anyway?

JOHNNA: I'm Johnna. I'm married to your son. All our children recently were killed.

NAOMI: Stop talking about your children, I heard you the first time. God, some people can't get over their own little personal tragedies, what a great big crashing boor. Lots of people have it worse, girlie, so eat shit! *(Calls off-stage)* Hey, John, where did you get this turd of a wife, at the Salvation Army? I'd bring her back! *(Laughs uproariously)* Ahahahahahahahaha!

JOHNNA: I think I want to go.

NAOMI: Boy, you can't take criticism, can you? Sit down, let's have a conversation. This is the conversation pit. You can't leave the pit until you converse on at least five subjects with me. Starting now, go: *(Waits expectantly)*

JOHNNA: I was reading about Dan Quayle's grandmother the other day.

NAOMI: That's one. Go on.

JOHNNA: She said there should be prayer in the schools . . .

NAOMI: That's two. (NAOMI *starts to remove her boots, or high heeled shoes, in order to massage her feet*)

JOHNNA: And that we should have a strong defense . . .

NAOMI: That's three.

JOHNNA: And that the Supreme Court should repeal the Wade vs. Roe ruling that legalized abortions.

NAOMI: That's four.

JOHNNA: And that even in the case of pregnancy resulting from incest, she felt that the woman should be forced to carry the child through to term.

NAOMI: That's four-A.

JOHNNA: And then she said she hoped the mother would be forced to suffer and slave over a horrible job and take home a tiny teeny paycheck to pay for some hovel somewhere, and live in squalor with the teeny tiny baby, and that then she hoped she'd be sorry she ever had sexual intercourse.

NAOMI: That's still four-A.

JOHNNA: Don't you think she's lacking in Christian charity?

NAOMI: That's five, kind of. Yes, I do. But then so few people are true Christians anymore. I know I'm not. I'm a psychotic. *(She throws her boot in* JOHNNA's *direction)* Get up off the couch, I want to sit there. (NAOMI *rushes over,* JOHNNA *has to vacate fast. Then* NAOMI *starts to luxuriate in sitting in the couch, moving sensuously.* NAOMI *luxuriates all over it)* Oh, couch, couch, big couch in the living room. I have room to spread. Couch, couch, you are my manifest destiny. Mmmmm, yes, yes. *(Calls out)* Edward, hurry out here, I'm about to have an orgasm, you don't want to miss it. *(Back to herself)* Mmmmmm, yes, couch, couch pillows, me sitting on the couch in the living room, mmmmm, yes, mmmm. . . . no. *(Calls)* Forget it! It's not happening. *(To* JOHNNA*)* Tell me, can you switch moods like I can? Let me see you. (JOHNNA *stares for a moment)* No, go ahead, try.

JOHNNA: Very well. *(Happy)* I'm so happy, I'm so happy. *(Screams)* AAAAAAAH! Do you have chocolates for me? *(Desperate)*

I'm so sad, I'm so sad. Drop dead! *(Laughs hysterically)*
Ahahahahahahahaha! That's a good one! *(Looks at* NAOMI *for feed-back)*

NAOMI: Very phoney, I didn't believe you for a moment. *(Calls off-stage)*
Herbert! Are you there? *(To* JOHNNA*)* Tell me, do you think Shubert is
dead?

JOHNNA: You mean the composer?

NAOMI: Is he a composer? *(Calls out)* Lanford, are you a composer?
(Listens) He never answers. That's why I sometimes worry he might be
dead and, as I said, I don't have a room for a dead person. We might
build one on, and that would encourage the economy and prove the
Republicans right, but I don't understand politics, do you?

JOHNNA: Politics?

NAOMI: Politics, politics! What, are you deaf? Are you stupid? Are you
dead? Are you sitting in chair?

(Enter JOHN. *He is dressed just like* JOHNNA—*the same dress, pearls, stock-ings, shoes. He has shaved off his moustache, and he wears a wig that
resembles her hair, and has a bow in it like the one she has in her hair.
They look very similar)*

JOHN: Hello again.

NAOMI: You took off your moustache.

JOHN: I just feel so much better this way.

NAOMI: Uh huh.

JOHNNA: *(Deeply embarrassed)* John and I are in couples therapy because
of this. Dr. Cucharacha says his cross-dressing is an intense kind of co-
dependence.

NAOMI: If this Dr. Cucharacha cross-dresses, I wouldn't see him. That's
what John here is doing. Too many men in women's clothing, nothing
gets done!

JOHNNA: *(To* JOHN*)* Why do you humiliate me so this way?

JOHN: I want to be just like you. Say something so I can copy you.

JOHNNA: Oh, John. *(Does a feminine gesture and looks away)*

JOHN: Oh, John. *(Imitates her gesture)* That doesn't give me much. Say something else.

JOHNNA: Maybe it's in your genes.

JOHN: Maybe it's in your genes.

(JOHNNA, *in her discomfort, keeps touching her hair, her pearls, shaking her head, etc.* JOHN *imitates everything she does, glowing with glee. His imitations drive her crazy, and is undoubtedly part of what has them in couples therapy)*

NAOMI: This is a disgusting sight. *(Calls)* Sherbert, our son is prancing out here with his wife, you should really see this. *(To them)* I find this uncomfortable. This makes me want to vomit.

JOHNNA: Maybe we should go.

JOHN: Maybe we should go.

NAOMI: *(Upset)* How come you don't dress like me? How come you dress like her?

JOHN: I want to be noticed, but I don't want to be considered insane.

JOHNNA: John, please, just stay quiet and pose if you must, but no more talking.

NAOMI: Insane? Is he referring to someone in this room as insane? *(Calls)* Sally! Gretchen! Marsha! Felicity! *(To them)* I'm calling my army in here, and then we'll have some dead bodies.

JOHNNA: Maybe we should go.

JOHN: Maybe we should go. *(Keeps imitating* JOHNNA's *movements)*

JOHNNA: Will you stop that?

(NAOMI, *very upset and discombobulated, stands on the couch and begins to pace up and down on it)*

NAOMI: Insane, I'll give you insane! What's the capital of Madagascar? You don't know, do you? Now who's insane? What's the square root of 347? You don't know, do you? Well, get out of here, if you think I'm so crazy. If you want to dress like her and not like me, I don't want you here.

(NAOMI *lies down on the couch in a snit to continue her upset.* JOHN *begins to walk back and forth around the room, pretending he's on a fashion runway.* JOHNNA *slumps back in her chair and covers her eyes*)

I can have Christmas by myself, I can burn the Yule log by myself, I can wait for Santa by myself. I can pot geraniums. I can bob for apples. I can buy a gun in a store and shoot you. By myself! Do you get it? *(Stands and focuses back on them)* You're dead meat with me, both of you. You're ready for the crock pot. You're a crock of shit. Leave here. I don't need you, and you're dead!

(Pause)

JOHNNA: Well, I guess we should be going.

JOHN: Well, I guess we should be going.

(JOHNNA *and* JOHN, *looking the same and walking the same, leave the house.* NAOMI *chases after them to the door*)

NAOMI: Fuck you and the horse you came in on!

(JOHN *and* JOHNNA *exit.* NAOMI *comes back into the room and is overcome with grief. She sits back on the couch and lets out enormous, heartfelt sobs. They go on for quite a bit, but when they subside she's like an infant with a new thought, and she seems to be fairly contented)* Well, that was a nice visit.

(END)

THE MAN WHO CLIMBED THE PECAN TREES

Horton Foote

Horton Foote

Horton Foote has written plays, screenplays, and television plays. His plays include *Only The Heart, The Chase, The Trip To Bountiful, The Traveling Lady, John Turner Davis, The Midnight Caller, Tomorrow, A Young Lady of Property, Night Seasons, Courtship, Valentine's Day, 1918, A Coffin in Egypt, The Road to the Graveyard, Blind Date, The Land of the Astronauts, The Roads to Home, Pilgrims, Lily Dale, The Widow Claire, Cousins, The Death of Papa, The Habitation of Dragons, Dividing the Estate* and *Talking Pictures.*

His screenplays include *To Kill a Mockingbird, Baby the Rain Must Fall, Tomorrow, Tender Mercies, 1918, On Valentine's Day, Courtship* and *Convicts.* He received Academy Awards and Writer's Guild awards for *To Kill a Mockingbird* and *Tender Mercies.*

The Widow Claire was included in *The Best Plays of 1986–1987* and *John Turner Davis* and *Blind Date* in *Best Short Plays of 1953–54* and *1988,* respectively.

Cast:

MRS. CAMPBELL
BROTHER
DAVIS
STANLEY
BERTIE DEE

Place:
Harrison, Texas

Time:
September 1938

Scene:
The living room of the CAMPBELL house. MRS. CAMPBELL, 52, is there with her oldest son, BROTHER, 35.

MRS. CAMPBELL: Murray St. John just called and said Davis and Stanley had driven him to Iago and were on their way here.

BROTHER: Why did they take Murray St. John to Iago?

MRS. CAMPBELL: I don't know. I didn't ask him. *(She looks out the window)* The lights are on at Stanley's house. Bertie Dee is still awake. I would call over and tell her Stanley is with Davis, but I never know what kind of mood I'll find her in.

BROTHER: How long has Stanley been acting so strangely?

MRS. CAMPBELL: Well, he's been drinking heavily for a while. He comes over usually after supper to have a visit with me and the last few months I couldn't help but notice he was very full every time he came over. A number of times he would just go to sleep sitting right on that chair, and then after he would visit or sleep for a while, he would get up and say he had to go down to the office and do some work. I don't sleep too well since Daddy died and I would lie in bed after, listening for his car to come home. I would be nervous, you know, because of his drinking, afraid he'd get in a wreck. Anyway it would be later and later and later when I'd finally hear his car drive into his garage. Sometimes not until four in the morning and finally I called Davis and I said,

"Davis, come over here, I have to have a talk with you. Stanley is not getting home until four in the morning." "I know that," he said, "and we have certainly to face something. He is behaving peculiarly." "In what way?" I asked. "He is drinking," he said. "I am aware of that," I said, "although I pretend not to notice even when he goes off to sleep right in front of me." "Well," he said, "when he gets drunk late at night he goes down to the courthouse square and climbs the pecan trees. Someone saw him doing that one night, and now word has gotten around town," Davis said, "and people stay up all night just to watch him." "Does Bertie Dee know about this?" I asked. "Yes," he said. "And how does she take it?" "She told me," he said, "that she hoped he would fall and break his neck." And he said, "I said, 'Bertie Dee, you don't mean that.' 'Yes, I do,' she said." *(She cries)* I'm so glad Daddy didn't live to see how this marriage has turned out. She's very bitter and hard, you know. She does nothing at all to keep him from drinking. "Please ask him not to drink," I said to her the other day. "I don't care what he does," she said. "Think of your son," I said. "He shouldn't see his daddy drink all the time." "You ask him not to drink," she said, "since it worries you so much." *(He gets up)* Where are you going?

BROTHER: I'm going back to Houston.

MRS. CAMPBELL: Why? I thought you had come to spend the night.

BROTHER: I did. But I'm too nervous. All these troubles get me wild. I come down here to get away from my own troubles and all I hear are Stanley's troubles. Anyway I shouldn't come here.

MRS. CAMPBELL: Why, it's your home.

BROTHER: I lost seventy-five thousand dollars.

MRS. CAMPBELL: You didn't do it on purpose.

BROTHER: How could I have been such a fool? How could I have let Phil Beaufort deceive me so?

MRS. CAMPBELL: We were all deceived. I was. Davis. Stanley. Sarah . . .

BROTHER: But I was the original sap. I got you all involved. Why out of all the people in Harrison, Texas, did he pick me out to get involved in his scheme?

MRS. CAMPBELL: Don't look back.

BROTHER: Seventy-five thousand dollars!

MRS. CAMPBELL: I never look back. I have two wonderful daughters. One dead. Three wonderful sons . . .

BROTHER: I am a failure. A stupid failure!

MRS. CAMPBELL: You were president of the oil company for two years.

BROTHER: A fraudulent oil company.

MRS. CAMPBELL: Shh, I hear a car. Let's talk of happy, pleasant things in front of Stanley. (A pause) I miss Daddy. Those were happy times, when Daddy was alive and we were all living at home. "Who's your favorite?" Mrs. Harper asked me once. "I have none," I said. "Don't hand me that," she said. "You have a favorite. Everybody does." "I don't know about everybody," I said, "but I have five children and I love each one just as much as the others. Daddy and I live for our children," I said. "Our deepest wish is to see them all well and happy." (She cries)

BROTHER: Now, Mama. Please don't cry. You have been so brave.

MRS. CAMPBELL: I know. I don't mean to cry. I know everything is going to turn out all right. Baby Sister and Daddy are in heaven, so they are at peace. Davis is married and has a sweet, hardworking wife, a little sarcastic, but I don't let that upset me and he has two lovely sons. Stanley has this drinking problem. But if we're patient and understanding he'll overcome that, and you will soon land on your feet again. And you may not be president of an oil company, but you will be very successful. I am sure of that. And though your first marriage wasn't a success, your second marriage is a happy one. So let's all count our blessings. Let's don't just look on the gloomy side. Let's . . .

(DAVIS, 26 and STANLEY, 30, enter)

DAVIS: I asked Murray St. John to call you. Did he?

MRS. CAMPBELL: Yes. Why were you and Stanley in Iago with Murray St. John?

DAVIS: He was on the courthouse square when I got there. He needed a ride home.

MRS. CAMPBELL: Stanley, your brother is here. Say hello to your brother.

STANLEY: How is Phil Beaufort?

BROTHER: How would I know? I haven't seen him since the bankruptcy proceedings.

MRS. CAMPBELL: Now let's don't bring up unpleasant things. I want us all to count our blessings. I was doing that with Brother just before you came in.

STANLEY: Guess what Davis and I did.

DAVIS: Not Davis! You did. I had nothing to do with it.

MRS. CAMPBELL: What did you do? If it's something terrible I don't want to hear about it.

STANLEY: I called the Houston operator and I said, "I want the number in Houston of Philip Beaufort," and she found it for me, and I called him up.

MRS. CAMPBELL: When?

STANLEY: Just now. Davis took me by the office and I called him.

BROTHER: Oh, Jesus!

MRS. CAMPBELL: And what did he say?

STANLEY: He said, "What in the hell do you mean waking me up at this time of the night? Are you drunk?" "Drunk enough," I said, "to ask you a few questions. Why did you involve my brother in a fraudulent scheme that took all my mother's reserves? You have known us all your life. Why did you do this to us, Phil Beaufort? You are a monster," I said. "I am drunk enough to tell you that. We are all aware in this family the kind of monster you are. You married a sweet girl, named Marjorie Halliday, from Harrison, took her to Houston, bullied and mistreated her, and when her father tried to interfere you stabbed and killed him and hired a slick lawyer to get you off, saying it was self-defense."

MRS. CAMPBELL: And what did he say?

STANLEY: He hung up on me. I'm going to call him back.

DAVIS: No you're not!

STANLEY: The hell I'm not! I'm going to call him every day. I will never let him forget what he has done. Seventy-five thousand dollars! (STANLEY *sings*) "In the gloamin', Oh, my darlin' . . ." *(A pause)* Where is Marjorie Halliday?

MRS. CAMPBELL: She's in Houston. Dora Vaughn does social work and she says Marjorie and her children applied for relief. She says she has broken. She has married again. *(A pause)*

BROTHER: I have failed you all.

DAVIS: Oh, come on, Brother.

BROTHER: I can never get over my feeling of shame.

STANLEY: *(Singing)* "In the gloamin', Oh, my darlin' . . ." *(He gets up)* I am going back downtown. I have to write my editorial.

DAVIS: No, Stanley. You have done all your work for the week. You told me that.

STANLEY: Except for one editorial, I forgot.

DAVIS: Do it tomorrow.

STANLEY: No, tonight. *(He passes out)*

MRS. CAMPBELL: Was he up in the pecan trees when you got down there?

DAVIS: Yes.

MRS. CAMPBELL: Was he hard to get down?

DAVIS: And it's embarrassing, let me tell you. I feel like a fool standing there and begging him to come down out of the tree.

MRS. CAMPBELL: Oh, I hated to call you and ask you to go down there, but I didn't know who else to turn to. The night watchman called me and said he was drunk on the square and we'd better come for him. "I'll call Davis," I said. "I hate like sin to do it, but I will."

BROTHER: *(To DAVIS)* Did he call Phil Beaufort?

DAVIS: Yes.

BROTHER: Oh, Jesus!

DAVIS: I'm going home. I have to get up early in the morning.

BROTHER: Don't you think we'd better take him home first?

DAVIS: Bertie Dee won't let him in the house when he's drunk.

MRS. CAMPBELL: Let him sleep on the couch. He'll be all right there. (DAVIS *goes*) He stays here almost every night now. He just goes to sleep there on the couch. I said to Philip Beaufort once, you know, "How could you have done this to us? My sons trusted you. You've taken everything we have in a worthless scheme." "I did not think it was worthless," he said. "I lost too. I am bankrupt." "You will never prosper," I said. But he has. He has prospered. I understand he has a fine new house, a lovely car and is back in the oil business.

BROTHER: Yes, he is. I am leaving Houston, because everywhere I turn I see signs of his prosperity. It's making me sick. I am moving to Galveston, or Dallas, so I won't be constantly reminded of his prosperity.

(STANLEY *wakes up*)

STANLEY: Mama, I apologize.

MRS. CAMPBELL: Shh, now. That's all right.

STANLEY: I have not behaved like a gentleman and I apologize. Where is Brother?

MRS. CAMPBELL: Here he is.

STANLEY: Brother, please accept my apology.

BROTHER: You owe me no apology. I owe you one.

STANLEY: Why?

BROTHER: You know.

STANLEY: Forget it.

MRS. CAMPBELL: I am moved to tears by the sweetness of you both. You were always extremely loyal brothers growing up. Daddy used to say, "We should be very thankful our boys are so loyal to each other. They never think of themselves first, but only of each other. You never see one without the other."

STANLEY: (*Singing*) "In the gloamin', Oh my darlin' . . ." (*A pause*) I want to start all over. I want you and me and Davis to move back in here and start all over.

MRS. CAMPBELL: What about the girls?

STANLEY: What about them?

MRS. CAMPBELL: Don't you want them here too, with you starting all over?

STANLEY: Baby Sister is dead. Sarah is married to Wesley Cox and you know about Wesley Cox and Bertie Dee.

MRS. CAMPBELL: Oh, my God! Don't start that, Stanley!

STANLEY: I called him up too. I said, "Wesley Cox, I know all about you and Bertie Dee."

MRS. CAMPBELL: Oh, my God!

STANLEY: Let's start all over. Sarah, Baby Sister, Davis, Brother and me. How do you do that?

BROTHER: What?

STANLEY: Start all over.

BROTHER: I don't know.

STANLEY: *(Singing)* "In the gloamin', Oh my darlin' . . ."

(BERTIE DEE, *30, enters*)

MRS. CAMPBELL: Hello, Bertie Dee. Stanley just got here. Davis brought him. He was very tired so I told him to spend the night on the couch here. I was going to call you and tell you. I knew you hadn't gone to bed because your light was still on. Davis just left. He has to get up at five-thirty every morning. Brother, Stanley and I were just having a little talk about old times. Brother, say hello to Bertie Dee.

BROTHER: Hello, Bertie Dee. How's Son?

BERTIE DEE: Son is all right.

BROTHER: I guess he's grown quite a bit since I saw him last.

BERTIE DEE: I don't remember when you saw him last.

BROTHER: It's been at least three months. Is he asleep?

BERTIE DEE: Yes.

BROTHER: It seems every time I come to visit Mama, he's asleep.

BERTIE DEE: Stanley . . . *(He doesn't answer)* Stanley . . .

MRS. CAMPBELL: I think he's asleep, Bertie Dee. He was very tired. Davis said he was working late meeting a deadline for the paper.

BERTIE DEE: Stanley, don't play possum with me. *(She goes over to him. She shakes him)* Open your eyes! I said don't play possum with me. You don't fool me.

MRS. CAMPBELL: Stanley, are you asleep? See, I think he is asleep.

BERTIE DEE: He is not. He's pretending.

BROTHER: How is your father, Bertie Dee?

BERTIE DEE: What?

BROTHER: How is your father?

BERTIE DEE: He's all right.

MRS. CAMPBELL: Daddy and Mr. Graham were the closest of friends. They had coffee every morning together and every afternoon. They would go to Outlar's Drugstore in the morning for their coffee and to Rugeley's in the afternoon, so as not to hurt anyone's feelings. Their fondest wish was to see Bertie Dee and Stanley married. That was a happy day for the both of them, for all of us, let me tell you. Everyone said, "Aren't they young to be married?" I was married to Daddy at sixteen. We had many happy years together. If you remember, it was Mr. Graham who came here to tell me Daddy had died. He was crying like his heart would break, he was crying so he could hardly speak the words. He grieved so, Mr. Graham said, he lost ten pounds.

BROTHER: Bertie Dee, how is your mother?

BERTIE DEE: What?

BROTHER: How is your mother?

BERTIE DEE: She's all right.

MRS. CAMPBELL: She is a homebody just like me. Neither of us care for society.

BERTIE DEE: I'm not leaving here, Stanley, until you talk to me.

MRS. CAMPBELL: What do you want to talk about, Bertie Dee? Can't it wait until morning?

BERTIE DEE: No!

BROTHER: Maybe we should go into the other room, Mama, so they can have a private conversation.

BERTIE DEE: No. You both stay here. I want you to be witnesses to this conversation. *(She goes to* STANLEY. *She shakes him)* Stanley! Open your eyes! *(He does so)*

STANLEY: Well? . . .

BERTIE DEE: Are you crazy? I think he is. I think he should be locked up in the asylum in Austin.

MRS. CAMPBELL: Now don't say that, Bertie Dee.

BERTIE DEE: I do. Do you know what he just did? He called Wesley Cox in Port Arthur, waked him out of a sound sleep to accuse him of having an affair with me.

MRS. CAMPBELL: Oh, my God!

BERTIE DEE: He's crazy! He's insane!

STANLEY: Wesley Cox, Robert Ferguson, Willy Davis, I've called them all. I've called them all and told them no wool was being pulled over my eyes.

BERTIE DEE: He's insane, he's crazy, stark raving mad! Your son, your precious son, is crazy, insane!

MRS. CAMPBELL: He didn't know what he was doing or saying in the condition he's in. I'll get him to call them all up in the morning and explain the condition he was in. I'll call Wesley Cox now myself, to explain. Wesley Cox is very understanding. He's a fine boy, like one of my own sons. Now you go home and get your rest, and Stanley will get his rest, and in the morning I'll have a good long talk with Stanley. And Davis will and Brother will and I am sure we can once and for all get him to see how foolishly he is behaving. *(A pause)* We all have our troubles. Mrs. Lehigh was here this afternoon to tell me about the Jacksons. She said she thought it would make me feel better to learn that we were not the only ones taken advantage of by a crook. It seems that Mrs. Stone Taylor was having an affair with Mr. Haus and she and Mr.

Stone Taylor were closest friends of the Jacksons. Of course, many people thought that Mr. Jackson and Mrs. Stone Taylor had had an affair earlier. Anyway, Mr. Haus and Mrs. Stone Taylor got the Jacksons to invest four hundred thousand dollars of the money Mrs. Jackson had inherited from her father and they made Mr. Jackson vice-president of some corporation Mr. Haus was president of . . . and . . .

(BERTIE DEE *cries*)

BERTIE DEE: I'm going crazy. I'm the one that's going crazy. I'm the one that will end up in the Austin insane asylum.

MRS. CAMPBELL: Now, now . . . it's going to be all right. Your father was Daddy's first friend here, you know. His first friend and his best friend. When he came here to start the paper he came home that first week and he said, "I've met the nicest fellow, name of Graham. And guess what?" he said. "He has the prettiest little girl, nine years old." And he looked over at Stanley, who was lying on the couch just as he is now, and he said, "I think she's just about right for Stanley." And Stanley blushed so we all had a good laugh.

BERTIE DEE: What's my life like? Married to a man drunk all the time?

MRS. CAMPBELL: Not all the time, honey. I'm very sensitive to his being in that condition and sometimes he comes over here and I smell nothing on his breath. I tell him if only he knew how wise and intelligent he is when sober . . .

BERTIE DEE: Getting drunk, climbing pecan trees . . .

STANLEY: I want to start all over again. I want me and Davis and Brother all living here again, so we can start all over . . .

(BERTIE DEE *gets up*)

BERTIE DEE: I'm going home. *(She leaves.* STANLEY *gets up)*

STANLEY: I'm going home too.

MRS. CAMPBELL: Are you sure she'll let you in, Stanley?

STANLEY: I'm sure. *(He leaves)*

(MRS. CAMPBELL *goes to the window*)

MRS. CAMPBELL: I hope she'll let him in, but I doubt it.

BROTHER: She did have an affair with Wesley Cox.

MRS. CAMPBELL: Change the subject please. I don't care to hear that. I knew it. She won't let him in.

BROTHER: Where will he go?

MRS. CAMPBELL: He'll come back here. *(She walks away from the window)* I don't want him to think I was spying on him. That would embarrass him if he thought we were watching. When he comes back in here, we'll just pretend like we didn't know what had happened.

BROTHER: What happened to the Jacksons?

MRS. CAMPBELL: The Jacksons? Oh, yes. Well, that Mr. Haus took them and their four hundred thousand dollars, just like Phil Beaufort took our seventy-five thousand dollars. They are very bitter and very upset, Mrs. Lehigh says. "I wish they could take it in the Christian way you have," she said. "How did you take your loss so calmly?" she asked. "Because," I said, "I know that money isn't everything. I have my health. I have four wonderful living children, a beloved husband and a daughter that are dead and lots of wonderful memories." Peek out the window and see if Stanley is still in the yard.

(BROTHER looks out the window)

BROTHER: No.

(STANLEY comes back in)

MRS. CAMPBELL: Hello, Son. Glad you came back. (STANLEY *doesn't answer. He goes to the window and looks out)* Do you all remember when Daddy built this house? We came here with nothing from Lake Charles and we rented a sweet little frame house across from the Cochrans, and I was certainly very happy there, but one day Daddy came in and he said, "Guess what? I am going to build you a two-story brick house on a nice lot and it will have everything in it you ever wanted, rooms for all the children and a big living room with a piano so they can bring their friends and sing and dance." "Won't it be very expensive, Daddy?" I said. "Yes," he said, "but I want to do it." And he did. And I thought it would take all our money and it did. But when Daddy died, I found that he had seventy-five thousand in insurance money and we were rich . . .

BROTHER: Rich, until Phil Beaufort convinced me to ask you for it to invest in his worthless schemes.

MRS. CAMPBELL: Don't look back now, don't look back. And if you do only think of the pleasant things. . . . When Stanley married Bertie Dee, Daddy said, "I want them living right next door to us. I am going to the bank and arrange a loan so they can build their house." And he did.

STANLEY: *(Singing)* "In the gloamin', Oh, my darlin' . . ."

MRS. CAMPBELL: "Because we have been so happy in our house I want them to have a house of their own to be happy in," Daddy said.

STANLEY: You know what I just saw?

BROTHER: What?

STANLEY: I just saw my brother-in-law, Wesley Cox, go into my house. What do you think of that?

BROTHER: I don't think anything of it, because you couldn't have seen him. Wesley Cox is ninety miles away in Port Arthur.

STANLEY: Who did I see go in there if it wasn't Wesley Cox?

BROTHER: No one went in there, Stanley.

STANLEY: They go in there all the time. Ask Mama. She'll tell you. Don't they go in there all the time, Mama?

MRS. CAMPBELL: I don't think so, Son.

STANLEY: You may not think so, but I know so. Do you have a gun in this house, Mama?

MRS. CAMPBELL: Now you know I don't keep guns here. I hate guns. I used to say to your daddy, "I want my boys to be real boys. I want them to play football, baseball, go out for track, but I don't want them near guns." We have had such tragedy from guns. That oldest Beck boy went out hunting with the Peebles boy, who was his best friend, and the Peebles boy's gun went off by mistake and shot and killed the Beck boy, and . . .

(BERTIE DEE *comes in*)

BERTIE DEE: Do you have an aspirin?

MRS. CAMPBELL: Yes, I do. Upstairs in my bathroom. Do you have a head-ache?

BERTIE DEE: Yes. *(She starts out)*

MRS. CAMPBELL: I'll get them for you. *(She goes)*

STANLEY: Who was it I saw go into my house? (BERTIE DEE *doesn't answer. She looks at* BROTHER *and sighs)* Was it Wesley Cox? Was it Robert Ferguson? Was it Willy Davis? They are all having affairs with her, you know. Everybody in town is switching. Rebecca and Jack Harris, Virginia and Douglas, Laurie Borden and anybody she can grab, Rosanna and Doc, Jenny and Brother Polk. I could have affairs, you know. All I want. Plenty of women want me. I would name them all for you if I wasn't such a gentleman. Who was that went into our house? Who was that went into our house? Who was that went into our house?

BROTHER: Tell him, for God sakes, Bertie Dee, that nobody went into your house.

BERTIE DEE: It don't do any good to tell him anything. I'm talked out. Worn out. Beat! *(She turns on him savagely)* Look, mister, if you can believe this tired old body can do anything except get to work in the morning and home at night, you'll believe anything.

STANLEY: I see you at the dances. Dancing with all the men. I see how you hold them . . . I see . . .

BERTIE DEE: What dances? We haven't been to a dance in ten years except the Christmas dance. I go nowhere now, because I'm worn out slaving at the paper, because you're so drunk you can't attend to it.

STANLEY: *(Singing)* "In the gloamin', Oh, my darlin' . . ."

(MRS. CAMPBELL *comes in with a box of aspirin. She goes to* BERTIE DEE.)

BERTIE DEE: Thank you. Come on home, Stanley. I'm dead for sleep and I can't get to sleep with you peeking through the windows. You woke Son up just now. You almost scared him to death. "What is Daddy doing outside looking in the window?" he asked. "Is he drunk again?" "Yes, unfortunately," I said. Come on with me, Stanley. I'll put you to bed.

STANLEY: I don't want to go to bed.

BROTHER: You have to go to bed, Stanley. You can't sit up all night talking. We all have to be up early in the morning.

STANLEY: Then go on to bed if you want to. I don't need you to stay with me. Fortunately, I have friends that will be happy to see me anytime . . . night or day . . .

BERTIE DEE: Name me one.

STANLEY: What did you say?

BERTIE DEE: I said name me one. You don't have a friend left in this town that doesn't run the other way when they see you coming. And you know it.

STANLEY: Oh, sure.

BERTIE DEE: Sure!

MRS. CAMPBELL: Well, why don't we just change the subject. Do you know what tomorrow is?

STANLEY: Valentine's Day.

BERTIE DEE: *(Shaking her head in disbelief)* He's really gone. Valentine's Day!

STANLEY: Christmas?

BERTIE DEE: Oh, shut up, Stanley. You're just making a fool of yourself.

MRS. CAMPBELL: It's Daddy's and my wedding anniversary. If he was with us we would have been married forty years. I want us all to go out to the cemetery tomorrow and put flowers on his and Baby Sister's graves, so they will know we haven't forgotten them.

STANLEY: Who was the best man at my wedding? Was it Davis or Brother?

MRS. CAMPBELL: Stanley, how can you forget something like that? Mr. Graham gave Bertie Dee away and Daddy was your best man. Brother and Davis were ushers. Sarah was a bridesmaid and Baby Sister was the flower girl. Daddy wasn't here for Sarah's wedding and Brother gave her away, because he was the oldest.

STANLEY: Michael Dalton . . .

MRS. CAMPBELL: What about Michael Dalton?

STANLEY: I could walk into his house right now, even if he and his wife and children were sound asleep in bed, and he would welcome me.

BERTIE DEE: The hell he would! Just try it and see!

STANLEY: Les Hines.

BERTIE DEE: Les Hines. He thinks you're crazy. Every time I meet him uptown he says, "Where is Stanley? Up in the pecan trees?"

STANLEY: Vernon May.

BERTIE DEE: He's dead.

STANLEY: Who is?

BERTIE DEE: Vernon May.

STANLEY: When did he die?

BERTIE DEE: Five years ago.

STANLEY: What happened?

BERTIE DEE: I don't know what happened. He just died.

STANLEY: Well, if he were alive I could go see him anytime . . . day or night.

BERTIE DEE: Well, I can't answer for Vernon May because he's dead, but I know what his wife thinks. She told me day before yesterday that if it were her husband getting drunk and climbing pecan trees in the courthouse square she would have him put away.

MRS. CAMPBELL: He's always been crazy about climbing trees. Ever since he was a little boy. Do you all remember that? Whenever his daddy and I couldn't find him, he would be high up in some tree.

BERTIE DEE: Well, a lot of boys like to climb trees, but name me one grown man, besides this fool, that climbs them on the courthouse square at all hours of the night.

BROTHER: Mama, when was the last time you heard from Baby Sister's children?

MRS. CAMPBELL: At Christmas. I wrote and asked them if they could come here for a visit this summer, but her husband hasn't answered my letter. He's very peculiar, you know. He didn't want Baby Sister to have anything to do with her family. I'm surprised he let us bring her back here to be buried beside Daddy. That would have finished me off, let me tell you, if he had refused to let her be brought back here. I've had many a cross, but that would have just finished me off. *(She reaches for a picture off a table)* Look at Daddy in his Shriner's cap. I remember the day he had that taken. Oh, it was a happy day for him when you both joined the Masons. "My cup runneth over," he said. "My two oldest boys are both Masons." He wanted you both so to become first-degree Masons, but that wasn't to be. Like I told him, "Let's look on the bright side. They are at least Masons and someday you will inspire them to become first-degree Masons. You have inspired them in so many ways to marry young, to go into business, to build nice, comfortable houses for their families . . ."

BERTIE DEE: Stanley, are you coming home?

STANLEY: No.

BERTIE DEE: Then don't ever come home.

MRS. CAMPBELL: Now, Bertie Dee.

BERTIE DEE: I mean it! Don't ever come home, because from now on day or night I won't let you in.

STANLEY: I'll kick the goddamn door down. Whore . . . I know why you won't let me in, so you can whore with every man in town. That's why I have no friends. You've taken them all with your whorish ways. You think you can keep me out? I'll kick the goddamn door in and I'll have a gun with me when I do and I'll shoot you and the bastard I catch you in bed with. I don't care if it's Wesley Cox or Davis or Brother.

BROTHER: Leave me out of this.

MRS. CAMPBELL: Bertie Dee, I wish you and Stanley could go and talk to the preacher.

BERTIE DEE: Let your crazy son go talk to the preacher. I don't need to. *(She gets up)* But you better keep him over here from now on, because if he tries to get in my house again I'm calling the law and I'm going to have him arrested. *(She goes)*

BROTHER: Whose name is their house in?

MRS. CAMPBELL: It is in both their names. Daddy and Mr. Graham built it for them as a wedding present. Remember? He laughed and told Mr. Graham, "I'm going to be selfish and put them right next door to me." He had a dream of one day having you all live in houses next to each other, that way he said we could all go through life together. "And when they have children," he said, "we'll build their houses next to our houses." Well, it didn't work out that way. Daddy died and you, Brother, moved into Houston to go into the oil business with Phil Beaufort. Sarah and Wesley Cox preferred Port Arthur.

STANLEY: *(Singing)* "In the gloamin', Oh, my darlin', When the lights are soft and low . . ."

MRS. CAMPBELL: I want you to promise me one thing in front of your brother. That you will never climb those pecan trees in the courthouse square again no matter how drunk you get. You can fall and break your neck when you're in that condition. Can't he, Brother?

BROTHER: He sure can. I would hate to try and climb them sober. Much less drunk.

MRS. CAMPBELL: Will you promise me that?

STANLEY: *(Singing)* "In the gloamin', Oh, my darlin', When the lights are soft and low . . ."

MRS. CAMPBELL: He was always the climber in the family, you know. He climbed every tree in our yard. He went down to the river and climbed the live oaks and the pin oaks. Whenever I wanted to find Stanley I would always look for him somewhere up in the trees. "What are you doing up there?" I once asked him. "Trying to get to heaven," he said. He was joking, of course. "Don't fall," I said, "and hurt yourself or you might land in the other place." I was joking, of course. That's one thing about us, I'll have to say, we've always had a sense of humor. We've always had time for a good joke. We've never minded a little fun.

STANLEY: *(Singing)* "In the gloamin', Oh, my darlin' . . ."

MRS. CAMPBELL: The main thing is that none of us get discouraged. We have our troubles, certainly. Everybody does. But if we try to look on the bright side as much as possible . . .

STANLEY: Do you remember when the old courthouse was there and they had long slides out of the upstairs windows to be used in case of fire and when we were boys we used to go into the courthouse yard and slide down those slides by the hour? And then when we got tired of that we played football on the lawn. *(A pause)* Why do I get so drunk, Mama?

MRS. CAMPBELL: Oh, I don't know that, honey. I wish I did.

STANLEY: I did go see the preacher, but he wasn't home. His wife was there and she asked me what I wanted to see him about and I said, "First, my drinking," and she said, "He'll pray for you about that, but don't get your hopes up as his own brother is a drunkard and he prays for him twice a day and he still drinks same as before." And then I told her about Bertie Dee and she said it didn't surprise her one bit, no one was faithful to their wives and husbands anymore. She says the things that go on at the dances over at the opera house was enough to turn your hair green if you were a Christian woman. She said she knew of ten women all friends of Bertie Dee's all having affairs with married men, and that the wives and the husbands of the men and women involved didn't mind as they were all having affairs themselves. "Well," I said, "some of them are going to mind one of these days and then there is going to be a killing like when Ted Bowen found out about his wife and the Garland boy, and shot him down right in front of the Palace Theater." And Jordan Buchanan would have killed Luke Goddard when he found out he was having an affair with his wife if someone hadn't tipped Luke off and gotten him out of town before Jordan could get to him.

(BROTHER is asleep. He snores slightly)

MRS. CAMPBELL: Look at Brother. He's gone to sleep on us. We'd better all go to bed now.

STANLEY: Has Bertie Dee gone to bed?

MRS. CAMPBELL: Yes, don't you remember? She left a while ago.

STANLEY: Has she turned the light out?

MRS. CAMPBELL: Yes, she has.

STANLEY: We were married at eighteen. We were married in the Baptist Church to please Bertie Dee's father. The church was packed. She was crying like her heart would break. It was really embarrassing. I said to

Daddy, "Why is she crying?" "She's scared, probably," he said. "Scared of what?" I said. "You know," he said. But she wasn't scared of that. We went to Galveston on our honeymoon and she met another couple on their honeymoon and she danced every dance with him . . . holding him real close the way she liked to dance with everybody but me. And I could have danced every dance with his wife, only I didn't feel like dancing and she didn't feel like dancing . . . *(A pause)* I have been cheated. Married at eighteen and cheated.

MRS. CAMPBELL: I was married at sixteen. Tomorrow is our anniversary.

STANLEY: Daddy was my best man.

MRS. CAMPBELL: Yes, he was.

STANLEY: Help me, Mama . . .

MRS. CAMPBELL: I want to help you, Son. Any way I can. Brother does, Davis does.

STANLEY: Help me Mama. I'm going to fall out of one of those trees one night and kill myself.

MRS. CAMPBELL: I know that. That's what has me half-crazy.

STANLEY: Bertie Dee and Wesley Cox are having an affair.

MRS. CAMPBELL: Oh, I hope not, Son. I surely hope not.

STANLEY: Bertie Dee cried the day Wesley Cox married Sarah, let me tell you. I walked into her bedroom and she was crying and I said, "Why are you crying?" "Because the thought of a wedding makes me sad," she said. "I cried at my own. I had no childhood, no youth, no nothing . . . there should be a law against marriage at eighteen," she said. *(A pause)* When I was a boy I climbed the water tower once. I could see the whole town from up there. It was a clear day and I could see everything for miles. The river, the courthouse, the gin, the pumping plant, the houses in town, the farms . . . Help me, Mama . . . or someday I'm gonna fall and kill myself. *(He sings)* "In the gloamin', Oh, my darlin' . . ." *(A pause)* Am I falling now, Mama?

MRS. CAMPBELL: No, honey. You're right here beside your mama. I'm not going to let you fall.

STANLEY: Where are we, Mama?

MRS. CAMPBELL: In the dining room of our house. The house Daddy built for us all.

STANLEY: Is Bertie Dee here?

MRS. CAMPBELL: No, sweetheart. She's in your house.

STANLEY: Hold me, Mama. Don't let me fall.

(She holds him)

MRS. CAMPBELL: I'm holding you, honey. I'm holding you.

(He gives a cry of pain and terror)

STANLEY: Did I fall, Mama?

MRS. CAMPBELL: No, darling. You're right here. Beside me. Right here . . .

STANLEY: *(Singing)* "In the gloamin', Oh, my darlin' . . ."

(As the lights fade)

TEETH

Tina Howe

Tina Howe

Tina Howe is the author of *The Nest, Birth* and *After Birth, Museum, The Art of Dining, Painting Churches, Coastal Disturbances,* and *Approaching Zanzibar.* These works premiered at the Los Angeles Actors Theatre, the New York Shakespeare Festival, the Kennedy Center and The Second Stage. Her awards include an Obie for Distinguished Playwriting, 1983; an Outer Critics Circle Award, 1983; a Rockefeller grant, 1984; an N.E.A. Fellowship, 1985; and a Guggenheim Fellowship, 1990. In 1987, she received a Tony nomination for Best Play, and in 1988, she was awarded an honorary degree by Bowdoin College. Miss Howe teaches at N.Y.U., Hunter College and the Sewanee Writers' Conference. She also serves on the council of the Dramatists Guild. Her works can be read in *Coastal Disturbances: Four Plays by Tina Howe,* published by the Theatre Communications Group.

Characters

DR. ROSE, dentist.
AMY, his patient.

Scene:

A modest one-man dentist's office in midtown Manhattan. An FM radio is tuned to a classical music station. It's March 21st, Bach's birthday, and Glenn Gould is playing the rollicking Presto from his Toccata in C minor. The whine of a high powered dentist's drill slowly asserts itself. In black-out . . .

DR. ROSE: Still with me . . . ?

AMY: *(Garbled because his hands are in her mouth)* Aargh . . .

DR. ROSE: *(Hums along as the drilling gets louder)* You've heard his Goldberg re-issue, haven't you?

AMY: Aargh. . . .

DR. ROSE: *(Groans with pleasure)* . . . Unbelievable!

(The drilling gets ferocious)

AMY: OW . . . OW!

DR. ROSE: Woops, sorry about that. O.K., you can rinse.

(Lights up on AMY lying prone in a dentist's chair with a bib around her neck. She raises up, takes a swig of water, sloshes it around in her mouth and spits it emphatically into the little bowl next to her. She flops back down, wiping her mouth. She's in her forties. DR. ROSE is several years older and on the disheveled side)

DR. ROSE: Glenn Gould. Glenn Gould is the penultimate Bach keyboard artist of this century, period! Open please. *(He resumes drilling)* No one else can touch him!

AMY: Aarg. . . .

DR. ROSE: Wanda Landowska, Roselyn Turek, Trevor Pinnock . . . forget it!

AMY: Aarg. . . .

DR. ROSE: *(Drilling with rising intensity)* Andras Schiff, Igor Kipness, Anthony Newman . . . no contest!

AMY: Aarg. . . .

DR. ROSE: Listen to the man . . . ! The elegance of his phrasing, the clarity of his touch . . . The joy! The joy! *(He roars)*

AMY: *(Practically jumping out of her seat)* OOOOOWWWWWWW!

DR. ROSE: Sorry, sorry—afraid I slipped. *(His drilling returns to normal)* Hear how he hums along in a different key? The man can't contain himself . . . *(He roars again, then calms down for a spate of drilling. He idly starts humming along with Gould)* You know, you're my third patient . . . no, make that fourth . . . that's pulled out a filling with candy this week. What was the culprit again?

AMY: *(Garbled)* Bit O'Honey.

DR. ROSE: Almond Roca?

AMY: *(Garbled)* Bit O'Honey.

DR. ROSE: Ju Jubes?

AMY: *(Less garbled)* Bit O'Honey, Bit O'Honey!

DR. ROSE: Yup, saltwater taffy will do it every time! O.K., Amy, the worst is over. You can rinse. *(He hangs up the drill)*

(AMY rinses and spits with even more fury)

DR. ROSE: Hey, hey, don't break my bowl on me! *(Fussing with his tools)* Now, where did I put that probe? . . . I can't seem to hold on to anything these days . . .

(AMY flops back down with a sigh)

DR. ROSE: *(In a little sing-song)* Where are you? . . . Where are you? . . . Ahhhhh, here it is! O.K. . . . let's just take one more last look before we fill you up. Open. *(He disappears into her mouth with the probe)* Amy, Amy, you're still grinding your teeth at night, aren't you?

AMY: *(Anguished)* Aaaaarrrrrrrrhhh!

DR. ROSE: You've got to wear that rubber guard I gave you!

AMY: *(Completely garbled)* But I can't breathe when it's on!

AMY: *(Incomprehensible)* I feel like I'm choking! I've tried to wear it, I really have, I just always wake up gasping for air. See, I can't breathe through my nose. If I could breathe through my nose, it wouldn't be a problem . . .

DR. ROSE: I know they take getting used to, but you're doing irreparable damage to your supporting bone layer, and once that goes . . . . *(He whistles her fate)*

(A radio announcer has come on in the background during this)

RADIO ANNOUNCER: That was Glenn Gould playing Bach's Toccata in C minor, BWV listing 911. And to continue with our birthday tribute to J.S. Bach, we now turn to his Cantata BWV 80, "Ein Feste Burg," as performed by the English Chamber Orchestra under the direction of Raymond Leppard. *(It begins)*

DR. ROSE: *(Comes out of her mouth)* Well, let's whip up a temporary filling and get you out of here. *(He rummages through his tray of tools)*

AMY: Dr. Rose, could I ask you something?

DR. ROSE: Of course, today's March 21st, Bach's birthday! *(Some instruments fall, he quickly recovers them)* Woops . . .

AMY: I keep having this recurring nightmare.

DR. ROSE: Oh, I love this piece. I used to sing it in college. Mind if I turn it up?

AMY: I just wonder if you've heard it before.

DR. ROSE: *(Turns up the volume, singing along. He returns to his tray and starts sorting out his things which keep dropping. He quickly retrieves them, never stopping his singing)*

> Ein feste Burg ist unser Gott,
> Ein gute Wehr und Waffen . . . woops.
> Er hilft uns frei aus aller, Not,
> Die uns itzt hat . . . woops . . . betroffen.

AMY: I have it at least three times a week now.

DR. ROSE: I came this close to being a music major. *This* close!

AMY: I wake up exhausted with my whole jaw throbbing. Waa . . . waa . . . waa!

DR. ROSE: O.K. let's just open this little bottle of cement here. *(He starts struggling with the lid)*

AMY: You know, the old . . . TEETH-GRANULATING-ON-YOU-DREAM! *(She stifles a sob)* You're at a party flashing a perfect smile when suddenly you hear this splintering sound like someone smashing teacups in the next room . . . . . . ping . . . . . . tock . . . . . . crackkkkkkkkkk . . . tinkle, tinkle . . . "Well, someone's having a good time!," you say to yourself expecting to see some maniac swinging a sledgehammer . . .

(Having a worse and worse time with the bottle, DR. ROSE moves behind her chair so she can't see him)

DR. ROSE: Ugh . . . . . ugh . . . . . ugh . . . . . . ugh . . . . . . ugh!

AMY: So you casually look around, and of course there *is* no maniac! . . . Then you feel these prickly shards clinging to your lips. . . . You try and brush them away, but suddenly your mouth is filled with them. You can't spit them out fast enough! *(She tries)*

DR. ROSE: GODDAMNIT! *(He goes through a series of silent contortions trying to open it—behind his back, up over this head, down between his legs, etc. etc)*

AMY: *(Still spitting and wiping)* People are starting to stare. . . . You try to save face. *(To the imagined party goers)* "Well, what do you know . . . I seem to have taken a bite out of my coffee cup! Silly me!" *(She laughs, frantically wiping)*

DR. ROSE: GODDAMN SON OF A BITCH, WHAT'S GOING ON HERE!

AMY: That's just what *I* want to know!

DR. ROSE: IS THIS SOME KIND OF CONSPIRACY OR WHAT?

AMY: Why me? What did I do?

DR. ROSE: They must weld these tops on.

AMY: Then I catch a glimpse of myself in the mirror . . .

DR. ROSE: *(Starting to cackle)* Think you can outsmart me? *(He starts whacking a heavy tool down on the lid)*

AMY: You got it! My teeth are spilling out of my mouth in little pieces. I frantically try and moosh them back in, but there's nothing to hold on to. Then they start granulating on me . . . fsssssssssssssssss . . . it's like trying to build a sand castle inside an hour glass!

(DR. ROSE is having a worse and worse time. He finally just sits on the floor and bangs the bottle down as hard as he can, again and again)

AMY: My mouth is a blaze of gums. We are talking pink for *miles* . . . ! Magellan staring out over the Pacific Ocean during a sunset in 1520— *(As Magellan)* "Pink . . . pink . . . pink . . . pink!"

(DR. ROSE starts to whimper as he pounds)

AMY: What does it *mean*, is what I'd like to know! I mean, teeth are supposed to last forever, right? They hold up through floods, fires, earthquakes and wars . . . the one part of us that endures.

DR. ROSE: Open, damnit. Open, damnit. Open, damnit. . . .

AMY: So if they granulate on you, where does that leave you? *Nowhere!*

DR. ROSE: *(Curls into the fetal position and focuses on smaller moves in a tiny voice)* Come on . . . come on . . . Please? Pretty please? Pretty, lovely, ravishing please?

AMY: You could have been rain or wind for all anybody knows. That's pretty scary. . . . *(Starting to get weepy)* One minute you're laughing at a party and the next you've evaporated into thin air. . . . *(Putting on a voice)* "Remember Amy? Gee, I wonder whatever happened to her?" *(In another voice)* "Gosh, it's suddenly gotten awfully chilly in here. Where's that *wind* coming from?" *(Teary again)* I mean, we're not around for that long as it is, so then to suddenly. . . . I'm sorry, I'm sorry. It's just that I have this um . . . longstanding . . . Oh God, here we go . . . *(Starting to break down)* Control yourself! Control . . . control!

(DR. ROSE is now rolled up in a ball beyond speech. He clutches the bottle whimpering and emitting strange little sobs)

AMY: See, I have this longstanding um . . . fear of death? It's something you're born with. I used to sob in my father's arms when I was only

. . . Oh boy! See, once you start thinking about it, I mean. . . . *really* thinking about it . . . You know, time going on for ever and ever and ever and ever and you're not there . . . it can get pretty scary! . . . We're not talking missing out on a few measly centuries here, but boom! And back to dinosaurs again? . . . *(More and more weepy)* Eternity . . . Camel trains, cities, holy wars, boom! Dinosaurs, camel trains, cities, holy wars, boom!. . . . Dinosaurs, camel trains, cities, holy wars. . . . Stop it Amy . . . just . . . *stop it!*

DR. ROSE: *(Broken)* I can't open this bottle.

AMY: *(Wiping away her tears)* Dr. Rose! What are you doing down there?

DR. ROSE: I've tried everything.

AMY: What's wrong?

DR. ROSE: *(Reaching the bottle up to her)* I can't open it.

AMY: *(Taking it)* Oh here, let me try.

DR. ROSE: I'm afraid I'm having a breakdown.

AMY: I'm good at this kind of thing.

DR. ROSE: I don't know, for some time now I just haven't . . .

AMY: *(Puts the bottle in her mouth, clamps down on it with her back teeth and unscrews the lid with one turn. She hands it back to him)* Here you go.

DR. ROSE: *(Rises and advances towards her menacingly)* You should never . . . NEVER DO THAT!

AMY: *(Drawing back)* What?

DR. ROSE: Open a bottle with your teeth.

AMY: I do it all the time.

DR. ROSE: Teeth are very fragile. They're not meant to be used as tools!

AMY: Sorry, sorry.

DR. ROSE: I just don't believe the way people mistreat them. We're only given one set of permanent teeth in a lifetime. ONE SET, AND THAT'S IT!

AMY: I won't do it again. I promise.

DR. ROSE: Species flourish and disappear, only our teeth remain. Open please. *(He puts cotton wadding in her mouth)* You must respect them, take care of them. . . . Oh, why even bother talking about it, no one ever listens to me anyway. Wider, please. *(He puts in more cotton and a bubbling saliva drain)* O.K., let's fill this baby and get you on your way. *(He dabs in bits of compound)* So, how's work these days?

AMY: Aarg . . .

DR. ROSE: Same old rat race, huh?

AMY: Aarg . . . . .

(During this, the final chorus, "Das Wort sie sollen lassen stahn" has started to play)

AMY: *(Slightly garbled)* What is that tune? It's so familiar.

DR. ROSE: "A Mighty Fortress is Our God"

AMY: Right, right! I used to sing it in Sunday school 100 years ago.

DR. ROSE: Actually, Bach stole the melody from Martin Luther.

AMY: *(Bursts into song, garbled, the saliva drain bubbling)* "A mighty fortress is Our God . . ."

AMY:	DR. ROSE: *(Joining her)*
. . . a bulwark never failing	. . . Und kein' Dank dazu
Our helper he amid the flood	haben
Of mortal ills prevailing.	Er ist bei uns wohl auf dem
For still our ancient foe,	Plan
Doth seek to work us woe . . .	Mit seinem Geist und Gaben.
	Nehmen sie uns den Leib,
	Gut, Ehr, Kind und Weib. . . .

(Their voices swell louder and louder)

(BLACKOUT)

SURE THING

A Brief Comedy

David Ives

Sure Thing was originally produced by the Manhattan Punch Line, Inc., in New York. Steve Kaplan, artistic director.

David Ives

David Ives was born in Chicago and educated at Northwestern University and Yale Drama School. His one-acts have been a staple of the annual comedy festival of the Manhattan Punchline Theatre for several years. He has written for television, for Hollywood, and recently his opera *The Secret Garden*, written with composer Greg Pliska, premiered in Philadelphia.

Characters
BILL, in his late twenties
BETTY, in her late twenties

Setting:
A café table, with a couple of chairs.

Scene:
BETTY, *reading at the table. An empty chair opposite her.* BILL *enters.*

BILL: Excuse me. Is this chair taken?

BETTY: Excuse me?

BILL: Is this taken?

BETTY: Yes, it is.

BILL: Oh. Sorry.

BETTY: Sure thing.

   (A bell rings softly)

BILL: Excuse me. Is this chair taken?

BETTY: Excuse me?

BILL: Is this taken?

BETTY: No, but I'm expecting somebody in a minute.

BILL: Oh. Thanks anyway.

BETTY: Sure thing.

   (A bell rings softly)

BILL: Excuse me. Is this chair taken?

BETTY: No, but I'm expecting somebody very shortly.

BILL: Would you mind if I sit here till he or she or it comes?

BETTY: *(Glances at her watch)* They seem to be pretty late . . .

BILL: You never know who you might be turning down.

BETTY: Sorry. Nice try, though.

BILL: Sure thing.

(Bell)

BILL: Is this seat taken?

BETTY: No, it's not.

BILL: Would you mind if I sit here?

BETTY: Yes, I would.

BILL: Oh.

(Bell)

BILL: Is this chair taken?

BETTY: No, it's not.

BILL: Would you mind if I sit here?

BETTY: No. Go ahead.

BILL: Thanks. *(He sits. She continues reading)* Everyplace else seems to be taken.

BETTY: Mm-hm.

BILL: Great place.

BETTY: Mm-hm.

BILL: What's the book?

BETTY: I just wanted to read in quiet, if you don't mind.

BILL: No. Sure thing.

(Bell)

BILL: Everyplace else seems to be taken.

BETTY: Mm-hm.

BILL: Great place for reading.

BETTY: Yes, I like it.

BILL: What's the book?

BETTY: "The Sound and the Fury."

BILL: Oh. Hemingway.

(Bell)

BILL: What's the book?

BETTY: "The Sound and the Fury."

BILL: Oh. Faulkner.

BETTY: Have you read it?

BILL: Not . . . actually. I've read *about* it, though. It's supposed to be great.

BETTY: It is great.

BILL: I hear it's great. *(Small pause)* Waiter?

(Bell)

BILL: What's the book?

BETTY: "The Sound and the Fury."

BILL: Oh. Faulkner.

BETTY: Have you read it.

BILL: I'm a Mets fan, myself.

(Bell)

BETTY: Have you read it?

BILL: Yeah, I read it in college.

BETTY: Where was college?

BILL: I went to Oral Roberts University.

(Bell)

BETTY: Where was college?

BILL: I was lying. I never really went to college. I just like to party.

(Bell)

BETTY: Where was college?

BILL: Harvard.

BETTY: Do you like Faulkner?

BILL: I love Faulkner. I spent a whole winter reading him once.

BETTY: I've just started.

BILL: I was so excited after ten pages that I went out and bought everything else he wrote. One of the greatest reading experiences of my life. I mean, all that incredible psychological understanding. Page after page of gorgeous prose. His profound grasp of the mystery of time and human existence. The smells of the earth . . . What do you think?

BETTY: I think it's pretty boring.

(Bell)

BILL: What's the book?

BETTY: "The Sound and the Fury."

BILL: Oh! Faulkner!

BETTY: Do you like Faulkner?

BILL: I love Faulkner.

BETTY: He's incredible.

BILL: I spent a whole winter reading him once.

BETTY: I was so excited after ten pages that I went out and bought everything else he wrote.

BILL: All that incredible psychological understanding.

BETTY: And the prose is so gorgeous.

BILL: And the way he's grasped the mystery of time—

BETTY: —and human existence. I can't believe I've waited this long to read him.

BILL: You never know. You might not have liked him before.

BETTY: That's true.

BILL: You might not have been ready for him. You have to hit these things at the right moment or it's no good.

BETTY: That's happened to me.

BILL: It's all in the timing. *(Small pause)* My name's Bill, by the way.

BETTY: I'm Betty.

BILL: Hi.

BETTY: Hi.

(Small pause)

BILL: Yes, I thought reading Faulkner was . . . a great experience.

BETTY: Yes.

(Small pause)

BILL: "The Sound and the Fury" . . .

(Another small pause)

BETTY: Well. Onwards and upwards. *(She goes back to her book)*

BILL: Waiter—?

(Bell)

BILL: You have to hit these things at the right moment or it's no good.

BETTY: That's happened to me.

BILL: It's all in the timing. My name's Bill, by the way.

BETTY: I'm Betty.

BILL: Hi.

BETTY: Hi.

BILL: Do you come in here a lot?

BETTY: Actually I'm just in town for two days from Pakistan.

BILL: Oh. Pakistan.

(Bell)

BILL: My name's Bill, by the way.

BETTY: I'm Betty.

BILL: Hi.

BETTY: Hi.

BILL: Do you come in here a lot?

BETTY: Every once in a while. Do you?

BILL: Not much anymore. Not as much as I used to. Before my nervous breakdown.

(Bell)

BILL: Do you come in here a lot?

BETTY: Why are you asking?

BILL: Just interested.

BETTY: Are you really interested, or do you just want to pick me up?

BILL: No, I'm really interested.

BETTY: Why would you be interested in whether I come in here a lot?

BILL: Just . . . getting acquainted.

BETTY: Maybe you're only interested for the sake of making small talk long enough to ask me back to your place to listen to some music, or because you've just rented some great tape for your VCR, or because you've got some terrific unknown Django Reinhardt record, only all you'll really want to do is fuck—which you won't do very well—after which you'll go into the bathroom and pee very loudly, then pad into the kitchen and get yourself a beer from the refrigerator without asking me whether I'd like anything, and then you'll proceed to lie back down beside me and confess that you've got a girlfriend named Stephanie who's away at medical school in Belgium for a year, and that you've been involved with her—*off and on*—in what you'll call a very intricate relationship, for about *seven YEARS.* None of which *interests* me, mister!

BILL: Okay.

(Bell)

BILL: Do you come in here a lot?

BETTY: Every other day, I think.

BILL: I come in here quite a lot and I don't remember seeing you.

BETTY: I guess we must be on different schedules.

BILL: Missed connections.

BETTY: Yes. Different time zones.

BILL: Amazing how you can live right next door to somebody in this town and never even know it.

BETTY: I know.

BILL: City life.

BETTY: It's crazy.

BILL: We probably pass each other in the street every day. Right in front of this place, probably.

BETTY: Yep.

BILL: *(Looks around)* Well, the waiters here sure seem to be in some different time zone. I don't see one anywhere . . . Waiter! *(He looks back)* So what do you . . . *(He sees that she's gone back to her book)*

BETTY: I beg pardon?

BILL: Nothing. Sorry.

(Bell)

BETTY: I guess we must be on different schedules.

BILL: Missed connections.

BETTY: Yes. Different time zones.

BILL: Amazing how you can live right next door to somebody in this town and never even know it.

BETTY: I know.

BILL: City life.

BETTY: It's crazy.

BILL: You weren't waiting for somebody when I came in, were you?

BETTY: Actually I was.

BILL: Oh. Boyfriend?

BETTY: Sort of.

BILL: What's a sort-of boyfriend?

BETTY: My husband.

BILL: Ah-ha.

(Bell)

BILL: You weren't waiting for somebody when I came in, were you?

BETTY: Actually I was.

BILL: Oh. Boyfriend?

BETTY: Sort of.

BILL: What's a sort-of boyfriend?

BETTY: We were meeting here to break up.

BILL: Mm-hm . . .

(Bell)

BILL: What's a sort-of boyfriend?

BETTY: My lover. Here she comes right now!

(Bell)

BILL: You weren't waiting for somebody when I came in, were you?

BETTY: No, just reading.

BILL: Sort of a sad occupation for a Friday night, isn't it? Reading here, all by yourself?

BETTY: Do you think so?

BILL: Well sure. I mean, what's a good-looking woman like you doing out alone on a Friday night?

BETTY: Trying to keep away from lines like that.

BILL: No, listen—

(Bell)

BILL: You weren't waiting for somebody when I came in, were you?

BETTY: No, just reading.

BILL: Sort of a sad occupation for a Friday night, isn't it? Reading here all by yourself?

BETTY: I guess it is, in a way.

BILL: What's a good-looking woman like you doing out alone on a Friday night anyway? No offense, but . . .

BETTY: I'm out alone on a Friday night for the first time in a very long time.

BILL: Oh.

BETTY: You see, I just recently ended a relationship.

BILL: Oh.

BETTY: Of rather long standing.

BILL: I'm sorry—Well listen, since reading by yourself *is* such a sad occupation for a Friday night, would you like to go elsewhere?

BETTY: No . . .

BILL: Do something else?

BETTY: No thanks.

BILL: I was headed out to the movies in a while anyway.

BETTY: I don't think so.

BILL: Big chance to let Faulkner catch his breath. All those long sentences get him pretty tired.

BETTY: Thanks anyway.

BILL: Okay.

BETTY: I appreciate the invitation.

BILL: Sure thing.

(Bell)

BILL: You weren't waiting for somebody when I came in, were you?

BETTY: No, just reading.

BILL: Sort of a sad occupation for a Friday night, isn't it? Reading here all by yourself?

BETTY: I guess I was trying to think of it as existentially romantic. You know—capuccino, great literature, rainy night . . .

BILL: That only works in Paris. We *could* hop the late plane to Paris. Get on a Concorde. Find a café . . .

BETTY: I'm a little short on plane fare tonight.

BILL: Darn it, so am I.

BETTY: To tell you the truth, I was headed to the movies after I finished this section. Would you like to come along? Since you can't locate a waiter?

BILL: That's a very nice offer, but—I can't.

BETTY: Uh-huh. Girlfriend?

BILL: Two of them, actually. One of them's pregnant, and Stephanie—

(Bell)

BETTY: Girlfriend?

BILL: No, I don't have a girlfriend. Not if you mean the castrating bitch I dumped last night.

(Bell)

BETTY: Girlfriend?

BILL: Sort of. Sort of . . .

BETTY: What's a sort-of girlfriend?

BILL: My mother.

(Bell)

BILL: I just ended a relationship, actually.

BETTY: Oh.

BILL: Of rather long standing.

BETTY: I'm sorry to hear it.

BILL: This is my first night out alone in a long time. I feel a little bit at sea, to tell you the truth.

BETTY: So you didn't stop to talk because you're a Moonie, or you have some weird political affiliation—?

BILL: Nope. Straight-down-the-ticket Republican.

(Bell)

Straight-down-the-ticket Democrat.

(Bell)

Can I tell you something about politics?

(Bell)

I consider my self a citizen of the universe.

(Bell)

I'm unaffiliated.

BETTY: That's a relief. So am I.

BILL: I vote my beliefs.

BETTY: Labels are not important.

BILL: Labels are not important, exactly. Like me, for example. I mean, what does it matter if I had a two-point—

(Bell)

—three-point—

(Bell)

—four-point at college, or if I did come from Pittsburgh—

(Bell)

—Cleveland—

(Bell)

—Westchester County?

BETTY: Sure.

BILL: I believe that a man is what he is.

(Bell)

A person is what he is.

(Bell)

A person is what they are.

BETTY: I think so, too.

BILL: So what if I admire Trotsky?

(Bell)

So what if I once had a total body liposuction?

(Bell)

So what if I don't have a penis?

(Bell)

So what if I spent a year in the Peace Corps? I was acting on my convictions.

BETTY: Convictions are important.

BILL: You just can't hang a sign on a person.

BETTY: Absolutely. I'll bet you're a Scorpio.

(Many bells ring)

BETTY: Listen, I was headed to the movies after I finished this section. Would you like to come along?

BILL: That sounds like fun. What's playing?

BETTY: A couple of the really early Woody Allen movies.

BILL: Oh.

BETTY: Don't you like Woody Allen?

BILL: Sure. I like Woody Allen.

BETTY: But you're not crazy about Woody Allen.

BILL: Those early ones kind of get on my nerves.

BETTY: Uh-huh.

(Bell)

BILL: *(Simultaneously)* BETTY:
Y'know, I was headed to   I was thinking about . . .
the . . .

BILL: I'm sorry.

BETTY: No, go ahead.

BILL: I was just going to say that I was headed to the movies in a little while, and . . .

BETTY: So was I.

BILL: The Woody Allen festival?

BETTY: Just up the street.

BILL: Do you like the early ones?

BETTY: I think anybody who doesn't ought to be run off the planet.

BILL: How many times have you seen "Bananas"?

BETTY: Eight times.

BILL: Twelve. So are you still interested?

BETTY: Do you like Entenmann's crumb cake?

BILL: I went out at two o'clock this morning to buy one. Did you have an Etch-a-Sketch as a child?

BETTY: Yes! Do you like brussel sprouts?

BILL: I think they're gross.

BETTY: They *are* gross!

BILL: Do you still believe in marriage in spite of current sentiments against it?

BETTY: Yes.

BILL: And children?

BETTY: Three of them.

BILL: Two girls and a boy.

BETTY: Harvard, Vassar, and Brown.

BILL: And will you love me?

BETTY: Yes.

BILL: And cherish me forever?

BETTY: Yes.

BILL: Do you still want to go to the movies?

BETTY: Sure thing.

BILL and BETTY *(Together):* Waiter!

(BLACKOUT)

CHRISTMAS EVE ON
ORCHARD STREET

A Short Play

Allan Knee

Allan Knee

Allan Knee's most recent play, *The Man Who Was Peter Pan*, was performed at the American Repertory Theatre in Cambridge last year. Productions of his other plays include *Second Avenue Rag* at the Manhattan Punchline, *Santa Anita '42* at the Chelsea Theatre at BAM, and *The Minister's Black Veil* at Playwrights Horizons. On Broadway he was represented by the musical, *Late Nite Comic*. For television he wrote the four-part adaptation of Nathaniel Hawthorne's *The Scarlet Letter* and the special, *A Gorey Halloween*, based on the characters of Edward Gorey. His short film, *Journey*, won a Cine Eagle at the Washington Film Festival. He is currently working on a musical adaptation of *The Picture of Dorian Gray*. Mr. Knee is a graduate of the Yale Drama School.

Scene:

The time is 1910. The place is the workroom of a dressmaker's shop in lower Manhattan. ELIAS *is putting the finishing touches on a dress modeled by* GERT, *an attractive, lively, enthusiastic young woman.* ELIAS *is the master tailor, a mature man, settled in his ways. He is assisted by* SAMMY, *a young man, hopeful and realistic, with a passion for* GERT. *Outside the shop, carolers are singing.*

GERT: I love Christmas.

SAMMY: *(On his knees, adjusting* GERT*'s dress)* You shouldn't say that.

ELIAS: What if God is listening?

GERT: I hope He is.

SAMMY: It's not your holiday, woman.

GERT: All holidays are mine.

ELIAS: Listen to her.

GERT: I was born for holidays.

SAMMY: You were born to bear babies.

GERT: You know nothing about me. Nothing.

SAMMY: I know you've got a body I love to feel. *(He throws his arms around her waist)*

GERT: *(Smiling)* That tickles.

(They continue working)

SAMMY: How about you and me stepping out tonight? I'll show you a good time.

GERT: Maybe in the spring.

SAMMY: In the spring? I could be dead by spring.

GERT: I've made other plans.

ELIAS: She goes nowhere. She goes home. She lives in a dream world.

GERT: You men—you've got all the answers. I'll tell you something. I take long walks. I meet people. I study people. *(Looking at herself)* Yesterday I met a woman. Had sleeves puffed out to here. They almost draped to the ground. She walked—you should've seen her walk. Like this. With her head high. Like she was royalty.

ELIAS: It's money.

GERT: It's more than money. I passed her and said, "Merry Christmas, madam." And she looked at me and smiled. A radiant smile.

SAMMY: And for that she wants to be a shikse.

GERT: *(Goes to the window)* Look at them. Look at their faces. Look how happy they are. *(She turns back into the room)* Last Saturday I walked uptown and everyone thought I was a Catholic.

ELIAS: A Catholic?

SAMMY: How could they tell?

GERT: I went into a church. I lit a candle. I thought, they'll throw me out. But so what.

SAMMY: Did they throw you out?

GERT: No! They thought I was one of them.

ELIAS: Turn around, my little Jewish shikse. *(Looking at the dress)* What do you think, Sammy?

SAMMY: *(Looking at GERT)* Beautiful.

ELIAS: I mean the dress.

SAMMY: I like the bosom. How do you make a bosom like that? *(He goes to touch the bosom)*

GERT: *(Turns away, laughs)* Don't.

SAMMY: It's only business.

ELIAS: *(To SAMMY)* Go see if the man who's bought this priceless garment is here yet.

(SAMMY starts out)

SAMMY: *(Turns back to GERT)* Hey! Wanna go skating?

GERT: I don't skate.

SAMMY: I'll teach you. I'm very good.

GERT: Maybe some other time.

SAMMY: All the Catholics go skating.

GERT: Go see if he's here.

(SAMMY *goes*)

ELIAS: *(Continuing to work on the dress)* Shall I tell you something? I'm getting old. How old would you say I was?

GERT: Don't ask me. I really don't know these things.

ELIAS: C'mon, guess.

GERT: I'm bad with ages, Elias.

ELIAS: Guess.

(She looks at him)

GERT: 70.

ELIAS: 70? I look 70?

GERT: You asked me how old I thought you were. I told you.

ELIAS: I'm 53.

GERT: You look older.

ELIAS: It's true. I've begun to creak. *(He bends, making his own creaking sound. He straightens)* Still, something in me wants to live. Shall I tell you a secret? Sometimes when I see a woman I like, I follow her home.

GERT: You follow women home?

ELIAS: Mind you, I've no evil intentions. I just want to follow her—think about her—and should she be interested—maybe have a drink with her.

GERT: And what would your wife say if she knew?

ELIAS: My wife—she's a good woman, a wonderful woman. An excellent cook. Her noodles are the talk of Cherry Street. But she's got a very somber outlook on life. Living with her is like living with a judge. I walk through the door each night and cry out, "Not guilty!" . . . Another question. If I were Christian, would you go for me?

GERT: Absolutely.

ELIAS: I don't believe you. An older man?

GERT: You're a man of experience. You could teach me things.

ELIAS: I could . . . Once I followed you.

GERT: *(Surprised)* You followed *me*?

ELIAS: *(Smiles with embarrassment)* I didn't know it was you. All I saw was a beautiful woman. It's true, I don't see too well from a distance. So I followed. I imagined so many wild things with you, Gert. You wouldn't believe. From a distance, you truly inspired me. But when I saw it was you, my God, I got sick to my stomach.

GERT: I affect men that way.

ELIAS: Come here. Let me fix that collar. *(She goes to him)* You got a very nice neck, you know. First thing I noticed about you was your neck. You can tell a lot about a woman by her neck.

GERT: I've got a secret too, Elias.

ELIAS: My God, it's a night of confessions.

GERT: The man coming for the dress—

ELIAS: The great Hartman. The great liberal.

GERT: I *know* him.

ELIAS: We all know him. He comes into the shop.

GERT: No, I really know him. We've talked at length.

ELIAS: You and Hartman?

GERT: You won't believe this. You won't breathe a word to anyone—not even Sammy?

ELIAS: May my wife suffer shingles if I do.

GERT: We're going away together.

ELIAS: You and Hartman?

GERT: Shh! *(She dances about)* I can't tell you how happy I am. My things are all packed. Look. *(She shows him her valise)*

ELIAS: You don't own very much.

GERT: I'm not taking very much. My Jewish possessions I'm leaving behind. I didn't even take my lace.

ELIAS: He asked you to go with him?

GERT: *(Very deliberate)* He said—he would see me tonight. He said—he had something very important to tell me. Something that would make us both very happy. *(She looks out)* You dream of moments like this. You think they'll never come. And then one day—*(She turns to* ELIAS*)* I heard him speak once. He's a great speaker. *(She recites)* "Think what is true for you is true for all men and women. That is the stuff of genius."

ELIAS: He said that?

GERT: They call him a prophet. He has a truly magnificent face. *(Dreamily)* Tonight we'll sing Christmas carols together. And we'll go to the midnight mass. I've never actually been to a mass. *(She turns to* ELIAS*)* You think it's wrong of me?

ELIAS: I don't know.

GERT: Surely God understands. *(She turns away. Dreamily)* When he touches me—

ELIAS: He's touched you?

GERT: Politely. Like a gentleman would. Here. And here. And here. He said—I had the stuff in me to arouse a man's heart.

ELIAS: I think maybe he had another organ in mind.

GERT: *(Turns to him, excited)* He gave me a book to read. Look. *(She shows him a book)*

ELIAS: *(Reads)* "The Emancipated Woman."

GERT: I think he's buying this dress for me. Why else would he ask for me to model it? *(She sings)* "Silent night. Holy night—"

(SAMMY *comes rushing back in with a box of ribbons, which he drops before her*)

SAMMY: Here.

GERT: What's this?

SAMMY: I stole them for you.

GERT: Ribbons? What for?

SAMMY: I thought you might like them.

ELIAS: Put them back, Sammy.

GERT: I don't want his ribbons.

SAMMY: He's got millions of ribbons.

ELIAS: What are you doing?

SAMMY: *(Stuffing the ribbons in his mouth)* I'm eating them. I'm going crazy. *(He rushes to the window)* Those singers. I wish they'd stop. They're beginning to get on my nerves.

ELIAS: Did he come for the dress yet?

SAMMY: No.

ELIAS: Put the sash around her.

SAMMY: *(Going for the sash)* The boss says we have to work late tonight. Can you believe it? *(He puts the sash around GERT)*

ELIAS: Squeeze her in, Sammy.

SAMMY: Breathe in.

ELIAS: Tighter.

SAMMY: Hold your breath.

ELIAS: More.

GERT: I can't breathe.

ELIAS: Good. *(The sash is complete)* There. Go to the mirror. *(She does)*

SAMMY: I propose a toast. *(He fills three thimbles with schnaps)* To a masterpiece. And a master. Le'cheiim!

EVERYONE: Le'cheiim!

ELIAS: *(To* GERT*)* Let me see how it looks when you move.

(She walks about)

GERT: Once my father tried to force me to marry against my will. And when he wouldn't listen to my protests, I plunged my foot into a kettle of boiling water and held it there until it was nearly boiled raw.

SAMMY: *(Following after her fixing the dress)* Smart girl.

GERT: I didn't have to marry.

ELIAS: Hold your head a bit higher.

GERT: Of course my foot was scalded terribly, and I had to remain in bed for weeks.

ELIAS: Come this way.

GERT: But it was worth it.

SAMMY: *(Taking hold of her around the waist)* What other outrageous things have you done?

GERT: You don't take me seriously.

SAMMY: I do.

GERT: I still have the scars if you care to see them.

SAMMY: I'd love to see them.

GERT: You could never be what I want.

SAMMY: I'll change.

GERT: You'll always be a small little man working at Hein and Fox.

SAMMY: You're wrong. I'm thinking of going into junk.

GERT: Into junk?

SAMMY: They say there's a fortune to be made there. I've already talked to people. They all tell me one thing. Junk. *(He kisses her)*

(She smacks him hard across the face)

SAMMY: Merry Christmas.

ELIAS: He's here! I see him walking around.

GERT: Oh, my God!

ELIAS: Get out there!

GERT: I can't move.

ELIAS: Get out there!

GERT: I'm shaking.

ELIAS: Don't shake. Go.

(She starts off)

Stand straight. Head high, Gert.

(She goes)

She sleeps with him.

SAMMY: With who?

ELIAS: With that gentleman. Of course, it's just in her dreams. But I thought you'd like to know.

SAMMY: It's maddness, isn't it? It's like the whole world was inside out. Nothing makes sense. *(Returns to work)* There's a man in Yonkers says he'll give a thousand dollars for the conversion of a Jew to Christianity.

ELIAS: I'll take it.

SAMMY: Scratch a little Jew deep enough and you'll find a little Christian in him.

ELIAS: Scratch a little Jew deep enough and you'll kill him.

SAMMY: I'll make a fortune in junk.

ELIAS: *(Working)* My wife insists I work. "All right," I say, "You want me to work, I'll work. But don't expect love." She looked at me like I was out of my mind. "Love?" she said. "When have I ever expected love?" I couldn't believe I married such a woman. I used to spend my days reading the Talmud. Such days. My wife had a nice little business. Sold manure.

SAMMY: What sort of business is that for a woman?

ELIAS: A good business, believe me. We ate good. We slept good. And she rejoiced in the fact she was married to a man of learning. Now it's all greed. We've got twelve of everything. Twelve plates. Twelve cups. Twelve chairs. Twelve towels. And there's just two of us. I keep asking her, "Who are you expecting?"

SAMMY: I'll never marry.

ELIAS: You never know. Everyone makes mistakes.

SAMMY: I know. I'll never marry.

(GERT *walks back in. The men turn to her. The carolers continue singing.* ELIAS *looks at her. She seems to be in a daze*)

ELIAS: Well?

SAMMY: Say something.

(*She continues to walk as if in a trance*)

ELIAS: Gert, tell us.

SAMMY: What was said?

GERT: He wasn't alone.

ELIAS: Who was with him?

GERT: He introduced me to—to—

SAMMY: To who?

GERT: His fiancee.

ELIAS: What about the dress?

GERT: The dress?

ELIAS: What did he say?

GERT: He didn't remember my name. I had to tell him.

ELIAS: But what about the dress?

GERT: He said—he said—it was perfection.

ELIAS: He liked the dress!

GERT: *(Explodes)* I hate it here! I hate being a Jew! I hate being stuck in this shop! Working twelve hours a day! I hate the two of you!

(Silence. They listen to the singing)

SAMMY: I wish they'd shut up!

GERT: I want to be out there with them.

SAMMY: *(Stopping her)* I understand your feelings. I do.

ELIAS: It's begun to snow. Look.

(They look out. The singing continues)

SAMMY: What do you say—we go out? The three of us?

ELIAS: The three of us?

SAMMY: Why not? We'll be like Christians tonight. We'll do big things. We'll pretend we're rich, uptown people. We'll celebrate and give gifts. And we'll love one another. Like a brotherhood. I mean for one night, why not? *(The singing continues)* Gert? What do you say? *(The singing continues. They listen)*

GERT: Yes! Yes! You're right. We'll sing. We'll do something wonderful for ourselves. We needn't be stuck here forever. America is a big place.

SAMMY: Of course it's big. It's enormous. We'll sing carols.

ELIAS: I've never sung a Christmas carol.

SAMMY: We'll sing! And for one night, we'll love each other. Le'cheiim!

EVERYONE: Le'cheiim!

(The carolers continue singing, as the lights lower)

AKHMATOVA

A Play in One Act

Romulus Linney

Romulus Linney

Romulus Linney is the author of three novels and twenty-eight plays, which have been seen, over the past twenty years, in resident theatres across the United States, as well as in New York, Los Angeles, London and Vienna. They include *The Sorrows of Frederick, Holy Ghosts, Childe Byron, April Snow* and *Three Poets*. Five of his one act plays have appeared in *Best Short Plays*, *Time* magazine picked *Laughing Stock* as one of the ten best plays of 1984, his adaptation and direction of his 1962 novel *Heathen Valley* won the National Critics Award and appears in *Best Plays of the Year 1987–88*, and his play *2* won the same award for the season of 1989–90 in its Humana Festival production at the Actors Theatre of Louisville, and appears in *Best Plays of the Year 1989–90*. He has received two fellowships from NEA, as well as Guggenheim, Rockefeller, and National Foundation for the Arts grants, an Obie Award, three Hollywood Drama-Logue Awards, the Mishima Prize for Fiction, and in 1984, the Award in Literature from the American Academy and Institute of Arts and Letters. He has directed his plays for the Milwaukee Repertory, the Alley Theatre, the Philadelphia Festival for New Plays, the Whole Theatre Company, the San Francisco Bay Area Festival, the Actors Studio, and the Theatre for the New City. He is a member of the Ensemble Studio Theatre, the Executive Board of American PEN and a Director of the Corporation of Yaddo. A graduate of Oberlin College and the Yale School of Drama, he teaches playwriting, screenwriting and fiction at Columbia and the University of Pennsylvania. He lives in New York City.

Characters

PECDOV

MARYA

RUDINSKY

KLARINA

ANNA AKHMATOVA

Place:
Moscow

Time:
10 a.m. March 6, 1953

Scene:
A red flag on the black wall. An elegant carpet. A sturdy table with two chairs on each side. On the table is a cigarette box and ashtray, matches. Two other chairs downstage on each side.

Morning light. A deep bell tolls.

PECDOV *stands in the light, at ease, relentlessly cheerful.* MARYA *sits. She is terrified, trying not to show it.*

PECDOV: Stalin, dead. Difficult to believe. Hard to grasp. *(He mimes closing a window. The bell is shut out. He turns to* MARYA*)* It is about ten pages long. Divided into many sections. A poem. We don't know the title.

MARYA: I see.

PECDOV: It is about a woman standing in front of a prison.

MARYA: I see.

PECDOV: She is waiting.

MARYA: I see.

PECDOV: *(Smiling)* Please say something beside "I see." It sounds pedantic.

MARYA: I'm sorry.

PECDOV: Such poems, given out in pieces for different people to memorize, exist like that. Unwritten. To be assembled. The existence of this one is alarming. Why? We'll see. *(Pause. He stares at her a moment, smiling)* Well, old woman, standing in line. Thinking, probably, poetic thoughts. Anything wrong with that?

MARYA: If her thoughts are a danger to the state, yes.

PECDOV: How could they be? Some old bag of bones? But then, another woman becomes involved. She is also standing in the prison line. What does she say?

MARYA: How should I know?

PECDOV: Guess.

MARYA: How the old women could threaten the state?

PECDOV: That's better.

MARYA: They know something. State secrets?

PECDOV: They have no knowledge of anything about the government. Try again.

MARYA: One old woman is the poet?

PECDOV: Brilliant.

MARYA: And the other is like the reader. Audience. You and me.

PECDOV: You are capable of marvels.

MARYA: They have made someone in the government angry.

PECDOV: Exasperated, better word. Would you like a cigarette?

MARYA: No, thank you.

PECDOV: Do you mind if I smoke?

MARYA: Please do.

PECDOV: Well, maybe I won't. *(He doesn't smoke)* Try again. Personal life. Husband, say.

MARYA: The poet is married to the wrong person.

PECDOV: She was once but he died. You're getting close.

MARYA: She is accusing someone of something.

PECDOV: Stay where you were. Not marriage, but what comes next?

MARYA: Children?

PECDOV: Children. Exactly. This old woman, well, maybe not so old as I've made out, late forties, let's say, and in an oriental sort of way, quite handsome—she has a child. In the prison.

MARYA: Oh. *(Pause)* Akhmatova.

PECDOV: Good for you. *(Smiling)* Ever met her?

MARYA: You know I have.

PECDOV: I'm glad we're being straightforward with each other. One of the women in line: Anna Andreyevna Akhmatova. The other an old hag. Then, ten pages of poetry, saying we know not what, and at the very end, something overwhelming. Stupendous. But's all we know. Ever meet Gumilev, her son?

MARYA: After he was in prison.

PECDOV: The first time? That was in the thirties.

MARYA: When I was a child.

PECDOV: Set free to fight in the Army. War over, his grateful nation puts him in prison again. In and out and in, like that. I wonder why?

MARYA: His mother.

PECDOV: Um, and out of her son's tragedy she makes yet another poem, possibly treason. Poets are persistent, I'll say that for them. Now what? *(Pause)* Do you like this room? It has always been used for these polite discussions. One of my predecessors, years ago, had Turgenev here. He was a young man then. So handsome, enormous shocks of hair. So rich. Mama's enormous hunks of the motherland. A thousand slaves. He had written a story. Do you know what he was told? Right here?

MARYA: No.

PECDOV: Given a brandy first. A Minister of Culture, no doubt quite like me, congratulated him. "Welcome, Ivan Sergeevich, to Russian letters!" "Thank you." There was a moment: Turgenev waiting to hear what was to be cut from his story, and the Minister like me waiting to strike to the heart of the matter. Which he did.

MARYA: I see.

PECDOV: *(Quickly)* You *see?*

MARYA: I beg your pardon! I don't see! What happened then?

PECDOV: Turgenev finally blurted out, "Well, come now! What do you want cut?" Would you call that rude?

MARYA: Uh, yes.

PECDOV: I wouldn't. He asked an honest question. He got an honest answer. "We don't want to change a word of what you have written," said the man like me. "We just want to break its spirit." *(Pause) You see? (Pause)* Do you have any idea of what I'm saying?

MARYA: Not quite, no.

PECDOV: Well. We sit here in this same room, almost a century later, and I am saying the same thing, this time about a woman who stood in a line in front of a prison and then didn't write down a poem about it. Whatever that is, I want to break its spirit, but I don't know what that spirit is, or what it says. I only know who possesses it.

MARYA: Akhmatova.

PECDOV: But why should I call you in, someone who knows her only slightly?

MARYA: You know I know her very well.

PECDOV: Yes, I do know that. But still, why? To ask you what she wrote?

MARYA: To ask if it threatens you.

PECDOV: Absolutely, and not just in the spirit. A real threat, in revolutionary terms. You love your country, don't you?

MARYA: Yes.

PECDOV: You wouldn't do anything to hurt her, would you?

MARYA: Never.

PECDOV: Do you think Akhmatova would?

MARYA: No, I don't.

PECDOV: How do you know?

MARYA: Her patriotic poems mean what they say. She wrote poems in praise of Stalin, too.

PECDOV: I know she wrote them and I know why and it wasn't for the love of Comrade Stalin. It was to keep her son from being executed. At the end of this poem, there is something else. What? Don't know. But whatever it is, people weep at the thought of it. So moved, they give Akhmatova money. Food. They help her live. What is it?

MARYA: I don't know.

(Pause)

PECDOV: In her early poems there are always lovers. Lovers, lovers. Zhdanov called her half nun, half whore. Do you know many writers like that?

MARYA: I know many writers who would like to be like that.

PECDOV: Artistic wit is so delicious. When a country needs patriots. *(Pause)* Anna Akhmatova is a relic of the Russian past. Living on, because of a talent, gift, yes, remarkable, for writing artistic ditties. Impressive as verse, perhaps: accurate, specific, surprising, melodious in her blunt way, sticking in the mind. But what is it about? Personal superiority, that's what it's about!! Nostalgia for a childhood in the city of the Tsars, and how beautiful were the pine trees! Young lieutenants committing suicide! Great artists, mysterious doubles! All this bunk steaming in the rotten fumes of sick Christian mysticism, and the stink of Great Art. What could be worse for a Working People than a self-absorbed Nun/Whore Artiste! Our Soviet children, studying *her* in school? Today? Unthinkable! Stalin would get right out of his coffin! *(Smile)* But I am always ready to learn. *(Pause)* Who is the other old woman in her poem?

MARYA: I don't know.

PECDOV: I have asked you two questions. What revelation is at the end of the poem and who is the old woman at the beginning. You say you don't know. Can you anticipate the next question?

MARYA: No.

PECDOV: Simple. Have you read the poem? But, wait, I haven't asked you yet. I don't want to, because then if you say you haven't, we face real difficulties. I haven't asked you anything yet. Nothing can be done to you yet. All right?

MARYA: Yes.

PECDOV: You're shaking. You've said nothing wrong. You are a valued worker, a teacher, respected by your students. However, once I ask you that question, then—we're in the soup. Your job, husband, children and so on. Do I have to ask?

(Long pause)

MARYA: She gave me five words to remember. And I know the title. Requiem.

PECDOV: Requiem? *(Laughs)* Not for Stalin, that's for certain. For her son? Maybe. For our government? Maybe. Only five words?

MARYA: That's all.

PECDOV: Do you expect me to believe that?

MARYA: It's the truth!

PECDOV: Why only five words?

MARYA: I don't know. Maybe she didn't trust me.

PECDOV: What are the five words.

MARYA: River. Cows. Doves. Rain. Statue.

PECDOV: What?

MARYA: Key words, maybe. I think for the ending of the poem, but she didn't say that.

PECDOV: This is all you have to tell me?

MARYA: It's all I know.

PECDOV: Statue. Whose?

MARYA: I don't know that, either.

PECDOV: Statue, statue. There is no statue in front of that prison.

MARYA: I didn't think so.

PECDOV: What else? What *else?*

MARYA: Anna Andreyevna told me nothing else. I swear it.

PECDOV: *(Smiling)* I see. Wait outside, with the others.

MARYA: You're smiling.

PECDOV: I begin my day with joy, and end it with joy. In between, I smile a lot. Wait outside.

(Exit MARYA, *as fast as she can*)

PECDOV: Hm.

(Blackout. Lights up on PECDOV *with* RUDINSKY, *a man in shabby, worn clothes)*

PECDOV: You'll have to do better than that!

RUDINSKY: He just won't talk about his mother.

PECDOV: But does he know about it?

RUDINSKY: You mean her poem?

PECDOV: No, *the end of the world.* Sit down!

RUDINSKY: You mean her poem?

PECDOV: *(Sighs)* God damn it.

RUDINSKY: Forgive me, but I have been given very peculiar instructions! Go to prison! Get to know a man! Find out about his mother! I am performing this duty to the very best of my ability but I can't threaten him! I can't work him over! I can't get *at* him! God damn it yourself! I beg your pardon.

PECDOV: Frustrated, are you? Have to know why you are doing what you are doing? *(Pause)* All right. Stalin died Sunday, after an all night

dinner with Beria, Bulganin, Khruschev, and Malenkov. A purge was
on. At the top. At the *very* top. Put it together. Well? *Well?*

RUDINSKY: *(Aghast)* They murdered Stalin?

PECDOV: It's possible. Cerebral hemorrhages can be brought about. Now,
a rising Minister of Culture, in my position, does what?

RUDINSKY: Something threatening none of them.

PECDOV: Of course, but what?

RUDINSKY: Nothing?

PECDOV: Fatal. It would be like I was waiting.

RUDINSKY: Some—ah—useful activity? Involving some general security?
Like that?

PECDOV: Maybe. One of them will take over, but who? Everything is in
the whirlwind. Anything can happen. Even a revolution, a real one this
time. Zhdanov always said Anna Akhmatova was a traitor. Now she is
writing an invisible poem about prisons and old women with endings
that make people weep. What could it mean?

RUDINSKY: My God, another revolution?

PECDOV: Maybe. Maybe. Does the son know about her poems?

RUDINSKY: He knows she writes about him. But he doesn't know what.

PECDOV: Does he still hate his mother?

RUDINSKY: Well, some. She farmed him out to his grandmother. She was
a poet instead of a mother. He remembers her with bitterness. I did
get that out of him.

PECDOV: Did you tell him Stalin is dead?

RUDINSKY: Yesterday. He won't talk to me at all now.

PECDOV: Did he believe something would happen upon the death of Stalin?

RUDINSKY: I think so.

PECDOV: Did he say anything about any specific poem? With something
overwhelming at the end of it?

RUDINSKY: No.

(Long pause)

PECDOV: Ah! Damn!

RUDINSKY: I did the best I could. With my hands tied behind my back!

PECDOV: I know that. Wait outside.

(PECDOV *shakes hands with* RUDINSKY, *claps him on the back. Exit* RUDINSKY. *Blackout. Light up on* PECDOV *and* KLARINA, *a well dressed woman in her forties. She is fierce and intelligent. She suffers from many psychological wounds)*

PECDOV: And the title of it, evidently, is "Requiem." What I need to find out is what happens at the end of it.

KLARINA: *(Paces)* And you think *I* can find out?

PECDOV: You of all people. Do you understand why?

KLARINA: Because she loved me, and doesn't know what I did to her.

PECDOV: *(Smiles)* Yes. Anna Andreyevna was so popular. The plainest people loved her steamy little verses, and I'll admit it, her. Stalin is dead. I want you to put those two things together? Can you?

KLARINA: No.

PECDOV: My dear woman, our great, vast, enormous land, our Soviet Russia, never had a revolution. Not a real one. Powers shifted. The backbone similarities between our government and the Russia of the Tsars are too obvious to need comment. We changed, yes, but not like France, or America. The thought of a truly popular revolution in our colossal country is not to be endured. Those who might bring it about must be dealt with. Now Stalin is gone. The one man who made a real revolution unthinkable is dead. And it is thinkable now. *(He stares at her)* Are you all right?

KLARINA: Yes, thank you. I just have a bit of a headache, is all.

PECDOV: Four popular artists. Friends. Mandelstam, Marina Tsvetaeva, Pasternak, Akhmatova. Only she survived. Why?

KLARINA: She is a great poet.

drove men crazy.

am very sorry to tell you that I am not the only one of your
rom the past to betray you! Others have too!

. The day Zhdanov attacked me, I hadn't read the papers. I
vent to market. I bought my fish, wrapped in a newspaper. I
ne, unwrapped my fish. Newspaper, article, Zhdanov. Death
et. My son in prison again. I thought it was you then.

d, my head!

RYA)

d afternoon.

, too?

You're getting nowhere. But stay.

the chairs downstage, facing ANNA)

u, Anna Andreyevna?

ank you.

I was.

arina told you what I've done?

em what I knew about Requiem.

imagine why.

boy.

do to my son what they did to yours. Or worse.

PECDOV: Of a sort, maybe.

KLARINA: People *love* the poems. Half Russia recites Akhmatova.

PECDOV: Good. Defend her.

KLARINA: She refused to emigrate. She wrote passionately about staying
with her country. She wrote a war poem praising Stalin.

PECDOV: All right. Mandelstam, labor camp. Tsvetaeva, suicide. Pasternak, muzzled. But Akhmatova remains, cooking up some deadly invisible opus called Requiem, of *what*, we may well ask! Do you follow me?

KLARINA: A revolution *after* after Stalin? That's very doubtful. We loved
Stalin. Didn't we?

PECDOV: *(Quickly)* Of course we did! But a group begins now. Establishes
something. Keeps on. In a year, five? I want you to talk to her again.

KLARINA: *(Paces)* You can't ask me to do that.

PECDOV: Why not?

KLARINA: When she stood outside the prison walls, in those awful lines,
she had time to think. She knows it was somebody's idea.

PECDOV: Which worked very well.

KLARINA: Do you know why I did that to her?

PECDOV: You love your country.

KLARINA: Yes, but something else.

PECDOV: She took a man away from you?

KLARINA: She is Dante!

PECDOV: And you are a Russian patriot. That's better than being Dante.
You will try again. Right now.

KLARINA: She's *here?*

PECDOV: In the next room. Waiting, she thinks, to see her son.

KLARINA: Oh my God.

PECDOV: When she comes in, she will find you here instead. Her friend who put him away in the first place. Elegant.

KLARINA: What do you have to know?

PECDOV: The old woman. That ending. Listen. Troops surround Moscow this instant. Tanks at every crossroad. This city is sealed off, but by an army ready to do God knows what under orders from God knows who!

KLARINA: Remember, she had a husband shot! She has a son in chains!

PECDOV: Oh yes, I know that. If Russia faces chaos, who cares? Here, smoke. If you get nowhere, don't worry. I'll be listening. *(Exit PECDOV)*

(Blackout. Lights up on ANNA AKHMATOVA. She has just entered the room. She is staring, stricken, at KLARINA. She sinks into a chair. She is a middle aged woman, once a slim, imperious beauty, now growing pleasantly fat. She is a little unkempt, but erect, and self possessed. For many, she is the greatest poet in Russia)

ANNA: Oh.

(She sits in the chair, devastated. KLARINA moves to the other chair, sits by her)

KLARINA: This is cruel.

ANNA: Yes.

KLARINA: I didn't send for you.

ANNA: I believe you.

KLARINA: I don't know where he is, or what is happening to him. Have you heard anything?

ANNA: Not in three years.

KLARINA: You're looking very—

ANNA: Thanks to you!

(Pause)

KLARINA: Anna! *(Pause)* You've known, all this time?

(Anna nods)

KLARINA: It wasn't just me, you know! It w[...] you. Stalin had so much trouble with h[...] gested to him, he said it was the perfec[...]

ANNA: He was right. You were right. It w[...]

(Pause)

KLARINA: Well. What are you writing no[...]

ANNA: Poetry in praise of Stalin.

KLARINA: I mean, anything else?

ANNA: Nothing else.

KLARINA: *(Paces)* Just tell me, please? [...] else can I do but ask you, my darli[...]

ANNA: Nothing.

KLARINA: So tell me!

ANNA: Nothing. I've written nothin[...]

KLARINA: They know about Requie[...]

ANNA: About what?

KLARINA: The old woman standin[...] a poem about her, and it is co[...]

ANNA: An old woman in a priso[...]

KLARINA: If the old woman is cr[...]

ANNA: Interesting, as always, h[...]

KLARINA: It is your mind and [...] worrying about!

ANNA: You are still beautiful.

KLARINA: What's in the poen[...]

ANNA: A boy once killed hir[...]

KLARINA: What overwhelmi[...]

ANNA: We[...]

KLARINA: I[...] friends f[...]

ANNA: Mos[...] slept in, [...] went hor[...] to the po[...]

KLARINA: G[...]

(Enter MA[...]

MARYA: Goo[...]

KLARINA: You[...]

MARYA: Yes. [...]

(They sit in[...] How are yo[...]

ANNA: Well, th[...]

MARYA: I wish [...]

ANNA: So do I. [...]

MARYA: Has Kl[...]

KLARINA: No.

MARYA: I told t[...]

ANNA: Oh.

MARYA: You can[...]

ANNA: Yes.

MARYA: It was a [...]

ANNA: So I heard[...]

MARYA: They can[...]

ANNA: Yes.

MARYA: So I told them my five words.

ANNA: I see.

MARYA: They think it's the old way of passing poetry on, but different, somehow, and worse.

ANNA: I see.

KLARINA: They think it is dangerous.

MARYA: They're afraid you are writing about something to come after the death of Stalin.

KLARINA: What happens at the end of Requiem, Anna? That's what they have to know!

MARYA: They'll take it out of you, when they want to!

KLARINA: They believe us when we say we don't know what happens!

MARYA: But that can change!

KLARINA: You know we *don't* know!

MARYA: We could die!

KLARINA: If they don't find out!

MARYA: It's only a poem!

KLARINA: They can shoot us all!

MARYA: Your son! Mine!

KLARINA: You have to tell us, Anna!

MARYA: You have to tell us something!

(Pause)

ANNA: I will tell you this. If you love Russia, you can dig for her.

MARYA: What?

KLARINA: Dig? For something buried?

KLARINA & MARYA: Where?

ANNA: In Petersburg. Where Mandelstam said it was.

KLARINA: Mandelstam?

MARYA: Petersburg?

ANNA: I'm tired now. We had many good times, the three of us. When you were little, Marya, and Klarina loved the voice of God. No more.

KLARINA: The voice of God?

ANNA: That's what poetry is. You've forgotten. Goodbye. *(She closes her eyes)*

KLARINA: Anna.

MARYA: Anna.

KLARINA & MARYA: Anna!

(Pause. ANNA *seems to be asleep. Enter* RUDINSKY*)*

RUDINSKY: I'll wake her up. *(He slams a chair down directly in front of* ANNA, *and sits in it)* I have been living with your son. In the same cell. He isn't where you think he is. He is here. In Moscow. Maybe five blocks from here. Look at me.

*(*ANNA *keeps her eyes shut)*

I can get to him in an hour. I can tell him things. Imagine.

*(*RUDINSKY *gets up, speaks directly into her ear)*

He is going free. He will rot in a camp 'til he dies. His mother has used him to write a poem, for which he can be shot!

*(*ANNA *opens her eyes)*

ANNA: Five blocks?

RUDINSKY: Five blocks. *(Satisfied, he sits down again)* You've been playing games with your son's life.

ANNA: Games? Do you think, after all these years, waiting to see him again, I would refuse to tell you anything on earth? You silenced me as no other human being who ever lived. Tell me I can see him, and I will tell you anything you ask me.

RUDINSKY: What happens to the old woman? What happens at the end of the poem? *That's* what you can tell us!

ANNA: All right, but do I see my son?

RUDINSKY: I can't promise, but yes, probably!

MARYA: Anna, you gave me rain, a cow, boats and a statue. Is it the statue? Of someone—revolutionary?

ANNA: If I tell you, will that set him free?

RUDINSKY: It might!

KLARINA: Tell us, Anna!

MARYA: Please, Anna!

(Enter PECDOV. *He carries a decanter of brandy and two glasses)*

PECDOV: "We will meet in Petersburg, around the grave where we buried the sun." She'll tell me now. Out.

(Exeunt MARYA, KLARINA *and* RUDINSKY. PECDOV *takes the chair* RUDINSKY *had set in front of* ANNA *and puts it back in place. He pours a brandy and hands it to her)*

Brandy?

ANNA: Thank you.

*(*PECDOV *pours himself a brandy)*

PECDOV: To a statue buried in the tomb of the sun. To your good health.

ANNA: To yours.

(They sip the brandy)

PECDOV: So. Here we are.

ANNA: You've done very well.

PECDOV: Yes, I have. The faithful disciple. Who sat at the feet of the master poets, with such humility. Such devotion to the great causes, until I discovered the great causes were the great egos of the great poets. Skillful parasites, just like Plato says, feeding on the state. So I became a Minister of the People, and slept well at night.

ANNA: I am glad you sleep well at night.

PECDOV: Let us go back to Petersburg. To the grave of the sun.

ANNA: All right.

PECDOV: I remember it, too. Better than you, perhaps. (PECDOV *closes his eyes and recites, broadly, in the Russian manner)* "We will meet in Petersburg, around the grave where we buried the sun—

(ANNA closes her eyes, and recites)

ANNA: "And then together we will say it for the first time, the wonderful word meaning nothing—

(Both, eyes closed, recite)

PECDOV: *(Reciting)* "In the new Russian night, soft and beautiful darkness, a black velvet nowhere, the beloved eyes of sacred women are still singing, flowers blossom that will live forever—

ANNA: *(Reciting)* "The city gathers itself like a lost cat, soldiers are stationed on the bridges, one automobile dashes blindly by, siren whooping like a screaming bird—

PECDOV: *(Reciting)* "Tonight I will not carry my credentials, I have no fear of the soldiers. I will pray in the new Russian night, for the wonderful word meaning nothing—

ANNA: *(Reciting)* "For fun we will stand by a fire, maybe time will fall apart, and the beloved hands of sacred women will sweep the ashes back together—

PECDOV: *(Reciting)* "Don't worry when the candles all snuff out, in the soft and beautiful darkness, the black nowhere. The bent shoulders of sacred women are still singing—

PECDOV & ANNA: *(Reciting)* You will not see the sun, still burning in the night."

(Pause)

PECDOV: Mandelstam.

ANNA: Mandelstam.

PECDOV: And poetry, the voice of God. Do you know how he died?

ANNA: No.

PECDOV: He died paranoid in a camp, certain his filthy grub was being poisoned. He tried to stay alive by stealing food from other prisoners. They beat him to death. Great poet of the Russian land.

ANNA: I am not surprised.

PECDOV: I denounced him to Stalin.

ANNA: I am not surprised.

PECDOV: He read ten of us a poem about Stalin, in which Stalin had cockroach eyebrows, and greasy fingers staining the pages of books by men he would kill. It was the single denunciation of Stalin ever written down by anyone, and that one poem did it. Now it is your turn. But you are different. Not as a poet. As a mother.

ANNA: How ingenious, the Devil. Killing a woman with her son. Mephistopheles, blush.

PECDOV: I always forget the Christian part of you. The nun within the whore. Never mind Mephistopheles. While Stalin lived, your son was safe. Kept in prison, used to torment you, but not to be killed. Now Stalin is gone, and others will make that decision. Who is the statue that makes people weep?

(ANNA *doesn't answer*)

I can let him go. You can be drinking champagne with him in half an hour. Or he can be shot. Not another second. Is there a statue?

ANNA: Yes.

(PECDOV *gets up*)

PECDOV: Of someone revolutionary?

ANNA: Yes.

PECDOV: Making Russia weep?

ANNA: Yes.

PECDOV: Who?

ANNA: I am the statue.

PECDOV: What?

ANNA: I stand in front of that prison. My metal eyes weep tears. In my poem, I am the statue.

PECDOV: I don't understand.

ANNA: Of course not.

PECDOV: You have built a statue to *yourself?*

ANNA: Yes.

(Pause. PECDOV *laughs, richly and loudly, sits)*

PECDOV: Made yourself a monument? Made yourself *an icon?*

ANNA: *(To him, explaining it)* I have made a statue of an old woman, standing in a line outside a prison, waiting every day to see her son. In the line are many other women, with sons, daughters, husbands, sisters, mothers and fathers. All in prison. And to my country I say, if in some future year, you mark my life with a statue, I consent to that honor. But I will not stand in the gardens of my love affairs, or in the company of the splendid artists I have known, or before the applauding crowds who loved me, but there, in a line of women, by the riverboats and the doves, before an iron gate, which was never, not once, opened to me. Russia can remember me there, if she pleases.

PECDOV: My God! All this fuss! Anna Andreyevna, you are not a dangerous revolutionary. You are a crazy old woman.

ANNA: And you are an insect of a single day.

(A long pause)

PECDOV: It's not his fault your son has a madwoman for a mother. If I make an issue of this, I'll put myself up for ridicule. Keep your mouth shut and go in peace.

ANNA: Will I ever see him again?

PECDOV: Soon, maybe. Stalin is dead, who knows what will happen. Never, maybe. Stalin is dead, who knows what will happen. Goodbye.

*(*ANNA *nods and starts to exit)*

Certainly—

(ANNA *stops*)

Statues will be made. But not of you. Of Stalin, and in time, perhaps, of me.

(ANNA *goes to him. He looks at her*)

ANNA: Perhaps.

(Exit ANNA. PECDOV *stands thinking. He opens the window again. The bell tolls for Stalin. Light fades on* PECDOV, *thinking.)*

UNPROGRAMMED

A One Act Play

Carol K. Mack

Carol K. Mack

Carol K. Mack, a New York playwright, is an alumna of New Dramatists, a member of The Women's Project, Dramatists Guild, The League of Professional Theatre Women/N.Y., and P.E.N. Her work includes:

Borders, recipient of The Beverly Hills Theatre Guild/Julie Harris Playwright Award, selected for Prima Facie 2 at The Denver Center for the Performing Arts, 1986; *Territorial Rites*, a Susan Smith Blackburn and FDG/CBS Finalist, produced at The American Place Theatre, starring Kim Hunter and Michael Gross, 1983; *Postcards* (University of Jacksonville One Act Award) produced at Ensemble Studio Theatre, New York City, 1983; *A Safe Place* (Stanley Drama Award) premiered at The Berkshire Theatre Festival in Association with the Kennedy Center, 1981; *Survival Games*, produced in the New American Play Series by The Berkshire Theatre Festival, 1980; *Esther*, produced by Lucille Lortel at The White Barn Theatre Foundation in 1976, and Off Broadway in 1977.

Two commissions by the Actors Theatre of Louisville resulted in her one acts: *Hi Tech* and *Half Time at Halcyon Days*. *The Magenta Shift*, commissioned by the "Difficult Women's Project" funded by NYSCA, won the Playwrights' Forum Award, Theatreworks, University of Colorado, 1986. *A.K.A. Marlene* and *Postcards* were produced in 1989 at the Producers' Club, New York City. All the above one acts have received hundreds of productions ranging from the Theatre of the Open Eye, New York City to Los Angeles showcases to university and community theatre productions throughout the United States and abroad.

Current plays include: *Necessary Fictions*, nominated for a 1988 Rockefeller Fellowship; *Last Resorts* (a duo of one acts); songs for a political cabaret, The Snicker Factory, 1988; *Unprogrammed*, a new one act play, performed at The Westport Theatre Artists' Lab, 1989 and selected for *Best Short Plays*, 1990.

Carol K. Mack's earlier appearance in this series was in the 1985 edition with *Half Time at Halcyon Days*, a comedy about five women in a health spa. For the past six years, Ms. Mack has taught "Life Stories," a fiction-writing class, at New York University, where she is now completing her Master of Arts degree in Religious Studies with a concentration on the traditions of the East.

Characters

GEORGE, edgy, insecure, very intelligent computer programmer.

HAROLD, suburban space salesman, GEORGE's drinking buddy.

CAPRICE, beautiful, candid, young woman. Has a subtle, unplaceable accent.

Set:

Downstage Left is a bar, with two stools upstage of it that face the audience; Upstage Center there is a small table and two chairs; Stage Right there is a rock. All the above seating areas are preset. Handprops are carried on and off by actors.

Time:

Summer in suburbia.

(Lights up. GEORGE and HAROLD lean on bartop Stage Left. GEORGE is cold sober and HAROLD is cosmically drunk)

GEORGE: *(Intensely)* Harold. Listen to me, Harold. Am I your friend?

(No response)

Am I your friend or am I NOT your friend?

HAROLD: What?

GEORGE: Am I or not?

HAROLD: Sure.

GEORGE: Right! Now, did I, *how* many times, how many times did I tell you, Harold?

HAROLD: Huhnh?

GEORGE: *Never*, Rule Number One, *never* do you give up *what* in a relationship?

HAROLD: What?

GEORGE: Control, Harold, control!

HAROLD: I love her, George, I love her!

GEORGE: This is what I'm *saying*. Tell me if this isn't what I'm telling you: What're you doing? You're reacting to re*actions*! You're not even *you*. You're a chain reaction. This is what you want out of life?

HAROLD: I want Brenda back.

GEORGE: Brenda, Jesus, Harold, Brenda! You should *know* by now! We're talking offense, not defense. With Brenda, you re*act,* she walks on your face!

HAROLD: Yeah.

GEORGE: I'm trying to *help* you!

HAROLD: I see what you're saying.

GEORGE: Good.

HAROLD: But Brenda . . . no listen, I can read Brenda already. Did I tell you there'd be a note when I got home? This is *what?* The third time! *(He takes nuts from bowl places them one by one on bartop)* She loves me, she loves me not, she took the Volvo.

GEORGE: *(Eats nuts as they hit)* You don't have to go through this, Harold. You don't have to *feel!* That should be your goal, Harold: numbness.

HAROLD: If she'd only give me one more chance I'd . . . I'd be, it'd be totally different. I'd go straight home from the train.

GEORGE: Get hold of yourself.

HAROLD: I GOTTA get Brenda back.

GEORGE: You've got one chance. Did I make you an offer that could save your life, huh?

HAROLD: *(Confusedly, trying to remember)* You know where she went?

GEORGE: NO. I told you I could put Brenda in my database and get you a printout on her every move.

HAROLD: Oh yeah! How do I do that again?

GEORGE: *I* do it! *I* do it! I'm the computer programmer. You're a space salesman, Harold, remember?

HAROLD: Oh yeah! You wanted me to tell you . . .

GEORGE: Facts! Hard facts. For my database. I programmed all variables in over two million relationships. A trillion gigabytes of female behavior! I can calculate their any move. It's all in there. No woman can take us by surprise. I'll get you a printout on Brenda by morning.

(HAROLD *passes out on the floor.* GEORGE *watches his body fall with some disgust)*

This is what happens when you're unprepared!

(GEORGE *steps over* HAROLD *and* HAROLD *remains corpse-like for the following scene.* GEORGE *begins jogging as he leaves the bar area and loops around the stage. He soon hears a voice (offstage)—a woman's voice singing a French folksong. He jogs slowly as he hears. The* WOMAN *enters singing. She is very beautiful. She sits calmly on a rock Stage Right and hums, oblivious)*

GEORGE: *(Upon seeing the* WOMAN, *startled, to himself, flatly, while jogging)* A Student, Undergrad, French Major, *no!* Maybe exchange student. Try Exchange Student, post grad, or an *act*ress. Possible. Possible. Retry! *Act*ress, memorizes part in . . . NO. Try Pseudofrancophile, spots ME, *genuine* Francophile jogging, NO. How would she know? But gorgeous, wow, whoa! Why so pale? Age? Age? Age? *(He slows near her, nonchalant)* Qu'est-ce-que vous chantez, Mademoiselle?

CAPRICE: *(Full of wonder, as if awakening)* Where am I?

GEORGE: *(Nonplussed by her full direct gaze)* You were, uh, singing something.

CAPRICE: It's *you* then . . . !

GEORGE: Right. Well, I thought I recognized the melody.

CAPRICE: *(Still delighted)* You heard me! You heard me singing!

GEORGE: Right. That's why I asked.

CAPRICE: I don't know the name, but if you'd like I'll sing it from the beginning. It has over a hundred verses. It's about a maiden who . . .

GEORGE: It's O.K. Just thought I recognized it. I have a small collection of obscure European folk tapes.

CAPRICE: Really!

GEORGE: Some old, some new. Some C.D.'s

CAPRICE: Oh I would so love to hear them. May I come to your home?

GEORGE: *(To himself, overwhelmed)* Careful . . . mind click. Boot *up!* Come on! . . . She could be homeless.

CAPRICE: What?

GEORGE: You're not from around here, huh?

CAPRICE: No, are you?

GEORGE: *(Sotto voce)* Toulouse. No. Try Canada. Not Connecticut. Not Connecticut.

CAPRICE: *(Smiling delightedly as if at a toy)* What did you say? You have such a nice whisper.

GEORGE: My name's George Appleman. I'm in computers.

CAPRICE: Nice to meet you George. *Very* nice. *(Shakes hands, moving closer)* My name is Caprice.

GEORGE: *(Backs off)* Uh, you just get to town?

CAPRICE: Yes!

GEORGE: You a . . . *dancer!* You look like a dancer! Am I right?

CAPRICE: Uh, yes. I do dance.

GEORGE: Bingo! Caprice what?

CAPRICE: What?

GEORGE: You have a last name?

CAPRICE: Just Caprice.

GEORGE: *(To himself)* Stage name. Getting there. Chill out. Take your time, George. *(To her, suddenly avuncular)* Look, I don't know how it is where you come from but here, I mean, *I'm* O.K., but do yourself a favor, don't talk to just any guy who . . . I mean there are a lot of creeps around.

CAPRICE: Oh . . . but you're O.K.?

GEORGE: Yeah, sure. I'm O.K.!

CAPRICE: Then would you help me to find my way?

GEORGE: *(Helpless from direct appeal. His eyes dart from side to side)* Some remake of Candid Camera. Sure! Maybe Letterman? No, then *what?* A hidden camera someplace. GOTta be. Keep smiling. Practical joke. *(Smiles in all directions for camera)*

CAPRICE: George? You're O.K.?

GEORGE: *("Cheerfully" suave for camera)* Sure. No problem. Where to?

CAPRICE: *(Hands him slip of paper)* Here is where I will live.

GEORGE: *(Stares at paper)* Not far from me. I jog along there sometimes just to look . . . very pretty neighborhood. *(Embarrassed at revealing anything)* Is it a sublet or . . .

CAPRICE: It has many trees?

GEORGE: Yeah. A lotta trees. Why?

CAPRICE: I was wondering.

GEORGE: *(Sotto voce)* Why THAT? Who IS this? What accent? Au Pair? Au Pair? *(To her)* You could walk it from here, unless you've got a car . . . ? *(She shakes her head "no")* I'll make a little map . . .

(She stands very very close watching. He is aware of her closeness, writes)

On paper you can see the layout better. Now we are "Here." Get that so far?

CAPRICE: George, excuse me . . . ?

GEORGE: What?

CAPRICE: Do you, could you, spare me a few moments to walk with me there?

GEORGE: *(Swallows as he sinks into her eyes)* Uh, sure. Sure, why not?

(They exit together. HAROLD *simultaneously stands at bar, rising from the floor drink in hand.* GEORGE, *who doesn't complete the "exit," loops around jogging back to bar, speaking as he does)*

GEORGE: What was I supposed to say, *no?* Somebody asks you for help crossing a street you say *no?* I just can't believe it.

(Arriving at HAROLD, *directly)*

I meet this girl . . . no. Girl is *wrong* . . . a *wom*an, no. Woman is wrong.

HAROLD: Person?

GEORGE: Person is wrong.

HAROLD: A *what?*

GEORGE: A WHAT? I don't know! A . . . what would she *be*—with a name like that? First I think she's playing with my mind, right? She's gorgeous, and she's gotta know it. You don't walk around gorgeous and not know, you know? But she's like, *surprised* I hear her singing. The only broad on the whole road singing, right? So why's she surprised? WHY?

HAROLD: You better have a drink.

GEORGE: O.K., O.K. But why no last name?

HAROLD: You asked her?

GEORGE: Yeah, Caprice what? Nothing. Where you from? Too long a story. Just . . . Caprice . . . who's got a fantastic body and navy blue eyes! (GEORGE *collapses)*

HAROLD: George, what's the matter?

GEORGE: I gotta find out *who* this chick is! Crack the source code! She's from . . . outta nowhere, Har! Maybe a *hooker,* enter that. But No, NO, she's a *kid* and like out of some old painting, like a Botticelli . . .

HAROLD: French. You said French. Not Italian.

GEORGE: It doesn't compute. She acts like she doesn't know what fork to use. Not a hick but like from Sherwood Forest, you know?

HAROLD: No . . .

GEORGE: Spacey?

HAROLD: Oh. Maybe she's *on* something.

GEORGE: *(A burst of Romantic enthusiasm, a very different tone)* There were all these little yellow butterflies, Harold. Like they all hatched at the same time and they're flying all over the road and then: there she *is* with this . . . *face!*

HAROLD: You didn't tell about the butterflies.

GEORGE: They mean something? Should I enter them? WHAT?

HAROLD: How would I know.

GEORGE: What'd you say it for?

HAROLD: Sounds *weird.* A whole bunch hatching like that. This whole thing sounds real weird, George.

GEORGE: Yeah! And another thing, she's so *pale.* I figure maybe she's out on a weekend pass . . . But then, she's so . . . she *looks* at you. I'm talking *enormous* eye contact. Delete mental. Delete. Delete.

HAROLD: So whaddya got?

GEORGE: *Nothing* is what I've got on her . . . except she doesn't know her way around and it makes you kind of want to . . .

HAROLD: Watch out, George!

GEORGE: What?

HAROLD: You're in over your head with no variables. You know, re*a*cting?

GEORGE: *(Straightens tie)* Don't worry about me. There are ways to format for aberrant behavior. I mean we are living Post Surprise, man! Post post.

HAROLD: If you say so . . .

GEORGE: With the right data everything's predictable! Halley's Comet is a *routine,* Harold. An eclipse? You don't have time for it live, you stick it on the VCR. This is an Age Beyond Reason! Thank God.

HAROLD: I see what you're saying. But this Caprice . . .

GEORGE: *(Snaps)* What?! What about her?!

HAROLD: Why not relax and enjoy, huh? So you can't figure every move . . . makes it kind of interesting, huh?

GEORGE: Interesting! A *tarantula* is interesting! You, of all people . . .

HAROLD: *(Shrugs)* Takes the fun out of . . .

GEORGE: Fun?! Look at the guy who lives near the volcano and *knows* when it's gonna blow. Then look at Pompei!

HAROLD: But maybe this once . . .

GEORGE: Once is all it takes. I've been moving too fast. It's all processing. Let this chick feed me hard facts. I'll take notes. She'll slip. She'll cross reference herself right into my program. Trust me, Harold, I'm at the controls.

HAROLD: But George . . . listen! . . . Brenda came home! What do I do? . . . hey?

(HAROLD, *slightly glazed, watches as* GEORGE *leaves his side, shakes his head and exits with glass, while* CAPRICE *enters from opposite side, her arms laden with flowers.* GEORGE *follows her glumly, notebook in hand)*

CAPRICE: There are flowers everywhere you look in this town, isn't it *wonderful,* George? Even in the grocery stores where you buy the food, and they also play music.

GEORGE: *(Grimly)* They didn't have flowers where you come from, Caprice? Or they didn't have food?

CAPRICE: *(Wide-eyed)* What, dear?

GEORGE: *(Startled)* Nothing. "Dear"?! *(Writes in notebook, aloud)* Too much too soon.

CAPRICE: George, tell me again about your work. It's so *intricate.* You seem so dedicated. Always taking notes, always thinking about your work.

GEORGE: She's trying to escape!

CAPRICE: Excuse me?

GEORGE: *(A benediction)* I want you to know, whatever you did or wherever you came from, I wouldn't hold it against you.

CAPRICE: Thank you!

GEORGE: I've heard just about everything. Nothing you could tell me would make headlines in my brain. So feel free to tell me anything at all about your past, all right?

CAPRICE: Thank you. And thank you for these beautiful flowers!

GEORGE: Anytime.

CAPRICE: We should put them in water.

GEORGE: All right then, forget the past. How about *now?* I'm not pushing but I was wondering . . . you have a job or what?

CAPRICE: You want me to "haf a job"?

GEORGE: ME? I mean hey, you're paying the rent and, I mean you said you were a dancer?

CAPRICE: I dance. Yes. I do and also I sing.

GEORGE: But what do you *eat?* I mean are you a medical illustrator or a *what?* Look, Caprice, whenever I get off the train, you're at the station. If I was some other guy I'd think you were maybe following me . . . *(Thinks, writes notes)* Hired to tail me, but *why?* Am I in some top secret program I don't know about? Being cleared for government work . . . *(To* CAPRICE*)* Are you C.I.A.?

CAPRICE: *(Laughs, delighted)* You are such a funny man, George. . . . C.I.A. You make me laugh.

GEORGE: I do, huh?

CAPRICE: Yes. You, how do you say? Break me up. But about my job . . .

GEORGE: Yes?

CAPRICE: Could I become a computer programmer like you?

GEORGE: That's it! Count me out. I don't like this game. I'll tell you what, Caprice, I'll give you a call sometime, we'll do lunch.

CAPRICE: I think you are angry.

GEORGE: You *think* I'm angry?

CAPRICE: Because I'm interested in your work?

GEORGE: Oh please don't look at me like that!

CAPRICE: I said something wrong. I am so sorry. Don't go, George . . . please! Would you like to come and stay with me? We'd have much more time to talk.

GEORGE: You mean . . . uh . . .

CAPRICE: Come live with me, George.

GEORGE: I . . . uh . . . let me think about that um option, O.K.? I'll uh get back to you. (GEORGE *stumbles to the bar, a broken man, while* CAPRICE *exits with flowers and* HAROLD, *notably sober, in new jacket, enters and observes his friend drinking*)

GEORGE: Data data data data dammit . . . damn her. She can't have my body!

HAROLD: Hey look, if you're not interested, I'll take her number.

GEORGE: Harold, you don't get it. I move onto her turf it's over. I watch you slobbering over Brenda like some sub-neanderthal, YES, this is the difference. Outta the ooze step by step from the amoeba to *me*— no backsliding now.

HAROLD: I never met a broad with navy blue eyes. Brenda's got . . . jeeze I don't know what color Brenda's eyes are, I can't believe it . . .

GEORGE: *(Already in a construct)* O.K. Who's paying the rent? A husband maybe. Ex? Traveling? Yes, enter Diplomat, which explains . . . I got it: he's stationed in some remote . . . but how about *her?* She's setting me up! I move in, some embassy guy shows up and . . . of *course.* Third world, gotta be! She learned English as a second language and that's why she talks funny. Yes! This could be big. I could be getting sucked into *espionage.* Sure, blackmail me for my computer program for some whoa! . . . I mean Harold otherwise . . . I mean *look* at me. Why would she pick *me*, huh? Why ME?

HAROLD: *(Has listened with increasing alarm)* Uh, George, what does your doctor say?

GEORGE: What?!

HAROLD: Your shrink. Did you tell him?

GEORGE: It's AUGUST, Harold. Why do you think I'm talking to you!?

HAROLD: O.K. O.K. Chill out. You want me to meet her. Just to give you a second opinion, huh?

GEORGE: *(Miserable)* I know what you'll say. Anybody would live happily with her forever and that's where *your* head is.

HAROLD: Does she play the piano?

GEORGE: Course she plays the piano. What do you care if she plays the piano?

HAROLD: I always thought it was a nice thing . . . you know, to play the piano. Brenda plays the piano. I think her eyes are hazel.

GEORGE: Caprice plays the piano, flute, cello and lute. She speaks at least four languages and she doesn't know how to drive.

HAROLD: Now there's a lotta data right there! How come you can't find her in your program?

GEORGE: I keep getting error messages. Abort. Retry.

HAROLD: Why not just marry her?

GEORGE: That is the *sickest* advice I've ever heard! She nearly burned out my motherboard!

HAROLD: Could you let go of my tie, George? Brenda likes me very neat. She says that was a major pothole in the relationship . . . me being a slob. So you know what, George? We made these lists, see, of all our likes and hates and priorities and we're building a compatibility column. Uh, how do you like my new jacket? Brenda picked it out. Tassel loafers . . . ?

(GEORGE, *totally preoccupied has let go of* HAROLD*'s tie and exits, thinking*)

HEY, George? Where are you going? I want to explain how we're working it all out, George . . .

(But GEORGE *has exited and* HAROLD *follows.* CAPRICE *enters and sits at a small table Upstage with a glass in one hand, a menu in the other.* GEORGE *enters, carrying a menu. Sits, keeping a close eye on* CAPRICE. *He crosses his legs and smiles a phoney smile at her. She smiles back a genuine one)*

CAPRICE: *(Raising her glass)* To us!

GEORGE: *(Raises glass, clinks, tightly)* I found this restaurant last winter. Very understated. Food is remarkable. Food people haven't found it yet. When they do, you won't be able to get in the door.

CAPRICE: I *love* it here!

GEORGE: You *do?*

CAPRICE: Oh yes!

GEORGE: *(Not too sure)* Well what it lacks in ambience, it makes up for in the paté.

CAPRICE: Oh, George, you *know* so much!

GEORGE: Not enough.

CAPRICE: And you're so modest.

GEORGE: Caprice, there's something I want to discuss with you.

CAPRICE: Yes?

GEORGE: I've known you for almost, what, three months? And I don't know the first thing about you.

CAPRICE: But I . . . I am just, myself.

GEORGE: Oh, no, you're not!

CAPRICE: I'm not?

GEORGE: No. You change all the time. Like whenever I think you're gonna say one thing you say something else. And also I don't believe anybody can be happy all the time. Why are you always happy!?

CAPRICE: Oh, George, have I done something to make you unhappy?

GEORGE: You've made me very happy, Caprice. You make me ecstatically happy. But I don't know *why.*

CAPRICE: Oh?

GEORGE: So you see, this relationship needs *work.*

CAPRICE: So you . . . won't just let us *be,* George?

GEORGE: I think it's perfectly *normal* for me to be a little curious about your childhood, your roots, other men in your life.

CAPRICE: *(Clear as water)* There is no other man in my life.

GEORGE: *Before,* Caprice.

CAPRICE: I'm afraid for us. I must warn you that . . . if you can't accept me now, you won't accept my origin.

GEORGE: Anything. Tell me anything!

CAPRICE: *(Sips wine, looks at him)* George . . . ?

GEORGE: Trust me.

CAPRICE: Well, in a sense, I'm . . . only an illusion.

GEORGE: Then let's have the truth.

CAPRICE: That's what I'm saying, George. I am, in a sense, a figment of your imagination.

GEORGE: That your first drink?

CAPRICE: I'm sorry, George. I am . . . like the reach of your mind to, uh, the other side . . . like "word-wrap," George. *(Pause)* I'm the parts that fell out of your database. The perfect parts.

(Long pause)

GEORGE: *(Quietly nods)* I know that *you* know that my analyst is away and I'm without support . . .

CAPRICE: I'm so sorry George. I have no power to change your mind . . . I'm only *part* of it.

GEORGE: Did you order that wine from the waiter over there?

CAPRICE: Yes?

GEORGE: So that guy sees you too, huh?

CAPRICE: *(Nods, simply)* Because you do.

GEORGE: *(Nods)* That's good, that's very good.

CAPRICE: *(Hopefully)* But all you have to do is believe in me. Is that so much to ask?

GEORGE: Now she's quoting Tinkerbell!

CAPRICE: I thought that you'd never accept it.

GEORGE: All I wanted was the regular stuff. Where you went to school, your last name, where you were born, single, married, divorced, who you voted for in the last election, nothing personal, hobbies. And what do I get? This FANTASY!

CAPRICE: I wish I could tell you what you want but . . . um . . . I was never here before so I didn't get to vote.

GEORGE: Right. Keep it up. You realize I don't remember my dreams. I've never had a daydream.

CAPRICE: Don't blame me, George, I was born for you.

GEORGE: I deal exclusively with reality chips.

CAPRICE: You heard me singing!

GEORGE: You're telling me I hallucinate daily and at the same time function brilliantly as a computer programmer. Give me a break, babe.

CAPRICE: I don't know how all these invisible forces operate, but I am sure there's a logic to them, if that makes you feel better. I suppose *some* part of your mind must have wanted . . . something you couldn't program.

GEORGE: Have you ever spent a real long time in any kind of institution?

CAPRICE: *(Last shot)* I'm telling you the truth! You're my destiny. My beginning. My end. I exist only so long as you believe in me.

GEORGE: It's original. Not a line you hear much around here. Brigadoon maybe. Not here! I have to hand it to you. *(Stands)* I'd like you to see my shrink if he ever gets back from Hawaii. I'm going to write his name and number here for you. *(Writes while speaking)* Meanwhile, it's better for both of us, assuming there *are* two of us—we just, don't see each other for a while.

CAPRICE: Oh . . .

GEORGE: It won't work. I can't go along with this creation myth of yours. Tell me you're a channel, maybe I'd buy it, but this—this is too much. I don't want to hurt you but . . . *(Lights flash)* I don't believe in you babe, O.K.? I've said it!

(GEORGE is startled; CAPRICE isn't there)

Caprice!?

(Immediately GEORGE, in shock, heads to the bar area. HAROLD, enters area with glass in hand, meets him there. As if electrified)

Before the PATÉ, Har! Not a sound, nothing. *Gone!*

HAROLD: Like Brenda.

GEORGE: She leaves notes. She doesn't vanish.

HAROLD: So she walked fast. She was pissed off.

GEORGE: Yeah? . . . Listen to this, Harold. I wait a couple of days. No calls. I call. No answer. I go by her house . . . all right. Say what you want, but Harold, it's gone. There's this construction pit and the foundation's in already.

HAROLD: They work fast. You know my view? That fantastic view I'm paying for in blood? Last Sunday I pull the shade up, half a condo is smack in the view. What're you gonna do?

GEORGE: She *vanished,* O.K.? I'm not gonna delude myself. I'm gonna *commit* myself. Should I commit myself, Harold, huh?

HAROLD: Over some broad? This is like an allergic reaction—get it together.

GEORGE: It's all over. I'm a failed system.

HAROLD: You're overreacting. Look at me. Have you happened to notice what I'm drinking? Perrier. And here's the good news. Toast: George I want you to be the godfather!

GEORGE: Congratulations. I better tell you something first.

HAROLD: Yeah?

GEORGE: *(Drinks in one shot)* You may not want me.

HAROLD: You didn't kill her, did you George? What'd you do—bury her in this construction pit?

GEORGE: I didn't *do* anything. *(Looks around nervously)* It's what I *saw.* This morning. See I . . . I'm trying to jog again. Work up my endorphins. Get over *her,* whatever she was . . . so I'm jogging, I'm sweating, I'm breathing hard and suddenly all these yellow butterflies . . .

HAROLD: The butterflies!

GEORGE: Why do you keep harping on them!

HAROLD: They sound like killer bees. Sci fi. You should carry bug spray.

GEORGE: *(Nods dreamily)* A cloud of them. Same spot. Same road. Same time. I look up and expect to see Caprice . . . like maybe she's got a box of butterflies she lets out, like magicians with the pigeons.

HAROLD: A box of butterflies?

GEORGE: *(Carried away into his thought)* I'm thinking PLEASE, please give me one more chance! I won't question. I'll just *accept!*

HAROLD: Yeah, and?

GEORGE: This is gonna sound a lot worse than it is, Harold . . . there's this, well, it looks *almost* like a regular white horse standing on top of the hill looking at me. But it's not a horse, Harold. It's a centaur.

HAROLD: A senator!?

GEORGE: No. A . . . half horse, half man . . . not in a bush or anything. Right out there! I figure it could've come from some stable, only it's not a horse. It's a centaur.

HAROLD: *(Snaps his fingers)* They're shooting a Greek film!

GEORGE: I look for the cameras, the crew. Nothing. I'm being honest with you Harold, I even thought my reflector glasses were defective. But when I take them off the thing's still there and it's looking at *me!* *(Pause)*

HAROLD: Yeah, well, George, I'd like to help you out here, but I can't afford to get involved with this level of fantasy. I just got my life together. I'm having the house painted . . . we have crabgrass and uh, other problems—priorities. *You* understand.

GEORGE: *(Grabs* HAROLD's *sleeve, desperate)* Why ME, Har? Why would these imaginary things . . . why would they single me out like this?! First *her,* then some mythical *beast*—it's like a *conspiracy!*

HAROLD: *(Slowly, humoring him)* Who could be behind it, you think?

GEORGE: *(Crazed)* Like a competitor maybe trying to drive me over the edge . . . *motive:* I'm thinking what if one of the chicks on the database figures I'm developing an ultimate gender weapon and she gets together with other chicks . . . to them my program could wipe them out. Enter that!

HAROLD: So you think there's some large Feminist Consortium behind it.

GEORGE: Who else? Who'd want to drive me crazy?! I know women with the means and the motive, why not, why not?

HAROLD: *(Straightening out his sleeve)* I don't know, George, it's not my field. I'm a space salesman, remember?

GEORGE: Who do I look like? Merlin!?

HAROLD: Look . . .

GEORGE: *(Pulling himself together)* I'm a scientist, a complete empiricist, I don't touch this stuff.

HAROLD: That's better, man!

GEORGE: You've known me how long? Did I ever once interface with anything metaphysical?! Forget it!

HAROLD: Good, good. Whew . . . I thought for a minute there you . . .

GEORGE: *(Evenly)* No I'm fine. I'm fine. I'm perfectly fine.

HAROLD: Great. *(Beat)*

GEORGE: So you know what I told it, Harold?

HAROLD: Not the centaur?

GEORGE: The, *yeah,* the thing with the half and half, yeah.

HAROLD: *(Carefully)* No, George, what did you tell it?

GEORGE: *(Pleased, calmly, completely insane)* I said: go find some *crackpot* that believes in you! Find some jerk out there, I'm not your man! This is the *wrong* century and the *wrong* season. You're out of *season!* That's what I told it. It's AUGUST!

(HAROLD *exits*)

Where are you going Harold? I *told* it I didn't believe in it. What would *you* have said? Harold, I'm your best friend, I taught you everything you know . . . Harold?

(BLACKOUT.)

THE CHERRY ORCHARD

Richard Nelson

Richard Nelson

Richard Nelson's stage plays include *Some Americans Abroad* (Royal Shakespeare Company, Lincoln Center Theatre Company, New York), *Principia Scriptoriae* (RSC, Manhattan Theatre Club, New York), *Between East and West* (Hampstead), as well as *The Vienna Notes, Rip Van Winkle or the Works, An American Comedy,* and *The Return of Pinnochio* which have been produced by many theatres in the United States. He is the author of numerous adaptations and translations which have been seen at theatres across the United States and on Broadway, and he wrote the book for the Broadway production of the musical, *Chess*. Richard Nelson has won many awards, including two Obies, a 1987 *Time Out* Award, a Guggenheim Fellowship and the 1986 ABC Television Playwriting Award. His television plays include *Sensibility and Sense* and *The Ending of a Sentence* (both American Playhouse, Public TV, United States). *Two Shakespearean Actors* was performed by the RSC in the Swan Theatre, Stratford in September, 1990.

PROJECTION
1986
THE CHERRY ORCHARD

Scene:
A room in a house that has been closed up; a few chairs, with dust covers.
LIBBY, *her brother,* FRANK, *and his wife,* JUDITH *sit and wait.*

(Pause)

LIBBY: Have you been watching the Irangate hearings?

(FRANK *shakes his head*)

Neither have I.

FRANK: What a ridiculous name.

(Short pause)

JUDITH: I watched a little. I couldn't take more. You watch and end up asking yourself—. Well—. *(She looks at* FRANK) I don't know. *(Beat)* Why *do* we have to tear everything down? We're just not happy unless we're destroying, are we?

FRANK: No, I don't think we are. *(Beat)* Though not everyone anymore. I wouldn't include everyone.

(JUDITH *nods. Short pause. To* LIBBY) By the way I brought different color stickers. We each take a color, you, Tom and me, and mark what furniture we might each want to keep. Then, I guess, we sort of horse trade. *(He laughs)* There's a book about dividing things up. About estates. They have a lot of great suggestions like that. *(Short pause)* We could start—

LIBBY: Wait for Tom, he'll be off soon.

(Short pause)

JUDITH: Odd, sitting here without your mother. She'd never have let any of you three kids sit like this here, without her being a part of it.

LIBBY: She still is a part of it. She is the reason for it.

JUDITH: Of course, I didn't mean—

FRANK: Judy meant, Libby, that Mom would have really enjoyed this. All of us together; sitting around her living room. *(Beat)* She missed that. She always told me on the phone how much she missed that. *(Beat)* But of course she's here in spirit. *(To JUDITH)* And that's all Libby meant.

(Short pause)

LIBBY: *(To JUDITH)* I don't think I've thanked you for your note. I was very touched.

FRANK: She writes wonderful notes, doesn't she?

LIBBY: If this was any indication—

FRANK: The one she wrote to Tom, you could publish it, I think.

JUDITH: Frank—

FRANK: I'm serious. *(Beat)* Take a compliment. Libby was complimenting you.

(Short pause)

JUDITH: I figured that since because of the kids, I couldn't come right away, with Frank, then at least—Well—*(She looks at FRANK)* I wanted you to know that my thoughts were with you.

LIBBY: You made that clear, thank you.

JUDITH: I felt badly; if Pete hadn't just been getting over the—

LIBBY: Judy, please, you do not owe anyone an apology.

FRANK: That's what I told her too, Libby. Judy, come on now, just forget it. *(Beat)* We're all here now. *(Beat)* We all were at the funeral.

(TOM, LIBBY and FRANK's younger brother, enters)

TOM: That was Taylor. *(Beat; he sits)* He'll take the case. I told you Frank we'd get someone.

FRANK: As I said, I don't think we should—

TOM: Let me finish. He'll split what we win, so we pay him nothing. That *was* your concern, Frank, that we pay him nothing.

FRANK: *(To himself)* Shit.

JUDITH: *(Trying to calm him)* Frank—

FRANK: Where did he get this guy?

TOM: *You* said if we paid him nothing.

FRANK: But there is no case! I'm a doctor, Tom, there's no grounds here for malpractice. What kind of shit lawyer—

TOM: You went to high school with Taylor—

FRANK: From what I remember about the high school in this town that is not a recommendation. *(Beat. To* LIBBY*)* He's found an ambulance chaser. We're supposed to put ourselves through hell—

TOM: *(To* LIBBY*)* He's president of the Optimists Club. You've seen him. He's very well known in this town.

LIBBY: Taylor? What's his first name?

TOM: George. I think George.

FRANK: *(To* LIBBY*)* When I said, okay as long as it doesn't cost us anything, the estate anything—I also meant the emotional cost. Do you know, Libby, what the emotional cost of something like this can be? Do you have any idea?

JUDITH: *(To* LIBBY*)* A friend of Frank's was sued for malpractice. He'd done nothing. His wife, just her, lost about forty pounds; she was down to nothing—

TOM: I don't care about the doctor, Judith!!

FRANK: *(Yells)* Don't shout!! *(Beat)* Look, if all we're going to do is shout—

TOM: Look. It's not the money. I don't care about that. We can give that away. Flush it down the toilet.

FRANK: *(To* LIBBY*)* An intelligent comment. Tom always did have a peculiar way of managing his money, didn't he?

TOM: *(To* JUDITH*)* But come on listen to me, she goes in for a physical from this guy, he says he can find nothing wrong—This is a complete physical, or at least that's what she paid for—

JUDITH: I know all this, Tom.

TOM: *(Ignoring her)* And within four weeks, she's falling down steps, and she's got a tumor the size of a—

FRANK: That can happen!

TOM: Then we'll see in court, won't we? Taylor has no qualms about taking this all the way to—

FRANK: *(To LIBBY)* He's not going to get me sitting in a courtroom.

LIBBY: If you're talking to Tom, talk *to* him.

FRANK: *(To LIBBY)* I'm not going to listen to lawyers pick over an autopsy report of my mother!

TOM: You don't have to do shit, Frank. Fly back to Phoenix. Forget about everything. Forget about us. *(Beat)* Leave us in peace.

LIBBY: Tom—

TOM: I'll drive you to the airport. When do you want to go?! *(Beat)* Just say when.

(Short pause)

JUDITH: Our flight isn't for another four hours.

TOM: They've got a nice lounge there you could wait in. If that's what you want to do.

(Pause)

FRANK: She was my Mother too, Tom, you're not the only one who's upset.

(Pause)

JUDITH: *(Getting up)* Maybe your Mother left some coffee. *(Beat)* Of course there won't be any milk . . . *(She goes)*

(Pause)

FRANK: *(Gets up and walks around)* Why? Why do we always look for someone or something to blame? I guess that's just human nature, right? I do understand, Tom, I really do.

(TOM laughs)

What? What is humorous about that? *(Pause)* The facts are: our mother has died. And a malpractice suit is not going to bring her back, pal. I know that. *(Beat)* Libby knows that.

LIBBY: Speak for yourself, Frank.

FRANK: So speak, then. *(Short pause. He shrugs and continues)* Such a suit, I promise you, will only cause us all considerable pain. And for what? You've said it's not the money. So it must be to get even. Is vengeance what you're after, Tom?

TOM: *(To LIBBY)* Taylor also said that since Mom smoked throughout the fifties, he'd try to get her name on a class action against the tobacco companies. *(Beat)* They say it's only time before one of those is won. The tide seems to be turning, he says.

FRANK: Fuck!!! *(Short pause)* Will you ever grow up, boy? *(Beat)* So it has to be multi-nationals that killed our Mom. It's big business; so that's the murderer! Pretty soon, you're going to end up blaming President Reagan! Don't you see how pathetic you've become, Tommy?!! *(Beat)* Get off your high horse, and you'll see that this country is not as awful as you think. *(Beat)* But then again, I don't delude myself for a second that I can convince you of this. *(Beat)* So let's just say we see the world a little differently.

TOM: No argument there.

(Short pause)

FRANK: And as I said, she is my Mom too. So you can tell your shit lawyer to kiss off. *(Pause)* Hey look, when I walked into this house, ask Judith, I must have turned as white as a sheet. I don't want time to pass by either. I don't want people I love to die. But they do. It does. It has. *(Beat. Laughs to himself)* Having kids, you really get to see the time go by. I'm really sorry you both—. But there's still time. Mom loved grandkids, you know. *(Beat)* She doted on Pete. I'd say if we really cared about doing something for Mom—

LIBBY: Shut up, Frank. *(Beat)* You want a family. Fine. Fine. But just shut up. *(Long pause)* We have things we have to get done. Right? Frank and Judy have a plane to catch. *(Beat)* Here, I've written the thank-you notes; I thought it'd be nice if we all signed; that's how Mom always made us do it. *(Beat)* Even when she wrote our thank-you notes herself.

TOM: *(Smiling)* So you're Mom now? *(Beat)* I wouldn't object.

FRANK: Give me a stack, I'll sign. *(Beat)* You should be thanked for thinking of this, Libby. Thank-you notes never entered my mind.

LIBBY: Your wife reminded me.

(Pause as they begin to sign)

TOM: Does it matter who signs first? Should I leave a space?

LIBBY: No. No it doesn't matter.

(Short pause)

FRANK: *(Looking at one card)* The O'Hara's flowers I thought were especially beautiful. Maybe I should say that.

LIBBY: I did. *(Beat)* Did you read my note? Both of you are just signing your names without reading my notes? How do you know what the hell I've said?

FRANK: *(Trying to make a joke)* God Tommy, Mom makes us not only sign our names but we have to read what she writes too. *(He laughs; no one else does)*

TOM: Flowers. Mom I'm sure would rather have had the money go to—

FRANK: Mom loved cut flowers.

TOM: I didn't say she didn't. *(Beat)* When Dad died, we asked people to give donations to somewhere.

FRANK: That was your idea, not hers. One more thing you shoved down our throats.

TOM: Not true. You know that isn't true.

FRANK: *(Ignoring him; looking at a card)* Who's the Reverend William Hackler? He wasn't the new assistant minister I met—

TOM: He's the Reverend of the Baptist Church on First Street.

FRANK: That was a black church.

TOM: It still is.

(Short pause)

LIBBY: Mom did a lot of volunteer work there these past couple of years. I just found out about it myself.

TOM: A few weeks ago Hackler shows up at the hospital—And he and Mom begin to have this conversation . . . *(Beat)* She told no one what she was doing.

FRANK: *(Signs his name and goes to another card)* Mom. Dear Mom. *(He smiles and shakes his head)*

TOM: What does that mean? *(Beat)* What the hell does that mean?! *(Beat)* You think it was stupid or something for her to volunteer to work at a black—

FRANK: Get off my back!!! *(Beat)* I didn't say anything. *(Beat)* Mom was a character, okay? We all knew that. One lovable, a bit eccentric, maybe overly generous character.

(Short pause. To LIBBY*)* He wants to turn me into a racist now. *(Laughs)* Why?? Because I happen to disagree with him on a few things. Tolerant, aren't we, Tom? *(Beat)* What else are you going to beat your chest about? Next will it be that I'm anti-semitic because I don't happen to pray every morning in the direction of your *New York Times?!! (Laughs)* You should really see the rest of this country, Tom. You should see just what a dinosaur you have become.

(To LIBBY*)* I have a Chicano nurse and secretary, Libby. The son of one I'm helping through college. The University of Arizona.

(To TOM*)* I try to help where I can. What the hell do you do, besides lecture people?!! *(Beat)* You want to know who is really closer to Mom, to the kind of help she was trying to—

TOM: *(Yells)* You aren't!! You aren't!!

*(*FRANK *is laughing)*

LIBBY: Stop laughing Frank.

(Pause. They continue to sign cards)

TOM: *(To* LIBBY*)* Tell me, am I crazy or what, but wasn't there a time long ago when the word "conservative" meant something—*bad?*

(Beat. Then LIBBY *laughs and* TOM *laughs)*

FRANK: I don't know, was it ever bad to *eat* conservatively, *drive* conservatively, *drink* conservatively, which, after watching you these past two days, Tom, I suggest you begin to think about.

(Short pause)

TOM: *(To* LIBBY*)* First they appropriate the flag, now they're after "health." Incredible.

FRANK: The flag we didn't wait to appropriate, we grabbed it out of your hands to stop you from burning it.

TOM: The hypocrisy! *(Beat)* Or is it amnesia? *(To* LIBBY*)* You remember, don't you, sitting up with Mom and Dad and Frank and listening to them make plans for Frank to go to Canada?

FRANK: I didn't go, did I?

TOM: Because of the lottery. You got something like three hundred and thirty in the lottery!!

FRANK: You want to know what I think you people's problem is?

TOM: Who's "you people"?

FRANK: *(Ignoring him)* You have to make everything a world cause. Everyone has to join in. Everyone has to follow you. Think like you. Believe in what you believe. But things have changed, Tom. Look around. Take a trip. Come and visit us. *(Beat)* What you'll realize, I swear to you, is that you need to relax. I say this as a brother. Look at your drinking for Christ sake.

TOM: I don't drink—

FRANK: Mom was relaxed. You want to be like her? Keep her ideals alive? Okay. But she didn't try and change the world. She didn't make a big *show* out of what she did. You just said that yourself. *(Beat)* Why does one person feel the need to impose his beliefs on another person? This is what I do not get. People are not as dumb as you people in the East think they are. *(Beat)* Politics. Politics. Where does that get you? Lay off for a while; I promise you, it'll change your life. *(Beat)* Always attacking everything. Standing up for what? Attack attack blame blame. Like with Mom's death. She died for Christ sake, let her lie in peace. Let us live in peace. *(Beat)* Just get on with life. Move on.

TOM: Grow up?

FRANK: Your words, not mine, but I'm not arguing. *(Short pause)* So—yeh, grow and begin for a change to look at things positively. You'll be amazed what a relief it is to stop finding fault with everything. I promise, you'll feel good.

JUDITH: *(Entering with coffee)* Sorry I took so long with the coffee, but—

TOM: *(To FRANK, interrupting)* Is that the point now, Frank—to feel good?

FRANK: What is wrong with that? *(Beat)* I see nothing wrong with that.

(Short pause)

JUDITH: Uh, I did a little cleaning around the stove, that's why—If the real estate people are coming by—

LIBBY: What real estate people—?

FRANK: Just to set a price. Just so we can see what it's worth. I figured while we're still here—I know we haven't decided to sell. I'm not pushing anything. I'm just getting the facts.

(JUDITH sets down the coffee)

I'll get those colored stickers. They're in Tom's car.

TOM: It's open.

FRANK: *(Starts to leave, stops)* I'm glad we talked, Tom. *(Beat)* It seems like years, doesn't it? Don't misunderstand me, I know there are a lot of things wrong with the world, but—and this is a big "but"—things are also not as bad as you think.

TOM: Maybe not for you.

(Pause)

FRANK: So, I am one of the fortunate ones. You think I should be sorry for that?

(He goes. Short pause)

JUDITH: No one takes sugar, do they?

LIBBY: I do.

JUDITH: Oh. *(Beat)* I'll check in the pantry.

LIBBY: *(Without meaning it)* I can look if you—

JUDITH: No, no. Let me. It's been a hard day for all of you, I'm sure.

(She goes. Pause)

TOM: *(Finally)* Listen.

LIBBY: What?

TOM: Hear that?

LIBBY: What? No.

TOM: It's Mom and Dad. *(Beat)* They must have been listening. *(Beat)* Because they're crying now.

(BLACKOUT.)

HIDDEN IN THIS PICTURE

A Play in One Act

Aaron Sorkin

Aaron Sorkin

Aaron Sorkin received the Outer Critic Circle Award for his play *A Few Good Men*. He is the author of an expanded version of *Hidden In This Picture* titled *Making Movies*, which played off-Broadway at the Promenade Theatre. A 1983 graduate of the Syracuse University drama department, Mr. Sorkin has contributed to *Rolling Stone*, *New York Newsday* and *Playbill Magazine*.

A small, grassy hill overlooking a massive expanse of land. On this plateau sits a directors chair. Next to the directors chair sits a bottle of champagne and two glasses.

At rise:

ROBERT *is standing and surveying the scene before him. He is in his early thirties. He wears jeans, boots, a baseball cap, a windbreaker, and sunglasses. Around his neck on a piece of string is a camera lens. Although he shows all the signs of a man who has not had enough sleep, he is, at the moment, as content as he's ever been. He checks his pocket watch. After a moment,* REUBEN *enters. He is in his early forties and is inappropriately dressed in a jacket and tie. Mud has begun to cake to his shoes and the bottom of his slacks. He's out of breath.*

REUBEN: Uh . . . Robert . . . What are you doing?

ROBERT: *(Not paying much attention)* Hm?

REUBEN: *(Shouting Off-Right and down)* He's up here!

ROBERT: This is perfect, did you know that?

REUBEN: *(Shouting)* Sylvia! He's up here!

ROBERT: This is a perfect shot.

REUBEN: Robert—

ROBERT: This is an Academy Award winning shot.

REUBEN: Robert, what are you doing up here?

ROBERT: Looking at my Academy Award winning shot.

REUBEN: They give Academy Awards for *movies,* Robert, not shots. And if they gave Academy Awards for shots, it's a pretty good bet that the shot would actually have to be down on *film.* It's not like we can invite the members of the Academy out here to the location and say "Look at this shot," am I making sense? Robert, we have four minutes to sunset.

ROBERT: Four minutes and ten seconds.

REUBEN: Oh, good, sorry, I didn't know. Let's go square dancing.

ROBERT: Don't bug me, Reuben. I'm happy right now. I'm trying to make believe you're not here right now.

REUBEN: Robert—Bobby—Lindstrom and Sachs were serious. They were dead serious, I know what I'm talking about. There's no more money. There is no more money. There was no more money two weeks ago when you were three weeks behind and six and a half million over. There was no money *then*. There is now *officially* no more money. I don't like being an asshole, but it's my job. I'm the Production Manager. I'm here to see that things run on schedule and at budget.

ROBERT: Three weeks behind and six and a half million over?

REUBEN: That's right.

ROBERT: You've been doing a good job, Reuben.

REUBEN: The final shot, Robert, *one shot*, and then the crew, the cast, the six-hundred and ninety-four extras, the cameras, the lights, the food, the trailers, they all go home.

ROBERT: We're gonna go home Reuben, it's under control, trust me.

REUBEN: You've said that before.

ROBERT: I was lying.

REUBEN: There's no re-take, here, you understand that, don't you? We can't ask the sun to come back and set again because we screwed it up the first time.

ROBERT: We can't?

REUBEN: No.

ROBERT: What if we asked nicely?

REUBEN: Goddamit—

ROBERT: What if we call the sun's agent?

REUBEN: I'm not fuckin' around.

ROBERT: Neither am I. Call William Morris, find out who handles the sun, say we need a little favor. Say there's the possibility that we might have to re-take a shot and, in the event that we do, is there any chance the sun would be willing to come back up and set again. I mean, you know, we'll owe him one.

REUBEN: Three and a half minutes, Robert. Don't you think you should be down with the crew?

ROBERT: The crew knows what to do.

REUBEN: How the hell do you know?

ROBERT: *(For the first time, he stops gazing out in the distance. He takes his sunglasses off and speaks directly to* REUBEN*)* Because we've been rehearsing for the past six hours. Because despite the fact that this is my first film, a fact that you've seen fit to remind me of four times a day since pre-production, despite that fact, I'm not an idiot. Because, whether you know it or not, and I suspect you don't, this is the most important shot in the movie and I have no intention of screwing it up. Because I have left absolutely no room for human error, Reuben. At seven thirty-seven the sun will begin to set. At seven thirty-seven the cameras will roll, three of them. Two Pana-flex 8-80's and an Aeri-BL. There is film in the cameras and the focus is pulled, I've checked them all six times. There are security guards posted by the cameras at the foot of the hill and there are twenty-six kids out of UCLA with walkie-talkies posted around the perimeter of the shot. Eleven minutes and thirty seconds. The cameras will roll for eleven minutes and thirty seconds. And during that eleven minutes and thirty seconds, our six-hundred and ninety-four extras, already costumed and approved in their uniforms, will, in a slow, trickling, symphonically theatrical stream, trot the four-thousand, five-hundred and sixty foot diagonal from the ridge of those trees, down past the blue flag and out of camera range. Roll credits. Six hours we rehearsed, Reuben, you should've been here. I ran them, and I ran them, and I ran them. And they got it right the first time. Craig is down on the deck, he'll be calling it. And when he does, there isn't a man, woman, or child who doesn't know what they're supposed to do. So I staked out this hill, and Jeff's gonna join me, and together we're going to watch art being made.

REUBEN: They're serious, Robert, this is it. Whatever you've got goes in the can and if it's not releaseable, they'll eat it, I swear, they can afford it.

ROBERT: I thought you said there was no more money?

REUBEN: Not for this. Not for a movie about disillusioned Marines in Guam playing war games that everyone in the industry knows is not going to make doo-dah at the box office!

ROBERT: *(Pause)* If they didn't *like* the movie, why'd they *make* the movie?

REUBEN: The hell did they know, they liked your plays.

ROBERT: They weren't my plays, they were Jeff's plays.

REUBEN: Your plays, Jeff's plays, who gives a shit?

ROBERT: Jeff, probably. Jeff's mom.

REUBEN: They went to New York, they went to the theatre, they saw a play. You directed, Jeff wrote it, they said "You guys wanna make a movie? Here's some money." They gave you money, a crew, equipment, actors—

ROBERT: Actors—

REUBEN: You have a problem with the actors?

ROBERT: No, sir.

REUBEN: These actors were pussycats, Robert, lemme tell you, these actors were dolls.

ROBERT: The actors never liked me, Reuben.

REUBEN: The actors loved you. You couldn't remember their names. *You* didn't like the *actors*.

ROBERT: That's right, I forgot.

REUBEN: And I'm asking you, did you have a problem with these actors? Did you have one attitude case? One star trip? One prima donna? Can you tell me that they were really a problem?

ROBERT: No, they were not a problem. Talentless and vacuous, sure. Vapid, facile, a little insipid . . . Good looking, though. Some of the best looking actors I've ever seen, I swear. But no, they weren't hard to get along with.

REUBEN: I'm sorry, my friend, but there was a limit to what could be done with the material.

ROBERT: Jeff worked very hard on this screenplay.

REUBEN: Yeah? Well it's lousy. It's full of Yale Drama crap. He should've stayed in church basements in SoHo where if the audience doesn't understand what the fuck is going on, they give him a plaque. I got news for you, welcome to the movies, if the audience doesn't understand what the fuck is going on, they leave. And they tell their friends. And they don't rent the video cassette. And we lose the European market. And there's no sequel. And there's no ancillary sales. And if you think I'm some kind of mercantile, anti-artist, studio-puppet, who only sees dollars and cents, you're right. But that's my job. And all I have to say is that if you expect to be handed seventeen-million dollars to make a movie, with another ten-million to promote it, you better be pretty damn sure that someone in Des Moines is gonna buy a ticket. You have two minutes and twenty seconds.

(JEFF *enters. He's around the same age as* ROBERT *and wears jeans, sneakers, and a fatigue jacket*)

JEFF: Reuben! Great! I have a question for you. Those people down there with the walkie-talkies . . . they work for us?

REUBEN: Yes.

JEFF: Good. I've fallen in love with one of them. I don't know her name, but she's got red hair and she's wearing blue pants and a white sweatshirt. If you could casually mention some impressive things about me to her, I would genuinely appreciate it. (REUBEN *stares at him.* JEFF *takes out a note pad and pen*) I'll jot some down.

ROBERT: Reuben's in a bad mood, Jeff.

JEFF: Why?

ROBERT: He thinks I've spent too much time and too much money making a movie about disillusioned Marines in Guam and he thinks your screenplay is full of Yale Drama crap and he thinks that no one in Des Moines is gonna buy a ticket.

JEFF: I'm not sure I'd say the Marines are disillusioned.

REUBEN: I'm going back down to the deck. You have two minutes.

JEFF: *(Calling after him)* Reuben! (JEFF *scribbles something on a note and hands it to him*) This is important to me. Red hair, blue pants, white sweatshirt. Tell her I have a reputation. *(To* ROBERT, *who has gone back to staring off in the distance)* Champagne?

ROBERT: Oh yeah.

*(*CRAIG *enters. He's about the same age as* ROBERT *and* JEFF. *He wears glasses and carries a walkie-talkie in his belt)*

CRAIG: Bob, we're at stand-by.

ROBERT: How's it look?

CRAIG: No problems.

ROBERT: It's your call.

CRAIG: I wanted to thank you for this.

ROBERT: Thank me for what?

CRAIG: Well, for giving me control like this. For letting me call a shot. It really means a lot to me.

ROBERT: You've done a real good job, I mean that. Nothing to thank me for.

CRAIG: It's just that I was a production assistant for four years, and all I've ever really gotten to do was organize background.

ROBERT: I'm sure you can handle it, Craig.

CRAIG: And I wanted to express my appreciation for your confidence in me, Bob.

ROBERT: Don't mention it.

CRAIG: It's just that I wanted you to know that you're the first person who's ever really considered that I might have, you know, some sort of personal career goals beyond being an A.D.

ROBERT: Craig, I hate to seem cold right now, 'cause I can tell you're opening up a little to me and I think that's great, but you are planning on going back down to the deck and call the shot aren't you?

CRAIG: Sure. *(He doesn't move)*

ROBERT: I mean you understand that the cameras are not gonna roll unless you call action, you understand that, don't you?

CRAIG: I'm not stupid, Bob.

ROBERT: *(Pause)* No, of course not. I just wasn't sure whether or not you realized that we were inside two minutes.

CRAIG: *(Checks his watch)* Yeah, one thirty-five.

ROBERT: I need help, Jeff.

JEFF: Craig, Bobby wants you to go down to the deck right now. He wants you to go down there because you have an extremely important job to do and he wants to be sure that you do it as well as he knows you're able.

CRAIG: Well that's what I was just saying to Bob. That I'm grateful to be given this responsibility and that I genuinely appreciate Bob's confidence in my ability to—

ROBERT: *GET DOWN ON THE DECK! RIGHT NOW! OR I WILL GO DOWN AND CALL THE SHOT MYSELF AND YOU WILL DIRECT TRAFFIC THE REST OF YOUR LIFE.*

CRAIG: Thank you, Bob. I mean it. *(He exits)*

ROBERT: He's sweet.

JEFF: Yeah, and very quick.

ROBERT: Yeah.

JEFF: Why're you letting him call the shot?

ROBERT: Craig can call the play by play of the Yankees game for all the difference it'll make, the cameras have been rolling for the last ten minutes.

JEFF: You're kidding me.

ROBERT: In a minute forty-five, Hillary will radio Michael who's standing by at the ridge, and Michael will cue the Marines.

JEFF: You've been letting the cameras roll for ten minutes?

ROBERT: Craig'll never know. What's the harm? He can go home and tell people he called the final shot of the film, and they will have sex with him.

JEFF: Bobby, three cameras rolling for ten minutes, and now they're gonna roll for another eleven and a half? At a thousand dollars a foot per camera?

ROBERT: You sound like Reuben, Jeff, it's not your money.

JEFF: It's *somebody's* money and it's being spent irresponsibly.

ROBERT: I want this shot.

JEFF: You'll get this shot.

ROBERT: I'm making sure.

JEFF: You're becoming obsessive.

ROBERT: If not now, when, Jeff? In the editing room? You know how many people get to cut this movie before I do? About the same number who get to cut it *after* I do. The unit caterer has more artistic control over this project than I've been given. Well fuck it, Jeff, I'm getting this shot. I've created a picture here, I've communicated with an image. I've communicated an idea, an emotion, *my* idea, and I've done it as succinctly as a well written sentence and as powerfully as a symphony. The rest of this film may end up looking like Beaver Goes to War, but this shot, this image, is gonna work.

JEFF: Good luck.

ROBERT: *(Checking his watch)* Forty-five seconds.

JEFF: *(Pause)* Who's Hillary?

ROBERT: Red hair, blue pants, white sweatshirt.

JEFF: Hillary.

ROBERT: *(Pause)* Thirty-five seconds. Thirty-five seconds till my dream comes true. How many times can you say that, Jeff?

JEFF: You mean, how many times can you say it really fast? I've never been good at that.

ROBERT: Please, God. Please be perfect, God. Just nice and slow and easy, God. No mistakes. I'm not asking any special favors of you, God, I'm not asking you to interfere. I've got all the bases covered, God, now please just let me have this. God, for the next eleven and a half minutes, just make the sun go down behind that hill and then mind your own business.

JEFF: Bobby—

ROBERT: Ssh. *(Pause. Whispering)* Action. *(Pause)* Oh yeah. Oh. Oh my. This is for my children, Jeff. This is for my little daughter. This is for Jennifer who'll watch it with her friends and say "My Daddy did that." This is for my unborn son who'll look at this and say "I want to be just like my Dad." This isn't for the actors, Jeff, this isn't for Lindstrom and Sachs, this isn't even for you. This one's for me. Look at it, Jeff, look at it.

JEFF: I'm looking.

ROBERT: Yeah, but are you seeing it?

JEFF: I think so. I'm looking at it.

ROBERT: Try and see it. Put a frame around it and see the picture.

JEFF: *(Pause)* Yeah.

ROBERT: Are you looking at it?

JEFF: I'm seeing it, Bobby.

ROBERT: Communicating an idea. Causing emotion. No words. No sounds. No paints. No brushes. Just twelve-hundred acres in Central New York, Six-hundred and ninety-four extras jogging down a hill, three, four, six at a time, and a perfect sunset. I don't know that I've ever been more fulfilled than I am right now.

JEFF: *(Pause)* You don't happen to know if Hillary's married or anything, do you?

ROBERT: Jeff.

JEFF: Sorry.

ROBERT: Jesus.

JEFF: I was looking, I was looking.

ROBERT: You know, when you've written a scene, and you're excited about it, I like to think that I'm pretty supportive. I like to think, you know, when you've created something that pleases you, that I share your enthusiasm whether it's genuine or not.

JEFF: Whether it's genuine or not?

ROBERT: Yes, Jeff. I'm not always as bowled over by your dramaturgy as I, perhaps, have sometimes led you to believe, on occasion. But that's not the point. The point is that I'm your friend, and I'm an artist, and I know how important it is to have an inspiration or whatever, you know —what?

JEFF: Nurtured?

ROBERT: Yeah.

JEFF: Whether it's genuine or not?

ROBERT: Yes. I encourage you. I support you. I celebrate with you.

JEFF: Except that in addition to being my friend and being an artist, you've also directed the last three plays that I've written. You've been the director, Bobby. And as the director, I depend upon your skilled, trained, experienced, and objective eye to guide me through a very crucial polishing, a focusing process prior to and during the rehearsal period. I appreciate the gesture, but in the future I'd like it, and I'll think you'll find in the long run that it will be more valuable and rewarding, if you told me exactly what you thought of my work.

ROBERT: I think your work has a tendency to be long winded and cynical, I think you have difficulty handling exposition, I think you take forever to introduce the inciting action, and I think your female characters talk and behave as if they just stepped off of the Love Boat.

JEFF: I said "In the future," Bobby. In the *future* I'd like you to be honest, and *specific*, about problems you might have with my work, so that I may reasonably ascertain whether I should heed your suggestions or seek another director. In the future, Bob. Not while I'm watching, sorry, seeing this communication of emotion. *(Beat)* And let me just say that while I give you full credit for creating this, the final scene of the picture, without sounds, without paints, without brushes, but for the 127 pages of dialog which precedes your creation, this would be a scene about a bunch of guys running down a hill. For eleven and a half minutes.

(CRAIG enters)

CRAIG: So far, so good.

ROBERT: Doin' a great job, Craig. Everything looks perfect.

CRAIG: Everything's goin' smooth as can be, Bob.

ROBERT: Love to hear it. How's the timing?

CRAIG: The starting pace was about ten seconds fast, I called up to Michael and we straightened it out.

ROBERT: What'd you tell him?

CRAIG: I told him to have the Marines slow down a little.

ROBERT: Good call, Craig, you did the right thing.

CRAIG: Thank you, I appreciate that.

ROBERT: Well . . . I'm glad I have you down there. *(Beat)* Down on the deck.

CRAIG: No, I mean it. I know you've got a lot on your mind right now and that, I mean, you could use some, you know, you're really tired, but I just think it's nice that you took the time and had the inclination to, you know . . . say that.

ROBERT: Craig, I need you on the deck.

CRAIG: I just came up to tell you that everything was going fine.

ROBERT: And I appreciate that. But I can see that everything is fine from right here. I can see everything from here. That's why I'm here. If all three cameras burst into flames at once, I'll know the moment that you know.

JEFF: Maybe even sooner.

ROBERT: The thing that I can't do from up here, is get timings from Hillary and relay instructions to Michael.

CRAIG: You want me to rig you up with a walkie-talkie?

ROBERT: I want you to—*(Resigning and asking for help)*—Jeff.

JEFF: I don't know, Bobby, why don't you try communicating an emotion to Craig with an image. You don't need words. Long winded, cynical, clumsily expository, tensionless, sexist, soap operatic words.

CRAIG: Bob, I'm gonna get back down to the deck. I'll check the timings.

ROBERT: Thank you. (CRAIG *exits*) Jeff, I apologize. I didn't mean to hurt your feelings. I don't—I just made that all up, I'm sorry, it was nasty and inappropriate. Jeff, we're coming up to the real meat of the sunset and I'd just like to watch it. *(Throughout this,* JEFF *has been staring at a spot off in the distance and to the right)* Jeff, just let me live this next ten minutes with your blessing and your forgiveness and then we can fight if you want. I'll do whatever you want, I'll tell Hillary you've got a three picture deal at Warners. Please, shake hands with me and watch my scene.

JEFF: Bobby?

ROBERT: Jeff?

JEFF: *(Pause)* Three cows have walked into the shot.

ROBERT: *(Long pause. He must have heard wrong)* I'm sorry, what did you say?

JEFF: Three cows have walked into the shot.

(ROBERT *turns and looks out*)

ROBERT: There are cows in the shot.

JEFF: Three.

ROBERT: Three cows are in the shot.

JEFF: Yeah.

ROBERT: I don't understand.

JEFF: Three cows are grazing in the middle of the shot.

ROBERT: Jesus Christ Almighty. *(He runs off. We hear him yelling, getting fainter and fainter in the distance)* YOU'RE IN THE SHOT! GET OUT OF THE SHOT! COWS! GET THE HELL OUT OF THE SHOT!

(Long pause. ROBERT *returns)*

ROBERT: Before I even begin to try and solve this problem, I want you to tell me, Jeff, you wrote the screenplay, you did research, you did months of research, you read books, tell me, are there cows on Guam?

JEFF: Not on Marine bases.

ROBERT: Fuck. *(Beat)* Fuck, fuck, fuck. *(Beat)* Never?

JEFF: No, never. There are no cows on Marine bases. Anywhere. Guam, Nicaragua, Berlin, there are no cows.

ROBERT: Don't tell me there are no cows, there are three cows standing in the middle of the shot!

JEFF: That's because we're ten miles outside of Schenectady on a farm. We're only pretending we're on a Marine base. The cows aren't screwin' around, they're on a farm. Bobby, it's okay. Just have some guys run out there and kinda shoo away the cows.

ROBERT: Shoo away the cows?

JEFF: Yeah, get a couple a guys to run out there and sorta herd 'em off to the left.

ROBERT: Jeff, an entire Marine infantry unit is running toward them with machine guns. They're not moving anywhere.

JEFF: It's 'cause they're all running past them. The cows probably can't even see them. Send some people out to run right towards them and herd 'em off that way to the left. You can edit this stuff out and the scene'll be nine minutes instead of eleven minutes. *(Pause)* Bobby, it's the only thing to do.

ROBERT: Those cows have gotta be three-quarters of a mile away. We've got eight minutes left. Do you know how long it's gonna take to get a film crew to run three-quarters of a mile up hill, clear the cows from the shot and then clear themselves from the shot? *What the fuck are they doing there?*

JEFF: It looks like they're eating.

ROBERT: Oh, good. And on this twelve-hundred acre farm in the middle of *nowhere,* it was important that these cows eat *that* particular spot of grass. And I'm sure that it was *very* important that they eat right *now.* I'm sure that they have many appointments later in the evening, leaving them no choice but to grab a quick bite during *this* particular eleven minute period.

(CRAIG *enters*)

CRAIG: Bobby, three cows have walked into the shot. I think it's pretty noticeable.

ROBERT: Oh? What makes you say that, Craig, what makes you say it's noticeable?

CRAIG: Well . . . everybody noticed.

ROBERT: Jeff—

JEFF: Listen to me, just sit tight.

ROBERT: The sun is setting, Jeff. Seemingly faster than it's ever set before.

JEFF: You might be able to salvage enough ending footage and then fudge around with the continuity on the sunset.

ROBERT: If the cows move. If they decide to move back out of the shot.

JEFF: Right.

ROBERT: And if they don't?

JEFF: You're screwed.

ROBERT: What's goin' on, God? Why are you doing this to me? Please move the cows, God. Move 'em over seventy-five yards to the left, God, what's the big deal? I'm not kidding, I'm really at a complete—I don't know what I'm supposed to do? Are you—Wait, wait, wait, what are they doing? They're bobbing their heads or something. What does that mean? Do you think that means they're ready to leave? Does it seem to you that they're about ready to leave?

JEFF: I don't—I'm not a livestock psychologist, Rob, I don't know if the cows seem ready to leave.

CRAIG: I think they're about ready to leave.

JEFF: Craig, on the other hand, has a very strong sense that the cows will be leaving soon.

ROBERT: Would you look at those guys? Just trotting by these cows like they weren't there. Doing it exactly the way we did it in rehearsal. You'd sorta think that one of 'em would say to himself "Hm, I'm an actor and I'm supposed to be imitating life. Right now I'm playing a Marine on my way back to the barracks. There's a cow. If I were a

Marine, I'd probably think it was somewhat out of the ordinary to see a cow on my way back to my barracks. I should use what's around me. I should use what's really happening, both externally and internally." You'd think one of those guys would somehow acknowledge the fact that they're running past three cows on the way down the hill.

CRAIG: Should I call Michael?

ROBERT: Please.

CRAIG: What should I tell him?

ROBERT: Tell him to tell whoever is left up there, that the scene now includes three cows. Tell him to tell whoever is left, that there's no point ignoring the cows, it only makes us look stupid.

CRAIG: I left my walkie-talkie down on the deck.

ROBERT: Go. (CRAIG *begins to leave*) Hold it. Don't bother. The extras have discovered the cows. They're acting with the cows. The extras are doing bits of business with the cows. I hate those cows. *(Beat)* You know what I think? I think that it's not nearly as big a problem as we think it is.

JEFF: Truly, Robert, that's the attitude you gotta have.

ROBERT: 'Cause you know why? 'Cause I don't think anyone in the audience is gonna notice. I mean, sure, they're gonna notice, they're gonna see these three cows in silhouette against a sunset while 694 Marines file back to their barracks after having spent the most difficult day of their lives engaged in a war game, sure the audience is gonna see these cows, *but I don't think they're gonna find that strange.*

JEFF: You don't?

ROBERT: No.

JEFF: Why not?

ROBERT: Why should they? They're just cows. Everybody's seen cows. What's the big scream? They're cows.

JEFF: On a Marine compound? In Guam?

ROBERT: You think people are gonna pick that out?

JEFF: I hope so. I mean if they've just sat through a two hour movie and they don't know that it took place on a Marine compound in Guam, hell, I think we can put Rocky and Bullwinkle out there and it won't make a difference.

ROBERT: I don't know, call it instinct, I don't think people are gonna find that strange.

JEFF: I find it a little strange. You find it strange.

CRAIG: I find it strange.

JEFF: Craig finds it strange, you wanna talk about playing to the lowest common denominator.

ROBERT: *(To* CRAIG*)* You find it strange?

CRAIG: Pretty strange, yeah.

ROBERT: *(Makes up his mind)* I want you to call down to the deck. Talk to Hillary. Get one of the policemen, one of the Schenectady Police guys, are they still around?

CRAIG: Yeah.

ROBERT: Good. I want you to radio down to the deck. Tell Hillary to have the policemen shoot the cows.

JEFF: Bobby—

ROBERT: Call!

JEFF: Craig, stop. Bobby, you can't tell the police to shoot the cows.

ROBERT: Why not?

JEFF: Why not? For about ten different reasons.

ROBERT: I don't have time for ten, gimme one.

JEFF: You can't kill cows to make a movie.

ROBERT: We kill cows to make hamburgers, why can't I kill cows to make a movie, what's the difference?

JEFF: What's the difference between food and a movie? Are you serious?

ROBERT: They don't have to kill the cows, they don't have to shoot to kill, just drop 'em. Wound 'em for crying out loud, I'm running out of time.

JEFF: Bobby, allow me a very quick hypothetical. Let's assume for a moment that Schenectady police officers carry pistols that can fire three-quarters of a mile and that the officers are accurate at that range so as to be able to wound and not kill a cow. Fast forward a year. Don't you think, now come on, don't you think that even the people who *don't* find it a little strange that three cows have wandered into Guam are gonna be a little perplexed when the cows, for no apparent reason, fall down to the ground?

ROBERT: You're right.

JEFF: I know.

ROBERT: You're one-hundred percent right.

JEFF: So just relax. The cows'll leave, you'll salvage some footage. The scene was too long anyway.

ROBERT: I've been looking at this all wrong. Look at the cows. What do they look like to you?

JEFF: The cows?

ROBERT: Yeah.

JEFF: They look like cows.

ROBERT: Besides cows. What do they look like besides cows?

JEFF: I'm not sure I understand.

ROBERT: I'm saying look at the cows, and tell me what you think they look like other than cows.

JEFF: I'm sorry, Rob, I'm drawing a blank. I'm looking at the cows and the only thing leaping out at me is that they look like cows.

ROBERT: Don't you think they look a little like tanks?

JEFF: Tanks?

ROBERT: Tanks. Sherman tanks. Don't you think they look a little, in a way, off in the distance there in silhouette, like tanks?

JEFF: No.

ROBERT: What do you think they look like?

JEFF: I think they look like cows.

ROBERT: Forget about the cows. Cows aren't an option, you can't choose cows, they're not cows.

JEFF: But they are cows. And they look like cows. Which only makes sense, 'cause they are cows.

ROBERT: I'm asking you to use your imagination, Jeff. I'm asking you to, for once in your life, be emotional and not intellectual. I'm asking you to pretend, to reach back in your mind's eye and tell me what you see, other than cows, when you look at those cows.

JEFF: You want me to be emotional and not intellectual?

ROBERT: Please. Once. For me.

JEFF: I see love, Rob. I see children playing freeze-tag in a sunny meadow. I see Fifth Avenue at Christmas time. I see a rainy Sunday afternoon by the fireplace. I see a man at peace with himself.

CRAIG: Really? Kids playing freeze-tag?

JEFF: *I see cows, Bobby!*

ROBERT: You don't think they look like Sherman tanks?

JEFF: Rob, you're out of control.

ROBERT: I'm in complete control. I know what I'm saying. I can make this work. If you—listen to me—if you squint your eyes a little and kinda blur things up, you see, I swear, they look like tanks. And no one's gonna think that's strange, right? I mean, tanks on a Marine base are okay. *(Beat)* You don't think I'm right?

JEFF: No.

ROBERT: Why?

JEFF: Because I think that when the ushers in the theatre instruct the audience to squint their eyes a little bit, some of 'em, some of the audience, are gonna hold out. I think that some people in the audience will, just for curiosity's sake, not squint their eyes a little. I think it's even possible that some of the critics will not squint their eyes a little. And those people, the people who chose not to play along, will think the Sherman tanks look like cows. And they'll be right.

ROBERT: I'm not saying tell the audience to squint, Jeff. I'm not saying we have to have a guy go around the country shouting in dark movie theatres that the people should squint now.

JEFF: What are you saying?

ROBERT: We have footage of tanks. I mean, we already have the footage. We have feet and feet of footage of tanks. I just keep jump cutting for half a second at a time to these shots of tanks every couple of minutes, all the way through, just keep jump cutting to tanks, three, four frames a shot, they will be subliminally convinced that they're looking at tanks.

JEFF: Rob—

ROBERT: *They will be subliminally convinced!*

JEFF: Because you showed them tanks every once in a while they're gonna think those cows are tanks?

ROBERT: Yes!

JEFF: Who do you think your audience is?

ROBERT: Idiots, Jeff. I think the vast majority are lazy, stupid idiots who, I believe, can be convinced by a clever director with enough footage at his disposal that three cows are in fact Sherman tanks.

JEFF: Well you're wrong. The only person who thinks those cows are anything but cows is you.

ROBERT: Craig, what do the cows look like to you?

CRAIG: Those cows?

ROBERT: No, not those cows, Craig, other cows. Those cows.

CRAIG: I just didn't understand the question.

ROBERT: What do those cows look like to you? Those cows out there in the middle of the shot?

CRAIG: It's funny, I was just thinking, with the way they're sort of bobbing up and down while they eat—

ROBERT: Yeah, what Craig?

CRAIG: —and 'cause you can only really make them out in shadow,

ROBERT: Craig—

CRAIG: I was thinking that they looked a little like boats.

ROBERT: Boats.

CRAIG: Yeah. Boats tied to a mooring. Bobbing at their mooring.

JEFF: Do either of you have any sense of size? Do either of you have any sense of shape and proportion? Do either of you understand that a boat and a tank and a cow are three different things, or is it like, anything that can move is just sorta lumped into one big pile?

ROBERT: No, but we are film makers and we don't lock ourselves into conventional notions and labels. We give ourselves the freedom to explore and communicate our own surroundings and we don't file the world around us into little shoe-boxes and label them black and white.

JEFF: Those are cows, Bobby.

ROBERT: How do you know? Craig says they're boats.

CRAIG: I said they *looked* like boats.

JEFF: THEY LOOK LIKE COWS! They walk like cows! They eat like cows! They're cows! Accept that fact. I wouldn't lie to you about something like this. Boats float and tanks have guns and cows are standing right there. And they're noticeable. You can squint from now till Tuesday and they'll be cows. And I think they're the best thing in the movie.

ROBERT: *(Pause. Quietly)* You're right. You're right. They're cows.

JEFF: What?

ROBERT: They're cows! There's really no way of getting around that. I thought there might be, but there isn't. They're cows. They'll have to stay cows. So fine. Okay. There are three cows standing in the last shot of the picture. *(Pause)* What did I mean by that? What was I trying to say, I wonder? I need to examine this. What are cows? What *are* cows? Cows are cows. What do cows do? Cows give milk. Milk is life. Is milk life? No, not really. Milk is milk. But it's also life in a way. Sure. Milk. Mother's milk. The milk of life. *(Pause)* Young, disillusioned Marines . . . *Young* disillusioned Marines . . . what? . . . Sucking the milk of life . . . the last drops of the milk of life, right? . . . Sunset? Endings? The Last Drops? *(He's got it)* Young disillusioned Marines sucking the last drops of life from cows . . . Because their mother's aren't there with them in Guam! *(Beat)* What am I saying?

CRAIG: Bob?

ROBERT: *(Quietly)* Wrap it, Craig.

CRAIG: You sure?

ROBERT: Wrap it. I'll be down in a minute. I'd just like a minute before I go down there.

CRAIG: We still have about ninety seconds.

ROBERT: Don't waste film. Just cut it and let's go home.

CRAIG: Sure. *(He exits)*

ROBERT: Go ahead. Say it.

JEFF: Say what?

ROBERT: Tell me how I never had control on this movie. Tell me about how I got ahead of myself. Tell me about how I got all dreamy and lofty and "master-filmmaker" and "boy-genius" and it all came crashing down around me and it's all capsulized, every one of my screw-ups, every one of my failed shots at the moon, they're all capsulized in this eleven minutes, which, I would say, will be coming soon to a theatre near you, except that I'm only a little luckier than that, Lindstrom and Sachs are gonna burn the negative. Go ahead. Say it, Jeff.

JEFF: I'm sorry, what am I supposed to say again?

ROBERT: Thank you, Jeff. Your compassion and sensitivity are moving me in a way I don't know what to do.

JEFF: Rob—

ROBERT: No go ahead. I'm serious, really. Have a little fun at my expense, Jeff.

JEFF: Rob, I wasn't gonna say that. I was gonna say let's go home, Rob. I was gonna say that the only reason why this movie sucks, and it really does bite, Rob, is that you had nothing to do with it. You were never in control and neither was I. They made us change things, we didn't even

ERT: It's about three cows.

: No it's not. What's it about?

ERT: It's about the incongruity of—

: Nope.

ERT: It's about—wait—the difference, the contrast in—

: No, no, no.

BERT: Yes, how can you really, to a certain degree, juxtapose—

F: Bobby—

BERT: Jeff, I'm saying, what we're seeing is—

F: What was going on in the scene? Really. What was *actually* going on in the scene?

BERT: *(Pause)* Marines were running down a hill.

F: Who?

BERT: Marines.

F: Who were they *really?*

BERT: Really?

FF: Yes.

BERT: They were extras.

FF: They were *actors.* In . . . ?

BERT: A movie.

FF: When all of a sudden . . . ?

BERT: Three cows walked into the most important shot.

FF: Of . . . ?

BERT: The movie.

FF: Which is about . . . ?

BERT: Disillusioned Marines in Guam.

know why, we just did it. They'd ask for a scene in bed, I'd write a scene in bed and it wasn't—Rob, it wouldn't even be *germane*. They surrounded you with—Did you hire *one* of these people yourself? You didn't make this movie, Rob, Lindstrom and Sachs did. They wrote it too. I *typed* it, that's what I did. Three months ago we were laughing about this, Bobby, you had a sense of humor about it. Come on, it's a bad movie, that's all. And it's not your fault. It's just a movie. A child hasn't died, Bobby.

ROBERT: I wish you wouldn't do that.

JEFF: Do what?

ROBERT: Talk about every problem in the world relative to the *worst* problem in the world. Just because one thing isn't as bad as something else, it doesn't make it good. It doesn't become all right. The town of Beaumont, Texas is flattened by a tornado, but "What's the problem? A nuclear weapon didn't explode." That's a bad habit, Jeff.

JEFF: Not when we're just talking about a movie.

ROBERT: That's not the point.

JEFF: What's the point?

ROBERT: The point is that Lindstrom and Sachs might just release the movie.

JEFF: So what?

ROBERT: *MY NAME'S ON IT!* What is the matter with you? In New York you spend half an hour wondering whether or not to change a comma. You don't sleep when we're doing a play. We have to put you in a hospital after the opening. Why don't you give a damn now?

JEFF: Because I take no pride whatsoever in this piece of work. Because this piece of work was mangled beyond my ability or interest in repairing it, by forces beyond my ability or interest to reason with. But they were paying me a lot of money, so what the hell?

ROBERT: Jeff, this isn't supposed to be a hobby. This isn't a weekend tennis match. This is supposed to be our lives. This is supposed to be what keeps us going, and you just sit there like, "Win some, you lose some."

JEFF: That's right. But it's *not* my life. And it's not yours. It's what we do for a living. And we're really good at it. And it's what we like working at more than anything else. Your life is Nancy, and Jennifer, and the Knicks, and the boat, and your dad, and the tomatoes . . . my life is Hillary, . . . I can't really think of anything else off the top of my head, but the point is that it's really just a movie.

ROBERT: I understand what you're saying.

JEFF: But?

ROBERT: Look, okay, you're right. This isn't the biggest tragedy in the world, but it's at least as bad, I mean, wouldn't you have to say that it's on a par with, like, my boat sinking? I mean, don't you think that if I called you and said "Jeff, I just went down to go sailing and I looked in the water and saw that overnight, my boat, on which I've spent many wonderful hours with my wife and daughter enjoying the pleasure of the outdoors and upon which I've spent many invaluable hours alone with the soothing company of the sea and into which I've put my heart, muscle and soul, has sunk beyond retrieval," you would express sympathy?

JEFF: Yes. If your boat sank, I'd say I was sorry.

ROBERT: And you don't think that this, although certainly not a tragedy on the scale of, say, the assassination of Abraham Lincoln, is at least as bad as my boat sinking?

JEFF: Does the boat have passengers?

ROBERT: No, just the boat. *(Pause)* A forty-five thousand dollar boat that I haven't finished paying for yet that I named after my first dog.

JEFF: Yes. I think they are equally bad. I'm sorry your movie has cows in it.

ROBERT: Thank you.

JEFF: I *am* sorry.

ROBERT: Then help me.

JEFF: How?

ROBERT: Gimme some Yale Drama crap.

JEFF: What?

ROBERT: I need an explanation. I need an explanation fo

JEFF: An explanation.

ROBERT: Yeah.

JEFF: Why?

ROBERT: Why?

JEFF: Yes.

ROBERT: Why do I need an explanation?

JEFF: Yeah.

ROBERT: Because I asked God for a favor and he wasn't
I'm asking you. I'm asking you for an explanation for th
thing good. Something real.

JEFF: Something real. Like actors playing trained Marine
their hair is in place before the cameras roll. Like war a
killing being reduced to a series of wacky, zany scenes
somehow palatable to the 16 to 21 audience. You know,
year of this, I think it takes a certain amount of arrogar
that when three cows walk half a mile into the last scene
God wasn't listening.

ROBERT: You don't believe in God.

JEFF: No, I don't. And I don't believe in movies. I beli
There's some Yale Drama crap for you. *(Long pause. JEFF
toward the cows. He smiles)* Bobby, what's this scene abo

ROBERT: No, you're right. Let's go home.

JEFF: Listen to me. What's this scene about?

ROBERT: I give up.

JEFF: No, you're gonna like this. What's this scene about?

ROBERT: It's supposed to be about the end of the day, the
game.

JEFF: Yeah, but it's not anymore. What's it about now?

JEFF: A subject to which we did a . . . ?

ROBERT: Disservice.

JEFF: What kind of disservice . . . ?

ROBERT: A great disservice.

JEFF: Okay. Now. What's the scene about? Really? Not the Marines. Not the sunset. What was really happening?

ROBERT: A movie shot was being destroyed.

JEFF: And if you don't think that that's an appropriate ending for this picture, you don't know Yale Drama crap when it comes up and bites you in the ass.

ROBERT: *(Pause)* It's a scene about a movie shot getting destroyed.

JEFF: I truly could not have written it better if I had a hundred years.

ROBERT: The scene is about a movie shot being ruined by three cows.

JEFF: Yes it is. And you are the boldest director since Welles.

ROBERT: A bad film, which began as a good film, about a group of Marines who join the Corps with an idealized, one might even say Hollywoodized, image of the Marines, but whose fantasies come crashing down around them, is ending with three cows walking into the last shot of the film itself.

JEFF: And you're telling me God doesn't hang around upstate New York?

(REUBEN *enters*)

REUBEN: Robert, the buses are leaving. Robert?

ROBERT: I'm coming.

REUBEN: Those cows were a pain in the ass, huh? What the hell, we'll just matte 'em out when we cut it. Hell of a sight though. I swear, I almost pissed my pants.

ROBERT: Matte 'em out?

REUBEN: Yeah. Takes half a day.

ROBERT: Matte out the cows?

REUBEN: Yeah, you talk to Leonard next week.

ROBERT: Why would I want to matte out the cows?

REUBEN: What?

ROBERT: I rehearsed those cows, I auditioned over four-hundred cows. Those were my favorites, they were my first choice. You gotta admit, the camera loves 'em, Reuben.

REUBEN: You planned those cows?

ROBERT: You believe this guy? Reuben, don't you understand?

REUBEN: You mean—

ROBERT: The scene. The *scene*. It's the whole statement of the picture.

REUBEN: The cows.

ROBERT: Yeah.

REUBEN: Oh, you're talking about . . . Sure. I thought you were talking about something else. *(Pause)* I liked it. *(Pause)* I really did. *(Pause)* The buses are heading back.

ROBERT: I'm right behind you.

REUBEN: *(Stops before leaving)* I think it's gonna work. (REUBEN *exits*)

JEFF: You ready to go?

ROBERT: *(Staring off in the distance)* Hang on . . . now they're leaving. *(Calling off, as if to say "That's all!")* THANK YOU! THAT'S A WRAP!

(BLACKOUT.)

BOY MEETS GIRL

Wendy Wasserstein

Wendy Wasserstein

Wendy Wasserstein is a resident playwright at New York's Playwrights Horizons Theatre off-Broadway. Her plays produced at Playwrights Horizons include *Any Women Can't, Montpelier PaZazz, Uncommon Women and Others,* (staged reading prior to Phoenix Theatre production) *Isn't Romantic, Miami,* a workshop of a musical with music and lyrics by Jack Feldman and Bruce Sussman, and *The Heidi Chronicles.* For PBS, *Uncommon Women and Others, The Sorrows of Gin* and *Drive She Said.* Screenplays: adaptations of *The House of Husbands,* co-authored with Christopher Durang, and *The Object of My Affection* by Stephen Mc-Cauley. Ms. Wasserstein is a contributing editor of *New York Woman* magazine. She is author of *Bachelor Girl,* a collection of essays recently published by Knopf and *The Heidi Chronicles & Other Plays* published by Harcourt, Brace, Jovanovich. She is a recipient of NEA and Guggenheim grants and serves on the council of the Dramatics Guild. *The Heidi Chronicles* was written during a grant from the British-American Arts Association and the National Theatre Corporation of Washington, D.C. Ms. Wasserstein was awarded the 1989 Tony Award for Best Play, The Pulitzer Prize for Drama, The New York Drama Critics Circle Award, The Outer Critics Circle Award, The Drama Desk award, The Susan Smith Blackburn Prize and The Dramatists Guild's Hull-Warriner Award for *The Heidi Chronicles.*

Characters

MOLLY, thirty-three years old, single, successful, and quietly desperate. Every Saturday night, Molly sheds her doctorate in molecular microchips and slips into a Zandra Rhodes macromini. On the weekends, Molly is just another girl at The Trading Post, a popular café on the Columbus Avenue strip. Just another S.S.D.B.G. (Single/Successful/ Desperate/Bachelor Girl) waiting for a discriminating Root Canal Man to invite her for an unfulfilling weekend at his summer share in the Hamptons. Molly, a native New Yorker, has recently begun considering relocating to the Sun Belt.

DAN, a successful creative director at B.B.D.&O. advertising agency. He is thirty-two, single, and having a ball. Every night, after twelve hours of Clio Award-winning work for his clients, Dan goes to the Odeon, where he eats poached salmon on grilled kiwi fruit at a table crowded with visual artists, conceptual artists, and performing artists. And every night, after picking up the tab, Dan swears that he, too, will one day give up his job and devote himself to art.

DR. SUSAN, Molly's psychiatrist.

STANLEY TANNENBAUM, PH.D., Dan's psychologist.

HER MAJESTY, THE QUEEN, ruler of the Helmsley Palace.

NARRATOR

Prologue

NARRATOR: On a spring morning in 1972, a senior at the Spence School was in Central Park, completing her science project on the reproductive cycle of flowering plants, when she saw an unmarked bus drop off twenty women in silk suits, bow ties, and sneakers on the corner of Eighty-ninth Street and Fifth Avenue. The girl took note; when she was in sixth grade, sneakers and suits had been cause for suspension.

Meanwhile, on the West Side, a middle-aged but very nice lady was on her way to Barney Greengrass, the Sturgeon King, on Eighty-ninth Street, when three cars—a Volvo, a BMW, and a Saab with M.D. plates and a "Save the Whales" bumper sticker—pulled up to Eighty-seventh Street and Amsterdam Avenue. Fifteen young men, whom the lady thought she recognized from her son's protest days at the University of Wisconsin, emerged from the cars. Before the gracious lady could offer them an Entenmann's cake, they jogged into a dilapidated brownstone and immediately began exposing brick and hanging spider plants.

And the city embraced these pioneers, who were dressed in 100-per-cent natural fabric. They prospered and they multiplied. From the now infamous drop-offs grew a new breed of New Yorkers, the Professionalites. Only their ratio of men to women, three to four, has remained constant.

What follows is a Love Story in One Act and Six Scenes between two of these sabra Professionalites: Dan and Molly.

Scene one:

One night in late August, DAN *has a yearning to talk to someone who knows Donna Karan but has moved on to Issey Miyake.* DAN *slips into the Trading Post, where the number of single women is a plague to the West Side zoning committee. It is here that he first sees* MOLLY, *seated at the bar. She is young, she is urban, she is professional. He knows immediately that* MOLLY *is the kind of new-fashioned girl he could bring home to his analyst's couch.* DAN *sits next to her.*

DAN: Hi.

MOLLY: Hi.

DAN: Do you come here often?

MOLLY: Never.

DAN: I don't either.

MOLLY: I'm waiting here for a friend. She selected this place. I think what's happening to the West Side is outrageous.

DAN: This is really an East Side singles kind of restaurant.

MOLLY: Yes, but it's here on the West Side, so we have to deal with it.

DAN: You sound like a concerned citizen.

MOLLY: Did you ever read any Kenneth Burke? In college, maybe? Lit. Crit.?

DAN: *(Immediately)* Oh, sure.

MOLLY: He divides people into observers, spectators, and participants. I'm here strictly as a sociological observer. I love to watch people in New York. Otherwise I would never come to a place like this.

DAN: I wouldn't either. In my spare time I write film criticism.

MOLLY: *(More interested)* Oh, you're a critic! Who do you write for?

DAN: I write for myself. I keep a film criticism journal.

MOLLY: I love film. Women in film particularly interest me. My favorites are Diane Kurys, Doris Dörrie, and Lee Grant.

DAN: I love women in film too.

MOLLY: *(Impressed)* You're so direct and forthcoming. What do you do?

DAN: I'm a psychiatrist.

MOLLY: Individual, group, house calls?

DAN: Actually, I'm a creative director at the B.B.D.&O. advertising agency. But I think of it as psychology. Dealing with the individual's everyday dreams and desires. I'm in charge of the Scott Paper account.

MOLLY: Fascinating. I use tissues a lot. I've always wondered why.

DAN: What do *you* do?

MOLLY: I'm a systems analyst for American Express.

DAN: "Do you know me?"

MOLLY: *(Very straightforward)* Not very well. But I'd like to.

DAN: *(Looks at her intently)* Why don't we go somewhere a little less trendy to talk. I can tell these aren't your kind of people.

MOLLY: No, I don't belong here. This isn't my New York.

DAN: *(Helps her on with her coat)* That's a nice jacket.

MOLLY: Donna Karan. But I've moved on to Issey Miyake.

DAN: *(Putting on a multilayered karate jacket)* We have so much in common.

MOLLY: "It's a phenomenon." That's a quote from a song in *Gypsy*. "Small world, isn't it?" I love Stephen Sondheim.

DAN: I'm afraid I don't know much about theater. I'm a workaholic. You know, mid-thirties New York guy, longing for Real Relationship with Remarkable Woman, meanwhile finds fulfillment through his work.

MOLLY: I think I like you. But be careful, I have Fear of Intimacy.

DAN: The Bachelor Girl's Disease. I hear it's an epidemic.

MOLLY: I'm working with my shrink to get past it.

(Pause as DAN *looks at her)*

DAN: I think I like you, too.

(They begin to exit restaurant)

DAN: What about your girl friend?

MOLLY: Uh, ah, she told me if she wasn't here by now she wasn't coming.

DAN: Not a very reliable friend.

MOLLY: No, but she's working with her shrink to get past it.

(They exit)

Scene two:
Phil's Risotto, a risotto and cheese emporium. DAN *and* MOLLY *stroll over to the counter arm in arm. It is mid-September.*

DAN: *(Ordering at the counter)* We'll have lemon risotto, chanterelle risotto, spinach risotto salad, pesto tart, carrot ravioli, goat cheese, goat cheese with ash, and a half pound of American.

MOLLY: *(Surprised, almost disturbed)* American?

DAN: Have you ever had real American cheese? Not the stuff they sell at the supermarket, but real American. *(He gives her a piece)* Taste this.

MOLLY: *(Tasting)* Oh, that's marvelous!

DAN: I've been rediscovering American food: peanut butter, grape jelly, Marshmallow Fluff, Scooter Pies, Chef Boyardee, bologna. It is unbelievable! If it's done correctly.

MOLLY: *(Softly)* I love you.

DAN: Excuse me?

MOLLY: I love blue. I adore Kraft blue cheese dressing.

DAN: Well, if it's done correctly.

Scene three:
MOLLY *in the office of her psychiatrist,* DR. SUSAN. *It is October.*

MOLLY: *(Sneezes)* Excuse me. I'm getting a cold.

DR. SUSAN: How do you feel about that?

MOLLY: Terrible. Tissues remind me of him. He says people should live together before they get married.

DR. SUSAN: How do you feel about that?

MOLLY: Sigourney Weaver and Glenn Close are married.

DR. SUSAN: How do you feel about that?

MOLLY: Living together was for kids in the late sixties and seventies. I'm a thirty-three-year-old woman.

DR. SUSAN: How do you feel about that?

MOLLY: I need a commitment. I want a family. I don't want to take a course at the New School on how to place a personal ad. Meryl Streep has three children already.

DR. SUSAN: Why do you always compare yourself to movie stars? You're not an actress.

MOLLY: That's true. That's really true! That's an incredible insight. Maybe my mother wanted me to be an actress. I hate her.

Scene four:

DAN *in the office of his psychologist,* STANLEY TANNENBAUM, PH.D. *It is November.*

DAN: I don't think I want to make a commitment to Molly, but I'm afraid of what she'll say.

STANLEY TANNENBAUM, PH.D.: Well, let's put Molly in this chair, and then you can answer for her.

DAN: All right. *(Talking now to an empty chair)* Molly, I don't think I want to make a commitment.

(DAN *gets up and sits in chair to answer as* MOLLY *would)*

DAN: *(Pretending he's* MOLLY*)* That's okay. I'm an observer. This is all a sociological investigation. Kenneth Burke divides people into spectators, partici—

(DAN *runs back to his seat to answer* MOLLY*)*

DAN: *(Angry)* Who the hell is Kenneth Burke? That is so pretentious, Molly!

DAN: *(As* MOLLY*)* Not as pretentious as keeping a journal of film criticism.

DAN: *(Furious)* You resent my writing! You want to swallow me up. If I live with you, I won't be here anymore. I'll lose myself.

STANLEY TANNENBAUM, PH.D.: Did you hear what you just said?

DAN: I have it. Goddamn it! I have it. Fear of Intimacy. That Bachelor Girl's Disease. Why couldn't I just get burn-out?

Scene five:

Central Park West. The Thanksgiving Day Parade. DAN *and* MOLLY *are watching floats of Bullwinkle and Superman pass by.*

MOLLY: *(Overcome by the sight of the floats)* I love this parade. Gosh, I really love this parade. Reminds me of growing up here and of New York before there were Benetton shops and a Trump Organization.

DAN: I never imagined people actually grew up in New York.

MOLLY: It was different then. There were real neighborhoods. The ladies on Madison Avenue wore white gloves and ate mashed potatoes at the Kirby Allen Restaurant. Marjorie Morningstar and her family gathered for Sabbath dinners on Central Park West. All artists wore turtlenecks and played bongo drums in the Village. And every night at seven o'clock, men in top hats and tails tap-danced from Shubert Alley to the Winter Garden theater.

DAN: Really!

MOLLY: Well, I like to think so. Now everywhere I go all the women look like me.

DAN: What's so bad about that?

MOLLY: Nothing, it's just that it's all the same. I like the idea of a flower district, a theater district, a diamond district. The whole city is being renovated into Molly district. Dan, I have to confess. I hate goat cheese.

DAN: *(Softly)* Me, too. But I love you.

MOLLY: Hmmmmmm?

DAN: I hate goat cheese, but I love blue. Molly, with Bullwinkle as my witness, I want to marry you. And every Thanksgiving we can bring our children here. And someday they'll tell someone they met at The Trading Post, "I love this parade, I grew up here."

MOLLY: *(No longer wistful)* But will our children go to Trinity or the Ethical Culture School? They could probably learn Chinese at Trinity, but there are a lot of Wall Street parents. Ethical Culture is nice, but maybe it's too liberal, not enough attention to the classics. How 'bout Brearley? There's something to be said for an all-women's education. *(She kisses* DAN) Dan, just think! We can raise a family of women filmmakers!!!!!

Scene six:

The Helmsley Palace. The Grand Ballroom. An enormous wedding party.
DAN *and* MOLLY *are standing under the altar before* HER MAJESTY, THE QUEEN.

QUEEN: Dan, do you take this woman to be your wife? To love, be emotionally supportive of, have good dialogue with, as well as a country home in the Hamptons, Connecticut, or possibly upper New York State?

DAN: I do.

QUEEN: Molly, do you take this man to love, and at the same time maintain your career, spend quality time with the children, and keep yourself appealing by joining the New York Health and Racquet Club?

MOLLY: I do.

QUEEN: *(Addressing the wedding guests)* I've known this couple for two hours. But I've stood guard at their honeymoon suite. Molly will be able to see her makeup in soft light in the bathroom mirror. Dan will be put at ease by the suit hangers that detach from the closet. And if Dan and Molly decide to get remarried someday, and return to the honeymoon suite, I will keep a note of their room number. I wouldn't sleep in a new room, why should they?

DAN: *(Bows)* Thank you, Your Majesty.

MOLLY: *(Curtsies)* Thank you, Your Majesty.

QUEEN: And now by virtue of being Queen of all the Helmsleys, I pronounce you husband and wife. Congratulations! You may kiss the bride.

(DAN *kisses* MOLLY. *There are cheers and the band begins to play "Lullaby of Broadway." Five hundred men in top hats and tails begin to tap down the aisle)*

Epilogue

NARRATOR: Dan and Molly became bi-island (Manhattan and Long), with bi-point three children (a girl, a boy, and an au pair from Barnard), and bi-career (a shift into management for him, a cottage industry for her). As Molly approached middle age she began to consult crystals about her hormonal convergence and undertook frequent pilgrimages to Stonehenge. Dan continued to pursue his interest in early American comestibles, and was featured on the cover of *Just Say Cheese* magazine for his distinguished cellar of American pasteurized-cheese foods.

The fortunes of the Queen, however, followed a crueler path. After a long and glorious reign, she was found to be poaching, thereby violating the charter, and was forced to abdicate. Even a monarch must obey the laws of the realm. On the day she was dethroned, she received a monogrammed Cartier sympathy note from Molly.

> Dear Your Majesty,
> Dan and I send you our best wishes at this difficult time.
> Molly

P.S. Is your estate in Greenwich for sale? Also, did you get a kickback from the band at our wedding?

Molly's mother had taught her that a lady always sends a note.

Otherwise—apart from twenty years of couples therapy, his-and-her reconstructive surgery, one triple bypass, and four extramarital affairs —they lived happily ever after.

ABSTINENCE

A Turn

Lanford Wilson

"... Abstinence engenders maladies."
Love's Labour's Lost

Lanford Wilson

Lanford Wilson received the 1980 Pulitzer Prize for Drama and the New York Drama Critics Circle Award for *Talley's Folly*. He is a founding member of the Circle Repertory Company and one of twenty-one resident playwrights for the company.

His work at Circle Rep includes: *The Family Continues* (1972), *The HOT L Baltimore* (1973), *The Mound Builders* (1975), *Serenading Louie* (1976), *5th of July* (1978), *Talley's Folly* (1980), *A Tale Told* (1981), *Angels Fall* (1982), all directed by Marshall Mason, and the one-act plays *Brontosaurus* (1977) and *Thymus Vulgaris* (1982).

His other plays include: *Balm in Gilead* (1965), *The Gingham Dog* (1966), *The Rimers of Eldritch* (1967), *Lemon Sky* (1969) and some twenty produced one-acts. He has also written the libretto for Lee Hoiby's opera of Tennessee Williams' *Summer and Smoke,* and two television plays, *Taxi!* and *The Migrants* (based on a short story by Tennessee Williams).

Other awards include the New York Critics' Award, the Outer Critics Circle Award and an Obie for *The HOT L Baltimore,* an Obie for *The Mound Builders,* a Drama-Logue Award for *5th of July* and *Talley's Folly,* the Vernon Rice Award for *The Rimers of Eldritch,* and Tony nominations for *Talley's Folly, 5th of July,* and *Angels Fall.* He is the recipient of the Brandeis University Creative Arts Award in Theatre Arts and the Institute of Arts and Letters Award.

Mr. Wilson has recently completed an entirely new translation of Chekhov's *The Three Sisters,* which was commissioned and produced by the Hartford Stage Company. His play, *Talley and Son* (the third play in the Talley Trilogy) opened in New York on September 24, 1985.

His new play, *Burn This,* opened at the Mark Taper Forum in Los Angeles in January 1987 starring John Malkovich and Joan Allen and opened on Broadway in October 1987 with the same cast. He is currently writing the screenplay for the film version.

He makes his home in Sag Harbor, New York. *Burn This* was done in London, starring John Malkovich in 1990.

Characters

MARTHA, THE MAID, a maid.
LON, Winnie's husband. Thirty-five and mild.
WINNIE, thirty, sweet and charming. Always.
DANNA, thirty. Sharp and a little hysterical just tonight.
JOE, thirty. The All American Sweetheart of a man. Unfortunately crazy.

Scene:

*The very dark front hall of a New York apartment. Maybe track lighting.
Chic.*

(MARTHA, *the Maid, stands at the front door.* LON *enters, lighting a cigarette*)

LON: I think all the guests are here, Martha.

MARTHA: Is this the shoplifters or the smokers or the sex-offenders or the drunks?

LON: I think it's the weight-watchers, but just in case it's the smokers I stepped out here to have a cigarette.

WINNIE: *(Enters from another way)* Happy anniversary, darling. I'm so thankful you're here.

LON: Happy anniversary, Winnie. My helpful little helpless wife. I thought you were in with your guests.

WINNIE: I just popped up for a moment to tuck in the children.

LON: Why is it that every anniversary we have to give a party for one of your charity groups?

WINNIE: I just feel our life is so perfect we should help those less fortunate.

(They exit arm in arm)

MARTHA: *(To the audience)* Already you know we're in trouble, right?

(The doorbell rings. MARTHA *reaches to open it, turns to look at audience)*

One tip. Always bet on somebody named Winnie.

(She opens the door. DANNA *staggers in a step)*

DANNA: Thank God someone's here! You're not Winnie. You're . . . she talks about you all the time . . . you're Abigail or Eleanor or Lady Bird. . . .

MARTHA: Martha.

DANNA: Martha!

MARTHA: And whom should I say . . . ?

DANNA: Oh. I'm a friend. I've just come from a meeting—this is the closest place I could think of. Tell her—My name is—God, I knew it a minute ago. Danna! I'm Danna Walsh.

MARTHA: Danna Walsh. *(In one move* MARTHA *takes a book from nowhere, pages quickly to the back, checks, raises her eyebrows)*

DANNA: Now, Jackie, darling . . .

MARTHA: Martha.

DANNA: Martha, darling, you've got to get me a drink.

MARTHA: No way.

DANNA: I'll give you money. I'll give you my jewels. I'll give you my husband—no, I dumped him, I'll give you my mother.

MARTHA: I was weakening but you blew it.

WINNIE: *(Entering)* Martha, who was at—Danna, darling! I so wanted to be there for you tonight but we have this dinner party every year.

DANNA: I hate to burst in on you like this but you've always been so helpful. I have to talk to you alone.

WINNIE: Oh, Martha knows everything.

DANNA: You do?

(Beat. Goes to MARTHA*)*

What is a . . .

(Whispers. MARTHA *raises her eyebrows, whispers back into* DANNA'S *ear)*

Well, of course it is. It's absurdly simple if you think about it.

(To WINNIE*)*

Winnie, you've got to help me.

WINNIE: You don't look well at all. How did it go?

DANNA: How did what go?

WINNIE: The meeting. A.A. The first anniversary of your sobriety.

DANNA: Who remembers, it must have been twenty minutes ago. I was a wreck. I qualified. Everyone applauded. I could have ripped their hearts out. I was congratulated. The rich bitch who runs things called me a brick. I've never wanted a drink so badly in my life.

WINNIE: Don't be silly. We're all so proud of you! You've gone an entire year today without a drink.

DANNA: A year? Are you mad? What would be so unusual about that? This is leap year, you idiot. Three hundred sixty-six long tedious days. And three hundred sixty-six long hopeless nights. I've read over five hundred books. I've written four. I've knitted some things: a bed cover, wallpaper for the living room. Johnnie Walker Red! Now there's a man with spine. Aren't you going to ask me in?

WINNIE: You're in, darling.

DANNA: This is your apartment? This well? It's pitch in here!

WINNIE: Would you like a cup of tea?

DANNA: *(All hope gone. Musing)* Oh . . . no . . . I've been haunted all day by a scene in one of the Thin Man movies. Nick is at the table when Nora comes in late, and she asks him how much he's had to drink; Nick says he's had five martinis. And when the waiter comes over Nora says, "Would you please bring me five martinis?"

(Beat)

I want to live like that. I want charm in my life. I want my alcohol back. I used to have a wonderful life. I mean, I didn't have friends, but I didn't notice.

WINNIE: Why don't you come join us? Just twenty or so, they're sitting down to eat. They're Liars, I'm afraid, Liars Anonymous, but you know how charming they can be.

DANNA: Food? How shallow. People don't know? Without a drink? I'll just steady myself against the wall here—where is it?—and I'll be fine. If Dolly could just bring me a . . .

MARTHA: Forget it.

WINNIE: I know, love. I'm a drunk, too. I've had some—

DANNA: Ha! You call yourself a drunk? You haven't had a drink in three years. Put me in front of a bottle of Cuervo Gold and I'll show you a drunk.

WINNIE: You know what we say: One day at a time.

DANNA: I've experienced one day at a time for three hundred sixty-six days—end to end. Twenty-four hours in every day, eighty-six thousand four hundred seconds. I know, I counted them once. A year ago I could celebrate the Fourth of July, come home, go to bed, wake up, it would be November.

LON: *(Enters. Sees* DANNA, *maybe hesitates one step, smiles)* Winnie, are you coming back to the . . .

WINNIE: Lon, I want you to meet a dear friend of mine. This is Danna. We've been friends for, oh, my, how long is it?

DANNA: Three hundred sixty-six . . . endless . . .

WINNIE: Is it a year already? Danna, this is my husband, Lon.

DANNA: You don't happen to be carrying, do you?

WINNIE: Danna was just admiring the foyer.

LON: Yes, my wife did the entire apartment herself.

DANNA: I haven't seen it.

LON: I was just talking to the most remarkable man in there. He says he climbed Mount Everest completely by himself.

WINNIE: Let me just—oh, you know what a terrible organizer I am—I'll just get the next course started and then I'm all yours.

(She goes out, smiling. Just before she leaves she stops. Thinks. Looks at MARTHA, *then goes out thinking. A calm beat. You can't tell, but they are listening to* WINNIE's *retreat)*

DANNA: *(They stare at each other an intense moment. Then)* Alonzo!

(They kiss passionately, fall to the ground in a 69 position, LON's *head up* DANNA's *dress, both growling and barking like dogs. They sit up.* DANNA's *hair is a mess. They stare at each other a frozen beat)*

MARTHA: *(To audience)* I turned down a paying job to do this play.

LON: *(To* DANNA*)* Every moment without you has been hell!

DANNA: You can't possibly be Winnie's husband. You're that pompous miser she talks about? She said you were eighty! She said you had no teeth.

LON: Where did you meet Winnie?

DANNA: Ha! You think she really goes to ballet class five times a week? Have you once asked to see her plié? You told me your wife was Catholic, blind, and confined to a wheelchair.

LON: I didn't want to worry you.

DANNA: I mean she's a kind-hearted helpless thing, but you might have told me you were married to Miss Ripple of 1985.

LON: Don't be jealous, Danna. Winnie never drinks.

DANNA: Ha! I could tell you stories about that Sweet-pea that would turn your piss green. Ever wonder why she carried a sewing basket for twelve years without ever so much as darning a sock?

LON: Winnie is the most charitable woman in the city.

DANNA: If you mean she's known for giving it away.

LON: This is not becoming, Danna.

DANNA: She can't help it, poor dear. While you're down on Wall Street that poor helpless thing is down on half of Spanish Harlem.

LON: You could hardly know her.

DANNA: I know you have two olive-skinned sons with flashing black eyes.

LON: *(Moving closer, becoming aroused)* If anything, Winnie is almost too gentle and kind. She has none of the shocking terms of endearment that you have. Or the voracious appetite. None of the inventive positions . . . certainly none of the improvisationally creative—before I met you I had no idea of the things that could be done with raw vegetables. If I were to think one of you had a broad experience . . .

DANNA: I wasn't myself, Lon. I was sober. And as for the potato trick, I learned that one at . . . *(Remembering herself)* I mean to say . . . "Winnie" you said her name was? No, we've only met a couple of times. Meetings or something, a few friends. I had no idea she was your wife. I doubt that I could allow myself to see you again now that I know—*(Losing it)*—unless you either take me right here in this dungeon of a foyer or bring me a Manhattan. Oh, god! With a Manhattan who needs a man? A Manhattan asks nothing from you. It doesn't deceive or sulk or play games. And it has, God knows, more interesting conversation. A Manhattan . . . listens!

LON: *(Love talk)* You said to pick—

(LON shuts up as WINNIE enters. She notices but doesn't show it)

WINNIE: Now, I'm all yours.

DANNA: Winnie! You poor deceived darling. You weak and caring . . .

WINNIE: Could you wait just a little moment? *(She exits)*

LON: *(Adjusting back)* You said to pick up a zucchini . . . I got three. And a cucumber. And a baby eggplant. And a crooked necked squash. The mind boggles.

DANNA: *(Torn, but)* Woah . . . no, no Lon. It's not enough. The night with the pumpkin was fun, but it's not enough.

LON: Martha might ask the cook if she has any sherry.

MARTHA: This woman is loaded for bear, she'd blow a glass of sherry to hell.

LON: Really, I don't believe there's any alcohol in the house.

DANNA: You're goddamned right there isn't. You'll find there's no nail polish remover either. That tit-mouse wouldn't trust herself in the same room with vanilla extract. Why do you think the radiator kept freezing on your car? It's the trusting ones who need our help, Alonzo. She needs you. A charming intelligent dynamo of a man who inherited thirty-seven million and has parlayed that, now, into . . . how much?

LON: *(Proud)* Well . . . a little over twelve. But I could never leave you. You're special. Who else has a living room with cable-knit walls?

DANNA: *(Pleased)* For one, my mother. I did hers too.

LON: But, you're right. Winnie does need me.

DANNA: If it were anyone but that lovely, uncomplicated . . .

LON: But she doesn't have to know.

DANNA: The woman has gimlet eyes. She's been sober for three years, she can see through six feet of concrete.

(WINNIE *enters with* JOE, *a very handsome young man indeed*)

WINNIE: Danna, darling. I wanted you to meet Joe. Joe is a friend of Bill Wilson's too.

JOE: Sorry, Winnie, I'd love to meet the fellow but I don't know Bill Wilson at all. Sounds like a lovely guy. Do you?

DANNA: Know him? I've practically had his child. If he were here I'd sauté the sanctimonious son-of-a-bitch in Marsala. Whoever—*(She notices* JOE *for the first time and does not take her eyes off him again)* Oh. Hi, Joe.

JOE: Hi.

DANNA: You're leaving soon?

JOE: I don't know. My pilot had the jet warmed up to go to Buenos Aires, but I saw you in the hall here and called him to cancel the trip.

DANNA: And then, Buenos Aires is so . . . hot this time of year.

JOE: And I don't like to fly without a drink and my doctor says my liver's shot. All those years in the P.O.W. camps.

DANNA: You poor dear. What was your drink? Bourbon?

JOE: Well, since we have our own vineyards, I mostly just stick to Dom Perignon. Family loyalty and all that.

DANNA: With me it's a cold vodka martini. Or two.

JOE: Twist or an olive?

DANNA: Hold the garbage.

JOE: So this is your anniversary.

DANNA: My first. It's been little nervous-making.

WINNIE: Remember, you don't have to worry about tomorrow. You just have to get through tonight.

DANNA: Oh, suddenly, I don't think that's going to be such a problem. —I don't know though. You sound like a playboy.

JOE: Actually, I'm a physicist.

DANNA: My.

(WINNIE *is helping* JOE *on with his coat*)

JOE: And you live close by.

DANNA: Twenty or thirty blocks.

LON: Danna? Aren't you going to say goodnight? Danna? The crisper?

WINNIE: Oh. And Joe.

JOE: Yes, Winnie?

WINNIE: Happy anniversary.

JOE: Thanks.

DANNA: It's your anniversary too?

JOE: Well, I don't talk about it. My wife, the Duchess, had a passion for collecting Iranian pottery. Nothing would do but she had to go there just one more time.

DANNA: Oh, no.

JOE: Caught in a terrorist crossfire.

DANNA: You don't have to talk about it.

JOE: Should we walk?

DANNA: Let's take a cab.

(*They leave*)

WINNIE: *(After a beat)* I do hope she'll be all right.

LON: You worry too much about other people. She can look after herself. Not like my helpless darling. It's his anniversary, too?

WINNIE: Yes. Such a pity. But they let him out this one night every year. We must go in and join our guests . . . take my arm. Now, remember, this is my Liars Anonymous group; don't believe a word anyone says . . . Darling. I was looking in the refrigerator. You must show me what you plan to do with all those vegetables.

(MARTHA *is left alone as at the beginning. A pause)*

MARTHA: . . . "The night with the pumpkin . . . was fun? . . ." *(Beat)* Liars Anonymous. Wouldn't you know. I had two marriage proposals and a tip on the market from that group.

(Starts to go, stops)

I don't belong to any of those organizations. I don't have the constitution for self-denial. Pity about Joe not being a physicist. Just as well, though. I don't trust scientists. They say they can put your body in cold storage for a hundred years and thaw you out as good as now? Come on. I mean have you ever tasted freeze-dried coffee? *(Going)* What a nasty little play. I don't know about you but I'll never touch a crudité again. *(Gone.)*

THE

BEST

AMERICAN

SHORT

PLAYS

1991–1992

To Marianne, always

INTRODUCTION

This year's volume of *Best American Short Plays* is comprised of work by playwrights who have been contributing to the health of the American theater for the last fifty years. Arthur Miller's first Broadway production, *The Man Who Had All the Luck,* was in 1942; A.R. Gurney's first published play was in *The Best One-Act Plays of 1955;* Arthur Kopit was making major noises up in Cambridge, Massachusetts, in 1958 and then made his New York City debut in 1962; Frank Gilroy established himself in the same year; Murray Schisgal and Terrence McNally made Broadway appearances before 1965; Joseph Chaikin and Jean Claude van Itallie made their voices heard by the end of that decade. This year's selection brings them together only by chance. Nevertheless, our desire is to keep the narrative going, to maintain the continuity and to explore the dynamics of playwriting during the last half of the twentieth century.

Hindemith, the great German composer, once told his music composition students at Yale that the life of a composition teacher was fifteen years. "After that," he said, "you can't hear the sound." Such an observation, it would seem, could apply to playwriting as well as to the teaching of playwriting. How does a playwright keep abreast of the sounds? That new sound invading his ear both reveals and illuminates the new reality. Although the universals remain and the constants continue, the details which distinguish the decades, the epochs, the generations, change. How do those creative talents deal with the sound that the teacher, according to Hindemith, can no longer hear? Does the playwright manage to transcend Hindemith's observation? In recent years we have heard from both Arthur Miller and (before his death) Tennessee Williams that they no longer had an audience in their native America. Does Schisgal? Kopit? Gilroy? Gurney certainly does have a theater audience. In this context, the exception tries the rule rather than proves the rule. Whatever the explanation, the question remains a provocative one.

Within this volume we can see where the population of Miller, Gurney, Schisgal, Gilroy, Kopit and McNally is quite different from the population of Park, Cruz, Noojin, Silverstein and Chaikin. Oates and Bosworth have a cast of characters much more in the tradition of the older writers. The population has shifted from middle-class problems to a population of country-western failed songwriters, a displaced black people seeking some sort of refuge, a lower-class couple trying to deal with the learning of Spanish, two homeless people trying to survive in a subway station, and an aphasic. That population did not inform the theatrical reality of the earlier playwrights, despite the existence in the nation of such a population.

Within this volume we can see where the language used by the characters is considerably different. Scatological language is one of the obvious differences. For Cruz and Park and Silverstein, words do not create any self-consciousness. But when Miller and Gurney and Gilroy use what used to be considered "obscene words," one does sense self-consciousness. That language is not their language. A greater distinction exists in the attempt of Cruz, Park, Oates and Chaikin to use diction which will evoke a poetic effect. They attempt to transcend the prosaic level of social realism although they may be dealing with problems and experiences of social realism.

Within this volume we can also see where the vision which informed the older playwrights, a vision of hope, progress, melody, order and design, and future, is not nearly so powerful in the works of the newer playwrights. In *The Open Meeting*, Gurney brings into his traditional vision the word absurd and even the principle of absurdity, while Miller, Schisgal and Gilroy, while not conversing with the absurd, bring into their traditional vision the presence of the bizarre, the eccentric, the illogical, which influences the reality of their characters. Miller's play closes with the anxiety for the future of a nation which has abandoned its birthright. Miller's concerns are updated, they are "with it," but their connection is within reason and common sense, not illogicality. Schisgal's couple is, in part, saved by the lottery, a relatively recent addition to the American reality. Oates's people are trapped by the forces of television and mass media. The younger playwrights, in tune with the sound of their time, make no extra attempt to deal with the reality that they know. The older playwrights make accommodations in their attempt to hear the sound of today.

The traditional playwrights do not wish to repeat themselves, but their preoccupations remain what they have always been: human relationships, truth and deception, love, permanence, and work. For the newer generation, work plays very little, if any, role in the drama of the character; permanence has given way to that which is temporary; love is a question mark (any relationship could read "until love do us part"), and truth is hardly an objective. Survival is an objective, aloneness (isolation) is the condition, and love is a suspicious connection always on the brink of crashing to the ground. These plays offer a panoramic view of the values, the perception and the reality of the lst half of the twentieth century.

The older playwrights, whether taught by Kenneth Thorpe Rowe (Arthur Miller's teacher at Michigan) or by Marc Connely and Boyd Smith (Gurney and Gilroy's possible teachers at Yale in the 50s), were most likely taught that a play required three characters minimum. In Gibson's *Two For the Seasaw,* the third character was the wife on the telephone! However, in this volume we have a number of plays with only two (two-handers) and two plays with only one character. The temptation to explain this phenomenon by economic necessity is very great. But a more realistic explanation might be that in our solopsistic reality of 1992 we are much more inner-directed, much more isolated and much more preoccupied with the individual life than we are with the community life. The question I would leave with the reader is, "Is the loneliness of 1992 different from the loneliness of 1952?"

HOWARD STEIN
Columbia University
April, 1992

MAKING CONTACT

Patricia Bosworth

Patricia Bosworth

Patricia Bosworth is a member of The Women's Project in New York, where *Making Contact* was first performed in November of 1990 at the Judith Anderson Theater. It has since been done in workshop at the Renegade Theater in Hoboken, New Jersey, and at the Lenox Theater Lab in Lenox, Massachusetts. Ms. Bosworth's other plays include *Choices,* which was also done originally at The Women's Project off Broadway.

Ms. Bosworth is on the board of the Actors Studio. She has been a contributing editor of *Vanity Fair* magazine and she writes frequently for *The New York Times* and *The Nation,* mainly on the arts.

She is the author of *Montgomery Clift, A Biography* (just reissued by Limelight Editions) and author as well of *Diane Arbus, A Biography* (published by Knopf and Avon).

Ms. Bosworth is currently writing a memoir/biography for Simon & Schuster of her father, Bartley C. Crum, a lawyer who defended the "Hollywood Ten."

A native of San Francisco, Ms. Bosworth is a graduate of Sarah Lawrence College. She is on the executive board of Pen American Center and a member of the Biographers Seminar at New York University. She teaches writing workshops at Barnard and a graduate program at the School of the Arts at Columbia University. She is the winner of a Columbia/Doubleday writing fellowship.

Characters:

POLLY HENDERSON

ABNER KYND

Scene:

The curtain rises on the world's ugliest sublet on New York's upper east side. There is nothing attractive about this apartment. It is one room four flights up—in a converted brownstone. It is supposedly a "duplex." Translation: a platform has been built at one end of the room—on that platform—or balcony—rests a bed. You can only get there by a rickety ladder.

The rest of the room is crammed with furniture of wildly varying styles. There's a funny little ship captain's desk—a couple of bar stools covered with zebra—an art deco lamp. On one wall—for no reason—an oil painting of a flying donut. Under it is a sagging couch—and on another wall a small mirror. The windows are shuttered. There is a wall kitchen with a small bar in front of it crowded with wines and liquors; off this room is a dressing room not visible to the audience and from it one can hear strange sounds emerging—female sounds—a female voice—constricted—wailing—crying—cursing: "Oh fuck—shit—damn it to hell where are my decent shoes?" A drawer bangs shut—more curses—and then POLLY HENDERSON enters, carrying a plastic makeup bag and a string of pearls. She stops; puts stuff down on the couch.

POLLY is a woman of "indeterminate years." She is on the brink of laughter —or tears. POLLY is a writer, so she's self-reliant—feisty—inquisitive—but there is a sadness—her manner most of the time is ironic. POLLY has been a widow for close to two years and she is still adjusting—moving from a state of shock through psychic numbness to a new reality for herself.

After a moment POLLY walks over to the mirror and surveys her reflection; her hair is in curlers; she is wearing a plain rather unflattering high-necked blouse and skirt—and scuffie slippers. She begins yanking off the curlers and methodically combing her hair; she turns to get lipstick and rouge from the makeup bag—applies both to her face—then stands back to study the results. As she does, she addresses her image in the glass:

POLLY: In a dim light I don't look so bad . . . who am I kidding? *(Smears more lipstick on her mouth—then removes it with Kleenex she pulls out of a pocket)* Could I still pass for forty? That's a laugh. *(Long pause)* Jesus . . . Oh shut up you nut. Stop worrying. This is not the end of the world.

(A crack of thunder is heard—lightning flashes—the sound of rain pelting down)

Great. Now my hair will go totally limp and I'll look like hell . . .

(Just then the doorbell rings and POLLY *jumps—runs over to open the door and reveal* ABNER KYND—*a round bearded man in rumpled chinos, filthy army jacket, baseball cap and muddy workboots.* ABNER *could be described as an "oddball" or an "eccentric." He is not your ordinary guy— now he is loaded down with camera equipment, portable lights, tripod, battered Bloomingdale's shopping bags; he is grinning genially; in his fist an enormous dripping umbrella)*

ABNER: Hello, Polly!

*(*POLLY *gazes at him in astonishment as he shakes water off umbrella, puts it in a corner and begins to unload his equipment)*

I'm just gonna put my stuff anywhere. *(And he does—setting up lights, putting down cameras in a row on the floor—at one point he marches off to the dressing room with a couple of bags—returns momentarily to continue setting up lights)*

POLLY: *(Watching)* Sure—Absolutely—Anywhere—. I'm Polly Henderson by the way. *(Laughs shortly)* But then who else would I be?

ABNER: Right. And I'm Abner Kynd. *(He is now prowling about the place with narrowed eyes—holding up a light meter—he unfolds a portable tripod)*

POLLY: You sure have a lot of stuff.

ABNER: *(Chuckling)* I come prepared for any emergency. I was in the Philippines right after Aquino was assassinated and there was this big power failure in Manila—but I had my emergency lighting equipment with me so I was able to shoot the body in the morgue and get these fantastic shots—sold 'em all over the world—to *Paris Match* and *Der Stern* and . . .

POLLY: Oh, dear. Well, that must have been . . .

ABNER: It was a little hairy but . . . *(He finishes arranging his equipment —goes to one of his shopping bags and pulls out a book—waving it at her)* Look what I have!

POLLY: My god. My first book. *(He hands it to her; she caresses it)* It's been out of print for years . . .

ABNER: I bought it at Strand. Wanted to see your author photograph. They had one copy way in the back . . .

POLLY: This book had a very small sale.

ABNER: I hear it's a great novel.

POLLY: It isn't a novel—it happens to be a series of essays.

ABNER: *(Slapping his head but not at all embarrassed by his gaffe)* Oh yeah! Sure, lady! Essays—not a novel—sure, I know that!

(Slight pause—POLLY hands book back to him)

I'm gonna treasure this, lady! *(Puts it back into the shopping bag with great flourish—turns around—paces about the room sizing it up . . . his eye finally lights on the oil painting of the flying donut)* Interesting work.

POLLY: Oh, stop it. That painting is terrible. The entire apartment is god-awful. Nothing of mine is here. It's a sublet. I had to take it. I couldn't find anything else. *(Her voice rises)* It is not to my taste!

ABNER: *(Soothing, quietly)* Take it easy, lady. I believe you.

POLLY: Sorry. I didn't mean to get upset . . . would you like something to drink?

ABNER: I never drink when I'm on the job. Maybe after I take your photograph.

POLLY: Well, I wish you weren't going to take my photograph! *(Fluffs her hair nervously)*

ABNER: Why not?

POLLY: Because I take a terrible picture, that's why.

ABNER: Well, I take a wonderful picture. OK? Don't worry. Relax. *(Starts putting film into a camera)* Say, why don't you have a drink?

POLLY: Great idea. I think I will. *(Goes to fridge—takes a bottle of vodka out; pours some into an espresso cup and raises it in his direction)* Cheers! *(Swigs some down—makes a face—takes another swig)* You notice I'm drinking out of an espresso cup? There is nothing else here. No glassware—no dishes. I eat off paper plates. I just moved in last month—took the place over from a woman who lives in Rhode Island most of the time. She calls this her *pied a terre*—are you ready for that?

ABNER: How'd you find it?

POLLY: From an ad in the *Village Voice.* I was desperate. But then I'm often desperate. I've been in four sublets in the past year and a half. Each one more hideous than the last . . .

ABNER: So why haven't you found an apartment of your own?

POLLY: I just can't seem to find what I want.

ABNER: In this market? It's a buyer's market.

POLLY: Yes, I know that—but at the price I want . . .

ABNER: Maybe you're being too particular.

POLLY: Maybe, but . . . *(She pauses, uncertain about whether or not she should continue her thought—then she decides she will)* You see—my husband and I lived in this wonderful brownstone floorthru—a rent-controlled floorthru—for twenty years. Then our landlord began dying of AIDS and he called us into his bedroom and told us he couldn't give us another lease—he was going to have to sell the brownstone to pay for his hospital bills . . . so naturally we said we understood. Then—bizarrely—not long after that my husband died suddenly . . .

ABNER: Hey, lady. I'm sorry. My sympathies—my deepest sympathy . . .

POLLY: Yes, well . . . thanks . . . well, anyhow . . . suddenly the house was sold and I was evicted. I stayed with friends for a while and then I began this crazy sublet hopping—*(She stops, realizing she is starting to relive the horror of the last year and a half)* Anyhow. I am about to move out of *this* place—it was just a month sublet—I have to be out of here and I still haven't found anything . . .

ABNER: Have you seen anything halfway decent?

POLLY: Well, I found one I sort of liked except it was inhabited by two midgets . . .

ABNER: Midgets?

POLLY: No, I'm not serious—they were just a very small couple and their place was crammed with furniture—

ABNER: I once photographed a midget. A dwarf, I mean. Do you remember Michael Dunn—he was an actor—in *Ship of Fools?* Nominated for an Oscar?

POLLY: Sure, I remember him. But didn't he die?

ABNER: Yeah, a long time ago. But when I photographed him in the 1960s he was a very hot actor . . . he was in this show on Broadway based on a Carson McCullers story—forget the name . . . so *Look* magazine asks me to follow Mike around for a while photographing him— you know, a day in the life kinda thing . . . Well, this little guy had something going every fucking minute. We start off at his tailor's— somewhere on 42nd Street—where he is being fitted for this spiffy little suit—Christ, I remember how mean he was to that tailor—he kept chewing him out—"Take it in here! Take it in there!" Then we go over to his barber's—"He trims John F. Kennedy's hair," he tells me out of the side of his mouth . . . After that we hop a cab and end up at his astrologist's . . . Christ—it's in this big cavernous apartment house on West End Avenue—the place smells of cockroach spray . . . the door is opened by some gypsy wearin' a fright wig and lotsa junk jewelry—Mike and I both have to pee but she won't let us use the john! "It is bad for your chart," she tells Mike. "Well, it'll be bad for your bank account, buby, if you don't let us take a piss!" he yells and then he starts shrieking with laughter—P.S. we get to use the john . . . By the end of the afternoon we pick up his co-star Lou Antonio at Lou's pad—somewhere on West 45th—at this point Mike crawls onto Lou's back and proceeds to ride him like a horse to the Martin Beck Theatre, beatin' him and cussin' him all the way and Lou puts up with it—thinks it's a gas . . . I shot two—three rolls of film of them galloping down the block—the damndest sight . . .

POLLY: It must have been . . .

ABNER: Mike had a lot of fantasies about himself which nobody disputed even though they sounded too extreme to be true. He told me as a kid he'd been a musical prodigy—on the piano—better than Van Cliburn he said. He'd almost played Carnegie Hall but the night before he'd got the mumps. Then before he became an actor he said he'd joined the Paratroopers—yeah, Paratroopers, which I find hard to believe but anyway—he said he was so small that whenever he jumped out of a plane on maneuvers, he'd wear one of those teeny-weeny parachutes they put on packages of food . . . (ABNER *chuckles at the thought*) He was a funny little guy. He had huge ambitions. He wanted to play Richard the Third. He wanted to play classic villains—like Boris Karloff or Peter Lorre . . .

POLLY: That is sad . . .

ABNER: No, I don't think it is sad. He had big aspirations but he lived up to a lot of them. Women found him tremendously sexy. He had dozens of girlfriends. I'd photograph him at Downey's—a different one every night—I remember once photographing him standing at the bar—oh, he drank like a fish—really put it away—well, he was kissing this broad a mile a minute—she had to go on her knees to get to his mouth . . . Afterwards she told me Michael is a great kisser—the greatest . . .

POLLY: I see . . .

ABNER: The last time we were together was at the opening of *Ship of Fools*—he was all dolled up in this little tux—he'd doused himself with cologne—he was beside himself with excitement—bouncing up and down on his seat—waving at the rest of the cast—Simone Signoret—Oscar Werner—Vivian Leigh—Then the lights go down and the movie comes on and suddenly he is gripping my hand so hard it hurt. "Oh my God, Abner, you never told me I looked like *that,*" and I think he is almost crying and he repeats, "You didn't tell me I looked like *that!*" And I gaze up at the screen and there's his face—grimacing at us—like a Weegee photo—all distorted and twisted—and suddenly I realized he didn't—he honestly hadn't been aware of how he *looked*—how *deformed*—and tiny—it was really something—all his life he'd had this fantasy built up in his head about how he appeared—He drank himself blind after that opening and so did I . . .

POLLY: That is some story.

ABNER: Yeah . . . *(He stops)* Would you mind if I took my shoes off? I photograph better in my stocking feet.

POLLY: *(Laughing)* Be my guest.

ABNER: *(Sits down—removes battered muddy workboots—reveals he is wearing one red sock—one yellow—his toes are protruding from both)* Woops. *(He grins—eyes her—but is not the least embarrassed)*

(POLLY *laughs*)

You have a nice smile, lady.

(POLLY *doesn't answer, shrugs.* ABNER *jumps up—begins to prowl about room*)

Now—let's see—where would be the best place for you to pose? Maybe against that wall? There is nothing on it—go over and stand against that wall . . .

(POLLY *does so, feeling a bit self-conscious.* ABNER *studies her with narrowed eyes*)

Nice but . . . don't like it—maybe this—*(He pulls out a stool from in front of the bar)* Sit on that and look straight at me . . .

(POLLY *sits on the stool—stares at him blindly.* ABNER *squats in front of her with camera*)

Maybee . . . maybe not. Christ the light is lousy in here. *(He gets up —plugs in portable light—the room is suddenly ablaze)*

POLLY: *(Watching him)* How long have you been a photographer? My publisher says you're terrific.

ABNER: I been taking portraits for a couple of years. But I became a photographer during the 1960s—Chicago—Days of Rage—Vietnam protests—Vietnam War finally.

POLLY: You were a war photographer?

ABNER: Yeah. I saw action. Blood. Death. I photographed for United Press International. Now I'm strictly free-lance. Do anything to survive. Editorials for magazines. I teach dark room technique at the New School. String for a German newspaper. Yesterday I photographed an ad for a balloon company—took some pictures of the homeless for a brochure—*(Pauses—studies her)* Think you could change that blouse?

POLLY: Well, it happens to be one of my favorites.

ABNER: Maybe so, but the neckline isn't particularly flattering. Have you got something more off the shoulder? Something that would show more of you . . .

POLLY: Well, maybe I . . .

ABNER: Lemme see some of your clothes. Gimme a few choices, OK?

POLLY: OK. *(She exits to dressing room—returns seconds later with an armful of shirts and blouses)*

ABNER: *(Riffles through them—pulls out a black silk top with a V-neck)* Try this one on. *(Hands it to her)*

POLLY: My husband gave this to me.

ABNER: He obviously had good taste. Try it on.

POLLY: All right. *(Exits offstage)*

ABNER: *(Calling to her)* I'm gonna take some Polaroids first.

POLLY: Is that necessary?

ABNER: Sure. Then I can see what I do wrong.

POLLY: *(Emerging from dressing room—fluffing hair)* How does this look?

ABNER: Better. I would still like to see more shoulder. More neck. You got good skin, lady.

POLLY: But this is just one picture for my book jacket.

ABNER: Yeah—yeah—but I'm a perfectionist. And besides, you could use it for publicity—and maybe if you write a bestseller . . .

POLLY: Maybe I will . . .

ABNER: What kind of books you write, Polly?

POLLY: *(Patiently—seeing he is something of a phony)* You *know* what I write—I write nonfiction books . . .

ABNER: *(Slaps his head again)* Oh yeah—yeah—I remember now—sure! Say—what's your definition of the difference between fiction and nonfiction, lady?

POLLY: Well, fiction is all about using the imagination. In nonfiction you can't change the facts—facts are your basic material but you can imagine the form you put them in.

ABNER: Yeah—*(Listening to her, grinning)* I like that—imagining your form—yeah . . .

POLLY: And *when* you do that . . .

ABNER: Don't say anything more. Just look at me.

(POLLY *looks at h᾿ ᾿η uneasily; sighs.* ABNER *gazes into the viewfinder*)

Christ, lady, it ain't that bad. Smile for the birdie.

(POLLY *smiles thinly; the camera clicks*)

Relax. You're not in front of a firing squad.

POLLY: Feels like it.

ABNER: Quick. Off the top of your head. Who's the most surprising person you ever interviewed?

POLLY: *(Thinks a minute)* That's easy. John Lennon.

ABNER: *(Camera clicking away)* OK. Why—how so?

POLLY: *(Resists answering)* Well . . . I . . .

ABNER: *(Coaxing—as camera clicks away)* Tell me more—I'd love to hear . . .

POLLY: Oh—OK . . . it was in 1965. The Beatles were world-famous. They were making a movie in London called *Help.* I had to fight my way into the studio at Elstree—because there were literally thousands of fans milling around outside. I ended up interviewing each Beatle separately—between takes. Oh, and I had to be passed through a phalanx of bodyguards. John Lennon's bodyguard was the scariest—a big bozo in leather and sporting brass knuckles. I interviewed John Lennon last. He served me tea and we had this quite amazing conversation. About the American blues and how black singers like Joe Turner had influenced his music. He even described a meeting he'd had with Elvis Presley where they'd discussed their lost mothers. When we finished he suddenly said to me: "My bodyguard didn't ask you out, did he?" And I said, "Oh, no." And Lennon said, "I am so glad because I would have told you not to go out with him—the man is a PIG."

ABNER: *(Repeats—as camera clicks away)* The man is a PIG . . .

POLLY: *(Laughing)* Could I see some of those, please?

ABNER: Sure thing. *(He hands her sheaf of photographs)*

POLLY: *(Goes through them)* Hey, these are very good.

ABNER: *(Looking at them with her)* They are better than good—they are sensational. Now we can get down to real work . . . *(He gazes at her)* I wish you could show some skin—don't you have anything that's strapless?

POLLY: Only a strapless bra . . .

ABNER: Yeah—yeah—so put that on.

POLLY: Well, I . . .

ABNER: Lady, for Christ sake . . . I am a guy with two wives . . . yeah, two wives—not one—and a couple of kids I don't see too often 'cuz they don't know I'm their father. I lead a very complicated life . . .

POLLY: You have two wives? How do you manage that?

ABNER: You really want me to tell you? —Just get that bra on and let's go to work.

(POLLY disappears behind screen; ABNER fiddles with camera and lights)

POLLY: *(Calling from behind screen)* I'm waiting.

ABNER: For what?

POLLY: For you to tell me how you juggle two wives!

ABNER: Simple. One lives in California, one lives in New York. I don't live with either one; I live mainly outa my truck. My New York wife cooks for me. We been married since I was seventeen. She's a school teacher. My other wife is my Muse. I don't see her too often—when I do I stay with her in her houseboat that's parked offa Sausalito . . . She reminds me of Laura Dern in *Blue Velvet*. Spacey but no nonsense . . . She used to be Thomas Pynchon's girl. Shacked up with him near Santa Fe, New Mexico during most of the 1970s . . .

POLLY: Hey—wait a minute! Thomas Pynchon—the novelist who wrote *Gravity's Rainbow* and who's a total recluse? Nobody has seen him for over twenty years.

ABNER: Well *I* saw him—not only that—I photographed him.

POLLY: Oh, come on! Where's the photograph? It would be worth a fortune—this guy's like Howard Hughes—nobody has any idea what he looks like . . .

ABNER: I tell you I do. I photographed him. But it was the damndest thing when I developed the film, his face was a blur—like a ghost—a shadow—it was like he willed himself not to be photographed.

(POLLY *emerges from behind screen in quite a form-fitting black strapless bra; she has draped a stole about her shoulders too—as if for protection*)

POLLY: That is the most preposterous story I ever heard.

ABNER: Scout's honor—it's the truth . . . You wanna hear Pynchon's theories about paranoia and art?

POLLY: Be my guest—go right ahead. *(She is amused by this whole bit)*

ABNER: The night I met him, Pynchon and I had this long rap about how most people think that art should redeem you—reaffirm you, but no way—true art excites—disturbs—great art is never rational . . . great art is always paranoid . . .

POLLY: Yeah—yeah, Pynchon's philosophy is life is chaotic—incoherent —crazy—art can't "save" us—it can only reflect what we are . . . Look I read *Gravity's Rainbow* too—every character in that novel is paranoid . . . every character . . .

ABNER: Well, I never read what is it—*Gravity's Sunset?*—but Pynchon and I talked all night about paranoia and its different forms—delusions of grandeur—narcissism—schizophrenia—erotomania . . . in between eating the most delicious pasta—he cooked it—I have ever eaten—I saved the tomato can he used. There's a plant in it growin' in my truck . . .

POLLY: I'm sure—now, let's get going . . .

ABNER: Right on, lady. Say, you look *nice.*

POLLY: Yes, thanks. But let's go . . .

ABNER: *(Getting the camera ready to go on the tripod)* Sit down. Look right at me. Lick your lips a little. *(He peers through the viewfinder)* You look absolutely terrific.

POLLY: *(Half-smiles—she doesn't quite believe it but she enjoys hearing it)* Thanks again.

ABNER: Think beautiful now.

(The camera click-clicks. POLLY *tries to relax and respond. A beat or two as* ABNER *clicks away murmuring "atta girl" "super" "hmmmm wonderful . . ." Continuing to click away)*

You know I been doin' most of the talking. Now you talk. Tell me a little about yourself.

POLLY: Well, I . . . what do you want to know?

ABNER: Who are you exactly?

POLLY: I'm a writer . . .

ABNER: Yeah—And? *(He is trying to pull more information out of her as the camera clicks away)*

POLLY: I'm a widow . . . and I'm a woman. Jesus, that's alliteration, which I hate . . .

ABNER: A writer first—a widow second and a woman third. Interesting.

POLLY: Not very.

ABNER: *(Camera continues clicking)* How does it feel to be a widow?

POLLY: Terrible. The pits.

ABNER: You must have loved your husband a lot.

POLLY: I did—very much . . . *(She moves silently)*

ABNER: Hold it! Beautiful expression!

(There is a long pause while POLLY *recovers herself)*

Go on—(ABNER *is wheedling now)* Go on with what you were saying . . .

POLLY: *(Continuing thought)* We—we grew up together—we became adults together. We were married for over twenty years.

ABNER: AWWWWWWWWWWWWW.

POLLY: Don't mock me, for God's sake!

ABNER: *(Clicking away with camera)* I wasn't mocking you. I envy you. You had something solid together. Few people do.

POLLY: We did have something . . . we were very lucky . . .

ABNER: So—how long has it been?

POLLY: Well, it's been over two years now. I still have periods of intense depression—of grief. I've only started feeling good every so often—but it never totally goes away—the loss is always with you . . . But I have started to feel myself again . . . only it is a different self . . . sometimes I feel totally unnecessary—sometimes—paradoxically I'll feel more alive than I've ever felt in my life. It's crazy. Oh, and I feel manic too. Can't sleep. I watch TV till four AM—and I talk to myself constantly, even when I'm on the street . . . see, my husband was ill for three years. That's a long time to watch someone die and I did—and it wasn't easy.

ABNER: *(Still clicking away)* What did he die of?

POLLY: Heart attack. I actually saw him die . . . the last breath . . . I'm glad I was there, though. One of the nurses told me when somebody is dying even if they're unconscious they still know you're there and it's comforting to have you talk to them . . . *(Pause)* Sometimes I can't remember what he looked like anymore. I still can't stand to have photographs around. Sometimes I think when I remember our times together I'm only beginning to understand him now—now that he's gone . . . He was a very loving, caring, complicated human being . . . a lot of people didn't understand how we got along because we seemed so mismatched—but . . . *(She starts fumbling for words—she is getting emotional, in spite of herself)*

ABNER: You look magnificent when you're sad.

POLLY: *(Snapping)* Oh, for Christ sake!

ABNER: I mean it. You got so much going in your face now. If you would just relax and release it . . . you are a very controlled woman, you know; very controlled.

POLLY: *(Briskly)* It is the only way I survive.

ABNER: Must be a strain . . .

POLLY: *(Ignoring that comment—gets up from the stool)* I am going to have another vodka. *(Crosses to bar)*

ABNER: Good idea. I need to put another roll in the camera . . .

(POLLY returns to the stool—sips vodka. ABNER *gazes at her)*

Listen—I wanna take a small break—OK? *(Puts the camera down—flops on the floor—performs a little bicycle motion with his legs—wiggles his toes)* My way of relaxing—

POLLY: *(Watching him, amused)* I still can't get over your two wives.

ABNER: Me neither.

POLLY: So how do you manage this double life?

ABNER: I lie a lot. I cheat a lot. I am a terrible guy, lady. I make a lot of promises I never keep. But all my women love me—well—correction —my two women love me. I guess I have something.

POLLY: What is this mysterious "something"?

ABNER: I can psych 'em out—I know what's bothering them before they do—I tell them to relax—stop wearin' a mask—stop fakin' . . . I have this antenna—had it since I was a kid—I knew when my mama was lyin'—It's like a sixth sense—I can smell trouble—I can smell panic before it happens—like if I'm in the A&P I know when somebody's gonna shoplift—when I'm at a cocktail party I can feel bad vibes—like I was at that party the night Mailer and Gore Vidal punched each other out . . . I knew it before it happened . . .

POLLY: I was there too and they did not punch each other out . . .

ABNER: Whatever. But like I know when somebody's bugged. An' I can usually help—like I know for example that you are freaked out of your mind right now. And you haven't said a thing.

POLLY: Oh, really.

ABNER: You *are* freaked out.

POLLY: Well, I wouldn't go that far . . .

ABNER: But you are not too happy . . .

POLLY: Being happy is a relative . . .

ABNER: You are fucking miserable . . .

POLLY: Look. Can't we just finish this picture taking?

ABNER: Yeah yeah yeah but I'm onto something—you are definitely bugged.

POLLY: Look—I . . .

ABNER: I'd say it's because you need to get laid. Am I right?

POLLY: I wish it were that simple. As a matter of fact I do not want to get laid.

ABNER: But I'm partially right—that you haven't been laid in a . . .

POLLY: Yes, you're right, I haven't been . . . *(Laughs angrily)* Jesus— why am I admitting this to you? I suppose you imagine you are the answer to my troubles?

ABNER: Absolutely not. I wouldn't lay a glove on you—you are inviolate —anyway I am on a job and I would . . .

POLLY: *(Sarcastically)* Oh I'm sure you never have seduced . . . Can we change the subject and finish up please. I am worn out!

ABNER: Sure we can change the subject. If you want to.

POLLY: Yes. I would like to. *(Hops off the stool—begins pacing around the room—trying to figure out a way of getting this guy out of there)*

ABNER: *(Watches, grinning)* Hey—lady—I'm not upsetting you, am I?

POLLY: Oh, no—not at all . . . now will you please finish up?

ABNER: Sure, sure lady. But I don't want to upset you.

POLLY: *(Shouting)* YOU HAVEN'T UPSET ME! Now for God's sake . . .

(ABNER *shooting pictures like crazy! Click! Click! Click!)*

Jesus! *(Laughs in spite of herself)* You are unbelievable.

ABNER: *(Still shooting pictures)* So how do you feel at this very minute?

POLLY: A bit unhinged.

(Camera continues clicking)

ABNER: OK. Great. Wonderful. We are practically finished . . . and we have some great stuff I can tell . . . but I have to ask you this one question—it's personal but . . .

POLLY: Oh come on—you'll ask it anyway . . . so what is it?

ABNER: Have you been with a man since . . . ?

(POLLY *downs the rest of the vodka—finally nods grimly but doesn't elaborate)*

Was it that bad?

POLLY: Well, it wasn't what you'd call romantic.

ABNER: Who's romantic in 1990?

POLLY: Someone who's gentle and tender and a good companion.

ABNER: Oh, that . . . *(He stares at her—as if daring her)*

POLLY: You really want to hear this.

(ABNER *nods)*

This guy was a friend of my husband's. Another professor at NYU. He called me about a month after the funeral and said he was worried about me. I guess I sounded manic over the phone so he asked what about dinner? I said wonderful—I hadn't been out at all. I had so much to do with the moving from the apartment . . . I was a basket-case . . . anyhow before I met him I agreed to go to a cocktail party —a book party for a friend . . . which I shouldn't have done because I got loaded. Drank two stiff vodkas and got smashed out of my skull. My friend asked me to meet him at his loft . . . I arrived drunk out of my mind—reeling around, giggling—my friend pours me another drink and suddenly he's telling me that he is so glad to see me because he has been so worried about me and how awful he feels because my husband died so young and what a great guy he was and how awful it must be for me etc. and bla bla bla . . . I usually don't feel sorry for myself. I hate self pity but all that vodka in me and him remembering my husband and the times we used to have together and suddenly I'm crying and sobbing in his arms and he is comforting me and kissing me and the next thing I know I am . . . in the sack with him and he is . . . it is awful . . . for me . . . it's like this strange dream because all the time I'm thinking of my husband and how much he liked this man—respected him—and how they used to play chess together and go to baseball games and we'd spend weekends at the Hamptons together . . . and you're not going to believe how this evening ended . . . by now I'm cold sober . . . after the love-making—if you could call it that—it was like for five minutes . . . slam bam thank you ma'am . . . the passion was nil—As I'm getting dressed—combing my hair . . . he hands me a cup of instant coffee and says, "I have always liked you, Polly. Maybe we can have an arrangement. I'd be glad to sleep with you again in say—six months? I have this arrangement with two other women—they find it perfectly agreeable. How's about it?" And I say thanks but no thanks and stumble off into the night . . . The next weekend so help me God this guy is phoning me and asking me to have brunch with him at the Sign of the Dove and he cannot understand why I say no!

ABNER: That is pretty heavy.

POLLY: Why am I telling you this?

ABNER: *(His voice crooning as he begins moving closer to her with his camera)* Photographers are good listeners.

POLLY: No—it's not that . . . I talk to myself too much. I have replayed that story over and over in the quiet of various sublets . . . it's a relief to finally tell it to another human being.

ABNER: *(Picking up another camera)* So you haven't dated since?

POLLY: Certainly no real dates. God, I hate that word. And for people our age to "date." It sounds almost obscene.

ABNER: For Christ sake! I use the word "date." I "date" young girls, divorcées—women I pick up at the Modern . . .

POLLY: In between your two wives . . .

ABNER: Yeah. Look, lady—don't patronize me—I live the way I live. Take me or leave me.

POLLY: *(Suddenly exasperated)* I wouldn't take you—or leave you.

ABNER: *(He is shooting pix now in deadly earnest)* Do you find me attractive?

POLLY: I suppose you're attractive—in a repulsive sort of way.

ABNER: YO! Finally openin' up . . . *(His eye is pressed to the viewfinder—zeroing in)* I bet in a few more minutes you'll be asking me to jump on your bones . . .

POLLY: *(Moving away from him, incredulous)* Are you crazy? I realize you're playing some kind of game with me; I'm not sure of the rules . . .

ABNER: *(Circling her with the camera; he is down on one knee—he is jumping on and off the couch clicking away)* I am not playin' games with you, lady, I am trying to take your picture!

POLLY: *(Jumping out of the line of vision)* Not any more you're not. I want you to leave. Now.

ABNER: *(Ignoring her demand, goes on photographing)* Hey—what a fabulous expression! Great eyes—sad eyes—lotsa secrets . . . so many . . .

POLLY: *PLEASE GO!*

ABNER: *(Still ignoring her)* You have had so much pain. And you've been all alone. No kids either. You didn't have kids to support you . . .

POLLY: *(That stops her—she forgets the camera)* We tried—not having kids is my biggest regret . . . *(Her voice trails off)*

ABNER: *(Pursuing—the camera clicks on)* But you did have *some* family here . . . A father—mother—inlaws—some blood kin to comfort you in your grief . . .

POLLY: I was all alone. I had friends but no family. I was by myself . . . nobody there . . . nobody to . . . *(Suddenly realizing her aloneness, it overwhelms her—the reality of it, and she starts choking up)*

ABNER: *(Clicking away)* Jesus, lady—that is so sad I feel awful for you—

POLLY: *(Breaking out of her reverie—turning on him angrily)* Stop it! Just stop it! What do you think you are doing to me?

ABNER: I am tryin' to take your picture, lady.

POLLY: No, you're not! You are trying to psych me out like you do your other women and it hurts!

ABNER: I swear, lady, all I been trying to do is take your picture.

POLLY: *(In a scary deep voice)* Pack your things and get the hell out of here.

(She grabs ABNER's *umbrella and brandishes it at him.* ABNER *scurries about—he knows she is serious so he hastily begins collecting stuff—puts on his workboots—leaves them unstrapped.* POLLY *watches him—holding his umbrella like a gun)*

This is something you do on a regular basis, isn't it? What else do you do—are you a peeping Tom—do you send anonymous letters—do you jerk off while watching *Midnight Blue??* I know your kind—you are a voyeur . . .

ABNER: *(Still packing)* Voyeur? What kinda word is that?

POLLY: You know what it means, you creep, and I *do* have you psyched out—admit it.

*(*ABNER, *folding up the portable lighting equipment, doesn't answer)*

Answer me! Are you happy now? Did it turn you on? Because you got to me—you really got to me. Before you arrived here tonight I was a zombie. I felt nothing. I didn't care whether I lived or died. I was completely numbed. But now I feel like a raw gaping wound. Maybe there's some hope for me. Maybe I'll eventually feel like getting laid . . . why I might even fall in love again . . .

ABNER: Oh, lady, it's much too soon for you to fall in love.

POLLY: *(In a forbidding voice that surprises even her)* DON'T TELL ME I CAN'T FALL IN LOVE AGAIN. WHO ARE YOU TO TELL ME ANYTHING? When I fall in love—if I fall in love again, it'll be a totally different love than I had for my husband—I was completely and utterly in love with him. I'll never love anyone the way I loved him.

ABNER: They all say that.

POLLY: You shit. I was really in love. But you wouldn't understand. *(She stares at him in fury but with some compassion)* I have you psyched out too Abner Kynd. You can manipulate—you can toy and probe but you never go beyond verbal foreplay. I bet you make dirty phone calls at three AM—am I right?

*(*ABNER *looks away; she may have gotten to him)*

And another thing—you have never experienced real love—not in
your life—because you're terrified—loving someone takes courage and
standards and . . .

ABNER: *(Groaning)* Spare me your holier than thou bit, lady, it is to barf.

POLLY: Oh, please let me tell you off for a while, Abner—you've been at
me for hours.

(ABNER *has gathered up all his equipment and is rushing for the door*)

Abner! (POLLY *shouts triumphantly, brandishing the umbrella*) Abner!
(She calls after him so loudly he stops in his tracks) After tonight I don't
think I'm ever going to feel sorry for myself again.

ABNER: *(Turning back to stare coldly at her)* With such self-awareness,
lady, you may finally be growing up.

POLLY: *(Deadly quiet)* Fuck you.

(ABNER *opens the door*)

Wait a minute. I want to see those contact prints.

ABNER: You'll see 'em—you'll see 'em. We got some great stuff tonight.

POLLY: *(Gesturing with umbrella)* Out, Abner! OUT!

ABNER: *(He grabs his umbrella away from her)* Goom bye, lady—this is the
last time I ever photograph a writer . . . *(He exits)*

(As soon as ABNER *leaves,* POLLY *lets out a huge sobbing laughing cry; it
sounds like a primal scream—she seems to be releasing some horrible
demon—some awful ghost from her heart and soul . . . then she begins
to cry—but in a different way—gulping, heart-wracking sobs—but not
anguished—it's the crying and grieving and mourning she's been needing
to release for some time now and she does . . . after a while she stops
crying . . . sighs . . . Lights dim . . .)*

DREAMS OF

Migdalia C.

Migdalia Cruz

Migdalia Cruz's work has been produced by En Garde Arts, Playwrights Horizons, INTAR, HOME for Contemporary Theater and Art, DUO, New York Shakespeare Festival's Festival Latino, Theater for the New City, the W.O.W. Cafe (New York), Old Red Lion (London, England), Latino-Chicago Theater Company (Chicago), Cleveland Public Theater (Cleveland), Frank Theater (Minneapolis), Theatre d'aujourd hui (Montreal), and American Music Theater Festival (Philadelphia). She has been nurtured by the Sundance Institute, Maria Irene Fornes' Hispanic Playwrights' Laboratory at INTAR, Midwest PlayLabs, the Mark Taper Forum's New Play Festival, and the Omaha Magic Theater. Her plays include *Miriam's Flowers, Lucy Loves Me, Dreams of Home, Fur, Cigarettes and Moby-Dick, Telling Tales, Occasional Grace,* and *Not Time's Fool.* She wrote the book and lyrics for the latin-jazz musicals *Welcome Back to Salamanca* and *When Galaxy Six and the Bronx Collide,* composed by Fernando Rivas; the libretto for an opera, *Street Sense,* composed by Linda Eisenstein; and lyrics/co-librettist for *Frida: The Story of Frida Kahlo.* She received commissions from Playwrights Horizons, WNYC-radio, Ballet Hispanico, Theater for a New Audience, Cornell University, DUO and INTAR. Her play *The Have-little* was the runner-up for the 1991 Susan Smith Blackburn Prize. Ms. Cruz is a 1990 NEA Playwriting Fellow, a 1988 McKnight Fellow, received her MFA degree from Columbia University, and is a member of New Dramatists. She was born and raised in the Bronx. Upcoming productions include *Lucy Loves Me,* Latino-Chicago Theater; *Frida,* Houston Grand Opera; *Running For Blood: No. 3,* WNYC/FM National Public Radio.

Characters

SANDRA, *a homeless woman in her late 30s, a ruined beauty*
PEDRO, *a homeless man in his late 30s, a ruined playboy*
DOLORES, *the angel of death, who looks like a Mexican movie star*
HOBIE, *an odd-looking angel, Dolores's apprentice*
JASPER/WOMAN, *a male corpse/a seamstress/male voice/Sandra's ex*
LETTIE/WOMAN, *a female corpse/a seamstress/female voice/Pedro's ex*

Place:
The 103rd Street and Lexington Avenue subway station, New York City.

Time:
The present.

Scene 1

PEDRO *and* SANDRA *are asleep at opposite ends of a subway platform. We watch them sleep for a moment, then a light hits* PEDRO *and we enter his dream.* DOLORES, *a beautiful woman in crimson, enters. She carries a covered tray. She uncovers the tray for* PEDRO *and he rejects the food. She goes out and comes back with a different food on the tray three times, and each time* PEDRO *rejects the food. When* DOLORES *returns with the fourth tray, she uncovers it and it is* HOBIE's *head with an apple in its mouth.* PEDRO *removes the apple and* HOBIE's *eyes pop open as he speaks.*

HOBIE: It takes great strength to plunge a knife through a man's heart. Or a woman's. But if you love him, you'll do it. If you hate to see her suffer, you'll learn to stuff it to the hilt.

(PEDRO *tries to put the apple back in* HOBIE's *mouth but he doesn't allow it*)

Not so fast my friend. Not till I'm done. Everything has a purpose. And the world's still round. Like me. Like my head and my eyes—you've got these same eyes. Wait. Dolores will speak now. Be civil. She's my boss.

(DOLORES *clears her throat and gets ready to speak. She adjusts her undergarments, straightens her seams, checks her make-up, etc.*)

DOLORES: *(To* HOBIE*)* You are here because I let you be here. I send you to do the simple things. The little ordinary things and what do you do? Chat. Mumble about knives and things. Come to the point Hobie or I will never let you speak again. Your job is to clarify the way not mystify. That's His job. Is that clear? And my job is to lead all people into the valley and let them reap there of the fruits of paradise. Don't you want to eat?

PEDRO: Sure I'll eat. I'll always eat . . .

DOLORES: *(Pointing at* HOBIE*)* Don't trust him. He tried to crush my skull once.

PEDRO: I'm sorry.

DOLORES: He's sorry.

(DOLORES *turns and exits into a dark part of the station)*

HOBIE: I'm sorry. Please follow her.

(PEDRO *moves to follow* DOLORES)

Well, take me with you.

(PEDRO *returns, picks up* HOBIE*'s tray and goes after her. Lights come up on that part of the station.* DOLORES *is now standing there in a black dress. Two women sew in the shadows)*

PEDRO: Your dress is very beautiful.

DOLORES: These are fine seamstresses. The very best. They'll make you something wonderful.

HOBIE: *(Speaking from beneath the covered dish)* EXCUSE ME! EXCUSE—

(PEDRO *lifts the cover)*

Aaahh! I love the air. It is my greatest joy.

DOLORES: You don't know joy, Hobie. *(She places her hand in* HOBIE*'s mouth)* Now, bite. Hard. That's it. Joy. Take bites from my flesh. Little ones. Good. Leave just the bone.

HOBIE: Can't I crack the bone?

DOLORES: No. No, that would be ecstasy. We're working exclusively on joy.

(PEDRO *tries to exit quietly,* DOLORES *and* HOBIE *turn on him*)

DOLORES AND HOBIE: Where do you think you're going?

DOLORES: Try on your suit.

(*The women hold up identical garments*)

PEDRO: No.

DOLORES: Put it on right now. Don't you want to experience joy?

HOBIE: Don't you want?

(PEDRO *runs out of the dream back to his sleeping area*)

PEDRO: It's so dangerous to fall asleep.

(*Lights fade on* PEDRO *and a spot comes up on* SANDRA*'s dream.* HOBIE, *now a complete person, enters with a stack of shoeboxes.* SANDRA *flips through them*)

SANDRA: I'll take those and those. Ohh, and those too. Oh, and those. And the black ones and—

HOBIE: Those run small. You'd better try them on.

(SANDRA *lifts up her right foot. It is diseased and bleeding.* HOBIE *sprays it*)

Foot mousse. It does wonders for bloody, stumpy messes. There we go. Slip it right in . . . and the other.

SANDRA: They're beautiful things. I want two of these.

HOBIE: They seem tight to me. I would never let you buy tight shoes. It's against store policy.

SANDRA: I gotta have these shoes. They're perfect.

HOBIE: You just think they're perfect cause you want them to be perfect. Believe me they would only cause you pain.

(HOBIE *pulls the shoes off* SANDRA. *She grabs for them*)

SANDRA: Please!

HOBIE: No! Don't shop if you can't go by the rules!

SANDRA: *(Crawling to him)* Please! Those shoes are gonna save me. With those shoes I can go anywhere. I can be with people again. Children won't spit on me, if I wear those shoes.

HOBIE: Sorry. Take it up with the manager.

(DOLORES *enters*)

DOLORES: Is there a problem?

SANDRA: Yes, my shoes—

DOLORES: Don't fit. I know. It's a tragedy . . . No one fits in those shoes. We'll just have to—

(DOLORES *holds a match to them and ignites them*)

SANDRA: No!!

DOLORES: I could never sell those shoes to anyone . . . It was time to move the merchandise.

SANDRA: I would've taken 'em as is . . .

(SANDRA *crawls away from* DOLORES *who follows her and stops her. Lights come up behind* DOLORES *to reveal two doors*)

DOLORES: Pick. There's this big door here and this other, little one. Which do you choose?

SANDRA: But they're both the same size.

DOLORES: Ah, hah!!! Perception is the devil's play thing. *(Touching her breasts)* Inside every man there's two of these. Enough said.

HOBIE: Yes, it's true.

SANDRA: *(Pointing to the door on the right)* That one.

DOLORES: So be it. *(She opens the door and light enters the room)* Go. Go on. It's yours. Enter it.

SANDRA: No—I—uh—I made a mistake. I want the other door.

(DOLORES, HOBIE *and offstage others laugh uproariously*)

Please, don't . . . Don't laugh at me. Don't—*(She runs into the light. The laughter becomes moaning)* I don't like lights. Turn them down. *(The lights dim)* Thank you. Why am I here? Don't you hear me? Why am I—Oh, I've been here before . . . I still don't like it. Open a window. I need air. Air heals. Air will heal my foot. I'll soon be without air. Air dries all my scabs—they stop hurting when they dry up. I can walk when it's dry.

(Water falls on SANDRA *from above;* DOLORES *enters with a towel)*

DOLORES: Here you are.

(She wraps SANDRA *tightly in the towel, puts her over her shoulder and carries her back to her sleeping place on the platform and dumps her there)*

SANDRA: I can't breathe . . .

DOLORES: Take a deep breath honey. When you breathe all the history of the world comes in through your nose. It's filtered like coins in a metal detector. Fine and complete. Everything you need to know you can smell around you—All you have to do is flare your nostrils, hold them tight, and in walks Antony and Cleopatra, Jesus and Barabbas, Ken and Barbie. Culture is yours. You got all diseases there. Typhoid, the Dipth, the Syph, Clap, Mumps, AIDS, plague, every conceivable Cancer, acute melancholia, psychosis, halitosis and PMS—Just keep your legs closed and your mind open and you'll be okay . . . honey. Because everything good comes to an end.

(SANDRA *and* PEDRO *fall back to sleep)*

Scene 2

SANDRA *and* PEDRO *sleep/sit on the subway platform.* PEDRO's *head bobs as he keeps slipping into sleep and awakening himself.* SANDRA *is sound asleep. They are covered with garbage and filth.* DOLORES *watches them for a minute, then speaks.*

DOLORES: Sleep almost never comes. But when it does . . . I'm waiting and ready for it. I watch over the sleepers . . . and those who can't sleep—I watch you too. Because I can help you to close your eyes. We'll take a trip together. A short one. Just perfume—the cheaper, the better. I think it's only fair—to warn you. Not that you listen. *(Pause)*

No. You are never scared until that moment when you close your eyes and take my hand. My hands are like ice. My touch will make all your hairs stand up on end. I'm God's electric eel. I bore a hole inside you and send you into cold shock. *(Pause)* Come with me and catch a thrill. Come with me and learn to love yourself. Love Dolores's winter. First the pain—then the glaciers gain. An inch closer every year. One day, all that's left will be ice.

(DOLORES *places a hand on* SANDRA, *who shivers but remains asleep. Then,* DOLORES *touches* PEDRO. *He awakens with a nightmarish scream*)

PEDRO: Nooooo!!!

(SANDRA *awakens when she hears his scream*)

SANDRA: Shut the fuck up, okay?! People are trying to sleep. *(She turns away from* PEDRO)

Scene 3

PEDRO *stands in front of* SANDRA. SANDRA *gets up and stands behind* PEDRO. *They are watching the sunset through the grating above them.* PEDRO *turns and is startled to find* SANDRA *so close behind him. He scares her and she begins to run away, dropping a shoe.* PEDRO *picks it up.*

PEDRO: Hey! Hey, you! You forgot something, stupid bitch!

SANDRA: *(Turns back and sees shoe in* PEDRO's *hand)* Gimme that back, stupid bastard! Gimme it now!

(She runs towards him and he throws the shoe back at her)

PEDRO: Who wants your stinkin' shoe anyway?! Take it! Take it and eat it!

SANDRA: *(Picks up the shoe lovingly)* Thanks.

PEDRO: What were you doing standing so close to a guy? Huh? What did you think you was doing?!

SANDRA: Nothing . . .

(She tries to put the shoe on but it hurts too much so she stops)

PEDRO: You hurt yourself?

SANDRA: Fuck you!

(DOLORES *freezes* PEDRO *and* SANDRA. *Then she speaks to* HOBIE)

DOLORES: I have a really lousy job.

HOBIE: Yeah.

DOLORES: I hate being an angel, especially around these kind of people. "It's your job to be merciful, Dolores. They'll thank you." They never thank me . . .

HOBIE: Yeah.

DOLORES: I want to change my life, Hobie. *(Pause)* I want to wear white.

HOBIE: Me, too.

(DOLORES *unfreezes them*)

PEDRO: I know how it is when you hurt yourself . . . I mean, how much it hurts and everything. *(Pause)* Can I help you get it on?

SANDRA: Keep your stinkin' hands off my shoe.

PEDRO: *(Sniffing himself)* It's not my hands.

SANDRA: *(Struggling to stand)* Hold on to me.

(PEDRO *moves to hug her, she pushes him off*)

Not like that. Up. So I can put it back on.

(PEDRO *holds her steady*)

I hate your stinkin' guts.

PEDRO: I hate yours and your mother's too. If you got one. You don't even got one, do you? If you do, I bet you don' even know who the fuck she is.

SANDRA: I don' got one.

PEDRO: I'm sorry. I'm sorry for scaring you. You like plastic mint containers?

SANDRA: Like for candy?

PEDRO: Yeah. Smells like candy. But jus' the plastic. You want one?

SANDRA: Yeah. Gimme.

(He hands her a plastic TicTac Mint box)

Oh . . . Don't you got sugarless?

PEDRO: You watch your weight? That's good. I'm natcherly skinny.

SANDRA: You're a lucky asshole. I gotta watch everything.

PEDRO: Thanks.

SANDRA: You want some bread?

PEDRO: What color?

SANDRA: Gray. Gray-blue. It's civil war bread! *(She laughs hysterically)* That's a little historical humor.

PEDRO: *(He doesn't get the joke)* Yeah, I'll take some.

(She hands him a tiny bit)

Thanks. *(They eat in silence)* Oh, my God!

SANDRA: What?!

PEDRO: The bread matches your eyes . . .

SANDRA: That makes it kinda hard to eat, huh? When I eat anything with eyes, I gotta first take out the eyes with my fingernails, when I got 'em, or else with this. *(She pulls out a steel nail file)* Works good.

PEDRO: Looks like it. *(Long pause)* Can I suck on your eyes?

SANDRA: Why would you want to do that?

PEDRO: They're the most beautiful eyes . . .

SANDRA: Men always talk about my eyes . . . For once I'd like to hear about my other parts. Especially the ones between my legs, now nobody ever pays that any compliments. It's hard to feel female when nobody notices your female parts, I mean, enough so to talk about 'em.

PEDRO: It's been so long since I sucked on a woman's . . . eyes.

SANDRA: Yes. Okay. (SANDRA *offers him her face. She laughs when he puts his tongue on her eye*)

PEDRO: What?

SANDRA: You look like my father when you do that.

PEDRO: He sucked on you?

SANDRA: He used his tongue for everything. He picked up pennies with it. I think he was almost famous.

PEDRO: Me too.

(He approaches her again, tongue extended. Lights fade)

Scene 4

SANDRA *stands alone on the platform facing the wall.*

SANDRA: I am a fine woman. My kids loved me. I played with them. I listened to them. But they didn't trust me. I don' know why. I say that, but now I've said it. I think it's true. I sewed all our clothes. They thought I couldn't see, that I was color blind—but I saw everything. Only different. I sewed a straight seam. I won a fair. I got a fine prize. Some silk . . . I made a dress. It seemed a dress born on me. Like my skin. They didn't like it. They thought it sealed me up and I wouldn't have room left for them. They were scared of me then. But they was wrong. I just wanted something nice—on my body, a dress to match my eyes—tight and small and tired . . . What could be scary about a dress? They was crazy. I am a fine woman. I have no more dresses. I wear what I find. I never find dresses. People just don' throw them out. You won't find nobody in this city throwin' out their eyes. People like to keep those things. Those things are personal. *(Pause)* I—I did see a dress once. But I had to turn my head from it . . . *(Turns and faces front)* It still had somebody in it, but she didn't have no arms. Somebody cut 'em right off her . . . So . . . so I couldn't lift her arms over her head to take off the dress anyway. So I didn't bother. I jus' turned my head . . . but I thought if she only had arms then I could rob her. It was my color too. I would've looked like a queen . . .

(SANDRA *sits back against the wall and lights fade on her and come up on* PEDRO, *who sits under a light fixture*)

PEDRO: I am so afraid at night. I cry sometimes. I cry thinkin' my eyes might close and I might fall asleep and wake up in the dark, by myself. I pray to Mary that I doesn't. I talk to Jesus when I am almost sleeping in the dark and he keeps me up. I stay up for a chat with the only begotten son. He knows how it is. He knows how important it is to stay awake. Things happen when you sleep. Your clothes disappear and you freeze. People touch you and stare. You gotta put on as many clothes as you can in case you nap and somebody tries to get you naked. A man don't let people see him naked in the street. That's weak. That's no good. He gets put someplace or somebody sucks on him. That's weak. You gotta suck first. You gotta look for people to suck on. That's why you got lips. That's why your nose fills up with dirt and you gotta breathe through your mouth . . . so you learn how to suck. Another thing I do is bite my fingers. That's how I know it's almost nighttime. I try to stay in the light, on a street corner, or in a building where rich people live . . . rich people always got lights. And they make loud noises at night. They grind their teeths together and it keeps me up. It's the same as biting my own fingers. *(Pause)* It hurts the same too. That's the only bad thing—but I don't need to sleep that much anyway. Not like some people. Some people get their feet beat on by people. And people shake they umbrellas in the sleeping people's faces and throw empty beer cans at them. That's the worst because they're empty. Who wants that? But you can make five cents. Unless it hit you just right—and then it just bounce away from you onto the tracks. And then it's goodbye. But I'm smarter than that. I stay awake. I sleep with one eye all the way open, like the Indians. I got Indian in me. I hold my liquor like an Indian—like this . . . *(He holds a pint of rum between his two hands like he's praying)* Like a gift from God.

(PEDRO *hits the floor with his palms like he's playing the congas as the lights fade*)

Scene 5

PEDRO *stands over* SANDRA

PEDRO: Hey. Look at my back. *(He turns his back to her. She doesn't look)* Hey! *(He hits her in the arm)* Look!

SANDRA: Okay! *(She hits him back)* What?!

PEDRO: Listen . . . listen. I got roaches on my back?

SANDRA: No.

PEDRO: Seriously. I feel like I got something crawling there. Knock it off, okay?

SANDRA: No.

PEDRO: Just like that. *(Rolls his arm down his back)* Please. Help me out.

SANDRA: No. *(She sits and scratches her butt)* Always an itch somewhere.

PEDRO: You're a dirty thing. You gotta keep yourself clean.

SANDRA: Look who's talking, scumball. You're the one don' wash. Hair don't stick up like that if it's washed.

PEDRO: You don't know nothing and God's gonna punish you for that. He's gonna put you somewhere. I been inside a place like that before.

SANDRA: Like what?

PEDRO: Like that. *(He points at her head)* It's an ugly place.

SANDRA: Look in a mirror, you want ugly.

PEDRO: At least, I'm clean enough to know when a roach is crawling on my back. You don' even know that. You so dirty it could crawl up you and leave eggs and a whole family with grandmother roaches and grandaddy roaches and all other kinds of relatives and you wouldn't even know it. Jesus is sad for you. You make him cry you so dirty. And Mary cries too.

SANDRA: Shows what you know—Jesus don't cry.

PEDRO: How would you know?

SANDRA: How do you know I don't know?

(Pause)

PEDRO: I know.

SANDRA: Uh huh.

PEDRO: *(Scratching himself furiously)* I can't stand it!! *(Rolls on the ground)*

SANDRA: Get up you fool. They'll see us if you do that. They'll see us and something will happen.

PEDRO: Roaches all over me!

(SANDRA *goes to him, stops his rolling with one foot and strokes his back*)

Oh, thank you! Thank you, Miss.

SANDRA: Get up.

PEDRO: Don't let me close my eyes.

SANDRA: Give me something.

PEDRO: Like—like flowers or something?

SANDRA: I want a bed.

PEDRO: *(Lies facedown on ground)* Here. I promise not to touch you.

(SANDRA *lies down on top of him. They close their eyes. Lights change.* DOLORES *enters and places two blankets on top of them*)

DOLORES: For two good soldiers . . .

PEDRO: *(Pushing aside* SANDRA, *who remains sleeping)* Don't!

DOLORES: You gotta stop being afraid, Pedro!

PEDRO: You don't know me.

DOLORES: Of course, I know you. You married me. We had four children, three are still alive. You used to sing to me . . . and bring me medicines. You sat by me and sucked on me. I wanted five breasts so you could all suck on me at once. I wanted to be a good mother, a good wife, a good Christian.

PEDRO: You don't look like my wife.

DOLORES: Things got better once you left. I learned about hair spray.

SANDRA: *(Awakens and spots the blankets* PEDRO *now holds)* Gimme those!

DOLORES: Careful now, Sandra. Even babies know how to share.

SANDRA: That's not my name you stinkin' bitch!

DOLORES: Oh, now that I have your attention, there are some people I'd like you to meet.

SANDRA: I can't go anywhere. I can't walk.

DOLORES: I'll bring them here. (DOLORES *exits and returns wheeling two corpses on a table*) There. *(Moves to the woman corpse, takes the sheet off her face)* Her name was Lettie. She had four children, three survived, two could talk, one was dumb.

PEDRO: I don't like this one bit.

SANDRA: But it's so nice and cool here. They brought good air with them.

DOLORES: That's right. How are you today. Lettie? Letts, get up and tell us a story. She's a wonderful storyteller. Up, up, up.

(DOLORES *claps her hands and* LETTIE *begins to speak*)

LETTIE: I was born poor and I loved that. I had freedom. I played games. I liked playing in the park. I loved music. A man taught me to play the drums there. We played together all the time. We had four little ones. They were even poorer. I wondered what they were meant for. I wanted them to stay alive, but I got tired of watching them. They lived with my mother. She grew too old. One got past her. He went off the side of a bridge. We were sad but life goes on. And there's things down under the bridge, in the water, that needed him. That ate him up. He wasn't a waste. Nothing goes to waste in this world. There's always something to eat . . . So I played the congas and stayed alive. My girls are good still. They get charity. They smile and then they get something to take home with them. They feed their grandmother. But they don't give anything to anybody else. So I took a job. I ran a sewing machine. It didn't play like the congas, but it paid. People paid me money to make them dresses. I let them walk on me. For money, I'll do anything. You can't be free forever. With money, I could buy things . . . feminine hygiene deodorant spray, feminine napkins, feminine shaving cream. I could make a lady out of myself. I was so happy about that. I forgot about my children; he helped me forget. We drank, I worked, he slept . . . until I got to be too much of a woman for him, too much of a lady. He said I lost my smell, the smell he loved. And he walked into a needle and made me buy his medicine. He was sick and I couldn't say no. I gave up all my perfumes. I waited in doorways taking on their smells of piss and blood. And other liquids spilled from broken people. He left me then. I was too much my own person. If you get

the time, it's easy to know your own smell. It's the smell that drives
people away. Enough said.

(LETTIE *lies back down on the table;* DOLORES *pulls the sheet over her*)

DOLORES: Lettie tells good stories when she's not depressed.

SANDRA: How can you tell when she's depressed?

DOLORES: By the story.

SANDRA: Oh . . .

(PEDRO *takes* SANDRA*'s arm*)

PEDRO: Let's go.

(JASPER, *the male corpse, sits up*)

JASPER: Wait a minute. I must speak. I must hear you listening to me
speak. My heart will sing for this. It waits and expands, waiting for
someone to happen by and see me. And here is all I have to say and I
will only say it once—so listen carefully. I am not what they say I was. I
am Jasper. I am myself. Thank you.

(JASPER *lies back down*)

PEDRO: I am myself too. But I am Pedro, not Jasper.

(JASPER *jumps back up*)

JASPER: We didn't like what happened. How she changed . . . She made
us cry. She didn't live for us anymore. She made a nest for other men
in her hair. The kids didn't like it. They were confused, but I told them
what to think. I went on a trip away from them all. Away. I took their
hands with me—how they felt—all on my arms and chest. And on my
back. Their fingernails tore at my flesh. Especially hers. Hers were
painted red now. She stole my blood through her fingers. I watched my
life shrink. The line used to wind down my palm, around my wrist and
up my arm. And now the holes are all that's left.

(*He lies down*)

SANDRA: He's a liar.

DOLORES: Aren't we all?

(JASPER *jumps up yet again*)

JASPER: Wait just a minute. I am more than myself. I am you. You bear this in mind. And when the tears come, don't bother to cry them. When they come, send them to your love canal and come them. Let your sadness be your pleasure. That's all that's sure in the world.

(He lies back down)

SANDRA: I'm not Jasper either.

DOLORES: I am Jasper, not Dolores, an angel from Paradise . . . Let's take a trip! Close your eyes and jump!

(DOLORES *jumps onto the tracks; Blackout)*

Scene 6

PEDRO *and* SANDRA *stand facing each other on the platform. They hold a once lit cigarette between them. They fight over it.*

SANDRA: Don't you see those lipstick marks.

PEDRO: Where?

SANDRA: This used to be a lady's cigarette—It is a lady's cigarette. It's gotta stay with a lady. No man can smoke this cigarette. If you smoke this cigarette, you're gonna be in big trouble my friend. Boys are gonna come after you. Big boys and they're gonna hurt you. I won't be able to help you with my bad foot and all. You're gonna be all alone . . .

PEDRO: That's not lipstick, it's tomato sauce. And tomato sauce ain't got no sex.

SANDRA: How do you know?

PEDRO: I never seen it smile.

SANDRA: My mother never smiled and she had me, so she musta had sex.

PEDRO: Maybe you was adopted. A lot of people are.

SANDRA: Not me.

(DOLORES *enters as* SANDRA*'s mother)*

DOLORES: Sandy! Sandy, darling! Dinner . . .

SANDRA: My mother was smart. She knew just what to call a person.

DOLORES: I made your favorite!

(DOLORES *exits*)

SANDRA: She always made my favorite food.

PEDRO: I didn't know my mother too well. She ran a beauty parlor and she was always—

(DOLORES *enters as* PEDRO's *mother*)

DOLORES: C'mere, Pepe. I wanna try a new haircolor on you. PEPE! It won't be like the last time, I promise. I'll take it off long before it sinks into your skin.

(DOLORES *exits*)

PEDRO: She never had time to cook. But if she did, I bet she, she woulda . . . *(Noticing* SANDRA's *hands)* You got nice hands.

SANDRA: *(Lighting the cigarette)* Yeah?

PEDRO: Yeah. I noticed 'em yesterday when you come out of the ladies room at Grand Central. They're nice hands.

SANDRA: Thanks.

PEDRO: That's the first time I saw the color of them. The real color I mean.

SANDRA: Yeah. I used soap.

PEDRO: It works good.

SANDRA: Yeah. I used to eat soap.

PEDRO: A person's gotta do those things sometimes—the streets get rough.

SANDRA: No, I mean when I was little. I liked the taste of it and I liked the bubbles that came out of my mouth.

PEDRO: That musta been something else.

SANDRA: It was.

PEDRO: Looks like it's still working good for you.

SANDRA: What?

PEDRO: The soap.

SANDRA: Yeah. I wash everything in there now. The guards leave at one o'clock. You can take a bath in there then. I seen all kinds of women in there taking down their clothes and washing everything. I mean, "everything," okay.

PEDRO: Okay. That's good. I like to keep myself clean too. When I got dirt under three fingernails of one hand, then I know it's time to wash that hand. I got rules like that for every part of my body. This way I never let things get too crazy. Because you know as soon as things get crazy, you can't find soap nowhere and you run out of water. That's how it works when you need something bad.

SANDRA: You really like my hands.

PEDRO: Sure. They look like baby pigs.

SANDRA: Shit!

PEDRO: I mean soft and pink like that . . . And chubby.

SANDRA: I'm getting so old.

PEDRO: How old are you?

SANDRA: Thirty-eight.

PEDRO: Shit! You are old. I'm thirty-six.

SANDRA: A young boy.

PEDRO: That's right. You don't look so bad for thirty-eight. You still got a waist that goes in and everything.

SANDRA: Do I?

PEDRO: *(Reaches out and touches her waist with one hand and with the other takes the cigarette and brings it to his mouth)* Right there. A good-sized waist.

SANDRA: What are you gonna do now?

PEDRO: What do you mean?

SANDRA: I mean now that you've got your hands where they ain't supposed to be unless we're dancing.

PEDRO: You wanna dance.

SANDRA: Sure. But we need music. Can you sing?

PEDRO: Yeah. But I only know one song.

SANDRA: That's okay. Sing it.

(PEDRO *hums the tune as they slow-dance and then begins to sing "America, the Beautiful" with some incorrect lyrics*)

PEDRO: *(Singing)* "Oh beautiful, for special skies for amber waves of grain . . . For purple mountains majesties above the fruity plains . . . America! America! God gave this land to me. And crowned thy hood with brotherhood, from sea to shining sea . . ."

(SANDRA *joins* PEDRO *in humming a few more bars as they continue to dance as the lights change to Scene Seven: The Dream Bar*)

Scene 7

The Dream Bar. DOLORES *is behind the bar.* HOBIE *serves drinks.* SANDRA *and* PEDRO *sit at one end, and* JASPER *and* LETTIE *at the other.*

DOLORES: The usual?

PEDRO: Uhh, yeah, sure.

SANDRA: Me, too.

DOLORES: Anything you say, honey.

(DOLORES *places glasses filled with something foul and steaming in front of* SANDRA *and* PEDRO. *The space fills up with bad-smelling smoke.* HOBIE *enters with wet, warm, white towels.* SANDRA *wipes her legs*)

HOBIE: These wipe away the blood so well, don't they?

(SANDRA *blows her nose into the towel;* PEDRO *does the same. They hand their towels to* HOBIE, *who smells them and displays them above their heads*)

The Honeymoon Towels.

(A neon light flashes on. It reads "Club Pedro")

PEDRO: It's my place.

SANDRA: I never dated a guy who had his own place before.

PEDRO: I treat a girl right.

(LETTIE *walks over to them. She's in a state of decay, but her hair is beautifully curled)*

PEDRO: No. Go away.

LETTIE: He doesn't remember. I was a girl once too. Now I'm this. And you know—you know what? Men like girls who take care of themselves. They are attracted to girls who comb their hair real pretty. Or who look like they want to be pretty. Even if they're not. Even if they got hair looks like something lives there. Like you. I can teach you to curl your hair. I'll get you looking like men follow you.

PEDRO: Go away.

SANDRA: Yeah, go away, you stinkin' bitch.

LETTIE: I smell just like you. *(Offers* SANDRA *her wrist to smell)* See? My whole body smells just like that. Like the blood I used to have. I know a joke.

SANDRA: Big fuckin' deal. So do I.

(LETTIE *moves back to* JASPER. DOLORES *places a tape deck on the imaginary bar, puts it on. Tango music plays)*

DOLORES: Welcome to Club Pedro's Tango Finals! We have two couples left. Our very own Pedro and his gangrenous partner, La Sandra, the half-footed terpsichorian. She smells bad—he smells bad. They swim in their own urine, but can they dance?! And then we have a team that will delight you with their delightfulness, if not their skill, Lettie and Jasper.

(The two couples stand and get into a tango position)

SANDRA: I don't like her.

lked down the tracks, to a very beautiful place. It had
r than you with meat for their petals. Clean, juicy, cook-
d we ate of those meat flowers and then fell asleep in this
s full of beer. Nice, fresh, imported beer.

ise.

t was paradise . . . Let's go for a walk today.

de?

t. My feet don't hold me no more.

e see them.

nds her legs for PEDRO to examine them)

y sick. We should get help for them.

Don't leave me alone. I can't go anywhere now.

n't just wait here. They won't come if we just wait. That's
e are—they want you to find them, to ask them to come.
they forget about you, it's easier.

t else happened in your dream?

e right back.

etter if I go. I promise, I'll be back soon. (PEDRO exits)

s not ever coming back. (The sound of footsteps) Pedro?

nters)

. . he left me alone.

u want company?

nt Pedro.

an get you some company.

away.

(They dance in two soft pools of light. JASPER and LETTIE's light shrinks
into nothing, as PEDRO swings SANDRA around. They are dancing like child
and father dance, her feet on top of his. He has to hold SANDRA up)

PEDRO: You dance like a dream.

SANDRA: My mother always said that if you got good posture, you can do
anything . . .

(DOLORES and HOBIE dance with just their hands, very passionately. Music
fades. PEDRO is left holding SANDRA in a pool of light which has changed to
a harsh fluorescent green. Everyone else has disappeared)

PEDRO: You look good in this light.

SANDRA: Yeah?

PEDRO: Yeah. Most people don't . . . most people don't look good in
the subway. But you do. You blend into it. Like oatmeal on marble.

SANDRA: It don't do much for you. Put me down.

PEDRO: Why?

SANDRA: I'm tired. I want to sleep.

PEDRO: Don't . . . not without me. You fall asleep here and the cops hit
on the soles of your shoes. They hit you to make sure you're not dead.
If you scream, they know you're not dead.

SANDRA: Ha! They couldn't even do that to me. I don't even got shoes.

Scene 8:
Lights up on PEDRO asleep in SANDRA's arms.

SANDRA: Wake up already, jerk. My arm's asleep.

PEDRO: What?

SANDRA: Get up.

PEDRO: What for?

SANDRA: You forgot something.

PEDRO: What?

SANDRA: You forgot to tell me how it was, jerk.

PEDRO: It was nice.

SANDRA: NICE! You ain't been with such a woman nice as me!

PEDRO: Sandra, you are beautiful and passionate and your love was sweet like cream and candy. Gimme your arm.

(She extends her arm to him. He puts his head on it and goes back to sleep)

SANDRA: Even though we did it with our clothes on, it was good. I didn't feel dirty with this man wriggling inside me. It just made me smile. I can make somebody feel something for me and that was something. He felt real hot. Ready to explode with being in me. Ready to crack open my heart along with my legs. You sleep so easy now, like you went back to where you belong . . . and the truth is, you did. I wanned your wendell inside me since I accidentally fell against it when that crowd of nicely dressed people rushed toward us to get on the train. I rammed myself up against you so as not to fall onto those people. They call you things when you do that, when you faint or fall on them by accident. And that's when I felt that hard, little wendell of yours and I thought, "Hmmm, is this the man for me?" Is he thinking about me? Looking at me? I saw myself in the window of the train then and I knew you were looking at somebody else. Somebody dressed nice and smelling of perfume. But she wasn't the lucky one. I was . . . I got to feel your wendell on my back. I followed you after that. It wasn't no accident that I found you here on one-hundred and third street. I knew this was a place for us to find love.

(The sound of rats squeaking and water dripping fills the space as SANDRA *pats* PEDRO's *cheek. Lights fade. When the lights are completely out,* PEDRO *begins to speak)*

PEDRO: I used to be afraid of the dark. I would fight to keep it away. Stand under bright lights and pray for morning . . . but I couldn't keep it away forever. One day I decided to let it in, to feel the darkness creeping under my nails, into my mouth, through my hair. It was so comfortable there, I thought it would never move. It was just the right place for it . . . so, I made friends . . . with the dark. I said welcome and it stayed awhile. It brought some of its friends to nest inside me.

Friends with six legs, the four-[...]ets. I was not alone in the da[...] and cracked and squeaked all [...] tell what they were feeling. A [...] my right arm—love. I got them [...] hungry and in love. Like me. Th[...] same. *(Pause)* Maybe I can ca[...] cook us dinner. We can have a [...] crawl in between the sheets, n[...] know it's true love—you crawl [...] ing else and when you're done [...] face and you rock together and [...] excited or tired or proud—just [...] without locks or guns or money.[...] tell you you're not where you [...] where you are.

Scene 9
DOLORES *enters with a wet umbrella,* [...] *and exits.*

SANDRA: *(Singing)* "It's raining, it's [...] Bumped his head as he went to [...] morning. Rain, rain, go away, con[...]

PEDRO: How can you do that? How [...]

SANDRA: I always did that. My father [...] and my sisters never wanted to get [...] out, if I sang to him—he wouldn't [...] had a terrible voice and Mama wou[...] wouldn't shut me up.

PEDRO: I had a good dream last night[...]

SANDRA: Me too.

PEDRO: For the first time in my life.

SANDRA: Me too.

PEDRO: We wa[...] flowers bigg[...] ing meat. A[...] river that w[...]

SANDRA: Parad[...]

PEDRO: Yeah. [...]

SANDRA: Outsi[...]

PEDRO: Yeah. [...]

SANDRA: I can[...]

PEDRO: Let m[...]

(SANDRA *ext*[...]

They're ve[...]

SANDRA: No! [...]

PEDRO: We c[...] how peopl[...] Otherwise[...]

SANDRA: Wha[...]

PEDRO: I'll b[...]

SANDRA: NO[...]

PEDRO: It's b[...]

SANDRA: He[...] Pedro!

(DOLORES [...]

It's you .[...]

DOLORES: Y[...]

PEDRO: I wa[...]

DOLORES: I [...]

SANDRA: G[...]

DOLORES: Men? Do you want the company of men?

SANDRA: No. Go away. Please.

DOLORES: Men it will be. But I warn you, not all men are as nice as Pedro. Most people are not moral. People don't know how to be good anymore.

(The sound of footsteps and laughter. Blackout)

Scene 10

PEDRO *enters and discovers* SANDRA *covered with blood, her clothing torn, her body mutilated.*

PEDRO: Sandra? I failed Sandra. I couldn't find anyone to—SANDRA!

(He runs to her and holds her head up)

SANDRA: I dreamed about Paradise, Pedro. And it was covered with blood. And people were laughing. And I wished I'd gone to hell.

PEDRO: I'll take care of you now. Don't worry anymore.

SANDRA: I'm afraid of the dark again.

PEDRO: Me too. We have to do something before dark. We have to take a trip. We'll pack our bags and buy train tickets and go someplace special. Our train will go through the water and up in the air and our friends will come with us. And we'll have a party on the way. Drink champagne.

SANDRA: No, beer.

PEDRO: Beer. We'll have beer. And anytime we want to stop we'll just say "Stop" and we'll get off and start a new life in that place and when we get tired of that life, we'll get back on the train. (PEDRO *picks* SANDRA *up and carries her to the edge of the train platform)*

Here it comes.

(The lights of the oncoming train flash on)

SANDRA: Let's get on and go someplace warm. A place with no blankets —only cool, comfortable sheets. Let's crawl in and be alone.

(PEDRO *jumps onto the tracks with* SANDRA, *they are silhouetted in a circle of lights for a moment, then there is a blinding flash and the screeching sounds of a train coming to a halt. Blackout)*

A WAY WITH WORDS

Frank D. Gilroy

A Way With Words was originally developed and presented by the Ensemble Studio Theatre, Curt Dempster Artistic Director, Dominick Balletta Managing Director.

Frank D. Gilroy

Frank Gilroy came on the theater scene with a bang in 1961–62 with the production of his script *Who'll Save the Playboy?*. That production, directed by Daniel Petrie, won the Obie Award for Best American Play of the Year in 1962. Its success helped pave the way for Mr. Gilroy's next major success, *The Subject Was Roses*, produced in 1964 on Broadway, a play which collected the Pulitzer Prize, the Tony Award, and the Drama Critics Circle Award. That play, which was made into a film starring Patricia Neal and Jack Albertson, both of whom were nominated for Academy Awards, was revived in New York City by the Roundabout Theater Company in 1991.

Mr. Gilroy has written three other plays that have been produced on Broadway: *That Summer—That Fall*, *The Only Game in Town* (again directed by Daniel Petrie), and *Last Licks*. In addition to *A Way With Words*, his short plays include *Dreams of Glory*, *Real to Reel* and *Match Point*, all of which have been presented at the Ensemble Studio Theater. Much of his career has been devoted to screenwriting. He wrote the screenplays for *The Subject Was Roses*, *The Only Game in Town*, *The Fastest Gun Alive*, and *The Gallant Hours*, and both wrote and directed the films *Desperate Characters*, *From Noon Till Three*, *Once in Paris*, *The Gig*, and *The Luckiest Man in the World*. His memoirs of the experiences making independent films, *I Wake Up Screening*, will be published by Southern Illinois Press in 1992.

Although he was born and raised in the Bronx, attended Dartmouth College and the Yale School of Drama, entered the Army at the age of eighteen where he served for two and a half years with the 89th Infantry Division—including eighteen months in the European Theater—Mr. Gilroy's dramatic education came from his work during TV's golden age of the 1950s and 1960s. He wrote for Playhouse 90, Studio 1, U.S. Steel, Omnibus, and Kraft Theater.

Characters:
FRED
ARTIE
LOUISE

Scene 1:
Place: A corner table in a Manhattan restaurant. Time: Present. Mid-day.

At rise, ARTIE *and* FRED, *early forties—drinks in hand.*

FRED: *I don't believe it. I do not fucking believe it.*

ARTIE: I'm sorry

FRED: Spare me.

ARTIE: I had no idea you'd take it like this.

FRED: What did you expect?

ARTIE: You look like I hit you.

FRED: That's how I feel.

ARTIE: I should have told you when it happened.

FRED: What stopped you?

ARTIE: I figured once she had her fling she'd come back. Why make waves.

FRED: And later? When you knew it wasn't a fling?

ARTIE: I was embarrassed.

FRED: So you kept lying.

ARTIE: I never thought of it as lying.

FRED: Every year I come to New York and we have lunch and I always ask how Louise is and you always say 'fine' . . .

ARTIE: Which she is.

FRED: . . . Until today when you announce that you and she aren't together any more . . .

ARTIE: It makes you feel better—I lied.

FRED: . . . "That's too bad," I say. "When did it happen?" And *you* say.

(Motions ARTIE *to speak)*

Say it.

ARTIE: I said it.

FRED: Say it again so I'm sure I heard right.

ARTIE: "Louise left me thirteen years ago."

FRED: Thirteen?

ARTIE: Thirteen.

FRED: I still don't believe it.

ARTIE: Nineteen seventy-eight.

FRED: Artie if this is a joke—

ARTIE: —It's on me.

FRED: How could you not tell me?

ARTIE: We see each other once a year.

FRED: You lied because it was easy?

ARTIE: We always talk about when we were kids. Good times. I didn't want to spoil it.

FRED: Bullshit.

ARTIE: You're right.

FRED: Why then?

ARTIE: Promise not to laugh.

FRED: Artie—please.

ARTIE: Because you thought she and I were still together made it seem true for a few hours.

FRED: Jesus.

ARTIE: Sometimes after our lunches I was so into it I expected to find her there when I got home.

FRED: Thirteen years and you're still carrying a torch?

ARTIE: Never changed the lock on the door or the phone number in case she—

FRED: —I get the picture. The Christmas cards with both your signatures?

ARTIE: Forged.

FRED: And that's why whenever I phoned I got *you.*

ARTIE: You didn't phone that often.

FRED: The phone works both ways.

ARTIE: You can only talk so much about boyhood memories.

FRED: We went separate ways—okay. But I always felt I could rely on you in an emergency.

ARTIE: I feel the same.

FRED: Your wife walking out wasn't an emergency?

ARTIE: What could you have done?

FRED: Provided a sympathetic ear at least.

ARTIE: I felt sorry enough for myself without encouragement.

FRED: Why did she do it?

ARTIE: I guess she wasn't happy.

FRED: You guess?

ARTIE: I come home from work. She's at the door, bags packed, cab waiting. Hands me a list of household things that need doing. Says it will be the best for both of us in the long run. The next thing I know the cab is turning the corner and I'm waving with a smile on my face like she's going to visit her mother in case any neighbors are watching.

FRED: There must have been warning signs.

ARTIE: If so I missed them.

FRED: "It will be best for both of us in the long run"?

ARTIE: Verbatim.

FRED: That's all she said?

ARTIE: From that day to this.

FRED: What's become of her?

ARTIE: Remarried. Has two kids. Maybe if we'd had kids.

FRED: Who's the guy?

ARTIE: Someone she met later. A lawyer. They live on Central Park West. A duplex. Plus a house in Connecticut. The boy's ten—the girl's seven. The dog's name is Skippy.

FRED: You keep in touch.

ARTIE: No.

FRED: Well how do you know all this?

ARTIE: She stayed friends with a cousin of mine.

FRED: What about *you?*

ARTIE: What about me?

FRED: Any women in your life?

ARTIE: Women—yes. Woman—close but no cigar.

FRED: You live alone.

ARTIE: Essentially. How's *your* family?

FRED: Fine.

ARTIE: Your youngest son was going to have a disc operation.

FRED: He's a hundred percent.

ARTIE: And your eldest?

FRED: I don't want to talk about them.

ARTIE: You're still upset.

FRED: Wouldn't you be if I said "Oh by the way, Ann and I split up thirteen years ago"?

ARTIE: No.

FRED: You wouldn't care?

ARTIE: I'd care but it's not the same. I never met Ann. You know Louise as long as I do—you were our best man.

FRED: Which you were supposed to be at *my* wedding until . . . Hold the phone.

ARTIE: A light dawns.

FRED: Louise left in seventy-eight?

ARTIE: April twelfth. A day that shall live in infamy.

FRED: I got married that May.

ARTIE: You're getting warm.

FRED: That's why you cancelled.

ARTIE: Head of the class.

FRED: The story about your mother too sick for you and Louise to come to California—

ARTIE: —The first of many deceptions.

FRED: Why did I never catch on?

ARTIE: I often wondered.

FRED: Implying I let you down somehow?

ARTIE: Not at all.

FRED: What then?

ARTIE: Some of the excuses I invented why Louise never joined us for lunch or why we didn't invite you to the house were pretty wild.

FRED: It's easy to fool people who trust you.

ARTIE: Maybe I missed my calling.

FRED: Meaning?

ARTIE: Maybe *I* should have become the writer and *you* should be the accountant.

FRED: Judging by the reviews of my last book you're not alone in that opinion.

ARTIE: I'm half-way through it.

FRED: Since it's been out eight months I gather that's a criticism.

ARTIE: I got bogged down in the long flashback.

FRED: Would you mind sticking to the subject at hand?

ARTIE: You're not interested in my opinion?

FRED: Not today. And *why* today after thirteen years?

ARTIE: You said you felt you could count on me in an emergency and I said the feeling was mutual.

FRED: What about it?

ARTIE: I've been seeing this woman and the time has come to legalize our relationship or end it. She's attractive, wealthy, got a good sense of humor and adores me.

FRED: But?

ARTIE: I've still got this thing for Louise.

FRED: That's ridiculous.

ARTIE: I'm not interested in your advice or opinion.

FRED: What then?

ARTIE: My cousin said Louise and her husband haven't been getting along.

FRED: Which you read as a favorable sign.

ARTIE: It's possible.

FRED: Talk about clutching straws.

ARTIE: I want to be sure it's over before I marry this other woman.

FRED: Artie take my word.

ARTIE: I want you to speak to Louise.

FRED: What?

ARTIE: I want you to sound her out and tell me if you think it's hopeless.

FRED: You can't be serious.

ARTIE: You said I could count on you in an emergency.

FRED: Emergency yes. This is craziness.

ARTIE: You won't do it.

FRED: If I saw any point I'd be glad to.

(ARTIE *rises, taking money from his wallet and throwing it on the table*)

What are you doing?

ARTIE: It's my year to pay.

FRED: We haven't eaten.

ARTIE: I lost my appetite.

FRED: Sit down.

ARTIE: Next time you're in town—don't call.

(*He would leave but* FRED *grabs his arm*)

FRED: *Sit down God damn it.*

ARTIE: What's the point?

FRED: Artie, we know each other longer than anybody else in our lives.

ARTIE: And the first time I ask a favor you turn me down.

FRED: I didn't turn you down.

ARTIE: You said it was crazy.

FRED: It *is* crazy.

ARTIE: But you'll do it?

FRED: I haven't seen or spoken to Louise in thirteen years. Do I phone? Knock at the door? Suppose her husband answers? Think about it.

ARTIE: *(Resuming his seat)* I have. And I've got it all worked out. Want to hear?

FRED: No. *(Hastily as* ARTIE *reacts)* But I will.

ARTIE: Every day, weather permitting, she jogs in Central Park from one to two o'clock.

FRED: Let me guess: I accidentally bump into her.

ARTIE: Right.

FRED: Then what?

ARTIE: You steer the conversation around to whether she has any regrets about leaving me.

FRED: Assuming there *is* a conversation.

ARTIE: Why wouldn't there be?

FRED: I never contacted her. She might be pissed.

ARTIE: Did *she* ever contact *you?*

FRED: No.

ARTIE: So you're even.

FRED: Why don't *you* "bump" into her and find out first hand?

ARTIE: I tried.

FRED: You spoke to her?

ARTIE: I went to the Park last week with every intention of doing so. Spotted her and got so choked up I couldn't go through with it.

FRED: It's not going to work, Artie. I'll do it if you insist but it's a mistake.

ARTIE: I insist.

FRED: Okay. But no accidental meeting. I'll tell her I just learned about the breakup and—

ARTIE: —*No way.*

FRED: Why not?

ARTIE: She thinks you've known from the beginning.

FRED: You told her you told me?

ARTIE: Yes.

FRED: Why?

ARTIE: I figured if I didn't *she'd* tell you and the more people who knew the less chance of our getting back together.

FRED: If I knew, why didn't I get in touch with her? What must she think?

ARTIE: That you blame her for what happened.

FRED: Why would she think that?

ARTIE: Because that's what I said.

FRED: You told her I blamed her for leaving you?

ARTIE: I thought it might carry some weight.

FRED: You know what I feel like doing right now?

ARTIE: You wanna poke me go ahead.

FRED: Where the hell do you come off—

ARTIE: —I was out of my mind.

FRED: I'm lucky she doesn't slug me.

ARTIE: I guarantee she'll be glad to see you.

FRED: On the basis of what?

ARTIE: If she was mad at you, would she buy your books?

FRED: She does?

ARTIE: My cousin says she has every book and story you ever published plus copies of interviews.

(Eyes his watch)

She should reach the reservoir in about ten minutes.

FRED: I bump into her by accident. "Is that who I think it is?" "It can't be." Then what?

ARTIE: You'll think of something.

FRED: How will I recognize her?

ARTIE: She'll be wearing a yellow or green jogging suit and a Mets baseball cap. Plus she hasn't changed.

FRED: The reservoir?

ARTIE: Yes.

FRED: *(Rising)* Here goes nothing.

ARTIE: I appreciate what you're doing.

FRED: Thanks.

ARTIE: I mean it.

FRED: Save it till you see what happens.

ARTIE: Whatever happens don't let on I put you up to it, or that you haven't known about the breakup from the beginning.

FRED: My lips are sealed on one condition.

ARTIE: Which is?

FRED: If I come back and say your chances with Louise are zero, will you marry that woman?

ARTIE: Deal.

FRED: You mean it?

ARTIE: My mother's head.

FRED: Yellow or green?

ARTIE: And a Mets cap.

(FRED *goes off.* ARTIE *sipping his drink looks after him)*

Scene 2:

Place: A bench in Central Park. Time: Thirty minutes later.

At rise, LOUISE, *late thirties/early forties, well preserved, vivacious, in a green jogging suit and Mets cap, shares the bench with* FRED.

LOUISE: If I'm staring like an idiot, it's because that's how I feel.

FRED: Same here.

LOUISE: I'm staggered.

FRED: Likewise.

LOUISE: It's really you.

FRED: As far as I know.

LOUISE: I don't believe it.

FRED: That makes two of us.

LOUISE: I knew our paths would cross. But Central Park? Me like this? How did you recognize me?

FRED: You haven't changed.

LOUISE: Why didn't *I* recognize *you?*

FRED: You were jogging.

LOUISE: I mean after you stopped me. I'm thinking I know this guy but who is he?

FRED: I haven't aged as gracefully as you.

LOUISE: You do look older.

FRED: Thanks.

LOUISE: Why shouldn't you? It's been thirteen years.

(She removes the Mets cap—frees her hair which she points to)

Look close—lots of gray. Feel better? The farewell party.

FRED: What?

LOUISE: The party when you moved to California. That's the last time we met.

FRED: You sure?

LOUISE: Positive. We spoke on the phone when you said you were getting married and asked Artie to be your best man. But the last time we saw each other was the going away party.

FRED: The only thing I remember about the party was a monumental hangover.

LOUISE: The Castle Grill on route seventeen. You thought you were going to a business meeting.

FRED: I remember getting there and being surprised. Everything after that is just a blank.

LOUISE: So here we are.

FRED: At long last.

LOUISE: Too long.

FRED: Much.

LOUISE: He called you right away.

FRED: What?

LOUISE: When I left, Artie said the first thing he did was phone you.

FRED: Yes.

LOUISE: You must have been jolted.

FRED: Yes.

LOUISE: Did he say why I left him.

FRED: He had no idea.

LOUISE: Subtext was never Artie's strong suit.

FRED: He said the only reason you gave was that it would be best for both of you in the long run.

LOUISE: What a bitch I was—huh?

FRED: I wouldn't say that.

LOUISE: You *did* say it.

FRED: Artie said I called you a bitch.

LOUISE: Among other less flattering things. Which is probably why I didn't recognize you. You don't expect a person who hates you to hail you with a smile on their face.

FRED: I never hated you.

LOUISE: Artie said you said—

FRED: —No matter what Artie said, I never hated you.

LOUISE: Then why didn't you call me?

FRED: Because . . .

(*About to level, he recalls his promise to* ARTIE)

I'm not sure.

LOUISE: Face it, you were angry. I'd "betrayed" your best friend.

FRED: Maybe I was a bit sore.

LOUISE: More than a bit or you'd have contacted me.

FRED: I was furious—okay?

LOUISE: "Was" meaning you're not any more?

FRED: Yes.

LOUISE: When did you stop?

FRED: Years ago.

LOUISE: Why didn't you get in touch with me *then?*

FRED: Too much time had passed. What could I say?

LOUISE: For openers you might have apologized for bum rapping me.

FRED: I apologize.

LOUISE: Too little—too late. But thanks anyway.

FRED: Why didn't *you* call *me?*

LOUISE: So you could repeat all the awful things you said personally?

FRED: Given your side of the story I might have felt differently.

LOUISE: There was only one side at that point.

FRED: What do you mean?

LOUISE: I shared the general opinion that in deserting such a decent, loyal, loving, hard-working man, I'd done a sinful thing.

FRED: You don't feel that way anymore.

LOUISE: Not for ages. How's Ann?

FRED: Ann?

LOUISE: Your wife. Isn't that her name?

FRED: She's fine.

LOUISE: Tim and Eric?

FRED: Also fine.

LOUISE: They look fine.

(His expression asks how she knows)

The jacket photos on your books.

FRED: You read my stuff?

LOUISE: Every word.

FRED: I'm flattered.

LOUISE: I didn't say I liked it.

FRED: Ouch.

LOUISE: Would you want me to lie?

FRED: Yes.

LOUISE: Actually I like most of your work a lot.

FRED: Thanks

LOUISE: But not your last book.

FRED: The flashback sucks.

LOUISE: In a word. Would you mind if I touched you?

FRED: *(Offering his hand)* Be my guest.

(She touches him playfully)

LOUISE: You know, I'm starting to think this is really happening.

FRED: And I'm starting to feel it's a dream.

LOUISE: How's Artie?

FRED: How should I know?

LOUISE: A cousin of his I'm friends with says you see him when you come to New York.

FRED: Not always.

LOUISE: You haven't seen him this trip.

FRED: No.

LOUISE: Are you going to?

FRED: Maybe.

LOUISE: I hope so.

FRED: Why?

LOUISE: His cousin said your visits mean a lot to him.

FRED: You keep tabs on him?

LOUISE: Just what his cousin tells me.

FRED: Did you ever regret leaving him?

LOUISE: Are you kidding?

FRED: I thought maybe—

LOUISE: —Artie is a sweet guy who might have had a happy life if he hadn't met me. I feel bad about that but that's all I feel.

FRED: You really have your act together.

LOUISE: Three and a half years on the couch—I should. Ever indulge?

FRED: Analysis?

LOUISE: Yes.

FRED: No.

LOUISE: You never felt the need or because you feared tampering with the creative process?

FRED: The latter mostly.

LOUISE: Nature abhors a vacuum.

FRED: So they say.

LOUISE: You get rid of old preoccupations new thoughts take their place.

FRED: Thus spake Sigmund.

LOUISE: Via Doctor Millstein.

FRED: In short, as a writer, I'm repeating myself?

LOUISE: Yes.

FRED: What about the science stuff in the last book?

LOUISE: More background for your usual concerns.

FRED: Serves me right for picking up a girl in Central Park.

LOUISE: It's only my opinion.

FRED: You left out "humble."

LOUISE: I don't feel humble.

FRED: Maybe you should give me Dr. Millstein's phone number.

LOUISE: If you like.

FRED: What I'd like is no more literary discussion.

LOUISE: In favor of what?

FRED: It's been thirteen years—fill me in.

LOUISE: What would you like to know.

FRED: You said you thought it would be best for both of you.

LOUISE: I was half right.

FRED: You're happy. Artie's not.

LOUISE: Right.

FRED: Why?

LOUISE: Why am I happy or why is he the keeper of the eternal flame?

FRED: You don't sound very sympathetic.

LOUISE: I married him knowing I didn't love him. Shame on me. He keeps a candle burning in the window for thirteen years. More fool he.

FRED: You never loved him?

LOUISE: Never.

FRED: Not even in the beginning when we used to double date?

LOUISE: Not even then.

FRED: You sure fooled me.

LOUISE: Not half as much as I fooled myself.

FRED: Artie said your husband's a lawyer—you have two kids.

LOUISE: Does he still think things would have worked out differently if *we'd* had kids?

FRED: He mentioned the possibility.

LOUISE: God what a horse's ass! I'm sorry. It's just that I've been hearing this pathetic crap from the day I walked out. How he's never changed the door locks or the phone number.

FRED: His cousin keeps you posted.

LOUISE: In painful detail.

FRED: Did she tell you he's been seeing someone and it's serious?

LOUISE: Yes. And once again I have my fingers crossed.

FRED: You'd like him to remarry.

LOUISE: More than anything.

FRED: The only thing stopping him is the hope that somehow, some day you'll go back to him.

LOUISE: What else is new?

FRED: I'm going to tell him I bumped into you and we had a long chat during which I realized there's no way on earth you'll every return.

LOUISE: Lots of luck.

FRED: I'll tell him your marriage couldn't be better.

LOUISE: Which is so.

FRED: I can see that and I'm glad for you.

LOUISE: If he needs more proof tell him I'm pregnant.

FRED: Really?

LOUISE: Three months.

FRED: Doesn't show.

LOUISE: Want to feel?

FRED: I'll take your word. Congratulations.

LOUISE: Thanks. *(Regards her watch)* I've got to pick my daughter up at school. Want to come along?

FRED: I'd love to but I've got an appointment.

(Both rise)

LOUISE: I'm glad we met.

FRED: So am I. *(Offering his hand)* Goodbye.

LOUISE: A far cry from our last parting.

FRED: What?

LOUISE: The farewell party. Artie went to get the car while you and I waited by the entrance.

FRED: And?

LOUISE: You kissed me . . . No memory at all?

FRED: No.

LOUISE: Suppose I told you I took that kiss to mean that you were moving to California because you felt distance was the only way to insure that you wouldn't make a play for your best friend's wife whom you secretly adored?

FRED: That must have been some kiss.

LOUISE: It started long before that.

FRED: It?

LOUISE: The crush I had on you.

FRED: You never let on.

LOUISE: You guys were pals. Plus I never detected the slightest interest on your part until that kiss when I convinced myself the feeling was mutual.

FRED: Why are you telling me this?

LOUISE: They say confession is good for the soul.

FRED: Feel better?

LOUISE: I'm not through. That kiss changed my life.

FRED: What?

LOUISE: When you called from California to say you were getting married I read it as an ultimatum to leave Artie or forever hold my peace.

FRED: Are you saying—

LOUISE: —Yes. I left him confident you'd contact me as soon as you heard. And we'd live happily ever after. But you didn't call. And as the date of your wedding neared I grew desperate. Called Artie on some pretext to be sure you knew we'd split. He said he told you right after I left and you pronounced me a bitch, et cetera.

FRED: I never said that!

LOUISE: What you said doesn't matter. The point is you didn't get in touch with me and I began to realize I'd been deluding myself. Went into a depression compounded by alcohol that saw me hospitalized the day after your wedding. Enter Dr. Millstein.

FRED: I can't tell you how bad I feel.

LOUISE: Why? If not for that kiss I might have stayed with Artie—missed out on the wonderful life I now enjoy. To quote the good doctor—I owe you.

FRED: Glad to have been of service.

LOUISE: If you mean that, there's one more thing you can do.

FRED: What is it?

LOUISE: Kiss me goodbye.

(He initiates a brief and tentative embrace)

I meant like you did that night at the party.

FRED: I don't remember what I did.

LOUISE: It was something like this.

(She cups his face in her hands and presses her lips to his in a kiss that is tender, passionate and probing. He, arms at his sides, the passive recipient at first. Then his arms slowly rise and he is about to enfold her when she breaks off)

Ring any bells?

FRED: No. Sorry.

LOUISE: What's to be sorry?

FRED: That I don't remember something that means so much to you.

LOUISE: Not "means"—*meant.*

FRED: *(Lightly)* It's over between us?

LOUISE: And has been for years. The kiss was just to make sure. Ciao.

(She goes off. He stands there)

Scene 3:

Place: Same as scene one. Time: Fifteen minutes later.

At rise, FRED *and* ARTIE *as before.*

ARTIE: And?

FRED: And what?

ARTIE: What else did she say?

FRED: That's it.

ARTIE: You were gone close to an hour.

FRED: It took most of that time to find her.

ARTIE: She was surprised.

FRED: Yes.

ARTIE: What did she say?

FRED: I told you.

ARTIE: I mean when you stopped her. What were her first words?

FRED: What difference does it make?

ARTIE: I'd like to know.

FRED: Why?

ARTIE: Maybe you missed something.

FRED: Artie look. She's never coming back to you. That's the bottom line.

ARTIE: *Fuck the bottom line!*

(Hastily apologetic)

I'm sorry. Just tell me everything so I can be sure. Please.

FRED: She and her husband are getting along fine.

ARTIE: She said that?

FRED: Yes.

ARTIE: I heard different.

FRED: You heard wrong.

ARTIE: You think she's going to bump into someone she hasn't seen in fifteen years and tell them personal problems?

FRED: She's pregnant.

ARTIE: Pregnant?

FRED: Pregnant.

ARTIE: My cousin never mentioned it.

FRED: She probably doesn't know.

ARTIE: Why would Louise tell you before my cousin?

FRED: She told me to tell you she was pregnant in the hope it would kill any hopes you had about her once and for all.

ARTIE: She actually said that?

FRED: Yes.

ARTIE: Wow.

FRED: Convinced?

ARTIE: That does sound pretty final.

FRED: I'd say so.

ARTIE: How did she look?

FRED: Remarkably unchanged.

ARTIE: Green or yellow? . . . The jogging suit.

FRED: Green.

ARTIE: Mets cap?

FRED: Yes.

ARTIE: Pregnant?

FRED: Three months.

ARTIE: *(Overwhelmed—wipes his eyes)* Forgive me.

FRED: No need.

ARTIE: Nice thing to lay on a guy comes to New York for a good time.

FRED: What are friends for?

ARTIE: Boyhood buddies. A secret revealed after thirteen years. Maybe you'll get a story out of it so it's not a total loss.

FRED: Maybe.

ARTIE: *(Blows his nose)* Does she know I'm thinking about getting married?

FRED: Yes.

ARTIE: And?

FRED: She hopes you go through with it.

ARTIE: Just what I always wanted—her blessing.

FRED: You said if I told you it was thumbs down—

ARTIE: —Want to be best man again?

FRED: You're going to do it?

ARTIE: Yes.

FRED: Congratulations.

ARTIE: Thanks.

FRED: You're doing the right thing.

ARTIE: It's a done deal. Don't sell me.

FRED: Sorry.

ARTIE: What's to be sorry? Actually I feel pretty good.

FRED: I'm glad.

ARTIE: Like a big weight's been lifted. Like . . . Like . . .

FRED: A sense of new beginnings?

ARTIE: Bullseye. Anyone ever tell you you have a way with words?

FRED: Not recently.

ARTIE: If you can get a story out of it, you'll change things so no one can point a finger.

FRED: Of course.

ARTIE: "A sense of new beginnings." That's exactly how I feel.

FRED: Suppose I loved Louise?

ARTIE: What?

FRED: Suppose I secretly loved Louise and would have told her if I'd known she left you. How's that for a switch? . . . Well?

ARTIE: I'm thinking. *(He ponders for a moment—then definitely)* I like it.

FRED: You don't think it's too farfetched?

ARTIE: Not for a story. I can't tell you how good I feel. You know what I'm going to do? I'm going to propose tonight. This calls for champagne!

(He beckons off)

Waiter.

(Freeze—ARTIE with his hand in the air)

THE OPEN MEETING

A. R. Gurney

A. R. Gurney

A. R. (Pete) Gurney was born in Buffalo, New York, in 1930. After his undergraduate education at Williams College and his graduate studies at the Yale School of Drama, he accepted a position as Instructor of Literature in the Humanities Division at MIT. Mr. Gurney remained in that post (with appropriate advances in rank!) until his career as a playwright catapulted to such heights in the 1980s that he could afford to take a leave of absence and confine his energies to writing. The theater has reaped great profit as a result of this radical transition.

Since devoting his entire professional life to writing, Gurney's plays have included *Love Letters, Sweet Sue, What I Did Last Summer, The Middle Ages, The Dining Room, The Cocktail Hour, Another Antigone, The Old Boy,* and *The Snow Ball,* the stage adaptation of his novel of the same title. He has written two other novels, *The Gospel According to Joe* and *Entertaining Strangers* and is presently at work on a fourth. Much of the playwriting he produced in the last twenty years was initiated while he was still at MIT. Those plays took on a new life, however, with his gigantic success beginning with *The Dining Room* in 1982. Gurney first appeared on the professional scene while still a student at Yale with his short play *Three People,* published in *The Best One-Act Plays of 1955* and again with a short play *Turn of the Century,* published in *The Best One-Act Plays of 1956.* His first major theatrical success in New York City was with *Scenes From American Life,* produced at Lincoln Center in 1971 and subsequently all over the country.

Following the New York success of *The Dining Room,* produced by Playwrights Horizons, A.R. Gurney has become one of the most produced playwrights in the U.S.A., a cinderella story for a dedicated playwright who was for so long on a university faculty and who wandered off into other forms. His most recent adventure has been the adaptation of *The Snow Ball,* a play which has been produced by the La Jolla Playhouse in San Diego and the Hartford Stage Company in Hartford, Connecticut.

Gurney had been honored with a Drama Desk Award (1971), a Rockefeller Award (1977) and a Lucille Lortel Award (1989), and in 1987 he received the Award of Merit from the American Academy and Institute of Arts and Letters.

Characters:
ROY, *a middle-aged man*
EDDIE, *a young man*
VERNA, *a woman*

Scene:
No curtain. A long, functional table, facing front. Four chairs behind it. Upstage, two crossed flags: the Stars and Stripes, and some local flag. On the table, a pitcher of water on a tray, with four tumblers. Before each chair, four placards, reading from the stage right to left: EDDIE, DICK, VERNA, ROY.

While the house lights are still on, EDDIE, VERNA, *and* ROY *come on. They stand upstage, to one side, arguing rather vehemently under their breath.* EDDIE *is a young man, casually dressed, carrying a worn paperback entitled* The Democratic Experience *into which are stuck a number of loose papers.* VERNA *is an attractive middle-aged woman, dressed efficiently, carrying a commodious purse.* ROY *is older, in an expensive business suit, carrying an elegant attaché case. Their discussions continue for some time, becoming more and more heated, until* VERNA *remembers the audience.*

VERNA: *(To audience)* We're discussing whether or not to begin.

EDDIE: *(To audience)* I think we should.

ROY: *(To audience)* I think we shouldn't.

VERNA: *(To audience)* I'm on the fence.

(They turn to each other and begin arguing again. Finally, to audience)

The issue is whether or not to begin without Dick.

EDDIE: *(To audience)* I think we should.

ROY: *(To audience)* I think we shouldn't.

VERNA: *(To audience)* I'm still on the fence.

(More ad-lib arguing, out of which EDDIE's *voice finally emerges)*

EDDIE: *(To* ROY *and* VERNA*)* Hey now look. This is May. It's our final meeting till fall. We've got a lot of ground to cover. It's about time we started sowing some seeds around here.

ROY: Without Dick?

EDDIE: Without Dick.

ROY: I don't buy that.

VERNA: *(To audience)* I really am on the fence.

EDDIE: Maybe you'd like to explain your objections to the group, Roy.

ROY: I'd be glad to. We asked Dick to go down to Washington. We asked him to meet with people in high places, sound them out, bring back documents. Now Dick is still down there working on these things. Until he comes up with answers, how can we possibly begin this meeting without Dick?

EDDIE: I like to think, Roy, I like to think that just occasionally in this country, in this so-called democracy, we can move ahead without either Dick or his documents.

VERNA: *(To audience)* I could go either way.

EDDIE: I mean, what do you propose to do, Roy? Just stand around, eyeing each other, until Dick shows up?

ROY: I propose we cancel.

EDDIE: *Can*cel?

VERNA: Oh my!

ROY: Until Dick returns.

EDDIE: *(Defiantly taking his chair)* Not me. I want to start this ball rolling.

VERNA: Just like that?

EDDIE: Just like that.

ROY: Fine. Very well. You roll the ball any way you want to, Eddie. I myself intend to do something more constructive with my time. *(He starts out)*

EDDIE: Hold it, pal.

ROY: *(Stopping)* Are you speaking to me, sir?

EDDIE: I've got something you might want to read, Roy. *(He rummages through his papers)* I've got something here which might interest you . . . Ah. Here. *(Waves a piece of paper)* Read this, Roy.

ROY: And what, pray tell, is that?

EDDIE: It's a note which was handed to me after our last meeting.

ROY: Ah. Well, I am delighted you are receiving communications, Eddie. You obviously are beginning to ingratiate yourself with the group.

EDDIE: *(Holding it out)* Just read it, Roy.

ROY: *(Holding his ground)* I am not at your beck and call, young man.

EDDIE: *(Waving it around)* I dare you to read it, Roy.

VERNA: Perhaps I can help here. *(She takes the paper)* Perhaps I can grease the wheels of progress here. *(She crosses to ROY)* Here, Roy.

ROY: Thank you, Verna. (ROY *takes the paper)*

EDDIE: Read it, Roy.

ROY: I will read it in my own sweet time. (ROY *slowly reads it)*

EDDIE: *(Low, to VERNA)* Notice how he is stalling.

VERNA: *(Low, to EDDIE)* I won't take sides in this, Eddie. I really won't.

ROY: Who wrote this?

EDDIE: A friend, Roy.

ROY: *(Folding the letter)* Some disgruntled job-seeker? Some left-leaning liberal?

EDDIE: I like to think it was a good friend.

ROY: You and I may have very different definitions of the word "good."

EDDIE: How about reading it out loud, Roy?

ROY: I don't see why I have to stand here, taking orders from the junior member of this panel. Is there any reason why I have to do that, Verna?

VERNA: Tell you what: *I'll* read it. *(Holds out her hand for it)* May I have it, please, Roy?

ROY: Verna, this is simply a . . .

VERNA: I'd like to read that piece of paper, if I may, Roy.

ROY: *(Reluctantly handing it over)* Very well, Verna.

VERNA: *(Taking the paper)* Now . . . *(She crosses down to the table, plunks down her purse, opens it)* If I can find my glasses. *(She rummages in her purse)* Eureka! *(She displays her glasses to the audience, then puts them on, opens the letter, clears her throat, reads carefully)* Here we go. *(She reads)* "Don't trust Dick."

EDDIE: See?

VERNA: Hmmm.

ROY: Some crackpot.

VERNA: *(Reading it again)* "Don't trust Dick."

ROY: Some trouble-maker.

EDDIE: You think so, Roy? What if I told you there are rumblings from others in this room about Dick.

ROY: Rumblings? From whom?

EDDIE: I'm not going to name names, Roy.

VERNA: People have the right to rumble, Roy.

ROY: Well it's nice to know that things are happening behind my back.

VERNA: *(Rereading the note)* "Don't trust Dick."

ROY: Now stop that, Verna! We all have heard what it says.

VERNA: *(Low, to ROY)* Please don't raise your voice at me, Roy. I mean that.

ROY: Look, people. I'm not going to stand around here listening to Dick being disparaged by a bunch of disgruntled trouble-makers. Sorry. I've got better things to do with my time. *Starts out again)*

VERNA: Actually, Roy . . . *(ROY stops)* I also received a note after our last meeting. It was thrust into my lap by a woman.

EDDIE: By a woman?

VERNA: Just as we were breaking up. I remember being quite taken aback by what it said.

EDDIE: Taken aback?

VERNA: Yes, I found it quite disturbing. (ROY *has remained hovering on stage*) But go on, Roy. Leave, if you must. You shouldn't stay if you don't want to.

ROY: What did your note say, Verna?

VERNA: Well I'm not sure it's even germane to the discussion.

EDDIE: Let's read it and see.

VERNA: All right. Let's do that. *(Starts groping around her purse again)* Let's see. I know I brought it. I remember thinking that it might come in handy during the evening. So when I changed purses, I distinctly remember putting it on the hall table right by my car keys and, Yes! Here it is! *(She pulls out a small, folded piece of paper)* Now, who— whom do I give it to?

ROY *and* EDDIE: *(Simultaneously)* Me!

VERNA: I'll read it myself. *(Looks around)* Now where did I put my glasses?

ROY *and* EDDIE: *(Pointing; simultaneously)* There!

VERNA: *(Calmly)* Thank you, gentlemen. *(She puts on her glasses, unfolds the note and reads)* Here's what it says: "Dick is a lousy lover." *(She looks from* EDDIE *to* ROY*)* I'll read it again: "Dick is a lousy lover." *(Pause)*

EDDIE: Wow.

VERNA: *(To* EDDIE*)* You can see why I was somewhat taken aback.

EDDIE: I'm glad to see the sisterhood is at last speaking up, Verna.

ROY: Oh for Chrissake!

VERNA: Roy, I will not have you swearing.

ROY: But I mean, Jesus . . .

VERNA: I'm serious, Roy. I won't have it. It offends me, and I suspect it offends a number of other people in this room.

EDDIE: Yeah, Roy.

ROY: But that note has nothing to do with the issues!

VERNA: I already said I wasn't sure it was germane.

EDDIE: The remark is about Dick, isn't it?

VERNA: It most certainly is.

EDDIE: It's about Dick's attitude toward other people, isn't it?

VERNA: It's about Dick's attitude toward women.

EDDIE: Well then I think it's germane as hell, frankly. It implies that Dick has trouble relating to women.

VERNA: That's a very good point, Eddie. Very sensitive to women's needs.

ROY: Well I'll tell you one thing. I do not intend to stand around while the mainstay of this meeting is made light of, through a series of sly cracks and undocumented innuendos. I will not be a party to that, and I suspect a number of other people here tonight feel equally uncomfortable. If Dick were here to defend himself, well and good. But since he's not here, since he's still in Washington, where he is working for our betterment and the betterment of democracy everywhere in the world, then I for one intend to go home and read a good book, and I invite everyone else to entertain the same notion. *(Starts out once again)*

EDDIE: Roy . . .

ROY: No, I'm sorry. Good night.

EDDIE: Roy, I just have one question. Then you can go.

ROY: *(Eyes closed; infinitely patient)* Ask away.

EDDIE: Have you yourself recently received any sudden or unexpected communications about Dick?

ROY: No.

EDDIE: You sure, Roy?

ROY: I am sure.

EDDIE: Roy, when you and Verna and I were waiting in the wings, you were suddenly approached by a delivery-person from Federal Express who put into your hands a large, stridently colored, glossy envelope, postmarked Washington, D.C., which required your immediate signature of receipt.

VERNA: That's true . . . I had forgotten that.

EDDIE: You signed for that envelope, Roy, and then you proceeded to slink off into a corner, where you opened it, read it furtively, gave a grim nod, crammed it into your briefcase, and then returned to our offstage deliberations.

VERNA: That's very well described, Eddie.

EDDIE: Was that letter about Dick, Roy?

(Pause)

ROY: It was not.

EDDIE: May I ask what that letter was about then, Roy?

ROY: Eddie, my inquisitive young friend, I hope you'll forgive me if I choose not to discuss my private mail in a public forum.

VERNA: Yes, Eddie. We all have lives of our own.

EDDIE: All right. But I think it would allow a number of us here to feel more comfortable, Roy, if you let us read that letter, or at least gave us a brief paraphrase of its contents.

VERNA: Yes, Roy. I do think that would make life easier, all around.

(Pause)

ROY: If you must know, Eddie, that letter was from Dick.

VERNA: But I thought you said . . .

ROY: Eddie asked me whether I had received a letter *about* Dick. I said no. Because it was *from* Dick. *About* something else. I believe I was being accurate in my response.

EDDIE: What did Dick's letter say, Roy?

ROY: Oh well, it was about some minor issue . . .

VERNA: Minor? When it arrives Federal Express at the last minute, right to this building?

ROY: Some personal business . . . Some legal technicalities having to do with various minor concerns . . .

EDDIE: May I read that letter, Roy?

ROY: You may not.

VERNA: May *I* read it, Roy?

ROY: I'd prefer you didn't, Verna.

VERNA: Then that's it.

EDDIE: WHAT?

VERNA: The subject is closed, Eddie. Roy and I outvote you on this one, I'm afraid. When it comes to questions of personal privacy, then I have to say that I stand foursquare with the strictest interpretations of the law. Dick wrote that letter to Roy, not to us. And we have absolutely no right to learn its contents unless Roy is willing to make them public. Which he isn't. For reasons which are his own business.

ROY: Thank you, Verna.

VERNA: And now you should feel free to leave, Roy. And you should feel confident that your private life will remain just that. Private.

ROY: Thanks, Verna. *(He starts out again)*

VERNA: *(To audience)* Dick's letter obviously makes some totally un-called-for remarks about Roy's personal hygiene.

ROY: *(Stopping)* It does NOT, Verna.

VERNA: Well then it probably makes some totally unnecessary insinuations about your tax returns, Roy.

ROY: It doesn't do that either!

VERNA: Well it must do *some*thing, Roy. Otherwise you'd let us read it.

ROY: ALL RIGHT! *(He comes down to his place, slams his briefcase onto the table, snaps it open angrily, takes out a Federal Express envelope, slams shut the case. He opens the envelope, takes out a crisp letter, reads it, shakes his head, and then slams it down on the table)* There. *(He walks upstage, sulkily)*

(EDDIE *and* VERNA *rush to the letter, and hover over it*)

VERNA: Today's date . . .

EDDIE: Washington, D.C. . . .

VERNA: Handwritten . . .

EDDIE: In what looks like Dick's pinched, ungenerous penmanship.

VERNA: I'll read it: "Dear Roy . . ."

EDDIE: "Try to abort the meeting."

VERNA: "Affectionately, Dick."

EDDIE: "Try to abort the meeting!"

VERNA: "Affectionately, Dick."

EDDIE: But "*abort* the meeting!" My God!

VERNA: I don't see what's so bad about that.

ROY: I don't either, frankly.

EDDIE: What? "Try to abort the meeting?" It means that Roy and Dick don't want this meeting to happen, Verna.

VERNA: Oh now . . .

EDDIE: They don't want any meetings to happen.

ROY: Oh look . . .

EDDIE: They'd be perfectly happy if none of us ever met again!

VERNA: Oh heavens, Eddie. Please!

EDDIE: I'm serious! Think of what Roy has done all winter long! With his tabling and postponing and subcommittees and points of order! Think of Dick with his fact-finding trips and constantly increasing absentee record! What are these guys up to? I'll tell you what. They are systematically trying to undermine the group process!

ROY: Oh Good Lord!

EDDIE: Lookit, pal. Look at the evidence here. (*He lines up the three documents on the table in front of him*) I get a note saying don't trust

Dick. Verna gets a note saying Dick is a lousy lover. And then you, Roy, get a secret communication from Dick down in Washington asking you to abort the meeting. I don't see much of a willingness to move forward in any of these documents, now do you, Roy?

ROY: And why, Eddie, for the sake of argument, do you think Dick and I don't want things to "move forward," as you so lamely put it?

EDDIE: Because you're scared of what might come out.

VERNA: *(Rereading* ROY's *letter)* "Affectionately, Dick." Did you and Dick have a sexual relationship, Roy?

ROY: We did NOT, Verna!

VERNA: Just *asking!* Honestly, Roy! No need to get so huffy!

EDDIE: I don't care whether they did or not. That's not the point. The point is that there are many things wrong with this country, many things radically, radically wrong, and it seems that Roy and Dick have spent the entire winter systematically preventing us from dealing with them.

(Pause)

ROY: Well. *(Taking his seat)* I can see I have to answer that.

VERNA: It might be helpful if you did, Roy. *(She takes her seat)*

EDDIE: *(Sitting down as well)* Let's hear it, Roy.

ROY: First, I'd like a glass of water, please, Verna.

VERNA: Yes. Oh yes, Roy. You deserve one, after having been in the hot seat for so long. *(Pours and gives him one)*

EDDIE: I'd like one, too, Verna.

VERNA: Yes, you should have one also, Eddie. Seeing as how you've been working so hard this evening. *(Pours and gives* EDDIE *one)*

ROY: *(Drinking his water)* Good water. Excellent water. Is this bottled water, Verna?

VERNA: It well may be. I have no idea.

EDDIE: He's just buttering you up, Verna.

ROY: It is first-rate water, Verna, and I thank you for it.

VERNA: Thank you, Roy.

EDDIE: He just wants your vote, Verna.

ROY: I am simply commenting on the excellence of the water.

EDDIE: I can envision a time when we'd get good, sweet water, right from the tap.

ROY: Here we go . . .

EDDIE: I can envision a time when our reservoirs and our lakes and our rivers and our groundwater would no longer be . . .

VERNA: That's enough, Eddie. Really. Now just simmer down . . . Now, Roy, I believe you had something to say to the group.

ROY: Yes, well, that is, I simply want to say that I as much as anyone believe that this nation should reap the benefits of the past even as we sow the seeds of the future. Yes, I see challenges ahead, but I view them as opportunities. Yes, mistakes have been made, but we must learn from our errors, and with both firmness and flexibility, with one eye on yesterday and the other on tomorrow, we must move firmly forward, bearing hope and freedom and democracy into all four corners of the globe.

EDDIE: Globes don't have corners, Roy.

ROY: It was a figure of—

EDDIE: It was a figure of bullshit, Roy.

VERNA: Now Eddie . . .

EDDIE: Are you paying Dick, Roy?

ROY: Am I paying Dick?

EDDIE: Or is Dick paying you? To distract us with that bullshit.

ROY: Now wait a—

EDDIE: Or are both of you on the payroll of someone else?

ROY: *(Getting up)* I am not going to sit here and listen to—

VERNA: Now Eddie, stop! And Roy, please! Sit down . . .

ROY: I do not have to stay here and—

VERNA: Now wait. Now listen. Here's an idea. Why don't we telephone Dick down in Washington and clear things up?

EDDIE: Just telephone him?

VERNA: Exactly. Just call him up. Say, "Hi, Dick. All of us up here are just kind of sitting around wondering what the heck is going on down there."

ROY: You can't just do that to Dick, Verna.

VERNA: Why can't you?

ROY: Because he's a busy man. Because he's preoccupied.

EDDIE: *(Getting up)* I'll do it. Right now.

ROY: No, all right. I'll do it.

EDDIE: What's his number, Roy?

ROY: I think I'd better do the telephoning around here.

EDDIE: Give me Dick's note there, Verna. Maybe it's on that.

VERNA: Eddie, I do not respond to people who just hold out their hands and say "gimme."

EDDIE: May I have Dick's note, please, Verna.

ROY: Don't give it to him, Verna.

EDDIE: *(Grabbing* DICK's *note)* Let me just look at this here.

VERNA: Nor do I respond to people who grab, Eddie!

EDDIE: But his number's written right here. *(He starts out)*

ROY: I want to do the telephoning, please.

VERNA: Let Eddie do it, Roy.

ROY: What? Why? Why him?

VERNA: Because he's younger.

ROY: But what will he say?

EDDIE: I'll simply say, Roy, that he should get the fuck back here toot sweet or we should know the reason why.

VERNA: No, Eddie. You will not say that. You will simply say that a number of us are becoming unhappy at what's happening in this country, and we'd appreciate it if he'd come up here and share with us his thoughts on the subject. That's what you will say, Eddie. And if you say anything else, I'm going to be very, very mad.

EDDIE: I'll find my own words.

ROY: That's what worries us.

EDDIE: There's a word or two I'm saving for you, Roy!

VERNA: Just GO, Eddie!

(EDDIE *goes off. Pause.* ROY *sits moodily.* VERNA *looks at him*)

VERNA: Roy . . .

ROY: Mmm?

VERNA: *(Indicating where* EDDIE *has gone)* That was calculated, Roy.

ROY: What?

VERNA: That. Getting Eddie to call Washington. I thought that up.

ROY: Mmm.

VERNA: And I did it for a very specific purpose. I did it because I wanted to talk to you alone. *(Remembers audience; smiles)* That is, without Eddie.

ROY: Mmm.

VERNA: *(Taking a deep breath)* Roy . . .

(EDDIE *returns, stands by the exit*)

EDDIE: I need a quarter. For the pay phone.

VERNA: Yes, all right, Eddie. I'll give you a quarter. *(Begins to rummage in her bag)*

ROY: Kid hasn't even got a quarter.

EDDIE: I'll bet you've got plenty of quarters, Roy.

VERNA: *(Rummaging nervously)* Where is that quarter? I know I had a quarter.

ROY: Yes I have plenty of quarters, Eddie. I earned them through good, hard work!

EDDIE: Robbing who, Roy? Who'd you rob for your dough?

VERNA: *(Desperately producing a quarter)* Here! Here's a quarter! Now go call, Eddie.

ROY: You'll never see that quarter again, Verna.

EDDIE: How many quarters did it take to buy off Dick, Roy? *(He goes out)*

ROY: *(Shouting after him)* You couldn't even earn an honest dime!

EDDIE: *(Coming back in)* I can envision a time when people could communicate freely and easily, back and forth, all over the earth, without enriching the coffers of the telephone company, Roy! *(Goes out again)*

ROY: *(Calling after him)* Communist! Fuzzy-headed pinko liberal wimp!

VERNA: Now stop it! (ROY *subsides moodily*) That is exactly what I wanted to talk to you about, Roy.

ROY: What?

VERNA: That. There is something going on between you and Eddie.

ROY: What do you mean?

VERNA: There is something extremely nonproductive, Roy. I've sensed it. I think everybody in this room has sensed it.

ROY: That kid accused me of bribery.

VERNA: That is just a symptom, Roy. We all know that. That is just the culmination of something which has been going on all winter long.

ROY: The hell with him.

VERNA: I won't accept that as a solution, Roy. I'm sorry, but we're not fooling around now.

ROY: He irritates me.

VERNA: He's young, Roy. He's a mere babe. Now tolerate him.

ROY: I've tried.

VERNA: No, Roy. No. You have NOT tried. Not really. Oh now look, my friend. I'm on the fence here. I'm in the middle. I'll make no bones about it. My role is the role of too many women these days. Namely, to Keep. The. Peace. Well, that's what I've done through all these long, dark, gloomy, winter months. They say that in Spain, Roy, to keep the bulls from fighting, they put cows into the pens. All right, I guess that's what I am, Roy. A cow. Mooo, Roy. Mooo.

ROY: Oh now, Verna . . .

VERNA: No, I am. And Dick, well maybe Dick is a steer. But it's no fun, Roy. Many's the time I wanted to lock horns with all of you. There are women who do, these days. There are cows who now go into combat. But I didn't. I went on trying to pour, well, milk on the troubled waters. *(She pours herself a glass of water)*

ROY: Verna, my dear friend . . .

VERNA: But I'm not sure I can do it much longer, Roy. I mean that. I'm getting torn apart by this tension. Look at my hand shake. Last week, after one of your battles with Eddie, I had to take a good stiff drink when I got home. I drank ALONE, Roy.

ROY: Verna . . .

VERNA: I'm not finished, Roy. Now you know, and I know, and I think everybody here knows, that there is something going on here. I don't know the name of it, and I'm not sure I want to know. But there is something under the surface here, and it is beginning to poison these meetings. They are becoming simply a ritual dance, a parody, a travesty of what they once were. And I won't have that, Roy. I simply won't have it. If the democratic experience is doomed to degenerate, then I want to get off the train.

ROY: But he—

VERNA: I'm almost finished, Roy. Now: all I want you to do is make an effort. I'm asking you personally to make a special effort. I'm asking you to fight whatever subterranean thing is tearing us all apart. When Eddie walks back into this room, I want you to treat him with warmth and affection, so that all of us can join hands in this thing the way we once did. There. I've said my say, Roy. And now I'd be very interested in your response.

ROY: Why don't you say these things to him?

VERNA: Because he's young, Roy. He doesn't know. And you do. Now. Promise me you'll make an effort. For the sake of all of us.

ROY: I'll . . . try.

VERNA: *(Kissing him on the cheek)* Good. Oh, good, Roy. I know you won't regret it.

(EDDIE *comes angrily back into the room*)

EDDIE: Want to know what happened?

VERNA: Sit down, Eddie.

EDDIE: I said, do you want to know what happened?

VERNA: We only do, Eddie, if it's relevant. If it's not relevant, if it's unpleasant, if it could irritate or embarrass anyone in this room, then no, we do not want to hear what happened.

(EDDIE *angrily takes his seat*)

EDDIE: He put me on hold.

VERNA: He what?

EDDIE: *(Shouting)* He put me on HOLD! He put me on HOLD!

VERNA: *(Covering her ears)* Eddie, do not shout in my ear. I don't like it.

EDDIE: Dick put me on hold.

VERNA: Well. Maybe he was busy, Eddie.

EDDIE: He left me hanging on hold. Listening to Muzak. Listening to the goddam love theme from *Doctor Zhivago*.

VERNA: Oh how ghastly!

EDDIE: Finally his assistant got on the line.

VERNA: His assistant?

EDDIE: He's got an assistant now.

VERNA: I'm not sure I like that.

ROY: What's wrong with that? The man's busy, he needs help . . .

VERNA: There's something about it I don't like, Roy.

EDDIE: Anyway, he put her on.

VERNA: Her? You said, "her?" His assistant is a "her." I knew there was something.

ROY: Now Verna . . .

VERNA: It bothers me, Roy, and I suspect it bothers a number of people here. When we delegated Dick to go down there, I don't recall anything about hiring a female assistant. I may be wrong, we can check the minutes, but I don't recall anything about that.

ROY: It simply means that Dick is working overtime and needs help.

VERNA: It may mean that, Roy. It may mean something very, very different. (To EDDIE) What did this so-called assistant say to you, Eddie? When she took you off hold?

EDDIE: She asked me what I wanted.

VERNA: And you replied?

EDDIE: I said I wanted answers to a few questions.

VERNA: And she?

EDDIE: She said she'd try to answer them.

ROY: See? What's wrong with that? Girl was doing her job.

VERNA: Now wait, please, Roy . . . Go on, Eddie.

EDDIE: So I asked her point blank. I said, how come our country is turning into a second-rate economic power? How come we have created an impoverished, drug-ridden, hopelessly miseducated under-class, with one of the highest infant mortality rates among the industrialized na-tions? I said how come we continue to spend huge amounts of our national treasure on totally unnecessary military armaments, while we go on contaminating the natural environment, perhaps irreversibly, for the generations that follow us?

VERNA: And how did this so-called assistant respond to *that?*

EDDIE: Oh, she hemmed and hawed.

VERNA: I'll bet she did. That little bimbo.

ROY: Oh hey, come on, Verna. Those were tough questions to answer.

EDDIE: She also said something else, Roy.

ROY: Oh yes? What else did she say?

EDDIE: She said tell Roy to keep those contributions coming.

VERNA: She said that?

EDDIE: That's what she said: keep those contributions coming.

VERNA: Now that also bothers me.

EDDIE: It does me, too, I'll tell you.

VERNA: Roy, have you been sending money to Dick on the side?

ROY: Well, I mean I've tried to see to it that he . . .

EDDIE: Let me put things a little clearer. No wonder Dick isn't here. No wonder he's goofing off in Washington with some second-rate bimbo. The thing is that Roy has bought him off!

ROY: *(Rising from his chair)* Hey, now just a minute!

VERNA: *(Restraining ROY)* Roy, you promised!

EDDIE: *(Pressing home)* And the reason Roy bought Dick off is that he wants to continue exploiting the poor and polluting the earth!

VERNA: Just ignore it, Roy.

EDDIE: And the reason Roy wants to continue doing these things is that he is motivated, no, *consumed* by simple, selfish, irresponsible greed!

VERNA: Just change the subject, Roy. Move blithely on to another topic.

ROY: *(Brushing her off; standing up)* No, Verna. I will not move blithely on to another topic! I'm going to answer that here and now!

VERNA: *(To* EDDIE; *through her teeth)* Eddie, I could strangle you with my bare hands!

ROY: Do you know what I think, Eddie?

EDDIE: No. What do you think, Roy?

ROY: I think you want to make me look bad out here.

EDDIE: Oh really, Roy?

VERNA: I won't have this!

ROY: Do you know what else I think, Eddie?

EDDIE: What else do you think, Roy?

ROY: I don't think you even bothered to call Dick out there.

VERNA: I will not have this!

ROY: I think you just pretended to call Dick out there. I think what you really did out there was think up bad things to say about me. And I think you pocketed Verna's quarter!

VERNA: *(Covering her ears)* I will not listen to this!

EDDIE: Roy, the only thing I'm going to pocket tonight is your fat ass!

VERNA: *(Pounding the table with her fists)* No, no, no, NO! I want the subject changed, do you hear me? CHANGED! Nobody's interested in these personal remarks! Now stop it! Eddie, you obviously need a laxative. Now go TAKE one, for heaven's sake!

ROY: Yes, Eddie!

VERNA: *(Wheeling on* ROY*)* And you, Roy, are obviously having trouble with your prostate again!

EDDIE: Yes, Roy!

VERNA: So cut it OUT! Honestly! I've never seen a meeting degenerate so completely! It's sophomoric! Now grow UP! Both of you!

ROY: It's up to him. One more crack from him and I leave. I'm serious. I've got better things to do with my time.

VERNA: Do you hear that, Eddie? Now it's up to you.

(Pause)

EDDIE: *(Quietly)* Roy . . . you know . . . in some ways, I respect you . . .

VERNA: Good, Eddie . . .

EDDIE: And come to think of it, you've run some good meetings this winter . . .

VERNA: Yes, he has, Eddie. Good . . .

EDDIE: Maybe you've held a little too much to the status quo, maybe you've been a little too skeptical of change, but that's your right, Roy, that's your privilege, and in a funny way, I respect you for it . . .

VERNA: That's very well put, Eddie. That's very mature . . .

EDDIE: BUT, Roy . . .

ROY: Here it comes . . .

EDDIE: BUT, Roy . . .

ROY: Come on, come on. Out with it . . .

EDDIE: Even though I respect you, Roy, I don't think I can rest, I really don't think I can rest, Roy, until I have presented to this assembled multitude your left ball!

(ROY *pushes his chair back from the table, stands up, and storms angrily out.* VERNA *groans and buries her head in her hands. Finally she turns to* EDDIE)

VERNA: Go apologize to that man!

EDDIE: No.

VERNA: I said go—

EDDIE: I said NO!

VERNA: I want to see Roy sitting in this chair!

EDDIE: I want to see Roy flat on the floor.

VERNA: Roy sat in this chair every week, all winter long. Wind, rain, and snow. There sat Roy.

EDDIE: Buying off Dick.

VERNA: I don't care. Dick ducked out. Roy stayed here. Here. Right in this seat. Feel. His seat is still warm from where he sat. Feel, Eddie.

EDDIE: Thanks but no thanks.

VERNA: Oh, and look: You made Roy so mad he left without his brief-case. *(Picks it up)* Look at this. This lovely old leather. These personal-ized initials, unobtrusively engraved in gold leaf. *(She weighs it in her hand)* Heavy . . . Heavy with homework . . . Work he planned to do on our behalf, Eddie . . . *(Puts it on the table)* Oh and look at the wear and tear! Here is that spot where he fell in a puddle, hurrying to one of our meetings! And here is that gash from when he was attacked by knife-wielding muggers in the parking lot. *(She tenderly wipes it clean with her handkerchief)* Oh Eddie, at least return his briefcase to him.

EDDIE: Let him come back and beg for it!

VERNA: Youth can be so cruel! *(She snaps open the briefcase, looks inside)* Oh look. It breaks my heart. *(Withdraws a large sheaf of papers)* Look at the work he's done over the years. Proposals, plans, budgets . . . *(Withdraws a large calendar)* And look at this calendar. Carefully marked with the dates of all our meetings. Blank for the summer, of course. And then all marked up again for next September, itemizing all the possible topics for discussion. Oh, say what you want to say, Eddie. You're not as hard-working as this, and you never will be.

EDDIE: *(Defensively)* I have a different style of approach.

VERNA: *(Continuing to poke around in the briefcase)* Oh, and look at these notes he wrote to himself: "Must do this" . . . "Ought to to that" . . . You're mentioned in these notes, Eddie.

EDDIE: I am not.

VERNA: You are! *(Reads)* "Remember to send Eddie a birthday card" . . . "Remember to buy Eddie a beer" . . . "Try to get Eddie a Gov-ernment Grant" . . .

EDDIE: Lay off, Verna. I feel bad enough as it is.

VERNA: *(Half withdrawing a folder)* I know, but look at—*(She sees folder's title, stops, puts it quickly back into the briefcase, slams it shut)*

EDDIE: What?

VERNA: *(Snapping the snaps on the briefcase)* Nothing, Eddie.

EDDIE: You saw something in that briefcase, Verna.

VERNA: *(Trying to hide the briefcase behind her back)* No, no . . .

EDDIE: *(Holding out his hand)* Give me that briefcase, Verna.

VERNA: This is Roy's private property, Eddie.

EDDIE: Hand it over! *(They struggle for it; finally he wrests it away from her. She collapses into her chair. He slams it down on the table in front of him, snaps it open, searches through it)* Now. Let's see. Papers, calendars, applications for government grants, and . . . Ah hah! *(He pulls out the suspicious file, reads the cover)* "For Dick's Eyes Only" . . . Ah hah. *(Opens the file, reads title page)* "Plans to turn America from a Democracy into an Oligarchy." AH-HAH!

VERNA: *(Exhaustedly)* What's an oligarchy?

EDDIE: An oligarchy is government by the rich, for the rich, and dedicated to the proposition that they get even richer.

VERNA: Oh Lord.

(EDDIE reads through the file)

EDDIE: Sure. Here it is . . . Tax breaks for the upper income brackets . . . Exorbitant salaries for corporation executives . . . sheltered retirement accounts . . . cutbacks on health care for the poor . . . permits on exploiting the environment . . . It's all here, Verna . . . And finally, this note, at the end, written in what is obviously Dick's handwriting! *(He slams the note down in front of her)* Read it, Verna. Read it and weep.

VERNA: *(Shaking her head)* I can't read it.

EDDIE: *(Taking it up)* Then I'll read it! *(Reads)* "Sic Semper Liberalis" . . . Translate it, Verna.

VERNA: I can't translate it.

EDDIE: Then I'll do that, too . . . "Thus always with liberals" . . . Written in Dick's pinched, ungenerous hand . . . Do you still want me to go apologize to Roy, Verna?

VERNA: *(Quietly)* Planted.

EDDIE: What?

VERNA: Planted! Someone could have planted that folder in Roy's briefcase.

EDDIE: Oh Verna . . .

VERNA: Why not? It's possible. Someone who hated Roy and the power structure he represents.

EDDIE: Are you accusing me, Verna?

VERNA: Not necessarily. I'm simply saying that in this country a man is innocent until he's proven guilty.

EDDIE: All right. We'll let him convict him*self.*

VERNA: I don't follow you, Eddie.

EDDIE: He'll convict himself in front of all these witnesses. *(Indicates the audience)* Listen. If Roy knows that this briefcase contains this incriminating folder, he'll come back for it almost immediately. The very fact that he comes back will prove he's guilty as sin.

VERNA: And if he doesn't come back? If he simply telephones and asks me to drop it by his office in the morning?

EDDIE: Then he's innocent, Verna, and I'll apologize to him personally.

VERNA: So we just . . . wait.

EDDIE: Yes. Wait. Wait while he drives home in his gas-guzzling, space-consuming stretch limousine, peering furtively from behind the tinted glass, making guilty and intrusive calls on his mobile telephone. We wait while he pulls into his exclusive, restricted, privately-protected neighborhood and pulls into the driveway of his insultingly ostentatious home. We wait while he gets out, deactivates his burglar alarm system, and sidles into his customized kitchen to stuff his face on a late-night snack of fat and unnatural food. We wait while he lumbers into his over-decorated den, farts, and then settles into his overstuffed chair to vicariously identify with a few minutes of violent commercial television. There he sits, festering, stewing, wallowing in his own depraved thoughts. Then suddenly he stiffens. He sits up. His beady, yellow little eyes narrow to slits. His tiny, tufted little ears prick to attention. He remembers! He remembers he's forgotten his briefcase! And with a sickening squeal of anger, he scampers back here, as fast as his cloven hooves can carry him! And we'll be waiting!

VERNA: That last speech was unnecessary, Eddie.

EDDIE: Necessary or not, baby, I made it, and I loved making it! And I'll make more of them to his fat face. *(Takes the incriminating folder, puts it on his chair)* Oh, Verna, this is exhilarating! I suddenly feel as if we've opened a door to a room which has been closed for years! It's as if we were all stepping back into the cave, when we knew who we were! Come on, Roy! Come home! I'm going to eat you for breakfast!

(Pause)

VERNA: I loved him, Eddie.

EDDIE: What?

VERNA: I loved him.

EDDIE: You loved ROY?

VERNA: It's hard to admit, particularly in public, but since this looks like our last meeting, I think it's time to tell all. *(Pause)* We had a thing going, Roy and I. Last fall, after these meetings, we'd drive out into the country. *(Pause)* We made love. Under the harvest moon. Among the squash and pumpkins.

EDDIE: You made LOVE? With ROY?

VERNA: Yes, Eddie.

EDDIE: *(Turning upstage)* I think I'm going to be sick.

VERNA: And I'll tell you something else, Eddie. Even before we ran these meetings, when Roy and I were both young, we copulated.

EDDIE: Roy was never young!

VERNA: He was, Eddie. He was once young. And liberal. And potent.

EDDIE: I never knew that.

VERNA: Oh there are lots of things you don't know, young man. For instance, I don't imagine you know that one spring, several years ago, he sired you in a newly planted cornfield.

EDDIE: You mean . . . Roy's my . . . father?

VERNA: If you want to put it that way.

EDDIE: And you're my . . . ?

VERNA: If you want to pin things down.

EDDIE: I always thought my *parents* . . . were my parents.

VERNA: Well, they're not.

EDDIE: I didn't know that.

VERNA: Nor does Roy. But he always liked you, Eddie. Dick used to irritate him with all his greed and ambition, but Roy always spoke fondly of you.

EDDIE: Are you saying Dick is . . . my . . . brother? Out of you? By Roy?

VERNA: I'm saying lots of things, Eddie. I'm saying Roy had a special feeling for you. And he watched your passage into puberty with pride and affection.

EDDIE: Gosh.

VERNA: Yes. Gosh. You can say gosh now, when that poor man is thrashing around his home, looking for his briefcase!

EDDIE: You know, Verna. All this time I thought that you loved *me*.

VERNA: I did. I do.

EDDIE: No, but I mean, all this spring, ever since Groundhog Day, I've been secretly hoping that you and I could drive out into the cornfields. And copulate.

VERNA: We can! We will!

EDDIE: But now I know about you and Roy, it changes everything. Everything becomes so much more complicated.

VERNA: But that's exactly what I'm *saying* Eddie! All I'm trying to do is get you—get all of us—to *think* about these things! There's so much in*volved!* Everything goes way, way back!

EDDIE: I'm beginning to realize that.

VERNA: I hope so, Eddie. Because now I'm going to give you something very difficult to do. *(Opens her bag, begins to take out various things and put them on the table in front of her)* I have sat here all winter long. *(Out comes gloves and hat)* I have tried to be an agreeable, accommodating woman. *(Out come lipstick, compact, perfume, a wig)* I have tried to hold things together, night after night. I have used every device in the book. *(Liquor, scotch tape, a sewing kit)* But I can't do it any more. Times change. People grow old. Institutions become atrophied. We simply don't—meet anymore, you and Roy and I. We've got to make a clean, fresh start. We've got to get back to the essentials. *(Overturns her bag on the table, pouring out a cornucopia of seed packages)* So you've got to do something about it, Eddie. *(Reaches down into the bottom of the bag, pulls out small, shiny revolver, holds it out to him)* Ah! Here! Take this. Use it on Roy. Do it simply and cleanly. Aim for the heart. Nothing—primitive, please.

EDDIE: *(Not taking the gun)* I can't kill my own father.

VERNA: Eddie, you've got to. *(She puts the gun down on the table)* There comes a point when men must act, and women simply have to step out of the way. *(Begins scooping things back into her bag)*

EDDIE: You're not leaving, are you?

VERNA: I'm afraid I must.

EDDIE: But where are you going?

VERNA: To take a bath.

EDDIE: There are no bathtubs in this building.

VERNA: There's running water somewhere upstairs.

EDDIE: Verna . . .

VERNA: Eddie, I think I hear Roy's stretch limousine pulling up to a side entrance. Now, please! Spread your wings and fly!

EDDIE: But Verna, if I do this, and if you get your bath, can we still drive out into the cornfields?

VERNA: Oh Eddie. Haven't you learned by now? I'm a woman. Doesn't that answer your question?

EDDIE: Yes, Verna, and I'm a man! That spring chicken, that young capon, that strutting little bantam cock who was crowing around here five minutes ago . . . He's grown up, Verna!

VERNA: Thank God! Otherwise these meetings have been fruitless, and we've all gotten absolutely nowhere! *(She goes out)*

(A noise is heard off, on the opposite side. EDDIE *looks off, quickly takes the gun, puts it in his pocket, turns and faces where the sound came from.* ROY *enters. Pause)*

ROY: I . . . um . . . forgot my briefcase.

EDDIE: Yes . . .

ROY: I believe that is it, right there.

EDDIE: Yes . . .

ROY: I'll just pick it up, then.

EDDIE: All right.

ROY: *(Looking around)* Where's Verna?

EDDIE: Taking a bath.

ROY: Taking a bath?

EDDIE: Trying to, Roy.

ROY: Then the meeting is . . . breaking up?

EDDIE: I'm afraid so. Yes.

ROY: *(Picks up his briefcase, starts off; stops; weighing it in his hand)* This briefcase seems lighter somehow.

EDDIE: Oh yes?

ROY: *(Lifting it up and down)* Lighter than when I brought it.

EDDIE: Oh really?

ROY: Maybe I'm just stronger.

EDDIE: I doubt that, Roy.

ROY: Or else everything isn't here.

EDDIE: Why don't you look and see?

ROY: All right. I will. *(Puts his briefcase back on the table, snaps it open, pokes around inside)*

EDDIE: *(After watching him for a while)* Perhaps this is what you're looking for, Roy. *(Produces the folder)*

(ROY goes to the folder, opens it, looks through it, closes it)

ROY: These are not my papers.

EDDIE: Roy . . .

ROY: This is not my folder.

EDDIE: You came back for that folder, Roy.

ROY: I came back to clear my good name.

EDDIE: You said your briefcase felt lighter, Roy.

ROY: That was a ploy.

EDDIE: A ploy, Roy?

ROY: An excuse to stay around. A sop to my pride. I wanted to rejoin the group.

EDDIE: I don't believe that, Roy.

ROY: I want Verna.

EDDIE: Verna's irrelevant to the discussion, Roy.

ROY: *(Calling off)* Verna!

EDDIE: She can't hear you, Roy.

ROY: *(Calling)* A little help here, Verna!

EDDIE: The splashing of water, that's all she can hear.

ROY: I'll go find her then. *(He starts off)*

EDDIE: *(Pulling out his gun)* She gave me this, Roy.

ROY: She gave you that? That's *my* gun. And my father's before me. That's a family gun. She had no right to give it to you, unless you're my own flesh and . . . *(Pause; then quietly)* Blood.

EDDIE: Hello, Pop.

ROY: You're not going to kill your old man, are ya, boy?

EDDIE: I'm afraid I have to.

ROY: Hey! Hey, kid! Come off it. I'm your pal. I'm your buddy, from way back.

EDDIE: Don't make it tough for me, Dad.

ROY: No, hey, listen, kid. It's not over yet. Want to make model airplanes together? Huh? Huh? I'll hit grounders to you with a fungo bat. I'll take you out in the woods, pal. You can shoot your first bear.

EDDIE: *(Painfully)* Oh Dad . . .

ROY: No, hey, listen. Tell you what. We'll go out on the town, then. You and me, kid. Make the rounds. Have a few beers. Get loaded. Listen to some tunes. Then we'll give Verna a ring. OK? OK, son? The three of us? You and me and Verna?

EDDIE: It's too late for all that, Dad. You should have thought of these things a long time ago. *(Points the gun at* ROY*)*

ROY: *(Protecting himself with his briefcase)* Couldn't we at least work out a compromise? Suppose I plead nolo, and you assign me some sort of community service?

EDDIE: Dad, let me tell you something: if this were a closed session, I suppose you and I could sit down together and work out some sort of a deal. But since it's an open meeting, I imagine everyone here wants and expects me to blow your brains out.

ROY: But why?

EDDIE: Because you have systematically betrayed our group, and the republic for which we stand. Now kneel, and pray, to the deity of your choice.

ROY: *(Dropping to his knees; praying)* Quo vadis . . . e pluribus unum . . . sic semper liberalis . . .

EDDIE: *(To audience)* Did you hear that last one? Is there any question NOW whether he's guilty?

ROY: *(Praying more desperately)* Caveat emptor . . . semper paratus . . . non illegitimis carborundum . . .

(EDDIE *puts the gun to* ROY's *temple. A moment. Then he lowers it slowly)*

EDDIE: I can't do it. *(He goes and slumps in a chair)*

ROY: *(Opening his eyes)* You can't . . . ?

EDDIE: Do it. Oh my God, is this what it all boils down to? The son killing the father while the mother waits offstage? Are we all caught in some grotesque Freudian parody, and is the democratic experience simply the sum of a series of petty patricides, commencing at the local level? How cruel! How horrible to contemplate! How can I contribute to such a grim charade? How can I pull this trigger, except on myself? *(Closes his eyes; points gun at his own temple)*

ROY: *(Slowly getting up; brushing himself off)* Then I win.

EDDIE: Nobody wins, Roy. It's an absurd and meaningless world.

ROY: Go see a psychiatrist, kid. And don't send me the bill, either. Get a job for a change. Start at the bottom, and stay there, for all I care. As for Verna, she's finished, pal. She's taken her last bath. That cheap two-timing whore! It's back into the kitchen for her. I'll have her waxing floors and darning socks. She'll be lucky if she has time to read *Good Housekeeping. (To audience)* And now for you folks: No more meetings! No more gatherings in groups greater than three! No loitering, no littering, no fornication for seventeen days! I'm in control now, gang. Permanently! I call the shots. The sun will rise on my say-so! The moon only shines if I approve. From here on in, I decide who gets into Harvard, who flies first class, and who gets a good review in *The New York Times.*

EDDIE: *(Taking a bead on* ROY *with the gun)* That does it, Roy! It's a meaningless world, Roy, but perhaps I can find meaning in an arbitrary act.

(He pulls the trigger. ROY *reels back.* EDDIE *shoots again and again, vindictively, as* ROY *reels, shudders, groans, collapses.* EDDIE *crosses, kneels and puts the gun on* ROY's *chest, à la* Tosca. VERNA *comes out jauntily, in a fresh, flowered dress. She looks much younger)*

VERNA: *(Brightly)* Oh Eddie, you were wonderful!

EDDIE: *(Kneeling by the body)* This is no time for crowing, Verna. I'm lost in a mood of sober contemplation and regret.

VERNA: Now don't be silly.

EDDIE: I've killed Roy, Verna.

VERNA: Nonsense. I put blanks in that revolver. I don't believe in the use of real bullets on stage.

EDDIE: But then . . . how . . . ?

VERNA: Perhaps I'd better explain.

EDDIE: Perhaps you'd better.

VERNA: First of all, *I* shot Roy.

EDDIE: You?

VERNA: I took a bead on him from off in the wings. See that smoking gun out there, leaning against that radiator? I used that. But I didn't *kill* him, Eddie. I got him in the right buttock with one of those tranquilizing darts they use on rhinoceri in the game preserves of Kenya. *(She reaches down, pulls the dart out of* ROY's *rear; holds it up)* See? *(She puts it in her purse)* Oh, he'll be a little sore for a while, but he'll end up fine. (ROY *stirs)* Look. He's coming around.

EDDIE: I'm confused, Verna. I need further explanation.

VERNA: Here's what happened. While I was out there, taking a bath, Dick telephoned and wanted to know what was going on. I told him what we had accomplished so far. He felt the meeting was getting out of hand. So he suggested neutralizing Roy. He had the tranquilizing gun sent over by the local chapter of the C.I.A.

(ROY *gets woozily to his feet, rubs his rear*)

EDDIE: So Dick was behind this?

VERNA: Exactly. He said these meetings are getting nowhere. He thinks we're constantly getting off the track. Enough is enough, he said.

EDDIE: I'm beginning to feel a little manipulated, Verna.

VERNA: I'm sure you do. But think how Roy must feel. (ROY *tries to sit down, can't*) Roy, darling, look what I have here. *(She takes an airline ticket out of her purse)* This is a plane ticket to Florida, sweetie pie. Business class. Now you go down there and find yourself a nice condo on some backwater canal, and putter around happily ever after. Here you go, sweetheart. *(Hands him the ticket)*

EDDIE: I suppose Dick also arranged for that plane ticket.

VERNA: No, I did. But Dick said he'd reimburse me later with taxpayer's money.

EDDIE: That irritates me too, Verna!

VERNA: Oh now, Eddie. Dick said he was perfectly willing to do favors for people, but in return he hoped we'd give up these open meetings, and leave the responsibilities of government to elected representatives like himself.

EDDIE: I consider all this extremely manipulative! It seems that Washington is totally pulling the strings. *(Puts his arms around* ROY) I feel a new sympathy for Roy here, jerked around as he has been by Dick. You also, Verna, seem to have become putty in Dick's hands.

VERNA: You may have a point.

EDDIE: These meetings may be inefficient, they may be confused, they may take us in strange directions, but we should all, all of us, take steps to preserve their viability.

VERNA: Well they do help us let off steam, don't they?

ROY: *(Woozily)* I want to go to Florida.

EDDIE: All right, old friend. I understand. Your days are over in this arena. I can see this is a battle my generation will have to fight by itself.

VERNA: *(Kissing* ROY *on the cheek)* There's a taxi waiting to take you to the airport, lovey. Have a wonderful trip. And don't flirt with the flight attendants. (VERNA *and* EDDIE *gently point* ROY *offstage)* Eddie, you mentioned something about taking steps.

EDDIE: Yes I did. I plan to go down to Washington and remind Dick, face to face, that democracy begins and ends at the grass roots level.

VERNA: Oh Eddie, don't go to Washington. I'm scared.

EDDIE: Are you scared Dick will have me killed?

VERNA: No, I'm scared you'll become just like him.

EDDIE: That will never happen, Verna.

VERNA: It might. After all, you're his brother.

EDDIE: I've learned tonight that every man is my brother, Verna. And every woman, too.

VERNA: Maybe so, but that kind of thinking can turn you into a lousy lover.

EDDIE: It's a chance I'll have to take, Verna. Good-bye for now.

VERNA: Good-bye, Eddie. *(They kiss, then* EDDIE *leaves. A pause. Then* VERNA *turns to the audience)* Well. That's that. All told, I think this has been a very successful meeting. We'll see you in the fall. Meanwhile, if anyone's interested in getting out into those cornfields, please see me afterwards. I'm beginning to think we could use a little new blood around here. *(She goes off)*

(Curtain)

SUCCESS

Arthur Kopit

Arthur Kopit

Arthur Kopit was the first of the wunderkind to appear in the American theater of the sixties. During his education in engineering and applied sciences at Harvard (McNally was at Columbia, Albee at Trinity, van Itallie at Harvard, Shepard at the bars, farms and beaches), he won two playwriting contests, had nine plays produced, directed six of his own plays, won a Shaw Traveling Fellowship for a post-graduate course in travel around Europe, had a play published by the *Harvard Advocate,* and had his play *Oh Dad, Poor Dad, Mamma's Hung You in the Closet and I'm Feelin' So Sad: A PseudoClassical Tragifarce in a Bastard French Tradition* produced by a Harvard undergraduate group in January, 1960. That production aroused the interest of the entire New York theater community, resulting in a pilgrimage to Harvard to see (and capture!) the work of the talent that was making such a fuss. A similar pilgrimage had taken place in 1923 when Thomas Woolf, at that time a student of George Pierce Baker, created exactly the same kind of response from the New York theater community with his play *Welcome to Our City.* In Kopit's case, Roger Stevens was the victorious producer, and he produced the play first in London and then off Broadway in 1962. Although the title became the subject of tiresome jokes, the play won the Vernon Rice and Outer Critics Circle Awards.

Kopit followed this success with a number of Tony-nominated plays: *Indians* in 1969, *Wings* in 1978, and the book for *Nine,* which won the 1982 Tony Award for Best Musical. His play *End of the World,* starring John Shea and directed by Hal Prince, was a major event of the 1983–1984 Broadway season, as his *Road to Nirvana* was a major project for Circle Rep in 1990, following its production at the Actors Theater of Louisville under the title *Bone-the Fish.* The musical *Phantom,* for which he wrote the book and Murray Yeston the music and lyrics, was produced in Houston in 1991 at the Theater Under the Stars and is scheduled to start touring the country in late spring, 1992. His latest play, *Discovery in America,* is scheduled for production by the Mark Taper Forum in Los Angeles. Mr. Kopit is married to the writer Leslie Garis and lives in Connecticut with their children, Alex, Ben and Kathleen.

Characters:

MRS. HOFFENSBERG
ELIOT ELIZALDE KRUM
WOMAN IN AUDIENCE

Scene:

At rise, we see a banquet room in a hotel, lectern downstage center, two chairs downstage right. At the rear, huge windows. Beyond, an iridescent blue sky. Because of this blazing light, at the moment, the objects on stage are in silhouette. Beyond the windows, sound of surf can be heard. Lights come up on the podium, as—

Two people enter from the wings. One is MRS. HOFFENSBERG, *stout, in her sixties at least. In one hand she clutches a book. Her other arm is linked through an arm of* ELIOT ELIZALDE KRUM, *a man of about forty, wearing a wrinkled raincoat.*

Applause greets their entrance. On hearing it, HOFFENSBERG *looks at the audience, then proudly at* KRUM, *smiles, and guides him to one of the two chairs downstage right. He takes off his raincoat, sits, folds the coat neatly across his lap, and stares out with an expression of some alarm—an alarm that grows by the moment.*

HOFFENSBERG *goes to the podium and adjusts some notes she has brought with her. Then she clears her throat and smiles to the assembled throng. Sound of applause is heard again. This time,* KRUM *applauds, too, though only slightly, as if it were merely an imitative action, of no meaning by itself.*

HOFFENSBERG: I had the great honor of meeting Eliot Krum two weeks ago at San Francisco State College where he was delivering a . . .

(Her words grow indistinct. The sound of the surf returns. Over this sound, the sound of thunderous applause at whatever MRS. HOFFENSBERG *is now saying. Presently, the sound of applause grows distant; then it and the sound of surf disappear)*

I found Mr. Krum at that time to be a man of both subtle . . .

(And again her words disappear behind the sound of surf. MRS. HOFFENSBERG *holds up her book and, smiling, glances toward* KRUM. *Then, looking back to her audience, opens the book to its last page, looks soberly out at her audience, then back at the book, and reads what is obviously to*

her a very moving last paragraph. Finished, she closes the book and looks up at the audience. Not a sound. Not a movement. Then . . . applause. MRS. HOFFENSBERG *looks over at* KRUM, *who does not move. Apparently, she has just introduced him. She says his name again. This time, it is barely audible. Then it comes through louder. He stirs. He has recognized the sound of his name. She smiles at him and he rises. As he does, she says—)*

. . . Eliot Krum!

(Wild applause as KRUM *assumes the lectern, spreads out his notes, arranges them, then looks over his audience. Smiles. Clears his throat. Opens his mouth. Nothing. Closes his mouth. Frowning, he reaches for a glass of water. Takes a sip. Puts down the glass. Ponders. Opens his mouth. Studies his audience for clues. Finds none)*

KRUM: Would someone be so kind . . . as to tell me . . . what . . . city . . . this is?

(Laughter)

VARIOUS WOMEN: *(Together)* SANTA MONICA!

KRUM: Santa Monica! Well, well—*(Laughter from audience)* And what . . . *organization* . . . might this be? *(Louder laughter, wild applause)*

HOFFENSBERG: *(To the audience, laughing)* Mr. Krum has been in such recent demand on the lecture circuit that it seems he no longer knows whereof he speaks! *(Laughter and applause)*

KRUM: Actually, it doesn't really matter. No one seems surprised that I'm here, so apparently I'm in the right place. *(Again, more laughter and applause. He shuffles his notes)* . . . I thought I'd just ramble on a bit this afternoon, explore a few areas suggested by my book, then open up the floor to relevant and exciting questions, if that meets with the approval of you ladies and—*(He peers around his audience for men; finds one)* . . . gentleman. First, however, I'd like to thank my gracious host, the lovely Miss, umm—

HOFFENSBERG: *(Sotto voce)* Mrs.

KRUM: Mrs., umm—

HOFFENSBERG: Hoffensberg.

KRUM: Hoffensberg, yes, for bringing me to this delightful spot, wherever it is, and . . . all of *you*, . . . whoever . . . you are. Indeed, had I not had the great fortune to meet Mrs., uh, . . . let me write that down.

HOFFENSBERG: Hoffensberg.

KRUM: "Hoffensberg." Indeed, had I not had the great fortune to meet Mrs.—*(He glances at his note)*—Hoffensberg some . . . while ago at . . . some . . . place or other, who knows where I'd be today? *(Pause)* To Mrs. . . . H then, my heartfelt thanks and solid reassurance that in the scrapbook of my mind, she will live forever. Certainly, I shall always cherish the memory of our first conversation. As I recall, immediately, upon taking me aside, she unbuttoned her blouse—

HOFFENSBERG: WHAT?

(Long pause)

KRUM: Ladies, . . . as the former president of a well-known West Coast university once aptly said—sometime, I believe, in the sixties: "It appears I am no longer in possession of my faculties." . . .

Now, I am not particularly *pleased* with this condition. Nor, obviously, are you. Certainly, when you invited me here today, as a leading literary light, you surely did not expect to find the light quite so flickering, if not dim. How has it come about, this dismal state?

Well, frankly, it's none of your business. Nonetheless, I will tell you, it has definitely not been helped by my recent madcap schedule, set up at the behest of my fiendish publisher, a relentlessly charming man, whom I shall try my very best to strangle the next time we meet. You see, for the past several months—six, seven, eight, who can say?—it seems I have been doing nothing but going from one strange place to another talking about this goddamn book of mine—a book I could hardly bear when I was writing, so imagine how I like it now! Which is why, today, I thought I would discuss football. *(He clears his throat)*

Football, as I see it, is one of our most—*(Pause)* . . . Or is it? *(Pause)* No! It's not at all, NOT AT ALL! Why would I think it *was*? QUESTION! YES! No? Thought I saw a hand, clutching, upwards. Ladies, for God's sake, I will give you back my fee, assuming you had planned to give me one, but let me out of this! It is an embarrassment to us all!

. . . Except, of course, to Mrs. H, who's shown herself to be beyond embarrassment, and whose bizarre bosom has, these last few weeks, played such a vital role in the continuation of my thought processes.

HOFFENSBERG: WHAT?

KRUM: Sorry. Slipped out. Didn't mean to mention it. Forget I ever said a word. So, what shall we talk about? MY BOOK! Yes. Why not? Ladies, in all candor, the extraordinary popular success of my book has not only taken me completely by surprise, but apparently, has taken my mind along with it. Surely ladies, *surely,* an eight-hundred-and-fifty-page book about suicide—*(He has a sudden and terrible coughing fit; reaches for some water; gains control; takes out a pill, pops it in his mouth, sips some water, puts the glass back down)*—about . . . suicide . . . would not seem, at first glance, a likely candidate for the bestseller list. And yet!—unless there is some enormous and rather peculiar hoax going on—there it is! Top o' the list! Thirty-fourth straight week! And I am rich. And getting laid like crazy. Mind you, not that sex means that much to me, but in my seven years as a rabbi in Bridgeport, and my three as a priest in New Rochelle, I would say I got laid no more than ten, twelve times maximum, and that includes four nuns and a mother superior I ravaged on my last official day, which, as those of you who've read my little volume know, was the first day of Lent, yes, question.

WOMAN IN AUDIENCE: Do you really expect us to sit here and listen to this crap?

KRUM: I'm sorry, I am *very sorry,* but I have not come all this way just to be insulted! To continue. After serving my three years as a priest in a mostly Jewish neighborhood, right on the heels of having served seven as a rabbi in a mostly Catholic, I made the first of my many suicide attempts. Ate seventeen of Mrs. Smith's jumbo apple pies, followed by twelve Sara Lee pound cakes. When this failed to finish me, I became a psychiatrist. In Mamaroneck.

SAME WOMAN: Mr. Krum!

KRUM: QUESTION!

SAME WOMAN: You don't seem to understand: we have all *read* your book. Which means we *know* your background. And your background is *not this.*

KRUM: . . . It's not?

SAME WOMAN: No.

(Silence)

KRUM: Are you . . . sure we're talking about . . . the *same book?*

SAME WOMAN: *The Gods of War,* by E. E. Krum.

KRUM: Or "Eeeek," as they used to call me in kindergarten!

SAME WOMAN: This *is* your book, then.

KRUM: Definitely. But please, feel free to keep it. To continue! As a psychiatrist, in Mamaroneck—

SAME WOMAN: MR. KRUM!

KRUM: Heavens, you're a pest.

SAME WOMAN: According to this book, you never were a rabbi. Never a priest. And never a psychiatrist.

KRUM: JUST WHAT ARE YOU TRYING TO SAY?

(Pause)

SAME WOMAN: That . . . you never were a rabbi. Never a priest. And never a psychiatrist.

KRUM: I see. *(Pause)* Well, this is certainly a very startling piece of news.

SAME WOMAN: To us, especially.

KRUM: Was I a . . . *baseball* player?

SAME WOMAN: No. Sorry.

KRUM: Dentist?

SAME WOMAN: Perhaps you should read your book.

KRUM: What, eight hundred pages, about suicide? You must think I'm mad!

SAME WOMAN: Mr. Krum, frankly, I was very moved by your book. It is really a most astonishing account of a man's constant battle against despair.

KRUM: Sounds amusing.

SAME WOMAN: It isn't.

KRUM: Was it illustrated?

SAME WOMAN: Not *my* copy.

KRUM: Well why'd you read it then? *(Silence)* Why'd *any* of you read it? *(Silence)* I don't understand this. Have you all nothing better to do with your time? *(Silence)* All right, come now, truthfully, game's over. How many of you actually read it, raise your hands. Let's go. Hands. Hands. *(He looks at what would appear to be a sea of hands)* Well, this makes no sense. No sense at all. And it's been the same everywhere. *What are you people doing?* I'd *NEVER* buy a book like that. It's the most lugubrious thing imaginable. You should be home, fucking. Not reading. You'll ruin your eyes! You wanna go blind? What's wrong with you people? *I can't take this anymore!* Yes. Question. Sorry. Thought you had a question. Oh God, this isn't right, isn't right. I'm fading, fading . . . *(Pause)* Fading . . . *(Very long pause) Faded.* *(Pause)* Ladies . . . Gentleman. Forgive me. But I find I just can't speak anymore today. *(He turns, goes to one of the windows and opens it. Sound of surf. He leaps. Lights to original position, with only the iridescent sky lit, all else in silhouette. No movement. Blackout)*

PRELUDE AND LIEBESTOD

Terrence McNally

Prelude and Liebestod was originally produced on the stage by the Manhattan Class Company.

Terrence McNally

Born in Florida in 1939, Terrence McNally was brought up in Texas and educated at Columbia. Although he had been smitten with the theater bug while in Texas, it was during his Columbia education that he became infected with the Broadway virus. Arthur Ballet, former head of the office for Advanced Drama Research project in Minneapolis, has written about McNally:

> His career is a chronicle of recent American theatrical action—starting off with some ill-fated Broadway productions, removing them to phenomenally successful runs off Broadway, and eventually into the mainstream of collegiate and regional theater in the United States. Finally . . . the process is reversing, and a major American dramatist is making his way back to the Big Time.

The last few years attest to the accuracy of Ballet's statement. *Lips Together, Teeth Apart* played to packed houses for months at the Manhattan Theater Club and then moved to the Lucille Lortel Theater, where it has continued to pack them in. After an extended run off Broadway, *The Lisbon Traviata* opened in San Francisco and Los Angeles in the fall of 1990, where it continued its successful run. His earlier play *Frankie and Johnny in the Clair De Lune* enjoyed great success at the Manhattan Theater Club and then opened in London's West End, where it was presented in a 1000-seat house. The screen adaptation of that play, written by Mr. McNally, was produced by Paramount, starring Al Pacino and Michelle Pfeiffer. McNally wrote the book for Kander and Ebb's musical adaptation of *Kiss of the Spiderwoman,* scheduled to open in Toronto during the summer of 1992 in a production directed by Harold Prince. His other major plays include *It's Only a Play, Bad Habits, Sweet Eros, The Ritz, Where Has Tommy Flowers Gone?, And Things That Go Bump in The Night, Next* and *Whiskey.* He wrote the book for the Broadway musical *The Rink* and a host of television plays including *Andre's Mother,* a 1990 Emmy winner. He is the recipient of two Guggenheim Fellowships, a Rockefeller Grant, a citation from the American Academy of Arts and Letters, and currently serves as vice-president of the Dramatists Guild Council.

Characters:

CONDUCTOR, *magnetic, animal, sexual, charismatic. Makes heads turn.*

CONDUCTOR'S WIFE, *beautiful, immaculate, somewhat unapproachable. Her looks are her defense.*

SOPRANO, *thinks she has all the answers and knows the score. Actually terrified of failure.*

CONCERTMASTER, *an excellent musician, though loaded with bile and spite.*

MAN, *his personality is defined by his attraction for the Conductor. A protogroupie.*

Scene:

The place of the play is various environs of a large concert hall. Though the setting is necessarily abstract, the individual playing areas should be sharply defined and specific. The time of the play is now. Lights come up on a conductor's podium, a small, square raised platform about fifteen inches high. There is a waist-high railing running the length of the upstage side of it. Sounds of a symphony orchestra tuning up at random. Spot up on a beautiful woman in a box seat somewhat upstage of the podium. She is the CONDUCTOR'S WIFE. She is perfectly dressed. She looks at her program. She looks at her watch. She looks at the orchestra in the orchestra level below her. She looks up at the higher tiers and balcony above her.

Spot up on a MAN in an orchestra-level seat stage left, also somewhat upstage of the CONDUCTOR'S podium. He is looking at the CONDUCTOR'S WIFE through a pair of opera glasses. She is not aware of this. Spot up on the CONCERTMASTER, who is seated in a chair just a little downstage right of the podium. He raps with his bow on his violin stand and gives the note. An unseen symphony orchestra tunes up to his note. The CONDUCTOR'S WIFE opens her purse and takes out a small box of mints. The MAN continues to stare at her through the opera glasses. At the same time, he reaches in his breast pocket and takes out a roll of Life Savers.

The houselights dim in the concert hall where the CONDUCTOR'S WIFE and MAN are sitting. At the same time, the lights will come up on the concert stage, that is, the theater itself. A spotlight hits a door leading to the backstage area. After a longer time than necessary, it is opened by unseen hands, and the SOPRANO enters to strong applause. She is in full regalia. As the SOPRANO moves towards the podium, she smiles at the unseen orchestra. The CONCERTMASTER taps his bow on his stand in approval. The SOPRANO turns her back to the orchestra (and us, in doing so) and bows deeply to heavy applause. Now the SOPRANO makes a great deal of arranging the panels of her dress and stole as she finally sits in a chair just left and a little downstage

*of the podium. Her back will be to us, but we will see her in profile as she
turns from time to time to take a sip of water from a glass on a low table next
to her chair or turns to the other side to smile at the* CONCERTMASTER.

*Silence. The spotlight has gone again to the door leading to the backstage
area. It waits there. Again the door is opened by unseen hands. No one
appears. Silence in the auditorium. Someone coughs. Someone else shushes
them. The door starts to swing shut, then is swiftly pulled wide open as the*
CONCERTOR *hurries through. Tumultuous applause. The* CONDUCTOR *moves
swiftly to podium and bows deeply. The* MAN *has risen and is clapping
wildly.*

MAN: Bravo! Bravo!

(CONDUCTOR'S WIFE *is applauding.* CONDUCTOR *leaps off the podium and
goes to* CONCERTMASTER *and shakes his hand vigorously. The ovation continues as* CONDUCTOR *crosses to* SOPRANO *and kisses her hand, then cheek.*
MAN *continues to stand and applaud)*

MAN: Bravo! Bravo!

(CONDUCTOR'S WIFE *has stopped applauding.* CONDUCTOR *has returned to
podium for final bow to audience (which means his back is to us) as
applause begins to diminish.* MAN *continues to stand and applaud. This
time his voice is especially prominent as the general ovation continues to
subside)*

MAN: Bravo! Bravo!

(CONDUCTOR *looks to* MAN. *Eye contact is made.* CONDUCTOR'S WIFE *looks
at* MAN. CONDUCTOR *looks up at* WIFE *and smiles, then turns his back to
concert-hall audience and faces orchestra (us).* CONDUCTOR *is delighted
with his reception. He gives orchestra members a self-deprecating grin and
raised eyebrows. Silence. He gets serious. He passes his hands over his
face. He takes a deep breath)*

MAN: *(Shattering the silence)* We love you!

(CONDUCTOR *ignores this. Angry shushes from audience.* CONDUCTOR
*reaches to music stand in front of him and closes the score. Gasps and
whispers from the audience. He picks up the baton. He raises both arms.
He waits. He throws the baton onto the music stand and raises both arms*

again, but this time gives the downbeat almost at once. Wagner's Prelude to Tristan und Isolde *is off and running)*

CONDUCTOR: *(After the fourth rest)* I love these pauses . . . Come on, you suckers, play for me. Play through me, music. Course through me. Surge. Fill me. I am you. This is it . . . God, that was good. Now we're off and running. I'm up here already. That was quick. I like it up here. The view is glorious. Fill, lungs. Heave, bosom. Burst, heart.

(At this point, the sound of the orchestra is considerably diminished and CONDUCTOR *will seem to be speaking from within his own private place. The music will be more of a "surround" than a presence)*

There were no empty seats. Clean as a whistle. There's no one better than me. Is there? No one even close. God, I love Wagner. That one in the fifth row. I've seen him. Where? In your dreams, asshole. We don't do that anymore. You wanna bet? Oh, shut up! Hey, third cello, look at me! Yes, you! Where did they find you? Yes, you're too loud. You think I'd be looking at you like this if you weren't? Jesus, where was I? Sometimes I think I do this on automatic. There we are, right on target! Somebody up there likes me. Yeah, Wagner, asshole. The big *Kraut in das Himmel* himself. I feel his eyes burning right into my back. He's mentally undressing me. They all are. All 2,187 of them plus the 131 in standing room. Maybe I could steal a look. Are you crazy? She's right up there in a box. She's always right up there in a box. I'd like to see her in a box. It's her box I'm sick of. You don't mean that. I don't mean that. You love her. I love you. *(He looks over his shoulder to* WIFE *who is reading something in her program)* She's reading! The fucking bitch is reading and you're conducting your fucking ass off. Fuck that shit. Bitch. You wanted to be married. No, you wanted to have children. You have to be married to have children. No, you have to be married to have children if you want to be the principal conductor of a big symphony orchestra with a big stuffy endowment. You're pissed off because you've got the hots for some groupie in the fifth row and *your* goddamn wife is right up there watching every move you make. Eagle eyes. Bionic ears. She can see and hear through lead walls if I'm talking to another man. It's one thing to be straight; it's another to be in a straight jacket. *(Suddenly aware of* CONCERTMASTER*)* What are you looking at, asshole? I swear to God, sometimes I think he's calling me an asshole under his breath through the whole concert.

CONCERTMASTER: Asshole.

CONDUCTOR: There! Right now! I'm positive he's doing it. I'd like to see him get up here and conduct, he thinks he's so great. They probably all think they can conduct better than me. Sorry to disillusion you, assholes! That's why I'm up here and you're down there. Whoever said it was right: it is lonely at the top. It's lonely anywhere.

MAN: Look at me. You know I'm here.

WIFE: *(Still looking at program)* Now that is what I call a stunning outfit. Oscar de la Renta. I should have guessed.

CONCERTMASTER: Asshole!

SOPRANO: Fuck you, too!

CONCERTMASTER: I wasn't talking to you.

SOPRANO: What did I do to him? I'm sorry, but we can't all be Kirsten Fucking Flagstad.

MAN: Turn around. You know you want to.

CONDUCTOR: He's talking to you. Go ahead. This climax. It's a perfect place. Shit! I can't. You blew it, asshole.

MAN: You know what I'd do if I had you alone with me? I have it all planned. I'd start with a button. This button. *(He touches his collar button)* Pop!

WIFE: Oh God, I hope Ralph can get away for that weekend when he's conducting in London. I don't think I can stand another week without him. I wonder what he'd do if he knew. Kill me. Punish me through the children. Both.

CONDUCTOR: Turn, turn, turn. To everything there is a season. The Beatles? The Turtles? Ten minutes with someone like that. Less. It doesn't take long. I want you so bad, fifth row.

CONCERTMASTER: Bloody, bleeding, blooming asshole.

CONDUCTOR: If I had a face like yours I'd kill myself.

SOPRANO: It's nearly me. There's got to be better ways to earn a living.

CONDUCTOR: Why did you have to be out there tonight, fatal beauty, or why did you have to be up there, faithful adoring wife? Why couldn't tonight be next week in London? I'm doing the Mahler Ninth. I'm always so drained after the Mahler Ninth. Drained and horny.

MAN: Look at me. They say if you stare at someone's left earlobe long enough eventually it begins to burn a hole and they turn around.

CONDUCTOR: It's all in the music. The longing, the learning. The impossibility. I am loved. I want to love. I've never found anyone as interesting as me. As lovable. As worthy of my undivided attention. Fifth row is one thing, her up there is another. I'm talking about a whole other kettle of fish. *(The Prelude is drawing to an end.* SOPRANO *stands and makes ready to sing)* Good God, it's her turn already. Come on, cow, sing it, swing it, shake it, bend it.

MAN: Maybe it's the right earlobe.

*(*SOPRANO *begins to sing. At first the music will be at concert-hall volume, then subside to the level of the Prelude. Although her back is to us throughout, it should be clear that* SOPRANO *is deeply involved with singing and communicating with her audience out front)*

CONCERTMASTER: You're flat. Get up there, get up there!

WIFE: Now that's a gorgeous voice.

MAN: Sharp as ever.

CONDUCTOR: You're singing through the wrong hole, honey. This is twat music. Listen to it. Listen to the words. God, if I had your instrument!

SOPRANO: Place the tone properly. Support it. Always legato. Thatta girl.

WIFE: If I could sing like that!

MAN: They like her! They actually like her!

CONCERTMASTER: That's more like it.

   (Surtitles will appear throughout)

SURTITLE: "Mild und leise wie er lachelt,
              wie das Auge hold er offnet,
              seht ihr's, Freund? Seht ihr's nicht?
              Immer lichter, wie er leuchtet,
              stern-umstrahlet hoch sich hebt?
              Seht ihr's nicht?"

CONDUCTOR: Do you know what the words mean? Sing it like you know what it meant. It's about love. It's about dying. It's about trans-fan-fucking-figuration. Sing it like you meant it.

SURTITLE: "Wie das Herz ihm mutig schwillt,
voll und hehr im Busen ihm quillt?
Wie den Lippen, wonnig mild,
susser Atem sanft entweht,
Freunde! Seht! Fuhlt und seht ihr's nicht?"

CONDUCTOR: This is not enough. Conducting it is not enough. Singing it is not enough. Writing it is not enough. Experience it. Love-death. Love-death. *Liebestod.*

CONCERTMASTER: What is he doing?

CONDUCTOR: You're behind, honey, catch up, catch up!

SOPRANO: This is not the tempo we agreed—!

WIFE: That man looks like Ralph.

MAN: He's losing you, lady.

CONDUCTOR: Who do you love the most? Who do you love the best?

SURTITLE: "Hore ich nur diese Wiese
die so wundervoll und leise,
Wonne klagend, alles sagend,
mild versohnend aus ihm tonend,
in mich dringet, auf sich schwinget,
hold erhallend um mich klinget?
Heller schallend, mich unwallend,
sind es Wallen sanfter Lufte?
Sind es Wogen wonniger Dufte?"

CONDUCTOR: What is transfiguration but an orgasm coupled with a heart attack?

SURTITLE: "Wie sie schwellen, mich umrauschen,
soll ich atmen, soll ich laushen?
Soll ich schlurfen, untertauchen?
Suss in Duften mich verhauchen?"

CONDUCTOR: Wagner knew a lot about fucking. I bet that guy in the fifth row does, too. My wife knows nothing about fucking. I'd like to fuck the entire world. No, I'd like to fuck every attractive man, woman and child in the world. Child over eleven. No, fourteen. Fifteen, fifteen. Fuck it.

SURTITLE: "In dem wogenden Schwall, in dem tonenden Schall,
in des Welt-Atems wehendem All
ertrinken, versinken—
unbewusst, hochste Lust—"

CONDUCTOR: It's over already. Shit. I don't even remember it beginning.

(Long pause as music fades to silence)

WIFE: Oh shit, now the Bruckner Fourth.

CONCERTMASTER: Oh shit, now the Bruckner Fourth.

SOPRANO: Isn't anybody going to clap?

MAN: Now he's got to turn around.

(Ovation begins. A tremendous one. CONDUCTOR *doesn't move. Instead, he remains with his back to concert hall-audience.* SOPRANO *accepts ovation with great humility)*

MAN: *(Above all the others)* We love you!

*(*CONDUCTOR *picks up baton and raps with it)*

CONDUCTOR: Again! From the top

CONCERTMASTER: But—!

*(*CONDUCTOR *gives downbeat.* SOPRANO *looks startled but takes her seat.* MAN *sits.* WIFE *remains standing in her box, looking concerned, but will eventually sit. The* Tristan Prelude *will seem very loud at first. It will finally settle at the same level of volume as previous rendition of it)*

CONDUCTOR: Give them profile. Feed it to them. They love your profile. Move the body. They come for body movement. Those fabulous, famous, far-reaching shoulders. Magnificent arms of a mighty torso. High flying adored. You and Evita! Wiggle your ass. Tight firm buttocks worthy of someone half your age. Make them think about your cock and balls. Are they large? Is he clipped? Is he good? I'm terrific, baby. Ask her. Ask him. Ask anyone who's had the pleasure of my acquaintance. It's them who don't measure up. It's them who fail me.

They're fucking me. Taking. Drawing my strength. Where's my equal? My match? I'm so alone. Up here. Everywhere. I really love this pause. What is this music really about? What is anything really about? I don't think this is such a great theme. I've written better, but he's Richard Wagner—big fucking deal—and I am Marie of Rumania—big fucking deal. This music always makes me think of certain kinds of sex. Hot late-afternoon damp sheets sweaty grunting people outside blinds drawn dark dirty make it last as long as you can come crazy, scream, rip the sheets, howl like a werewolf, hurt him, hurt her, ouchy kind of sex. This will be in all the papers tomorrow. For twenty-four hours I'll be the most famous person in the world. Forty-eight maybe. Seventy-two. Then next week, when the magazines come out, there will be a new spurt of fame. Then a gradual subsiding until the first major memorial service. A plaque will go up somewhere. Probably outside the hall. God knows, no one ever, anywhere, ever again will listen to this music without thinking of me. *(He glances at* WIFE. *Their eyes meet and hold)* You had the most beautiful skin and breasts and throat and everything when we met. They weren't enough. Nothing has ever been enough. The children. They're not real. Real in themselves but not real to me. Nothing, no one is real enough. I am the only person in the world, and I cannot bear the pain of being so alone. I'm only alive when I come—the way I want to be alive—ecstatic, half-conscious, eyes closed, brain flaring, words, thoughts inadequate. *(He glances at the* MAN*)* The only satisfying sexual experience I ever had was with a man.

MAN: Finally.

CONDUCTOR: The kind of sexual experience this music is about.

CONCERTMASTER: This is more like it.

WIFE: Go on.

SOPRANO: I hate it when they look at me.

CONDUCTOR: I was twenty-two years old, studying in Milan, already made my debut in Salzburg that summer, an instant sensation, the old fool got sick, I took over, the Bruckner Fourth and the *Pathetique* . . . God, that would have been next on the program, I loathe Bruckner! Who couldn't conduct the *Pathetique?* The toast of Europe. God, I was handsome that year. I could spend hours in front of the mirror talking to myself. I'd make faces. Scowl, smile. Flirt with myself. I could even get myself hard. This bastard—what was his name?—he was a journal-

ist, political. . . . The apartment was near the Piazza della Republica.
. . . It was over a pharmacy. . . . The steps were exhausting . . .
deep, steep Renaissance steps. . . . There was a terra-cotta Madonna
in the apartment. . . . He said it was a Lucca della Robbia, and I
wanted to believe him. . . . God, I was already so famous but I was
still so easily impressed! . . . What the fuck was your name?

MAN: Giorgio, Piero, Giacomo, Giuseppe, Gaetano.

WIFE: Does it matter?

CONCERTMASTER: Asshole!

MAN: Carlo, Mario, Fausto, Arturo, Vittorio, Fred.

CONDUCTOR: Guglielmo! Guglielmo Tell. Kidding, kidding. No, I'm not.
Guglielmo Bianchini. He knew who I was. He must have. Everyone
did. My picture was everywhere that summer. I was so beautiful that
year—I was perfect—I was all I wanted—all anyone could ever possibly want—and this cocksucker, this arrogant wop, this goddamn glorious dago, he led me on and on and on. A touch, a glance, a brush of
thigh, but no more. I wasn't even sure he was queer. Weeks went on
like this. Torture. No one knew why I was staying in Milan. I'm doing
research. What research? You know everything. It's true. I did. About
music. But the promise of this person kept me on.

WIFE: My poor darling.

MAN: After the concert, when I ask for your autograph, I will pass you a
slip of paper with my telephone number on it. No name, just a number. You'll know what to do with it.

SOPRANO: I better be paid twice for this. And I'm certainly not singing the
Tannhäuser for an encore.

CONCERTMASTER: Asshole, asshole, asshole.

CONDUCTOR: Finally, there was a weekend when his father, a widower and
some sort of famous judge or lawyer, would be out of town at their
place in Como. I went to the apartment. The door was ajar. There was
no sign of him. I wandered through the empty apartment. It had been
a palazzo. Everything was huge—molded, sculpted, ornate. I went into
a bedroom—it must have been the father's—yes, that is where the
Lucca della Robbia was and I stood looking at this enormous bed and

then I felt—I feel!—hands on me from behind. I didn't turn around. Don't want to.

(The SOPRANO *stands and begins to sing the* Liebestod *again. Only this time the surtitles will be in English)*

Hands here, hands there. Hands over my eyes, hands over my mouth. Four hands. Someone else is there. I didn't struggle. My clothes are being taken off—were being taken off—I don't know what tense I'm in —what tense I want to be in—The past is too painful, the present too forlorn—and I am being stripped and stroked and I am blindfolded and I am led to the bed and my cock is so hard and I am put on the bed and I let myself be tied spreadeagle to it—No one has ever done this to me and I do not resist—And when it is done I am left there for what seems like hours and my hard-on will not subside and once it even threatens to explode and I pray to the unseen Della Robbia Madonna above me not to let me come and I know this is blasphemy and I know that she forgives and understands because she is a good mother—all mothers are good mothers—and oh, it is so unimaginably tense to be there like that with him.

SOPRANO: "How gently and quietly he smiles,
　　　　how fondly he opens his eyes!
　　　　See you, friends? Do you not see?
　　　　How he shines ever higher,
　　　　soaring on high, stars sparkling around him?
　　　　Do you not see?
　　　　How his heart proudly swells
　　　　and, brave and full, pulses in his breast?
　　　　How softly and gently from his lips
　　　　sweet breath flutters:—
　　　　see, friends! Do you not feel and see it?
　　　　Do I alone hear this melody
　　　　which, so wondrous and tender
　　　　in its blissful lament, all-revealing,
　　　　gently pardoning, sounding from him,
　　　　pierces me through, rises above,
　　　　blessedly echoing and ringing round me?"

CONDUCTOR: And after a while I am unblindfolded and see my captors— Guglielmo and a young woman who can only be his twin sister; she is a feminine mirror image of him—and they are both nude and more beautiful than anyone I have ever seen—more beautiful than even I was that summer—and she straddles me and lowers herself on my cock very slowly just once and I almost come but I pray and then he— Guglielmo—what an absurd name!—puts his mouth on my cock and moves it up and down the length of it just once and again I almost come and have to pray and then they both just looked at me and I said, "Please, make me come." *"Prego, farmi morire"* is what I said. "Please make me die." I didn't know the Italian for "come," you see. *"Prego, farmi morire."*

SOPRANO: "Resounding yet more clearly, wafting about me,
         are they waves of refreshing breezes?
         Are they clouds of heavenly fragrance?
         As they swell and roar round me,
         shall I breathe them, shall I listen to them?"

CONDUCTOR: And they just smiled at each other. He kissed one of her breasts. She touched his cock. I knew they weren't really twins. I wondered if they were even brother and sister. She took her panties, pink, and ran them the length of my body, toe to head. Then she very slowly pushed them into my mouth, gagging me with them. I didn't resist. The whole time our eyes held. He blindfolded me again. I felt their hands on me, their mouths. Everywhere. And then I heard the door close. After a while I stopped thinking about the Madonna and praying to her, and when I thought of Guglielmo and Francesca—I'd named her by then, you see; I have a great need to know the name of things— adoring me, I couldn't hold back any longer. I didn't want to, and I came with an intensity that amazes me to this day and that I have never since even remotely equalled. I could feel my own semen on my lips, on my eyes, in my hair. Guglielmo and Francesca.

MAN: What are your secrets?

WIFE: I only deceive him sexually.

CONCERTMASTER: This is beautiful. I'll grant him that.

SOPRANO: "Shall I sip them, plunge beneath them,
         to expire in sweet perfume?"

CONDUCTOR: Of course, after I came I lost all interest in the game and wanted to be free. More importantly, I lost all interest in them. I lay there feeling the flood of semen grow watery, then dry and caked on my stomach, chest and face. Hours passed. I could not free myself. The blindfold, the gag, held firm. Once, I relaxed enough to mentally relive the episode and I immediately got hard and came again, though not nearly so much this time. The next thing I knew I heard a strange woman's scream, a man's angry voice and pretty soon I'm unblindfolded and the room is filled with people, most of whom are police, and an irate, bewildered couple in their sixties who had returned to their apartment after an outdoor performance of *Nabucco* in the Piazza del Duomo, and who was I, how did I get there, what was I doing? Translation: What had I done? I never saw Guglielmo or Francesca again. It wasn't their apartment, of course. Were they even real? The orgasm was.

SOPRANO: In the surging swell, in the ringing sound,
   in the vast wave of the world's breath—
   to drown, to sink
   unconscious—supreme bliss!

CONDUCTOR: Once I asked her to tie me to the bed and sit on me. She loved it.

WIFE: This is so beautiful.

CONDUCTOR: Once I tied her. She loved it.

CONCERTMASTER: I gotta hand it to you, asshole.

CONDUCTOR: Once I let a fan—someone like you, sweetheart—try it, but I'd had too much to drink or he'd had too much to drink or he smelled funny or he said something I didn't like—like Nixon wasn't such a bad President—or he was too big or too little or one of the ten million other things that don't let you connect perfectly with another person. That afternoon in Milan when I was young and first famous and still thought the answer to a good life was in my work, in other people, in success seems so long ago. There is no other person. There is a woman in a box who is my wife and bore me two children. There is a man in the fifth row who entertains fantasies about someone he thinks is me. There is a concertmaster who detests me but not half as much as I detest myself. There is a cow guest soprano who sings music that has no meaning for her in a perfectly ravishing voice. And so it goes. There are a lot of people. Five billion of us, I read just this morning, and pretty soon there will be six billion and the only time I ever felt connected to any of them was when I was twenty-two years old and tied spreadeagle to a retired Milanese optometrist's bed wanting to be made love to by two people I'm not even sure exist.

(The last measures of the Liebestod *are sounding.* CONDUCTOR *takes a small Japanese seppuko blade from the music stand in front of him)*

I know why I'm doing this. Wagner knew. Tristan and Isolde knew. That's four of us. Fuck the rest.

(He plunges the blade into his abdomen. Blood spurts onto the music stand. CONDUCTOR's *face is transfigured. Another standing ovation has begun.* SOPRANO *bows deeply to the audience in the concert hall. The* MAN *is already on his feet)*

MAN: Bravo! Bravo! We love you!

*(*WIFE *rises in her box, afraid.* CONDUCTOR *continues to stare straight ahead, blood spurting from him onto the music stand, the transfigured, ecstatic expression on his face. The ovation is mounting. The* CONCERTMASTER *is busily gathering his music, ready to leave the stage)*

CONCERTMASTER: Asshole.

(Fade to black)

THE LAST YANKEE

Arthur Miller

Arthur Miller

Arthur Miller was born in New York City in 1915. He went to the University of Michigan, where two plays were produced in 1934. When he graduated in 1938 he began work with the Federal Theater Project. His first Broadway production was *The Man Who Had All the Luck;* his next play, *All My Sons,* won the Drama Critics Circle Award. In 1949, Mr. Miller's *Death of a Salesman* was given the Pulitzer Prize and the Drama Critics Circle Award. *The Crucible* won a Tony Award four years later. *A View From the Bridge, A Memory of Two Mondays, The Price, After the Fall, Incident at Vichy, The American Clock, The Archbishop's Ceiling,* a novel, stories and essays are among his other works. *Timebends,* his autobiography, was published in 1987.

His screenplays include *The Misfits* and the play for television, *Playing for Time.* His newest original screenplay, *Everybody Wins,* which was released in the U.S. in January 1990, was directed by Karel Reisz and stars Debra Winger and Nick Nolte. Two books on reportage, *In Russia* and *Chinese Encounters,* were accompanied by photographs by his wife, the famed Inge Morath. His book *Salesman in Beijing* is based on his experience in China, where he directed *Death of a Salesman.* Recent productions of his plays include *A View From the Bridge* and *Death of a Salesman,* starring Dustin Hoffman, on Broadway, *Up From Paradise* and *After the Fall* off Broadway and two one-act plays called *Elegy for a Lady* and *Some Kind of Love Story (Two Way Mirror)* at the Young Vic in London as well as a revival of *An Enemy of the People,* which transferred from the Young Vic to the Playhouse Theater in London. The Young Vic in London did *The Price* in February, 1990. At the National Theater in London were productions of *The Crucible* and *After the Fall.*

His new play, *The Ride Down Mt. Morgan,* opened in London in October, 1991, directed by Michael Blakemore and starring Tom Conti.

Characters:

LEROY HAMILTON

FRICK

Scene:

A hospital waiting room.

The visiting room of a state mental hospital. LEROY HAMILTON *is seated on one of the half-dozen chairs, idly leafing through an old magazine. He is forty-eight, trim, dressed in subdued Ivy League jacket and slacks and shined brogans.*

MR. FRICK *enters. He is sixty, solid, in a business suit. He looks about, glances at* LEROY, *just barely nods, and sits ten feet away. He looks at his watch, then impatiently at the room.* LEROY *goes on leafing through the magazine.*

FRICK: *(Pointing right)* Supposed to notify somebody in there?

LEROY: *(Indicating left)* Did you give your name to the attendant?

FRICK: Yes. 'Seem to be paying much attention, though.

LEROY: They know you're here, then. He calls through to the ward. *(Returns to his magazine)*

FRICK: *(Slight pause)* Tremendous parking space down there. 'They need that for?

LEROY: Well, a lot of people visit on weekends. Fills up pretty much.

FRICK: Really? That whole area?

LEROY: Pretty much.

FRICK: 'Doubt that. *(He goes to the window and looks out. Pause)* Beautifully landscaped, got to say that for it.

LEROY: Yes, it's a very nice place.

FRICK: 'See them walking around out there it's hard to tell. 'Stopped one to ask directions and only realized when he stuck out his finger and pointed at my nose.

LEROY: Heh-heh.

FRICK: Quite a shock. Sitting there reading some thick book and crazy as a coot. You'd never know. *(He sits in another chair.* LEROY *returns to the magazine. He studies* LEROY*)* Is it your wife?

LEROY: Yes.

FRICK: I've got mine in there, too.

LEROY: Uh, huh. *(He stares ahead, politely refraining from the magazine)*

FRICK: My name's Frick.

LEROY: Hi. I'm Hamilton.

FRICK: Gladameetu. *(Slight pause)* How do you find it here?

LEROY: I guess they do a good job.

FRICK: Surprisingly well kept for a state institution.

LEROY: Oh, ya.

FRICK: Awful lot of colored, though, ain't there?

LEROY: Quite a few, ya.

FRICK: Yours been in long?

LEROY: Going on seven weeks now.

FRICK: They give you any idea when she can get out?

LEROY: Oh, I could take her out now, but I won't for a couple weeks.

FRICK: Why's that?

LEROY: Well, this is her third time.

FRICK: 'Don't say.

LEROY: I'd like them to be a little more sure before I take her out again.

FRICK: That fairly common—that they have to come back?

LEROY: About a third, they say. This is your first time, I guess.

FRICK: I just brought her in last Tuesday. I certainly hope she doesn't have to stay long. They ever say what's wrong with her?

LEROY: She's a depressive.

FRICK: Really. That's what they say about mine. Just gets . . . sort of sad?

LEROY: It's more like . . . frightened.

FRICK: Sounds just like mine. Got so she wouldn't even leave the house.

LEROY: That's right.

FRICK: Oh, yours, too?

LEROY: Ya, she wouldn't go out. Not if she could help it, anyway.

FRICK: She ever hear sounds?

LEROY: Oh, ya. Like a loud humming.

FRICK: Same thing! Ts. What do you know! How old is she?

LEROY: She's forty-four.

FRICK: Is that all! I had an idea it had something to do with getting old. . . .

LEROY: I don't think so. My wife is still—I wouldn't say a raving beauty, but she's still . . . a pretty winsome woman. They're usually sick a long time before you realize it, you know. I just never realized it.

FRICK: Mine never showed any signs at all. Just a nice, quiet kind of a woman. Always slept well. . . .

LEROY: Well, mine sleeps well, too.

FRICK: Really?

LEROY: Lot of them love to sleep. I found that out. She'd take naps every afternoon. Longer and longer.

FRICK: Mine, too. But then about six, eight months ago she got nervous about keeping the doors locked. And then the windows. I had to air-condition the whole house. I finally had to do the shopping, she just wouldn't go out.

LEROY: Oh, I've done the shopping for twenty years.

FRICK: You don't say!

LEROY: Well you just never think of it as a sickness. I like to ski, for instance, or ice-skating . . . she'd never come along. Or swimming in the summer. I always took the kids alone. . . .

FRICK: Oh, you have children.

LEROY: Yes. Seven.

FRICK: Seven! I've been wondering if it was because she never had any.

LEROY: No, that's not it. You don't have *any?*

FRICK: No. We kept putting it off, and then it got too late, and first thing you know . . . it's just too late.

LEROY: For a while there I thought maybe she had too *many* children. . . .

FRICK: Well, I don't have any, so . . .

LEROY: Yeah, I guess that's not it, either.

FRICK: I just can't figure it out. There's no bills; we're very well fixed; she's got a beautiful home. . . . There's really not a trouble in the world. Although, God knows, maybe that's the trouble. . . .

LEROY: Oh, no, I got plenty of bills, and it didn't help her. I don't think it's how many bills you have.

FRICK: What do you think it is, then?

LEROY: Don't ask me, I don't know.

FRICK: When she started locking everything, I thought maybe it's these Negroes, you know? There's an awful lot of fear around; all this crime.

LEROY: I don't think so. My wife was afraid before there were any Negroes. I mean, around.

FRICK: Well, one thing came out of it—I finally learned how to make coffee. And mine's better than hers was. It's an awful sensation, though—coming home and there's nobody there.

LEROY: How'd you like to come home and there's seven of them there?

FRICK: I guess I'm lucky at that.

LEROY: Well, I am, too. They're wonderful kids.

FRICK: They still very young?

LEROY: Five to nineteen. But they all pitch in. Everything's clean, the house runs like a ship.

FRICK: You're lucky to have good children these days. I guess we're both lucky.

LEROY: That's the only way to look at it. Start feeling sorry for yourself, that's when you're in trouble.

FRICK: Awfully hard to avoid sometimes.

LEROY: You can't give in to it, though. Like tonight—I was so disgusted I just laid down and . . . I was ready to throw in the chips. But then I got up and washed my face, put on the clothes, and here I am. After all, she can't help it, either, who you going to blame?

FRICK: It's a mystery—a woman with everything she could possibly want. I don't care what happens to the country, there's nothing could ever hurt her anymore. Suddenly, out of nowhere, she's terrified! . . . She lost all her optimism. Yours do that? Lose her optimism?

LEROY: Mine was never very optimistic. She's Swedish.

FRICK: Oh. Mine certainly was. Whatever deal I was in, couldn't wait till I got home to talk about it. Real estate, stock market, always interested. All of a sudden, no interest whatsoever. Might as well be talking to that wall over there. . . . Your wife have brothers and sisters?

LEROY: Quite a few, ya.

FRICK: Really. I even thought maybe it's that she was an only child, and if she had brothers and sisters to talk to . . .

LEROY: Oh, no—at least I don't think so. It could be even worse.

FRICK: They don't help, huh?

LEROY: They *think* they're helping. Come around saying it's a disgrace for their sister to be in a public institution. That's the kind of help. So I said, "Well, I'm the public!"

FRICK: Sure! It's a perfectly nice place.

LEROY: They want her in the Rogers Pavilion.

FRICK: Rogers! That's a couple of hundred dollars a day minimum. . . .

LEROY: Well, if I had that kind of money I wouldn't mind, but . . .

FRICK: No-no, don't you do it. I could afford it, but what are we paying taxes for?

LEROY: So they can go around saying their sister's in the Rogers Pavilion, that's all.

FRICK: Out of the question. That's fifty thousand dollars a year. Plus tips. I'm sure you have to tip them there.

LEROY: Besides, it's eighty miles there and back, I could never get to see her. . . .

FRICK: If they're so sensitive, you ought to tell *them* to pay for it. That'd shut them up, I bet.

LEROY: Well, no—they've offered to pay part. Most of it, in fact.

FRICK: Whyn't you do it, then?

LEROY: *(Holding a secret)* I didn't think it's a good place for her.

FRICK: Why? If they'd pay for it . . . It's one of the top places in the country. Some very rich people go there.

LEROY: I know.

FRICK: And the top doctors, you know. And they order whatever they want to eat. . . . I went up there to look it over; no question about it, it's absolutely first-class, much better than this place. You should take them up on it.

LEROY: I'd rather have her here.

FRICK: Well, I admire your attitude. You don't see that kind of pride anymore.

LEROY: It's not pride, exactly.

FRICK: Never mind, it's a great thing, keep it up. Everybody's got the gimmes, it's destroying the country. Had a man in a few weeks ago to put in a new shower head. Nothing to it. Screw off the old one and screw on the new one. Seventeen dollars an hour!

LEROY: Yeah, well. *(Gets up, unable to remain)* Everybody's got to live, I guess.

FRICK: I take my hat off to you—that kind of independence. Don't happen to be with Colonial Trust, do you?

LEROY: No.

FRICK: There was something familiar about you. What line are you in?

LEROY: *(He is at the window now, staring out. Slight pause)* Carpenter.

FRICK: *(Taken aback)* Don't say. . . . Contractor?

LEROY: No. Just carpenter. I take on one or two fellas when I have to, but I work alone most of the time.

FRICK: I'd never have guessed it.

LEROY: Well, that's what I do. *(Looks at his watch, wanting escape)*

FRICK: I mean your whole . . . your way of dressing and everything.

LEROY: Why? Just ordinary clothes.

FRICK: No, you look like a college man.

LEROY: Most of them have long hair, don't they?

FRICK: The way college men used to look. I've spent thirty years around carpenters, that's why it surprised me. You know Frick Supply, don't you?

LEROY: Oh, ya. I've bought quite a lot of wood from Frick.

FRICK: I sold out about five years ago. . . .

LEROY: I know. I used to see you around there.

FRICK: You did? Why didn't you mention it?

LEROY: *(Shrugs)* Just didn't.

FRICK: You say Anthony?

LEROY: No, Hamilton. Leroy.

FRICK: *(Points at him)* Hey, now! Of course! There was a big article about you in the *Herald* a couple of years ago. Descended from Alexander Hamilton.

LEROY: That's right.

FRICK: Sure! No wonder! *(Holding out his palm as to a photo)* Now that I visualize you in overalls, I think I recognize you. In fact, you were out in the yard loading plywood the morning that article came out. My bookkeeper pointed you out through the window. It's those clothes—if I'd seen you in overalls I'd've recognized you right off. . . . Well, what do you know. *(The air of condescension plus wonder)* Amazing thing what clothes'll do, isn't it. . . . Keeping busy?

LEROY: I get work.

FRICK: What are you fellas charging now?

LEROY: I get seventeen an hour.

FRICK: Good for you.

LEROY: I hate asking that much, but even so, I just about make it.

FRICK: Shouldn't feel that way; if they'll pay it, grab it.

LEROY: Well, ya, but it's still a lot of money. My head's still back there thirty years ago.

FRICK: What are you working on now?

LEROY: I'm renovating a colonial near Waverly. I just finished over in Belleville. The Presbyterian church.

FRICK: Did you do *that*?

LEROY: Yeah, just finished Wednesday.

FRICK: That's a beautiful job. You're a good man. Where'd they get that altar?

LEROY: I built that.

FRICK: That altar?

LEROY: Uh-huh.

FRICK: Hell, that's first-class! Huh! You must be doing all right.

LEROY: Just keeping ahead of it.

FRICK: *(Slight pause)* How'd it happen?

LEROY: What's that?

FRICK: Well, coming out of an old family like that—how do you come to being a carpenter?

LEROY: Just . . . liked it.

FRICK: Father a carpenter?

LEROY: No.

FRICK: What was your father?

LEROY: Lawyer.

FRICK: Why didn't you?

LEROY: Just too dumb, I guess.

FRICK: Couldn't buckle down to the books, huh?

LEROY: I guess not.

FRICK: Your father should've taken you in hand.

LEROY: *(Sits with magazine, opening it)* He didn't like the law, either.

FRICK: Even so.—Many of the family still around?

LEROY: Well, my mother and two brothers.

FRICK: No, I mean of the Hamiltons.

LEROY: Well, they're Hamiltons.

FRICK: I know, but I mean—some of them must be pretty important people.

LEROY: I wouldn't know. I never kept track of them.

FRICK: You should. Probably some of them must be pretty big. Never even looked them up?

LEROY: Nope.

FRICK: You realize the importance of Alexander Hamilton, don't you?

LEROY: I know about him, more or less.

FRICK: More or less! He was one of the most important founding fathers.

LEROY: I guess so, ya.

FRICK: You read about him, didn't you?

LEROY: Well, sure . . . I read about him.

FRICK: Well didn't your father talk about him?

LEROY: Some. But he didn't care for him much.

FRICK: Didn't care for *Alexander Hamilton?*

LEROY: It was something to do with his philosophy. But I never kept up with the whole thing.

FRICK: *(Laughing, shaking his head)* Boy, you're quite a character, aren't you?

(LEROY *is silent, reddening.* FRICK *continues chuckling at him for a moment)*

LEROY: I hope to God your wife is cured, Mr. Frick. I hope she never has to come back here again.

FRICK: *(Sensing the hostility)* What have I said?

LEROY: This is the third time in two years for mine, and I don't mean to be argumentative, but it's got me right at the end of my rope. For all I know, I'm in line for this funny farm myself by now, but I have to tell you that this could be what's driving so many people crazy.

FRICK: What is!

LEROY: This.

FRICK: This what?

LEROY: This whole kind of conversation.

FRICK: Why? What's wrong with it?

LEROY: Well, never mind.

FRICK: I don't know what you're talking about.

LEROY: Well, what's it going to be, equality or what kind of country? I mean am I supposed to be ashamed I'm a carpenter?

FRICK: Who said you . . . ?

LEROY: Then why do you talk like this to a man? One minute my altar is terrific and the next minute I'm some kind of shit bucket.

FRICK: Hey now, wait a minute . . . !

LEROY: I don't mean anything against you personally, I know you're a successful man, and more power to you, but this whole type of conversation about my clothes—should I be ashamed I'm a carpenter? I mean everybody's talking "labor, labor," how much labor's getting; well, if it's so great to be labor, how come nobody wants to be it? I mean, you ever hear a parent going around saying, *(Mimes thumbs pridefully tucked into suspenders)* "My son is a carpenter?" Do you? Do you ever hear people brag about a bricklayer? I don't know what you are, but I'm only a dumb swamp Yankee, but . . . *(Suddenly breaks off with a shameful laugh)* Excuse me. I'm really sorry. But you come back here two, three more times and you're liable to start talking the way you were never brought up to. *(Opens magazine)*

FRICK: I don't understand what you're so hot about.

LEROY: *(Looks up from the magazine. Seems to start to explain, then sighs)* Nothing. *(He returns to his magazine)*

(FRICK *shakes his head with a certain condescension, then goes back to the window and looks out)*

FRICK: It's one hell of a parking lot, you have to say that.

YOU CAN'T TRUST THE MALE

Randy Noojin

AUTHOR'S NOTE: In the Ensemble Studio Theater production, Harvey was played as a Polish immigrant with accent. We made him Harvey Kesselkovski. This is a wonderful option worth consideration.

Randy Noojin

Randy Noojin was born in Hammond, Indiana, on October 24, 1960, and attended Indiana State University where his focus was acting. He acted in repertory, dinner and children's theaters throughout the southeast before coming to New York in 1985 to intern at Circle Repertory. He is a member of Circle Rep's Actor's Lab and continues to act while writing. His first play, *Eat,* was produced at Indiana State. On the basis of his one-act play *Slaves,* he was commissioned by Actors Theater of Louisville to write *Boaz,* subsequently produced by ATL in the 1985 Shorts Festival and published by The Dramatic Publishing Company. Actors Theater then commissioned his one-act play *Unbeatable Harold,* also available through The Dramatic Publishing Company. He has just completed a full-length play, *Unhooked. You Can't Trust the Male* was produced at the Ensemble Studio Theater's 1991 Marathon of One-Act Plays.

Characters:

HARVEY KESSEL
LAURA SPIVEY

Scene:

A night class room. Chairs with desks for one arm face Down toward a teacher's desk. A door Up with frosted window. A piece of paper is taped to the window of the door on the outside. The sax solo in Tom Waits' "The One That Got Away" off the "Small Change" album plays as lights go to black. Lightning flash and, as the subsequent thunder rumbles, dim light fades up outside the door and night light through the windows of the fourth wall. Sound of rain. A figure approaches the door and tears the paper and tape off the window. He enters and turns on the lights.

HARVEY KESSEL *is a man in his mid-thirties and he's sopping wet. He takes the crumpled paper to the trash can by the teacher's desk, thinks better of it and pockets it. He shakes water from his hat and umbrella. He stands the umbrella up in the can and goes to a seat Up Left. He takes off his coat. He has a* Village Voice, *a cup of coffee and a notebook. He settles in and lights a cigarette* LAURA SPIVEY *enters. She's an attractive woman around* HARVEY's *age. She has an umbrella, a big bag, a purse and a Beginning Spanish book. She's wet and late.*

HARVEY: Hello.

LAURA: You can't smoke in here.

HARVEY: I'm sorry. I'll put it out.

LAURA: You can go out in the hall and smoke.

HARVEY: Nah, I'm done with it.

LAURA: It's the law.

HARVEY: Absolutely. It's the law. And it's a good law. Sorry if I stunk up the room already.

LAURA: It'll fade out. Intro to Spanish, right?

HARVEY: Si.

LAURA: Where the fuck is everybody? I thought I was late.

HARVEY: I don't know. I just got here.

LAURA: I cannot believe this shitty weather. Fuckin' thunderstorm in December. And then the goddamn D train goes local and even when they *make* a fuckin' announcement that they are—Surprise—fucked up, you can't understand a fuckin' word they say over the speakers at DeKalb. Are we in the right room?

HARVEY: 36A

LAURA: Well, it's five after.

(A distant thunder)

HARVEY: The weather maybe. *(Pause.* HARVEY *is looking at the paper)* Oh, no. Wouldn't you know it. Just my luck. Boy, oh, boy.

LAURA: What?

HARVEY: Oh, no, I was just realizing out loud that Andy and Red are playing at Dan Lynch's tonight. At eight. Great blues guys. And I'm stuck in an Intro to Spanish class. Darn it.

LAURA: So get outta here. The first class is always bullshit anyway.

HARVEY: Yeah, I guess I could do that.

LAURA: We got the right date? *(She checks her registration card)*

HARVEY: Friday the sixth. *(He browses the paper. Casually)* Yeah, nothin' like the blues to beat the devil outta ya.

LAURA: Huh?

HARVEY: No, I just remember I was in this relationship once, which I'm not now, this was a while ago, but we were almost up to two years together when from outta the blue she up and dumps me and I had all this—I don't know—anger that I couldn't do anything with so I did it to myself. I beat the shit outta myself. For like four months I went into this dark hole of sick mud where I felt like I wasn't a bit of good to anybody—and— *(She's looking at him and he now sees that she is)*— uhm—I'm sorry, what was I talking about?

LAURA: I don't—

HARVEY: Oh, and it took the blues—to, you know, at least make me feel like—I guess, that I wasn't the only one.

LAURA: Have we met before?

HARVEY: No, just—you know. Small talk. *(Pause)* I wonder where is everybody. *(He goes to the door and looks down the hall)*

LAURA: Yeah, this is ridiculous.

HARVEY: Maybe I'll get lucky and nobody'll show up. Still plenty of time to get to Andy and Red.

LAURA: It's supposed to start at seven, right?

HARVEY: Actually no. They start at eight but these guys are always late.

LAURA: No, I mean class starts at seven, right?

HARVEY: Oh, yeah. Class does. Yeah. Seven. I wonder what's goin' on.

LAURA: I know.

HARVEY: Maybe—I mean, if there's no class, I don't know—

LAURA: Why would there be no class do ya think?

HARVEY: No, I'm not sayin' there's not, but where is everybody?

LAURA: There was a lady in the office. I'll go check.

HARVEY: We should give 'em a while longer. We're in the right place at the right time.

LAURA: I'll go make sure.

HARVEY: Oh, you know what? Hold on. Lemme check something.

LAURA: I just checked the schedule.

HARVEY: No, I know. This is not the schedule. I know, I did get that too, but this is something else. I didn't really—oh, yeah, here we go. *(He finds a postcard in his jacket pocket)* Oh, no. Intro to Spanish is rescheduled for Tuesdays at eight!?

LAURA: What?

HARVEY: I shoulda read this.

LAURA: Lemme see that.

HARVEY: I thought it was just another something else.

LAURA: I NEVER GOT THIS! Goddamn it! What next?! How come everything is picking *now* to happen? *(She takes his card to her desk and copies the information)* These are the most incompetent, disorganized, stupid bunch of timid, foreign fuck-ups I ever had to deal with in my life.

(Thunder)

[No offense.*]

HARVEY: They probably sent you one, it's gonna come tomorrow.

LAURA: Yeah! Tomorrow! Why don't they *call* us? *(Her pencil lead breaks. She searches in purse for another pencil)* Shit. Would that be brilliant? A mailbox is a fuckin' wishin' well in Brooklyn.

HARVEY: Well, something's bound to fall through the cracks occasionally. Here. *(He hands her a pen)*

LAURA: Thanks. They don't need an occasion to fuck up in Brooklyn. They need a business day.

HARVEY: Well, this time a year, you know. Christmas cards and parcels pouring in. It's a flood.

LAURA: That's exactly why they should call. Everybody knows you can't trust the mail.

HARVEY: Well, it'll get there eventually, I bet, but you're right.

LAURA: What, is your dad a mailman or something?

HARVEY: No, no.

LAURA: Hold it—

HARVEY: He's a mechanic.

LAURA: Oh, my God, I'm sorry.

HARVEY: What?

LAURA: I thought I'd seen you before.

HARVEY: I doubt it.

---

* "No offense" added for the "Kesselkovski" version.

LAURA: Oh, God. Aren't you my mailman?

HARVEY: Your mailman?!

LAURA: You look jist like my mailman.

HARVEY: You're kidding?

LAURA: 294 Vanderbilt Avenue. Fort Greene.

HARVEY: Well, yeah, that's my route. I thought you looked—yeah, I guess maybe that might be it.

LAURA: I'm sorry.

HARVEY: No, no.

LAURA: I wasn't sayin' it was your fault.

HARVEY: No, I know.

LAURA: I didn't mean it was the mailmen. It's the post office probly.

HARVEY: You don't have to apologize. I know you didn't mean anything by it. It's funny. Ha. Forget it.

LAURA: You know what I mean.

HARVEY: Definitely. Forget it. I know what you mean. But, yeah, hey, I'm your mailman! Wow! How are ya? Nice to meet ya. I'm Harvey. Harvey Kessel.

(The rain stops)

LAURA: Laura Spivey.

HARVEY: Nice to meet you. Small world.

LAURA: Yeah.

HARVEY: Your thing'll probably come tomorrow. I just deliver what they give me.

LAURA: Well, they should call, anyway. Or at least tape up a sign or somethin'.

HARVEY: Yeah.

LAURA: It doesn't matter. *(Pause)* Well—

HARVEY: So we're both taking a Spanish class, huh?

LAURA: Yeah, weird, huh?

HARVEY: Why are you taking Spanish?

LAURA: I'm goin' to Mexico the end of February.

HARVEY: Really? That's great.

LAURA: Yeah, I love the sound of the language.

HARVEY: *(In Spanish)* My dog has no nose. How does he smell? Terrible.

LAURA: Hey, that's pretty good. What did you say? *(He resists)* It was dirty?

HARVEY: No. Just—

LAURA: What?

HARVEY: My dog has no nose. How does he smell? Terrible.

LAURA: Oh. Well—Okay.

HARVEY: Oh, so why are you taking Spanish?

LAURA: 'Cause I'm—you know—

HARVEY: Oh, yeah.

LAURA: —supposed to go to Mexico—

HARVEY: That's right. You said. Listen—

LAURA: Oh, ya know what? While I got ya here.

HARVEY: What?

LAURA: I know you're off and everything—

HARVEY: No, no.

LAURA: No, no. 'Cause I know after 5:30 I don't give two shits what happened to yer colored contacts.

HARVEY: No. What?

LAURA: Well, if ya think about it, could you shove the mail under the grating, that iron door—?

HARVEY: Sure.

LAURA: But only if it hasn't been rainin'.

HARVEY: Be glad to.

LAURA: 'Cause the drain clogs.

HARVEY: No problem.

LAURA: Just if ya think about it.

HARVEY: I'll think about it. I mean, I'm sure I'll think about it. It's my job to think about it.

LAURA: That would be great. *(She readies to go)* The kids upstairs, I think, or somebody's been opening my mail. *(She gets umbrella)*

HARVEY: Oh, no. *(She gives him back his notice and pen)*

LAURA: Thanks.

HARVEY: What makes you think that?

LAURA: Little rips. You know. It's no big deal, it's mostly just a feelin', but if it's no trouble.

HARVEY: Not at all. 294 Vanderbilt Avenue.

LAURA: Thanks. Well, you get your wish.

HARVEY: What?

LAURA: You can go hear your blues.

HARVEY: Yeah, what're you—? I don't know—you gotta—? I mean, it's early and it's Friday and everything and there's no class now and everything—I don't know. You gotta be somewhere?

LAURA: Yeah, I gotta meet my boyfriend uptown in a minute. You know.

HARVEY: Oh, okay. I was just wondering. Good night then.

LAURA: Or else I would.

HARVEY: No, that's cool.

LAURA: Maybe some other time.

HARVEY: Okay. You go ahead. I'm just gonna give 'em a few more minutes.

LAURA: Okay. Well—it's Tuesdays now, right?

HARVEY: Oh, yeah. That's right. I'm brain dead. No, I just wanna see what time these guys are playing. *(He gets the paper)*

LAURA: Eight o'clock.

HARVEY: Thanks. See ya Tuesday.

(LAURA *exits. A short beat. She re-enters*)

LAURA: That was a pretty bad lie, wasn't it?

HARVEY: No, no. It was an okay one. *(He's getting ready to go)*

LAURA: I mean, it wadn't even logical. I'm here for a two-hour class and now I all of a sudden gotta meet my boyfriend uptown in a minute? Bad lie.

HARVEY: We say whatever.

LAURA: I just wanna set the record straight. I do not have to be anywhere and I definitely do not have a boyfriend. I'm just—I'm a mess. So, believe me you don't wanna have anything to do with me right now.

HARVEY: What's wrong?

LAURA: Ahhh. I recently discovered I almost moved in with a lying prick from hell.

HARVEY: I'm sorry.

LAURA: Yeah, so I'm in a bad mood. But, thanks though. Some other time.

HARVEY: Fine. That's fine. You let me know.

LAURA: Sorry I lied.

HARVEY: Don't worry about it.

LAURA: No, 'cause if I haven't learned that lyin' is a dirty piece of shit thing to do from all this, then I ain't gained a thing.

HARVEY: Well—don't beat yourself up about it.

LAURA: Thanks. I'm not usually like this. I haven't slept. My brain against my will keeps playin' this dirty movie starring this guy and a beach fulla girls who're prettier than me.

HARVEY: Nobody's prettier than you.

LAURA: Oh, please. I'm a wreck.

HARVEY: I think you're takin' it better than I usually do.

LAURA: Yeah? You musta been a mess. What, did you check into the nut ward or somethin'?

HARVEY: I can't say I didn't think about it.

LAURA: I think about it every ten seconds, only I ain't got insurance till March.

HARVEY: Oh, boy, oh, boy, oh, boy, I was a lunatic. But I been through it a couple times now and I'm getting better at it. I've developed a sort of recipe of recuperation.

LAURA: Oh, yeah? Well, I'd like to know what it is. I'm goin' nuts here.

HARVEY: Okay, well, three things: a little booze—

LAURA: I did that by instinct—

HARVEY: Okay, a lot of Blues—

LAURA: Right—

HARVEY: —and Duck Soup.

LAURA: Uh, oh. I'm a vegetarian.

HARVEY: No, the movie.

LAURA: Oh. Marx Brothers.

HARVEY: Right.

LAURA: Just watch it?

HARVEY: You can fast-forward through Zeppo.

LAURA: Well, at this point I'll try anything.

HARVEY: You'll be fine. It passes eventually, but the only way out is through.

LAURA: I guess.

HARVEY: Oh, and one other thing. Never keep a Dear John letter. *(He gets pen and paper)* My advice is to burn it immediately if you haven't already. Here, lemme jot these down for ya. *(Pause)*

LAURA: Thanks.

HARVEY: How long were you together?

LAURA: Two years.

HARVEY: Yeah—

LAURA: Can I see that postponement thing you got? Make sure I wrote it all down right. *(He gives it to her)*

HARVEY: So, Tuesdays, huh? This should be fun.

LAURA: Yeah.

HARVEY: This pen's running out. *(He scribbles)*

LAURA: How did you know it was a letter?

HARVEY: Ah, there we go.

LAURA: I never said I got a Dear John letter.

HARVEY: Huh?

LAURA: How did you know it was a letter?

HARVEY: What was? No, I was just saying about *my* Dear John—that I burned it.

LAURA: Plus you got this thing that says there's no class tonight, that I didn't get, and you're my mailman.

HARVEY: What?

LAURA: Just how did you know it was a letter?

HARVEY: I didn't!

LAURA: Have you been reading my mail?

HARVEY: What're you talkin' about? I never read your mail. That's a felony! That's crazy. I was just talkin' to ya.

LAURA: Really?

HARVEY: God, you are so paranoid.

LAURA: I KNOW IT! That's exactly why you gotta tell me the truth now. Am I crazy? It's possible. Have I finally gone crazy? I won't be mad. Just tell me.

HARVEY: You're not crazy. Forgive me. I read Alan's last letter.

LAURA: I KNEW IT!

HARVEY: Can I at least explain?

LAURA: Stay away from me.

HARVEY: Oh, Jesus, don't be scared of me. Please don't think I'm dangerous 'cause I'm not. I'm a chickenshit. If I wasn't a chickenshit I could just *ask a girl out* like everybody else seems to be able to do.

LAURA: What?

HARVEY: I'm sorry. Oh, God, what an idiot. I just—I think you are so beautiful. You weaken my knees sometimes you're so beautiful. I swear to God I could faint from you sometimes if I stopped trying not to. And I been trying to think of a way to say something to you since I got your route. But no way seemed like the perfect way and then there was never really a good time and then I didn't want to bother you and then I didn't know what to say and then I got a fever blister and then—I just plain chickened out. I admit it. I'm scared of you. I am. I mean, you think *you're* scared—oh, boy, oh, boy, oh, boy. Okay. To make a stupid story short, I read your registration stuff for class. I mean, that's not really personal, really.

LAURA: Yeah, it is!

HARVEY: You're right, but it gave me the idea that—maybe we could meet in the class and I could maybe, I don't know—impress you maybe a little.

LAURA: Impress me?

HARVEY: I took two [years*] of Spanish in [high school*]. So I signed up and that was the plan. But then you started getting the airmails from Alan. And I thought for a while he might just be a friend or something but then he drew the little hearts in the corner that one time—

LAURA: I don't believe this.

HARVEY: So I was gonna cancel the class. I sold my book back. I was gonna do my best to just forget the whole thing, but—I was just—curious, I don't know—what kinda love letters a guy who could be with you would have to write—or something like that, I don't know. But what I read was not exactly a love letter.

LAURA: You read my Dear John letter!

HARVEY: Right, so last week when your postponement thing came, I didn't deliver it and I was gonna finally make myself, no matter what, ask you out tonight. I just—I screwed up. I know it was wrong. Everything I do is wrong, but I can't just not do anything anymore. So I just did *something,* anything, something, I didn't think and I'm sorry but I gotta be glad goddamn it 'cause it's better at least than what I been doing which is not a goddamn thing. But the last thing in the world I wanted was to add to your troubles and I hope you do whatever it takes to make yourself feel better about this. And turn me down if that's what it'll take. (*He writes a number down and gets out a quarter during*) My boss's name is Mrs. Menikos. She may still be there. There's a phone by the Coke machine. Here. Here's a quarter.

LAURA: You wanted a date?

HARVEY: I insist that you call. It'd make me feel a lot better. (*He lays paper and quarter down for her to take*)

LAURA: Well, too bad, 'cause I'm not going to.

HARVEY: Don't worry about me.

LAURA: I'm not worried about you.

HARVEY: I invaded your privacy and there's no excuse for that.

LAURA: There's excuses.

* If Harvey is played as Polish, substitute "units" for "years" and "secondary" for "high school."

HARVEY: You have every right to be furious and it's not good to keep that in.

LAURA: Will ya shut up about it? I can't turn you in.

HARVEY: I don't understand. *(Pause)*

LAURA: Well, see—uh—okay, Alan's a SEAL. In the Navy. So sometimes he goes out on these special maneuvers where there's no—whatever, telecommunications or somethin'. Least that's what he told me, and me, like a moron's been lappin' it up the last two years. Who *knows* what's really the truth, but when he does this we correspond. So he goes out this time and I wrote him and I'm expecting a letter and I'm gettin' nothin', so I figure my mail must be bein' sent to his place.

HARVEY: Why?

LAURA: I was gonna move in with him next month before Mexico, so I filled out one a those change of address things, but I figured they might coulda started it too soon. You know how they are over there.

HARVEY: You'd be surprised the job we do, but I know what you mean, go on.

LAURA: So I went to his place to see if my mail's in his box—and it's not —but guess what was? *(She produces an opened letter)* A fuckin' love letter from some bitch named Brenda. I could not fuckin' believe it.

HARVEY: Is that Alan's mail?

LAURA: Oh, shut up. You did it too.

HARVEY: Oh, boy, oh, boy.

LAURA: But what burns me is once I read this, I was gonna break it off with *him*. I was so proud a myself. I didn't wanna talk about it. I didn't wanna fight it out. I wrote this— *(She shows him a notebook)* —like, what is it, two-and-a-half pages of fuck-off. I was waitin' to buy a stamp. But I got his Dear John before I could mail him mine. Fuck-off interruptus. *(She tears pages from notebook and goes to trash can. Tears letter)* That is mostly what I'm pissed about. It is hard to feel like you have left some bastard who is already fuckin' *gone. (Pause)* I feel exactly like a piece of shit. Exactly. I can see why people use that.

HARVEY: I'd go through this for you if I could.

LAURA: I'd let ya.

HARVEY: Is there anything I can do?

LAURA: Nah, nobody can do anything.

HARVEY: I gotta tell ya, it's about all I can do to keep from kissing you right now. *(Beat)*

LAURA: What size shoes do you wear?

HARVEY: I know. I got giant feet.

LAURA: Are you a twelve? *(She gets shoes from her bag)*

HARVEY: Eleven-and-a-half, twelve. Depends.

LAURA: Try these on.

HARVEY: What're these?

LAURA: They're good shoes.

HARVEY: You don't want 'em?

LAURA: If they fit you, you can have 'em.

HARVEY: These are great.

LAURA: See if they fit.

(He tries them on)

HARVEY: I really love these. They're great. I don't know what to say. This is so nice of you. They fit perfect. Thank you.

LAURA: You're welcome.

HARVEY: How come you don't—*oh,* these are Alan's shoes!

LAURA: They were gonna be, but not anymore.

HARVEY: I can't take these.

LAURA: No, please, if you like 'em keep 'em. I was gonna throw them off the D train into the river but we went local.

HARVEY: I can't. What if—you know—what if you guys make up?

LAURA: I wouldn't worry about that. They look good on you.

HARVEY: Well, before you start givin' his stuff away—you should probably read this. *(He pulls an airmail letter from his notebook)* This came today.

(He holds the airmail letter out to her. She just looks at him)

LAURA: Ya know, if I were you I'd wonder if maybe I shouldn't be a mailman.

HARVEY: Believe me, every winter I wonder that.

(She takes it and looks at it)

LAURA: This came today?

HARVEY: Came and went.

(She looks at it a second then holds it out to him)

LAURA: Take it back. I don't even wanna hear it. I'm never speakin' to him again. I don't care if he begs on his hands and knees.

HARVEY: He does quite a bit of beggin' in there.

(She examines the letter for rips)

LAURA: What, steam?

HARVEY: The laundromat on your corner. There's an exhaust vent.

LAURA: You are so fuckin' lucky I had a recent fit of snoopiness.

HARVEY: I realize that. And I'm grateful as hell. But that's the end of it. I gotta smoke.

(She opens letter. Reads. HARVEY *smokes at the door)*

LAURA: Oh, sweet God. This is a miracle. *(Pause. She's in sweet relief)* This is—He wants me back. Oh, God— *(She reads that a ticket is enclosed and takes an airline ticket out)* Mexico. Oh, my God, I can't believe it! It's a miracle. Harvey! A miracle just happened. Listen, could you do me a big favor?

HARVEY: I know, you want the shoes back.

LAURA: Hell, no. I want to send this letter back first class. *(She writes on envelope)* Return to sender. Address unknown.

HARVEY: Oh.

(She salvages the letter from the wastebasket and sprinkles it into the airmail envelope)

LAURA: Eat shit and die, motherfucker. *(She holds out letter to him)*

HARVEY: Oh, boy, oh, boy, oh, boy. *(Pause)*

LAURA: You got any tape?

HARVEY: At my house.

LAURA: This is so great! You think we can still get into that blues place?

HARVEY: Sure, absolutely. *(Beat)* I really—love these shoes.

LAURA: They look good on you.

HARVEY: I really—would like to kiss you.

LAURA: I dunno. You just smoked a cigarette.

HARVEY: You got mints?

LAURA: No.

(Beat. She goes to him and reaches into his pocket and extracts a cigarette from his breast pocket and holds it near her face looking at him. He takes out a lighter and lights her cigarette. Lights fade as she blows out smoke. They're caught kissing for curtain call)

TONE CLUSTERS

Joyce Carol Oates

Joyce Carol Oates

Joyce Carol Oates has the rare distinction of having novels nominated for a National Book Award in each of three successive years: *A Garden of Earthly Delights* (1968), *Expensive People* (1969) and *them* (1970). *them* was the only one of the three to win the award, a nomination for which is already a considerable award. Best known as a novelist, Oates nevertheless is famous for five published volumes of poetry, books on critical writing, including *Edge of Impossibility: Tragic Forms of Literature,* and a number of plays published and produced. She has been a writer of plays for an extensive period of time, ever since the beginning of her writing career in the mid-sixties. Her play *The Sweet Enemy* was presented at the New York Actor's Playhouse in 1965, *Sunday Dinner* at St. Clements Church in New York City in 1970, *Ontological Proof of My Existence* at the Cubiculo Theater in New York in 1972 (then published in *Partisan Review*), *Miracle Play* at the New York Playhouse 2 in 1974, and *Presque Isle* at the Theater for the Open Eye in New York in 1984. E.P. Dutton recently published her *Twelve Plays* in both hardcover and paperback. Actors Theater of Louisville in the 1990 Humana Festival produced *In Darkest Africa (Tone Clusters* and *Eclipse),* plays that were staged for radio reading at the McCarter Theater in Princeton, New Jersey, in September 1991. Devoted to the theater, Oates has articulated her romance with that medium:

> To experience the play, the playwright must become a part of the audience, and this can occur only when there is an actual stage, living actors, voices other than one's own.

Oates is currently the Roger S. Berlind Distinguished Professor of the Humanities at Princeton University and is a member of the American Academy and Institute of Arts and Letters. Her novel *American Appetites* was published in 1989, and her novel *Because It Is Better, And Because It Is My Heart* was a finalist for the National Book Award in 1990. Ms. Oates lives with her husband in Princeton, New Jersey.

Characters:

FRANK GULICK, *53 years old*
EMILY GULICK, *51 years old*
VOICE, *male, indeterminate age*
These are white Americans of no unusual distinction, nor are they in any
self-evident way "representative."

Scene 1:

Lights up. Initially very strong, near-blinding. On a bare stage, middle-aged
FRANK *and* EMILY GULICK *sit ill-at-ease in "comfortable" modish cushioned
swivel chairs, trying not to squint or grimace in the lights (which may be
represented as the lights of a camera crew provided the human figures involved can be kept shadowy, even indistinct). They wear clip-on micro-
phones to which they are unaccustomed. They are "dressed up" for the
occasion, and clearly nervous: they continually touch their faces, or clasp
their hands firmly in their laps, or fuss with fingernails, buttons, the micro-
phone cords, their hair. The nervous mannerisms continue throughout the
piece but should never be too distracting and never comic.*

Surrounding the GULICKS, *dominating their human presence, are TV
monitors and/or slide screens upon which, during the course of the play,
disparate images, words, formless flashes of light are projected. Even when
the* GULICKS' *own images appear on the screens they are upstaged by it: they
glance furtively, with a kind of awe.*

The monitors always show the stage as we see it: the GULICKS *seated, glancing
uneasily up at the screen. Thus there is a "screen-within-a-screen."*

*The employment of music is entirely at the director's discretion. The opening
might be accompanied by classical tone cluster piano pieces—Henry Cow-
ell's "Advertisement" for instance. The music should never be intrusive. The
ninth scene might well be completely empty of music. There should certainly
be no "film-music" effect. (The* GULICKS *do not hear the music)*

The VOICE *too in its modulations is at the discretion of the director. In a way,
I would like* Tone Clusters *to be aleatory, but that might prove too radical
for practicality. Certainly at the start the* VOICE *is booming and commanding.
There should be intermittent audio trouble (whistling, static, etc); the* VOICE,
*wholly in control, can exude any number of effects throughout the play—
pomposity, charity, condescension, bemusement, false chattiness, false ped-
antry, false sympathy, mild incredulity (like that of a television m.c), affect-*

less "computer talk." The GULICKS *are entirely intimidated by the* VOICE *and try very hard to answer its questions.*

Screen shifts from its initial image to words: IN A CASE OF MURDER— large black letters on white.

VOICE: In a case of murder (taking murder as an abstraction) there is always a sense of the inevitable once the identity of the murderer is established. Beforehand there is a sense of disharmony. And humankind fears and loathes disharmony, Mr. and Mrs. Gulick of Lakepointe, New Jersey would you comment?

FRANK: . . . Yes I would say, I think that

EMILY: What is that again, exactly? I . . .

FRANK: My wife and I, we . . .

EMILY: Disharmony . . . ?

FRANK: I don't like disharmony. I mean, all the family, we are a law-abiding family.

VOICE: A religious family I believe?

FRANK: Oh yes. Yes,
We go to church every

EMILY: We almost never miss a, a Sunday
For a while, I helped with Sunday School classes
The children, the children don't always go but they believe, our daughter Judith for instance she and Carl

FRANK: oh yes yessir.

EMILY: and Dennis, they do believe they were raised to believe in God and, and Jesus Christ

FRANK: We raised them that way because we were raised that way,

EMILY: there *is* a God whether you agree with Him or not.

VOICE: "Religion" may be defined as a sort of adhesive matter invisibly holding together nation-states, nationalities, tribes, families for the good of those so held together, would you comment?

FRANK: Oh, oh yes.

EMILY: For the good of . . .

FRANK: Yes I would say so, I think so.

EMILY: My husband and I, we were married in church, in

FRANK: In the Lutheran Church.

EMILY: In Penns Neck.

FRANK: In New Jersey.

EMILY: All our children,

BOTH: they believe.

EMILY: God sees into the human heart.

VOICE: Mr. and Mrs. Gulick from your experience would you theorize for our audience: is the Universe "predestined" in every particular or is man capable of acts of "freedom"?

BOTH: . . .

EMILY: . . . I would say, that is hard to say.

FRANK: Yes. I believe that man is free.

EMILY: If you mean like, I guess choosing good and evil? Yes

FRANK: I would have to say yes. You would have to say mankind is free. Like moving my hand. *(Moves hand)*

EMILY: If nobody is free it wouldn't be right would it to punish anybody?

FRANK: There is always Hell.
I believe in Hell.

EMILY: Anybody at all

FRANK: Though I am not free to, to fly up in the air am I? *(Laughs)* because Well I'm not built right for that am I? *(Laughs)*

VOICE: Man is free. Thus man is responsible for his acts.

EMILY: Except, oh sometime if, maybe for instance if
A baby born without

FRANK: Oh one of those "AIDS" babies

EMILY: Poor thing

FRANK: "crack" babies
Or if you were captured by some enemy, y'know and tortured
Some people never have a chance,

EMILY: But God sees into the human heart,
God knows who to forgive and who not.

(Lights down)

Scene 2:
*Screen shows a suburban street of lower-income homes; the GULICKS stare at
the screen and their answers are initially distracted.*

VOICE: Here we have Cedar Street in Lakepointe, New Jersey neatly
kept homes (as you can see) American suburb low crime rate, single-
family homes suburb of Newark, New Jersey population 12,000 the
neighborhood of Mr. and Mrs. Frank Gulick the parents of Carl Gulick. Will you introduce yourselves to our audience please?

(Houselights come up)

FRANK: . . . Go on, you first

EMILY: I, I don't know what to say

FRANK: My name is Frank Gulick, I I am fifty-three years old
that's our house there 2368 Cedar Street

EMILY: My name is Emily Gulick, fifty-one years old,

VOICE: How employed, would you care to say? Mr. Gulick?

FRANK: I work for the post office, I'm a supervisor for

EMILY: He has worked for the post office for twenty-five years

FRANK: . . . The Terhune Avenue Branch.

VOICE: And how long have you resided   in your attractive home
on Cedar Street?

(Houselights begin to fade down)

FRANK: . . . Oh I guess, how long   if this is   this is 1990?

EMILY: (oh just think: 1990!)

FRANK: we moved there in, uh   Judith wasn't born yet so

EMILY: Oh there was our thirtieth anniversary a year ago,

FRANK: wedding
no that was two years ago

EMILY: was it?

FRANK: or three, I   twenty-seven years, this is 1990

EMILY: Yes: Judith is twenty-six,   now I'm a grandmother

FRANK: Carl is twenty-two

EMILY: Denny is seventeen, he's a senior in high school
No none of them are living at home now

FRANK: not now

EMILY: Right now poor Denny is staying with my sister in

VOICE: Frank and Emily Gulick you have been happy here   in Lakepointe raising your family like any American couple   with your hopes
and aspirations
until recently?

FRANK: . . . Yes, oh yes.

EMILY: Oh for a long time we *were*

FRANK: oh yes.

EMILY: It's so strange to,   to think of
The years go by so

VOICE: You have a   happy family life like so many millions   of Americans

EMILY: Until this, this terrible thing

FRANK: *Innocent until proven guilty*—that's a laugh!

EMILY: Oh it's a, a terrible thing

FRANK: Never any hint beforehand of   the meanness of people's hearts. I mean the neighbors.

EMILY: Oh now don't start that, this isn't the

FRANK: Oh God you just try to comprehend

EMILY: this isn't the place, I

FRANK: Like last night: this carload of kids
drunk, beer-drinking foul language in the night

EMILY: oh don't, my hands are

FRANK: Yes but you know it's the parents set them going   And   telephone calls   our number is changed now, but

EMILY: my hands are shaking so
we are both on medication   the doctor says,

FRANK: oh you would not believe, you would not believe the hatred like Nazi Germany

EMILY: Denny had to drop out of school,   he loved school he is an honor student

FRANK: everybody turned against us

EMILY: My sister in Yonkers, he's staying with

FRANK: Oh he'll never be the same   boy again,
none of us will.

VOICE: In the development of   human identity there's the element of chance,   and there is genetic determinism.
Would you comment please?

FRANK: The thing is,   you try your best.

EMILY: oh dear God yes.

FRANK: Your best.

EMILY: You give all that's in your heart

FRANK: you
     can't do more than that can you?

EMILY: Yes, but there is certain to be   justice.
     There *is* a, a sense of things.

FRANK: Sometimes there is a chance, the way they turn out
     but also   what they *are*.

EMILY: Your own babies

VOICE: Frank Gulick and Mary   what is your assessment of   American
     civilization today?

EMILY: . . . It's Emily.

FRANK: My wife's name is,

EMILY: It's
     Emily.

VOICE: Frank and EMILY   Gulick.

FRANK: . . . The state of the   civilization?

EMILY: It's so big,

FRANK: We are here to tell our side of,

EMILY: . . . I don't know: it's a,   a Democracy

FRANK: the truth is,   do you want the truth?
     the truth is where we live
     Lakepointe it's changing too

EMILY: it has changed

FRANK: Yes but it's all over, it's
     terrible, just terrible

EMILY: Now we are grandparents we fear for

FRANK: Yes what you read and see on t.v.

EMILY: You don't know what to think,

FRANK: Look: in this country half the crimes
are committed by the,   by half the population against the other half.
(Laughs)
You have your law-abiding citizens,

EMILY: taxpayers

FRANK: and you have the rest of them.
Say you went downtown into a city like   Newark, some night

EMILY: you'd be crazy if you got out of your car

FRANK: you'd be dead.   That's what.

VOICE: Is it possible,   probable   or in your assessment *im*probable that
the slaying of   fourteen-year old   Edith Kaminsky on February 12,
1990 is related to
the social malaise   of which you speak?

FRANK: . . . "ma-lezz"?

EMILY: . . . oh it's hard to,   I would say yes

FRANK: . . . whoever did it, he

EMILY: Oh it's terrible the things that
keep happening.

FRANK: If only the police would arrest the right person

VOICE: Frank and Emily Gulick   you remain adamant in your belief   in
your faith in your twenty-two-year-old son   Carl that he is innocent
in the death of   fourteen-year-old Edith Kaminsky
on February 12, 1990?

EMILY: Oh, yes,

FRANK: oh yes that is the single thing we are convinced of.

EMILY: On this earth.

BOTH: With God as our witness,

FRANK: yes

EMILY: Yes.

FRANK: The single thing.

(Lights down)

Scene 3:

Lights up. Screen shows violent movement: urban scenes, police patrol cars, a fire burning out of control, men being arrested and herded into vans; a body lying in the street. The GULICKS *stare at the screen.*

VOICE: Of today's pressing political issues   the rise in violent crime most
   concerns American citizens
Number one political issue of   Mr. and Mrs. Gulick tell our viewers your
   opinion?

FRANK: In this state
   the state of New Jersey

EMILY: Oh it's everywhere

FRANK: there's capital punishment supposedly

EMILY: But the lawyers   the lawyers get them off,

FRANK: you bet
   There's public defenders the taxpayer pays

EMILY: Oh, it's   it's out of control
   (like that what is it "acid rain")

FRANK: It can fall on you anywhere,

EMILY: the sun is too hot too:

BOTH: (the "greenhouse effect")

FRANK: It's a welfare state by any other name

EMILY: Y'know who pays:

BOTH: the taxpayer

FRANK: The same God damn criminal, you pay for him   then he   That's
   the joke of it *(Laughs)*
   The same criminal who slits your throat *(Laughs)*
   He's the one you pay bail for to get out.
   But it sure isn't funny. *(Laughs)*

EMILY: Oh God.

FRANK: It sure isn't funny.

VOICE: Many Americans have come to believe this past decade that capital punishment is one of the answers: would you comment please?

FRANK: Oh in cases of actual, proven murder

EMILY: Those drug dealers

FRANK: Yes *I* would have to say, definitely yes

EMILY: I would say so yes

FRANK: You always hear them say opponents of the death penalty "The death penalty doesn't stop crime"

EMILY: Oh that's what they say!

FRANK: Yes but *I* say, once a man is dead he sure isn't gonna commit any more crimes, is he. *(Laughs)*

VOICE: The death penalty *is* a deterrent to crime in those cases when the criminal has been executed

FRANK: But you have to find the right,
the actual murderer.

EMILY: Not some poor innocent some poor innocent.*

Scene 4:

Lights up. Screen shows a grainy magnified snapshot of a boy about ten. Quick jump to a snapshot of the same boy a few years older. Throughout this scene images of "Carl Gulick" appear and disappear on the screen though not in strict relationship to what is being said, nor in chronological order. "Carl Gulick" in his late teens and early twenties is muscular but need not have any other outstanding characteristics: he may look like any American boy at all.

VOICE: Carl Gulick, twenty-two years old the second-born child of Frank and Emily Gulick of Lakepointe, New Jersey How would you describe your son, Frank and Emily

---

* "Innocent" is an adjective here, not a noun.

FRANK: D'you mean how he looks or . . . ?

EMILY: He's a shy boy, he's shy   Not backward just

FRANK: He's about my height I guess   brown hair, eyes

EMILY: Oh! no I think   he's much taller Frank
he's been taller than you   for years

FRANK: Well that depends on how we're both standing.
How we're both   standing
Well in one newspaper it said six feet one inch, in the other
six feet three inches, that's the kind of

EMILY: accuracy

FRANK: reliability of the news media
you can expect!

EMILY: And oh that terrible picture of,
in the paper
that face he was making   the police carrying him
against his will   laying their hands on him

FRANK: handcuffs

EMILY: Oh that isn't *him*

BOTH: that isn't our son

(GULICKS *respond dazedly to snapshots flashed on screen*)

EMILY: Oh! that's Carl   age I guess about

FRANK: four?

EMILY: that's at the beach one summer

FRANK: only nine or ten, he was big for

EMILY: With his sister Judith

FRANK: that's my brother George

EMILY: That's

FRANK: he loved Boy Scouts

EMILY: but
Oh when you are the actual parents it's a different

FRANK: Oh it is so different
from something just on t.v.

VOICE: In times of disruption   of fracture   it is believed that human
behavior moves   in unchartable leaps   History is a formal record of
such   leaps   but in large-scale demographical   terms
in which the   individual   is   lost
Frank and Emily Gulick it's said your son   Carl charged in the savage
slaying of   fourteen-year-old shows no sign of   remorse that is to say,
awareness of the act: thus the question we pose to you
Can guilt reside in those   devoid of "memeory"

EMILY: . . . Oh the main thing is,
he is innocent.

FRANK: . . . Stake my life on it.

EMILY: He has always been   cheerful, optimistic

FRANK: a good boy, of course he has not
forgotten

BOTH: He is innocent.

EMILY: How could our son "forget" when he has nothing to

BOTH: "forget"

FRANK: He took that lie detector test voluntarily didn't he

EMILY: Oh there he is   weight-lifting, I don't remember
who took that picture?

FRANK: When you are the actual parents you see them every day,   you
don't form judgments.

VOICE: In every household in America   albums of family
lovingly preserved,   many Baby Books of course
Those without children elect to have   pets: a billion-dollar industry
Many young people of our time   faced   with rising costs in   housing
prefer to remain in the parental   home
And how is your son employed, Mr. and Mrs. Kaminsky?
Excuse me: GULICK.

FRANK: Up until Christmas he was working in
  This butcher shop in East Orange

EMILY: . . . it isn't easy, at that age

FRANK: Before that, loading and unloading

EMILY: at Sears at the mall

FRANK: No: that was before, that was before the other

EMILY: No: the job at Sears was

FRANK: . . . Carl was working for that Italian, y'know that

EMILY: the lawn service

FRANK: Was that before?   or after
  Oh in this butcher shop   his employer

EMILY: yes there were hard feelings, on both sides

FRANK: Look: you can't believe a single thing   in the newspaper or t.v.

EMILY: it's not that they lie

FRANK: Oh yes they lie

EMILY: not that they lie, they just   get everything wrong

FRANK: Oh they do lie!   And it's printed and you can't stop them.

EMILY: In this meat shop, I never wanted him to work there

FRANK: In this shop there was pressure on him
  to join the union.

EMILY: Then the other side, his employer
  did not want him to join.
  He's a sensitive boy,   his stomach and nerves
  He lost his appetite for weeks, he'd say "oh if you could see
  some of the things I see"   "the insides of things"
  and so much blood

VOICE: There was always a loving   relationship in the household?

EMILY: . . . When they took him away he said,   he was so brave   he
  said Momma I'll be back soon

I'll be right back,   I am innocent he said
I don't know how she came to be in   our house
I don't know,   I don't know he said
I looked into my son's eyes and saw   truth shining
His eyes have always been   dark green,
like mine.

VOICE: On the afternoon of   February 12 you have told police that no one was home   in your house?

EMILY: I, I was . . . I had a doctor's appointment,
My husband was working, he doesn't get home until

FRANK: Whoever did it,   and brought her body in

EMILY: No: they say she was   they say it,   it happened there

FRANK: No I don't buy that,   He brought her in carried her whoever that was,
I believe he tried   other houses
seeing who was home and who   wasn't
and then he

EMILY: Oh it was like lightning striking

VOICE: Your son Dennis   was at Lakepointe High School
attending a meeting of the yearbook staff,   your son Carl has told police he
was   riding   his motor scooter
in the park,

FRANK: They dragged him like   an animal
put their hands on him like
Like Nazi Germany,

EMILY: it couldn't be any worse

FRANK: And that judge
it's a misuse of power, it's

EMILY: I just don't understand.

VOICE: Your son Carl on and after   February 12 did not exhibit (in your presence)   any unusual sign of emotion?
agitation?   guilt?

EMILY: Every day in a house,   a household,
   is like the other days.   Oh you never step back, never *see*.
   Like I told them, the   police,   everybody, *He did not*.

(Lights down)

Scene 5:
Lights up. Screen shows snapshots, photographs of the murdered girl Kaminsky. Like Carl Gulick, she is anyone of that age: white: neither strikingly beautiful nor unattractive.

VOICE: Sometime in the evening of February 12 of this year forensic reports say   fourteen-year-old Edith Kaminsky daughter of
   neighbors 2361 Cedar Street, Lakepointe, New Jersey   multiple stab
   wounds, sexual assault   strangulation
   An arrest has been made but   legally or otherwise, the absolute identity of the murderer has yet to be

EMILY: Oh it's so unjust,

FRANK: the power of a single man
   That judge

EMILY: Carl's birthday is   next week
   Oh God he'll be in that terrible   cold place

FRANK: "segregated" they call it
   How can a judge refuse to set bail

EMILY: oh I would borrow a million dollars
   if I could

FRANK: Is this America or   Russia?

EMILY: I can't stop crying

FRANK: . . . we are both under medication you see but

EMILY: Oh it's true he wasn't himself   sometimes.

FRANK: But that day when it happened, that wasn't one of the times.

VOICE: You hold out for the possibility that   the true murderer   carried
   Edith Kaminsky into your house, into your basement
   thus meaning to throw suspicion on your son?

FRANK: Our boy is guiltless that's the main thing, I will never doubt that.

EMILY: Our body is innocent . . .   What did I say?

FRANK: Why the hell do they make so much of
Carl lifting weights, his   muscles
He is not a freak.

EMILY: There's lots of them   and women too, today like that,

FRANK: He has other interests he used to collect stamps   play baseball

EMILY: Oh there's so much misunderstanding

FRANK: actual lies
Because the police do not know who the murderer *is*
of course they will blame   anyone they can.

(Lights down)

Scene 6:

Lights up. Screen shows the exterior of the Gulick house seen from various angles; then, the interior (the basement, evidently, and the "storage area" where the young girl's body was found)

VOICE: If, as believed, "premeditated" acts arise   out of a mysterious
sequence of neuron discharges   (in the brain) out of what source   do
"unpremeditated"   acts   arise?

EMILY: Nobody was down in,   in the basement
until the police came.   The storage space is behind the water heater,
but

FRANK: My God if my son is   so shiftless   like people are saying just
look: he helped me paint the house last summer

EMILY: Yes Carl and Denny both,

FRANK: Why are they telling such   lies, our neighbors?   We have never
wished them harm,

EMILY: I believed a certain neighbor was my friend, her and I, we we'd go
shopping together   took my car
Oh my heart is broken

FRANK: It's robin's-egg blue, the paint turned out brighter than when it dried, a little brighter than we'd expected

EMILY: *I* think it's pretty

FRANK: Well. We'll have to sell the house, there's no choice the legal costs Mr. Filco our attorney has said

EMILY: He told us

FRANK: he's going to fight all the way, he believes Carl is innocent

EMILY: My heart is broken.

FRANK: *My* heart isn't,
I'm going to fight this all the way

EMILY: A tragedy like this, you learn fast who is your friend and who is your enemy

FRANK: Nobody's your friend.

VOICE: The Gulicks and Kaminskys were well acquainted?

EMILY: We lived on Cedar first, when they moved in I don't remember: my mind isn't right these days

FRANK: Oh yes we knew them

EMILY: I'd have said Mrs. Kaminsky was my friend, but
that's how people are

FRANK: Yes

EMILY: Carl knew her, Edith
I mean, we all did

FRANK: but not well,

EMILY: just neighbors
Now they're our declared enemies, the Kaminskys

FRANK: well, so be it.

EMILY: Oh! that poor girl if only she hadn't,
I mean, there's no telling who she was with,
walking home
walking home from school I guess

FRANK: Well she'd been missing overnight,

EMILY: yes overnight

FRANK: Of course we were aware

FRANK: The Kaminskys came around ringing doorbells,

EMILY: then the police,

FRANK: then
 they got a search party going, Carl helped them out

EMILY: Everybody said how much he helped

FRANK: he kept at it for hours
 They walked miles and miles,
 he's been out of work for a while,

EMILY: he'd been looking
 in the *help wanted* ads but

FRANK: . . . He doesn't like to use the telephone.

EMILY: People laugh at him he says,

FRANK: I told him no he was imagining it.

EMILY: This neighborhood:

FRANK: you would not believe it.

EMILY: Call themselves Christians

FRANK: Well, some are Jews

EMILY: Well it's still white isn't it a white neighborhood, you expect
 better.

VOICE: The murder weapon has yet to be found?

FRANK: One of the neighbors had to offer an opinion, something sarcastic
 I guess

EMILY: Oh don't go into *that*

FRANK: the color of the paint on our house
 So Carl said, You don't like it, wear sunglasses.

EMILY: But,
  he was smiling.

VOICE: A young man with a sense of humor.

FRANK: Whoever hid that poor girl's
  body
  in the storage space of our,
  basement well clearly it
  obviously it was to deceive
  to cast blame on our son.

EMILY: Yes if there were fingerprints down there,

BOTH: that handprint they found on the wall

FRANK: well for God's sake it was from when Carl
  was down there

BOTH: helping them

FRANK: He cooperated with them,

EMILY: Frank wasn't home,

FRANK: Carl led them downstairs

EMILY: Why they came to our house, I don't know.
  Who was saying things I don't know,
  it was like everybody had gone crazy
  casting blame on all sides

VOICE: Mr. and Mrs. Gulick it's said that from your son's room Lakepointe police officers confiscated comic books, military magazines,
  pornographic magazines a cache of more than one dozen
  knives including switchblades plus
  a U.S. Army bayonet (World War II)
  Nazi memorabilia including a "souvenier" S.S. helmet (manufactured
  in Taiwan)
  a pink plastic skull with light bulbs in eyes
  a naked Barbie doll, badly scratched
  numerous pictures of naked women
  and women in magazines,
  their eyes breasts crotches cut out with a scissors
  Do you have any comment Mr. and Mrs. Gulick?

FRANK: Mainly they were hobbies,

EMILY: I guess I don't,

FRANK: we didn't know about

EMILY: Well   he wouldn't allow me in his room, to vacuum or anything

FRANK: You know how boys are.

EMILY: Didn't want his mother

FRANK: poking her nose in

EMILY: So . . . (EMILY *upsets glass of water*)

VOICE: Police forensic findings   (bloodstains, hairs, semen)   and the DNA "fingerprinting"   constitute a tissue of circumstance   linking your son to the murder   but cannot rise   to revelation?

EMILY: Mr. Filco says   it's all pieced together
Circumstantial evidence, he says.

FRANK: *I* call it bullshit. *(Laughs)*

EMILY: Oh Frank

FRANK: *I* call it bullshit. *(Laughs)*

VOICE: Eye witnesses seem to disagree,   two parties report having seen Carl Gulick and   Edith Kaminsky   walking together in the afternoon, but   a third party   a neighbor   claims to have seen the girl in the company of a stranger   at approximately 4:15 pm
And Carl Gulick insists he was riding his motor scooter all that afternoon.

FRANK: He is a boy

EMILY: not capable of lying.

FRANK: Look: I would discipline him sometimes,

EMILY: you have to, with boys

FRANK: Oh yes you have to, otherwise

EMILY: He was always a good eater

FRANK: He's a quiet boy

EMILY: you can't guess his thoughts

FRANK: But he loved his mother and father

EMILY: always well behaved at home.
That ugly picture of him in the paper,

FRANK: that wasn't him.

EMILY: You can't believe the cruelty in the human heart.

FRANK: Giving interviews

EMILY: telling such cruel lies

FRANK: his own teachers from high school

VOICE: Mr. and Mrs. Gulick you had no suspicion no awareness
you had no sense of   the fact that   the battered and mutilated body
of
fourteen-year-old Edith Kaminsky
was hidden in your basement   in a storage space
wrapped in plastic garbage bags
for approximately forty hours,
no   consciousness of   any disharmony   in
your household?

EMILY: Last week at my sister's where we were staying,
we had to leave   this terrible place
in Yonkers I was crying,   I could not stop   crying
downstairs in the kitchen   three in the morning
I was standing by a window and there was suddenly   it looked like
snow!
it was moonlight moving in the window and there came a   shadow I
guess
like an eclipse?   was there an eclipse?
Oh I felt so, I felt   my heart stopped   Oh but I, I wasn't scared I was
thinking   I was seeing how the world is
how the universe *is*
it's so hard to say, I feel like a   a fool
I was gifted by this, by   seeing   how the world *is* not
how you see it   with your eyes, or talk   talk about it

I mean names you give to,   parts of it   No I mean how it *is*
when there is nobody there.

VOICE: A subliminal conviction of disharmony may be nullified by a transcendental leap of consciousness;   to a "higher plane"
of celestial harmony,
would you comment   Mr. and Mrs. Gulick?

EMILY: Then Sunday night it was,

FRANK: this last week

EMILY: they came again

FRANK: threw trash on our lawn

EMILY: screamed
Murderers! they were drunk, yelling   in the night *Murderers!*

FRANK: There was the false report that Carl was released on   bail
that he was home with us,

EMILY: Oh dear God if only that was true

FRANK: I've lost fifteen pounds since February

EMILY: Oh Frank has worked so hard   on that lawn,
it's his pride and joy and in the neighborhood everybody knows, they
compliment him,   and now
Yes he squats right out there, he pulls out crabgrass by hand
Dumping such ugly nasty disgusting things
Then in the A&P a woman followed me   up and down the aisles I
could hear people   *That's her, that's the mother of the murderer*   I
could hear them   everywhere in the store *Is that her,   is that the
mother of the murderer?*   they were saying   Lived in this neighborhood, in this town   for so many years we thought we were welcome
here and now
Aren't you ashamed to show your face!   a voice screamed
What can I do with my face,   can I hide it forever?

FRANK: And all this when our boy is   innocent.

VOICE: Perceiving the inviolate nature of   the Universe   apart from human suffering   rendered you happy, Mrs. Gulick   is this so?
for some precious moments

EMILY: Oh yes, I was crying but
  not because of
  no   I was crying because
  I was happy I think.

(Lights down)

Scene 7:
*Lights up. Screen shows neurological X-rays, medical diagrams, charts as of
EEG and CAT-scan tests.*

VOICE: Is it possible that in terms of   fracture, of evolutionary unease or,
  perhaps, at any time   human behavior mimics that of minute particles
  of light? The atom is primarily emptiness
      the neutron dense-packed
  The circuitry of the human brain   circadian rhythms can be tracked
  but never, it's said comprehended. And then in descent from
  "identity" (memory?)   to tissue to cells to cell-particles   electrical
  impulses axon-synapse-dendrite   and beyond, be-
      neath
  to sub-atomic bits
  Where is "Carl Gulick"?

*(GULICKS turn to each other in bewilderment. Screen flashes images;
kitchen interior; weight-lifting paraphernalia; a shelf of trophies; photographs; domestic scenes, etc)*

Mr. and Mrs. Gulick you did not notice anything   unusual
  in your son's behavior on the night of February 12   or the following
  day,   to the best   of your recollection?

EMILY: . . . Oh we've told the police this so many times

FRANK: Oh you forget what you remember,

EMILY: That night, before we knew there was anyone missing   I mean, in
  the neighborhood   anyone we knew

FRANK: I can't remember.

EMILY: Yes but Carl had supper with us like always

FRANK: No I think,   he was napping up in his room

EMILY: he was at the table with us:

FRANK: I remember he came down around nine o'clock, but he did eat.

EMILY: Him and Denny, they were at the table with us
I don't know any longer

EMILY: I'm sure it was Denny too. Both our sons. We had meatloaf ketchup baked on top, it's the boys' favorite dish just about isn't it?

FRANK: Oh anything with hamburger and ketchup!

EMILY: Of course he was at the table with us, he had his usual appetite.

FRANK: . . . he was upstairs, said he had a touch of the flu

EMILY: Oh no he was there.

FRANK: It's hard to speak of your own flesh and blood, as if they are other people
it's hard without giving false testimony against your will.

VOICE: Is the intrusion of the "extra-ordinary" into the dimension of the "ordinary" an indication that such Aristotelian categories are invalid? If one day fails to resemble the preceding what does it resemble?

FRANK: . . . He has sworn to us, we are his parents
He did not touch a hair of that poor child's head let alone the rest.
Anybody who knew him, they'd know

EMILY: Oh those trophies! he was so proud
one of them is from the, I guess the Lakepointe YMCA
there's some from the New Jersey competition at Atlantic City two years ago?

FRANK: no, he was in high school
the first was, Carl was only fifteen years old

EMILY: Our little muscle-man!

VOICE: Considering the evidence of thousands of years of human culture of language art religion the judicial system "The family unit" athletics hobbies fraternal organizations

charitable impulses   gods of all species   is   it   possible
that humankind   desires
not   to   know
its   place   in
the
food cycle?

EMILY: One day he said   he wasn't going back to school,
my heart was broken.

FRANK: Only half his senior year ahead
but you can't argue,   not with

EMILY: oh his temper!   he takes after,
oh I don't know who

FRANK: we always have gotten along together
in this household   haven't we

EMILY: yes but the teachers would laugh at him he said   girls laughed at
him he said   stared and pointed at him he said   and there was this
pack of   oh we're not prejudiced against Negroes,   it's just that
the edge of the Lakepointe school district
well

FRANK: Carl got in fights sometimes
in the school cafeteria and   I guess the park?

EMILY: the park isn't safe for law-abiding people these days
they see the color of your skin,   they'll attack
some of them are just like animals   yes they *are*

FRANK: Actually our son was attacked first   it isn't like he got
into fights by himself

EMILY: Who his friends are now, I don't remember

FRANK: He is a quiet boy, keeps to himself

EMILY: he wanted to work
he was looking for work

FRANK: Well: our daughter Judith was misquoted about that

EMILY: also about Carl having a bad temper   she never said that   the
reporter for the paper twisted her words

Mr. Filco says we might sue

FRANK: Look: our son never raised a hand against anybody let alone against

EMILY: He loves his mother and father, he respects us

FRANK: He is a religious boy at heart

EMILY: He looked me in the eyes he said Momma you believe me don't you? and I said Oh yes Oh yes he's just my baby

FRANK: nobody knows him

EMILY: nobody knows him the way we do

FRANK: who would it be, if they did?
I ask you.

Scene 8:
Houselights come up, t.v. screen shows video rewind. Sounds of audio rewind. Screen shows GULICKS *onstage.*

VOICE: Frank and Mary Gulick we're very sorry something happened to the tape we're going to have to reshoot Let's go back to, we're showing an interior Carl's room the trophies I'll say, I'll be repeating Are you ready?

(Houselights out, all tech returns to normal)

VOICE: Well Mr. and Mrs. Gulick your son has
quite a collection of trophies!

FRANK: . . . I, I don't remember what I

EMILY: . . . yes, he,

FRANK: Carl was proud of he had other hobbies though

EMILY: Oh he was so funny, didn't want his mother poking through his room he said

FRANK: Yes but that's how boys are

EMILY: That judge refuses to set bail, which I don't understand

FRANK: Is this the United States or　is this the Soviet Union?

EMILY: we are willing to sell our house to stand up for what is

VOICE: You were speaking of your son Carl having quit school, his senior year?　and then?

EMILY: . . . He had a hard time, the teachers　were down on him.

FRANK: I don't know why,

EMILY: we were never told
And now in the newspapers

FRANK: the kinds of lies they are saying

EMILY: that he got into fights, that he was

FRANK: that kind of thing is all a distortion

EMILY: He was always a quiet boy

FRANK: but he had his own friends

EMILY: they came over to the house sometime, I don't remember who

FRANK: there was that one boy what was his name

EMILY: Oh Frank　Carl hasn't seen him in years
he had friends in grade school

FRANK: Look: in the newspaper there were false statements

EMILY: Mr. Filco says　we might sue

FRANK: Oh no: he says we can't,　we have to prove "malice"

EMILY: Newspapers and t.v. are filled with lies

FRANK: Look: our son Carl never raised a hand against anybody let alone against

EMILY: He loves his mother and father,

FRANK: He respects us.

VOICE: Frank and,　it's Emily isn't it　Frank and Emily Gulick
that is very moving.

(Lights down)

Scene 9:
Lights up. Screen shows GULICKS *in theatre.*

VOICE: The discovery of radioactive elements in the late nineteenth century enabled scientists to set back the estimated age of the Earth to several billion years, and the discovery in more recent decades that the Universe is expanding, thus that there is a point in Time when the Universe was tightly compressed smaller than your tiniest fingernail!
thus that the age of the Universe is many billions of years uncountable
Yet humankind resides in Time, God bless us.
Frank and Emily Gulick as we wind down *our* time together. *What are your plans for the future?*

FRANK: . . . Oh that is, that's hard to that's hard to answer.

EMILY: It depends I guess on

FRANK: Mr. Filco had advised

EMILY: I guess it's,
next is the grand jury

FRANK: Yes: the grand jury.
Mr. Filco cannot be present for the session to protect our boy I don't understand the law, just the prosecutor is there
swaying the jurors' minds
Oh I try to understand but I can't,

EMILY: he says we should be prepared
we should be prepared for a trial

VOICE: You are ready for the trial to clear your son's name?

FRANK: Oh yes . . .

EMILY: yes that is a way of, of putting it
Yes. To clear Carl's name.

FRANK: . . . Oh yes you have to be realistic.

EMILY: Yes but before that   the true murderer of Edith Kaminsky
   might come forward.
   If the true murderer is watching this   *Please come forward.*

FRANK: . . . Well we both believe Carl is protecting someone, some
   friend   another boy

EMILY: the one who really   committed that terrible crime

FRANK: So all we can do is pray.   Pray Carl will come   to his senses
   give police the other boy's name, or I believe this: if it's a friend of
   Carl's
   he must have some decency   in his heart

VOICE: Your faith   in your son remains unshaken?

EMILY: You would have to see his   toes,
   his tiny baby toes in his bath.
   His curly hair,   splashing in the bath
   His yellow rompers or no: I guess that was Denny

FRANK: If your own flesh and blood looks you in the eye,
   you believe

EMILY: Oh yes.

VOICE: Human personality, it might be theorized, is a phenomenon of
   memory yet memory   built up from cells, and   atoms
   does not "exist":   thus memory   like mind   like personality
   is but a fiction?

EMILY: Oh   remembering backward is so hard!
   oh it's,

FRANK: it pulls your brain in two.

EMILY: This medication the doctor gave me, my mouth   my mouth is so
   dry
   In the middle of the night I wake up drenched in

FRANK: You don't know who you are   until a thing like this happens,
   then you don't know.

EMILY: It tears your brain in two, trying to remember
   like even looking at pictures
   Oh you are lost

FRANK: in Time you are lost

EMILY: You fall and fall,
. . . ever since the, the butcher shop
he wasn't always himself but
who he was then, I don't know.
It's so hard, remembering why.

FRANK: Yes my wife means thinking backward the way the way the police make you, so many questions you start forgetting right away it
comes out crazy.
Like now, right here I don't remember anything up to now I mean,
I can't swear to it: the first time, you see, we just lived. We lived in
our house. I am a, I am a post office employee I guess I said that?
well, we live in our, our house. I mean, it was the first time through.
Just living. Like the t.v., the picture's always on, if nobody's watching it
you know? So, the people were there then, I guess I'm trying to say
those actual people me and her the ones you see *here* aren't them
(Laughs)
I guess that sounds crazy,

VOICE: We have here the heartbeat of parental love and faith, it's a
beautiful thing Frank and Molly Gulick, please comment?

FRANK: We are that boy's father and mother.
We know that our son is not a murderer and a, a rapist

EMILY: We know, if that girl came to harm there is some reason
for it to be revealed, but

EMILY: They never found the knife, for one thing

FRANK: or whatever it was

EMILY: They never found the knife, the murderer could tell them where
it's buried, or whatever it was.
Oh he could help us so if he just would.

VOICE: And your plans for the future, Mr. and Mrs. Gulick of Lakepointe, NJ?

FRANK: . . . Well.
I guess, I guess we don't have any.

(Long silence, to the point of awkwardness)

VOICE: . . . Plans for the future, Mr. and Mrs. Gulick of Lakepointe, NJ?

FRANK: The thing is, you discover   you need to be protected from your own thoughts sometimes,   but who is there to do it?

EMILY: God didn't make any of us strong enough I guess.

FRANK: Look: one day in a family like this, it's like the next day and the day before.

EMILY: You could say it *is* the next day, I mean the same   the same day.

FRANK: Until one day it isn't.

(Lights out)

SNAILS

Suzan-Lori Parks

"Or as the snail, whose tender horns being hit,
Shrinks backward in his shelly cave with pain,
And there, all smoth'red up, in shade doth sit,
Long after fearing to creep forth again . . . ."
—*Venus and Adonis*

Suzan-Lori Parks

Ms. Parks started contributing to the professional theater very soon after her graduation in 1985 as a Phi Beta Kappa student from Mt. Holyoke College. Prior to attending Holyoke, she studied writing with James Baldwin at Hampshire College (1983), and during the year immediately following graduation, she studied at the Drama Studio in London. In 1987, she had her first production of a playscript in New York City, *Betting on the Dust Commander,* produced at The Gas Station (New York City) and subsequently produced at Company One in Hartford (1990) and at the Working Theater in NYC (1991). That play has been published by the New Dramatists Guild.

Major productions followed rapidly over the next five years: *Imperceptible Mutabilities in the Third Kingdom* (1989), *The Death of the Last Black Man in the Whole Entire World* (1990), *Devotees in the Garden of Love* (1992), *Poetry Spots* and *Alive From Off Center* (video), *Anemone Me* (film), and *Locomotive, The Third Kingdom, Pickling* (radio). During this period Ms. Parks received an Obie Award for *Imperceptible Mutabilities* as "The Best New American Play, 1990," Playwriting Fellowships from the National Endowment for the Arts (1990, 1991), a "New Forms" Grant from the National Endowment for the Arts (1990), a Rockefeller Foundation Grant (1990), a New York Foundation for the Arts Grant (1990), a Naomi Kitay Fellowship (1989) and a Mary E. Woolley Fellowship (1989).

Ms. Parks has been employed as an instructor in playwriting at the New School, Lang College, and Theater for a New Audience. Soon to be published are both *The Death of the Last Black Man in the Whole Entire World* (Applause Books) and *Imperceptible Mutabilities in the Third Kingdom* (University of Michigan Press).

With great anticipation the theater community looks forward to two current projects on which Ms. Parks is working: *Venus,* commissioned by The Woman's Project, and *The America Play,* commissioned by Theater for a New Audience. Suzan-Lori Parks, still in her twenties, has already made an indelible mark on this nation's theater.

Characters:

MOLLY/MONA
CHARLENE/CHONA
VERONICA/VERONA
THE NATURALIST/DR. LUTZKY
THE ROBBER

A.

Slideshow: Images of MOLLY *and* CHARLENE. MOLLY *and* CHARLENE *speak as the stage remains dark and the slides continue to flash overhead.*

CHARLENE: How dja get through it?

MOLLY: Mm not through it.

CHARLENE: Yer leg. Thuh guard. Lose weight?

MOLLY: Hhh. What should I do Cho-na should I jump should I jump or what?

CHARLENE: You want some eggs?

MOLLY: Would I splat?

CHARLENE: Uh uh uhnnnn.

MOLLY: 12 floors up. Whaduya think?

CHARLENE: Uh uh uhn. Like scrambled?

MOLLY: Shit.

CHARLENE: With cheese? Say with cause ssgoin in.

MOLLY: I diduhnt quit that school. HHH. Thought: nope! Mm gonna go on—go on ssif nothin ssapin yuh know? "SK" is /sk/ as in "ask". The-little-lamb-follows-closely-behind-at-Mary's-heels-as-Mary-boards-the-train. Shit. Failed every test he shoves in my face. He makes me recite my mind goes blank. HHH. The-little-lamb-follows-closely-behind-at-Mary's-heels-as-Mary-boards-the-train. Ain't never seen no woman on no train with no lamb. I tell him so. He throws me out. Stuff like this happens every day, y know? This isn't uh special case mines iduhnt uh uhnnn.

CHARLENE: Salami? Yarnt veg anymore.

MOLLY: "SK" is /sk/ as in ask. I lie down you lie down he she it lies down. The-little-lamb-follows-closely-behind-at-Mary's-heels . . .

CHARLENE: Were you lacto-ovo or thuh whole nine yards?

MOLLY: Whole idea uh talkin right ain't right no way. Ain't natural. Just goes tuh go. HHH. Show. Just goes tuh show.

CHARLENE: Coffee right?

MOLLY: They—expelled—me.

CHARLENE: Straight up?

MOLLY: Straight up. "Talk right or you're outa here!" I couldn't. I walked. Nope. "Speak-correctly-or-you'll-be-dismissed!" Yeah. Yeah. Nope. Nope. Nope. Job sends me there. Basic Skills. Now Job don't want me no more. Closely-behind-at-Mary's-heels. HHH. Everythin in its place.

CHARLENE: Toast?

MOLLY: Hate lookin for uh job. Feel real whory walkin thuh streets. Only thing worse n workin sslookin for work.

CHARLENE: I'll put it on the table.

MOLLY: You lie down you lie down but he and she and it and us well we lays down. Didn't quit. They booted me. He booted me. Couldn't see thuh sense uh words workin like he said couldn't see thuh sense uh workin where words workin like that was workin would drop my phone voice would let things slip they tell me get Basic Skills call me breaking protocol hhhh! Think I'll splat?

CHARLENE: Once there was uh robber who would come over and rob us regular. He wouldn't come through thuh window he would use thuh door. I would let him in. He would walk in n walk uhround. Then he would point tuh stuff. I'd say "help yourself." We developed us uh relationship. I asked him him name. He didn't answer. I asked him where he comed from. No answer tuh that neither. He didn't have no answers cause he didn't have no speech. Verona said he had that deep jungle air uhbout im that just off thuh boat look tuh his face. Verona she named him she named him "Mokus." But Mokus whuduhnt his name.

MOLLY: Once there was uh me named Mona who wanted tuh jump ship but didn't HHH. Chona? Ya got thuh Help Wanteds?

CHARLENE: Flies are casin yer food Mona. Come eat.

MOLLY: HELP WANTEDS. *YOU GOT EM?*

CHARLENE: Wrapped thuh coffee grinds in em.

MOLLY: Splat

B.
Lights up on stage with canned applause. At the podium stands the NATURAL-IST.

NATURALIST: As I have told my students for some blubblubblub years, a most careful preparation of one's fly is the only way by in which the naturalist can insure the capturence of his subjects in a state of nature. Now for those of you who are perhaps not familiar with the more advanced techniques of nature study let me explain the principle of one of our most useful instruments: "the fly." When in Nature Studies the fly is an apparatus which by blending in with the environment under scrutiny enables the naturalist to conceal himself and observe the object of study—unobserved. In our observations of the subjects subjects which for our purposes we have named "MOLLY" and "CHARLENE" subjects we have chosen for study in order that we may monitor their natural behavior and after monitoring perhaps— modify the form of my fly was an easy choice: this cockroach modeled after the common house insect *hausus cockruckus* fashioned entirely out of corrugated cardboard offers us a place in which we may put our camera and observe our subjects—unobserved—. Much like the "fly on the wall."

C.
Slideshow: Images of MOLLY *and* CHARLENE. *Actors speak as stage remains dark and slides flash overhead.*

MOLLY: Once there was uh me named Mona who wondered what she'd be like if no one was watchin. You got thuh Help Wanteds?

CHARLENE: Wrapped thuh coffee grinds in um. —Mona?

MOLLY: Splat. Splat. Splatsplatsplat.

CHARLENE: Mm callin thuh ssterminator for tomorrow. Leave it be for now.

MOLLY: Diduhn't even blink. I threatened it. Diduhnt even blink.

CHARLENE: They're gettin brave. Big too.

MOLLY: Splat!

CHARLENE: Mona! Once there was a little lamb who followed Mary good n put uh hex on Mary. When Mary dropped dead, thuh lamb was in thuh lead. You can study at home. I'll help.

MOLLY: Uh hunn! I'm all decided. Ain't gonna work. Can't. Ain't honest. Anyone with any sense don't wanna work no how. Mm gonna be honest. Mm gonna be down n out. Make downin n outin my livelihood.

CHARLENE: He didn't have no answers cause he didn't have no speech.

MOLLY: Wonder what I'd look like if no one was lookin. I need fashions. "SK" is /sk/ as in ask. The-little-lamb-follows-Mary-Mary-who . . . ?

CHARLENE: Once there was uh one Verona named "Mokus." But "Mokus" whuduhnt his name. He had his picture on file at thuh police station. 99 different versions. None of um looked like he looked.

MOLLY: Splat! Splat! Diduhn't move a muscle even. Don't even have no muscles. Only eyes. Splat! Shit. I woulda been uhcross thuh room out thuh door n on tuh thuh next life. Diduhnt twitch none. Splat! I can't even talk. I got bug bites bug bites all over! I need new styles.

CHARLENE: Once there was uh one named Lutzky. Uh exterminator professional with uh PhD. He wore white cause white was what thuh job required. Comes tuh take thuh roaches uhway. Knew us by names that whuduhnt ours. Could point us out from pictures that whuduhnt us. He became confused. He hosed us down. You signed thuh invoice with uh X. Exterminator professional with uh PhD. He can do thuh job for $99.

MOLLY: Mm gonna lay down, K?

CHARLENE: You're lucky, Mona.

MOLLY: He thuh same bug wasin thuh kitchen?

CHARLENE: Uh uhnn. We got uh infestation problem. You're lucky.

MOLLY: He's watchin us. He followed us in here n swatchin us.

CHARLENE: I'll call Lutzky. Wipe-um-out-Lutzky with thuh PhD. He's got uh squirt-gun. He'll come right over. He's got thuh potions. All mixed up. Squirt in uh crack. Hose down uh crevice. We'll be through. Through with it. Free of um. Wipe-um-out-Lutzky with thuh PhD. He's got uh squirt gun. He'll come right over.

MOLLY: Uh—the-cockroach-is-watching-us,-look-Chona-look! Once there was uh me named Mona who wondered what she'd talk like if no one was listenin.

CHARLENE: Close yer eyes, Mona. Close yer eyes n think on someuhn pleasant.

D.

The NATURALIST *at the podium.*

THE NATURALIST: Thus behave our subjects naturally. Thus behave our subjects when they believe we cannot see them when they believe us far far away when they believe our backs have turned. Now. An obvious question should arise in the mind of an inquisitive observer? Yes? HHH. How should we best accommodate the presence of such subjects in our modern world. That is to say: How. Should. We. Best. Accommodate. Our subjects. If they are all to live with us—all in harmony—in our modern world. Yeahs. Having accumulated a wealth of naturally occurring observations knowing now how our subjects occur in their own world *(mundus primitivus)*, the question now arises as to how we of our world *(mundus modernus)* best accommodate them. I ask us to remember that it was almost 25 whole score ago that our founding father went forth tirelessly crossing a vast expanse of ocean in which there lived dangerous creatures of the most horrible sort tirelessly crossing that sea jungle to find this country and name it. The wilderness was vast and we who came to teach, enlighten and tame were few in number. They were the vast, we were the few. And now. The great cake of society is crumbling. I ask us to realize that those who do not march with us do not march not because they will not but because they cannot . . . I ask that they somehow be—taken care of for there are too many of them—and by "them" I mean of course "them roaches." They need our help. They need our help. Information for the modern can not be gleaned from the primitive, information for the modern can only be gleaned through. Ex-per-i-men-tation. This is

the most tedious part of science yet in science there is no other way.
Now. I will, if you will, journey to the jungle. *Behavioris distortion-allus-via modernus.* Watch closely:

E.
On stage. During this part E the ROBBER *enters steals the roach and exits.*

CHONA: Verona? Hey honeyumm home?

VERONA: Chona Chona ChonaChonaChona. Mona here?

CHONA: Laying down.

VERONA: Heart broken?

CHONA: Like uh broken heart. Thuh poor thing. I'll learn her her speech.
Let's take her out n buy her new styles.

VERONA: Sounds good.

CHONA: She wants fashions. —We got roaches.

VERONA: Shit! Chona. That's uh big one. I got some motels but. I some
stickys too—them little rays with glue? Some spray but. Woo ya! Woo
ya woo ya?! They gettin brave.

CHONA: Big too. Think he came through that crack in thuh bathroom.

VERONA: Wooya! Wooya! Shit. You call Lutzky? Thuh PhD?

CHONA: On his way. We'll pay. Be through. He's got uh squirt-gun.

VERONA: We'll all split thuh bill. He gonna do it for 99?

CHONA: Plus costs. Mona duhnt know bout thuh Plus Costs part. Okay?

VERONA: —K. Maybe I can catch uh few for our Lutzky shows.

CHONA: Once there was uh woman who wanted tuh get uhway for
uhwhile but didn't know which way tuh go tuh get gone. Once there
was uh woman who just layed down.

VERONA: Traps. Place um. Around thuh sink corner of thuh stove move
move yer feet threshole of thuh outside door. Yeahuh. Mm convinced
they're coming in from uhcross thuh hall—slippin under thuh door at
night but I ain't no professional—see?! Lookit im go—movin slow-ly.

He's thuh scout. For every one ya see there are thousands. Thousands thousands creepin in through thuh cracks. Waiting for their chance. Watchim go. Goinsslow. We gotta be vigilant: sit-with-thuh-lights-out-crouch-in-thuh-kitchen-holdin-hard-soled-shoes. GOTCHA! Mona's got bug bites on her eyelids? Mmputtin some round her bed. Augment thuh traps with thuh spray.

CHONA: Once there was uh woman was careful. Once there was uh woman on thuh lookout. Still trapped.

VERONA: Vermin free by 1990! That means YOU!

CHONA: Wild Kingdom's on.

VERONA: YER OUTTA HERE!

CHONA: Yer show's on.

VERONA: Great. Thanks.

CHONA: Keep it low for Mona. K?

VERONA: Perkins never shoulda uhlowed them tuh scratch his show. Wildlife never goes outta style. He shoulda told em that. Fuck thuh ratings. Oh, look! On thuh trail of thuh long muzzled wildebeast: mating season. Ha! This is uh good one. They got bulls n cows muzzles matin close ups—make ya feel like you really right there with em. Part of thuh action. Uh live birth towards thuh end . . .

CHONA: You want some eggs?

VERONA: They got meat?

CHONA: —Yeauh—

VERONA: I'm veg. Since today. Kinder. Cheaper too. Didja know that uh veg . . .

CHONA: Eat. Here. Ssgood. Ssgood tuh eat. Eat. Please eat. Once there was uh one name Verona who bit thuh hand that feeds her. That's Lutzky. I'll get it.

VERONA: Mona! Our shinin knight's here!

MONA: THE-LITTLE-LAMB-FOLLOWS-MARY-CLOSELY-AT-HER-HEELS—

VERONA: Wipe-um-out Dr. Lutzky with uh P uh H and uh D. Baby. B. Cool.

MONA: B cool.

CHONA: Right this way Dr. Lutzky. Right this way Dr. Lutzky Extaordinaire Sir.

LUTZKY: I came as quickly as I could—I have a squirt-gun, you know. Gold plated gift from the firm. They're so proud. Of me. There was a woman in Queens—poor thing—so distraught—couldn't sign the invoice—couldn't say "bug"—for a moment I thought I had been the unwitting victim of a prank phone call—*prankus callus*—her little boy filled out the forms—showed me where to squirt—lucky for her the little one was there—lucky for her she had the little one. Awfully noble scene, I thought. You must be Charlene.

CHONA: Char-who? Uh uhn. Uh—It-is-I,-Dr.-Lutzky,-Chona.

LUTZKY: Ha! You look like a Charlene you look like a Charlene you do look like a Charlene bet no one has ever told that to you, eh? Aaaaaaah, well. I hear there is one with "bug bites all over." Are you the one?

CHONA: I-am-Chona. Mona-is-the-one. The-one-in-the-livingroom. The-one-in-the-livingroom-on-the-couch.

LUTZKY: What's the world coming to? "What is the world coming to?" I sometimes ask myself. And—

CHONA: Eggs, Dr. Lutzky?

LUTZKY: Oh, yes please. And—and am I wrong in making a livelihood—meager as it may be—from the vermin that feed on the crumbs which fall from the table of the broken cake of civilization—oh dear—oh dear!

CHONA: Watch out for those. We do have an infestation problem. Watch out for those.

LUTZKY: Too late now—oh dear it's sticky. It's stuck—oh, dear—now the other foot. They're stuck.

MONA: THE-LITTLE-LAMB—

VERONA: SShhh.

CHONA: Make yourself at home, Dr. Lutzky. I'll bring your eggs.

LUTZKY: Can't walk.

CHONA: Shuffle.

LUTZKY: Oh dear. Shuffleshuffleshuffle. Oh dear.

VERONA: Sssshhh!

LUTZKY: You watch Wild Kingdom. I watch Wild Kingdom too. This is a good one. Oh dear!

MONA: Oh dear.

CHONA: Here is the Extraordinaire, Mona. Mona, the Extraordinaire is here. Fresh juice, Dr. Lutzky Extraordiniare?

LUTZKY: Call me "Wipe-em-out."

MONA: Oh dear.

VERONA: SSSSShhhhh.

LUTZKY: Well. Now. Let's start off with something simple. Who's got bug bites?

MONA: Once there was uh me named Mona who hated going tuh thuh doctor. —I-have-bug-bites-Dr.-Lutzky-Extra-ordiniare-Sir.

LUTZKY: This won't take long. Step lively, Molly. The line forms here.

CHONA: I'll get the juice. We have a juice machine!

LUTZKY: I have a squirt-gun!

VERONA: He's got uh gun—. Marlin Perkinssgot uh gun—

MONA: Oh, dear . . .

LUTZKY: You're the one, aren't you, Molly? Wouldn't want to squirt the wrong one. Stand up straight. The line forms here.

CHONA: I am Chona! Mona's on the line! —Verona? That one is Verona.

LUTZKY: ChonaMonaVerona. Well well well. Wouldn't want to squirt the wrong one.

VERONA: He's got uh gun. Ssnot supposed tuh have uh gun—.

MONA: "SK" IS /SK/ AS IN AX. Oh dear. I'm Lucky, Dr. Lutzky.

LUTZKY: Call me "Wipe-em-out." Both of you. All of you.

CHONA: Wipe-em-out. Dr. Wipe-em-out.

LUTZKY: And you're "Lucky"?

VERONA: He got uh gun!

MONA: Me Mona.

LUTZKY: Mona?

MONA: Mona Mokus robbery.

CHONA: You are confusing the Dr., Mona. Mona, the Dr. is confused.

VERONA: Perkins ssgot uh gun. Right there on thuh Tee V. He iduhnt spposed tuh have no gun!

MONA: Robbery Mokus Mona. Robbery Mokus Mona. Everything in its place.

CHONA: The robbery comes later, Dr. Wipe-em-out Extraordinaire, Sir.

LUTZKY: There goes my squirt-gun. Did you feel it.

VERONA: I seen this show before. 4 times. Perkins duhnt even own no gun.

CHONA: Once there was uh Dr. who became confused and then hosed us down.

LUTZKY: I must be confused. Must be the sun. Or the savages.

MONA: Savage Mokus. Robbery, Chona.

CHONA: Go on Mokus. Help yourself.

LUTZKY: I need to phone for backups. May I?

VERONA: He duhnt have no gun permit even. Wait. B. Cool. I seen this. Turns out alright. I think . . .

CHONA: Juice? I made it myself!

MONA: I am going to lie down. I am going to lay down. Lie down? Lay down. Lay down?

LUTZKY: Why don't you lie down.

MONA: I am going to lie down.

CHONA: She's distraught. Bug bites all over. We're infested. Help yourself.

LUTZKY: You seem infested, Miss Molly. Get in line, I'll hose you down.

MONA: MonaMokusRobbery.

LUTZKY: Hello Sir. Parents of the Muslim faith? My fathers used to frequent the Panthers. For sport. That was before my time. Not too talkative are you. Come on. Give us a grunt. I'll give you a squirt.

VERONA: Ssnot no dart gun neither—. Holy. Chuh! Mmcallin thuh— That is not uh dart gun, Marlin!!!

MONA: Make your bed and lie in it. I'm going to lay down.

CHONA: Lie down.

MONA: Lay down.

CHONA: LIE, Mona.

MONA: Lie Mona lie Mona down.

CHONA: Down, Mona down.

MONA: Down, Mona, bites! On my eyelids! On-her-heels! Down Mona down.

VERONA: Call thuh cops.

LUTZKY: That will be about $99. Hello. This is Dr. Lutzky. Send 10 over. Just like me. We've got a real one here. Won't even grunt. Huh! Hmmm. Phone's not working . . .

VERONA: Gimmie that! Thank-you. Hello? Marlin-Perkins-has-a-gun. I-am-telling-you,-Marlin-Perkins-has-a-gun! Yeah it's loaded course it's loaded! You listen tuh me! I pay yuh tuh listen tuh me! We pay our taxes, Chona?

CHONA: I am going to make a peach cobbler. My mother's ma used to make cobblers. She used to gather the peaches out of her own back yard all by herself.

LUTZKY: Hold still, Charlene. I'll hose you down.

CHONA: Go on Mokus. Help yourself.

VERONA: HE'S SHOOTIN THUH WILD BEASTS!

MONA: Oh dear.

VERONA: He-is-shooting-them-for-real! We diduhnt pay our taxes, Chona.

LUTZKY: Here's my invoice. Sign here.

CHONA: X, Mona. Help yourself.

MONA: Splat.

CHONA: Cobbler, Dr. Lutzky? Fresh out of the oven????!!!

MONA: Splat.

LUTZKY: Wrap it to go, Charlene.

MONA: Splat.

LUTZKY: What did you claim your name was dear?

MONA: Splat.

CHONA: I'll cut you off a big slice. Enough for your company. You're a company man.

LUTZKY: With back-ups, Miss Charlene. I'm a very lucky man. Molly's lucky too.

MONA: Splat. Splat. Splatsplatsplat.

VERONA: Cops don't care. This is uh outrage.

LUTZKY: Here's my card. There's my squirt-gun! Did you feel it? I need back-ups. May I?

VERONA: Don't touch this phone. It's bugged.

LUTZKY: Oh dear!

CHONA: Cobbler, Verona?

LUTZKY: Well, goodnight.

VERONA: We pay our taxes, Chona?

LUTZKY: Well, goodnight!

VERONA: We pay our taxes, Chona??!!!!?

MONA: Tuck me in. I need somebody tuh tuck me in.

F.
Slideshow. VERONICA *speaks at the podium.*

VERONICA: I saw my first pictures of Africa on T.V.: Mutual of Ohmaha's Wild Kingdom. The thirty minute filler between Walt Disney's wonderful world and the CBS Evening News. It was a wonderful world: Marlin Perkins and Jim and their African guides. I was a junior guide and had a lifesize poster of Dr. Perkins sitting on a white landrover surrounded by wild things. Had me an 8×10 glossy of him too, signed, on my nightstand. Got my nightstand from Sears cause I had to have Marlin by my bed at night. Together we learned to differentiate African from Indian elephants the importance of hyenas in the wild funny looking trees on the slant—how do they stand up? Black folks with no clothes. Marlin loved and respected all the wild things. His guides took his english and turned it into the local lingo so that he could converse with the natives. Marlin even petted a rhino once. He tagged the animals and put them into zoos for their own protection. He encouraged us to be kind to animals through his shining example. Once there was uh me name Verona: I got mommy n dad tuh get me uh black dog n named it I named it "Namib" after thuh African sands n swore tuh be nice tuh it only Namib refused tuh be trained n crapped in corners of our basement n got up on thuh sofa when we went out n Namib wouldn't listen tuh me like Marlin's helpers listened tuh him Namib wouldn't look at me when I talked tuh him n when I said someuhn like "sit" he wouldn't n "come" made im go n when I tied him up in thuh front yard so that he could bite the postman when thuh postman came like uh good dog would he wouldn't even bark just smile n wag his tail so I would kick Namib when no one could see me cause I was sure I was very very sure that Namib told lies uhbout me behind my back and Namib chewed through his rope one day n bit me n run off. I have this job. I work at a veterinarian hospital. I'm a euthenasia specialist! Someone brought a stray dog in one day and I entered "black dog" in the black book and let her scream and whine and wag her tail and talk about me behind my back then I offered her the humane alternative.

Wiped her out! I stayed late that night so that I could cut her open because I had to see I just had to see the heart of such a disagreeable domesticated thing. But no. nothing different. Everything in its place. Do you know what that means? Everything in its place. That's all.

(Lights out)

EXTENSIONS

Murray Schisgal

Murray Schisgal

Murray Schisgal was born in New York City in 1926, attended Thomas Jefferson High School and then continued his education at the Brooklyn Conservatory of Music, Brooklyn Law School, New School for Social Research, and New York University Graduate School. He served in the United States Navy, played saxophone and clarinet in a small jazz band in New York City, practiced law from 1953 to 1956 and taught English in private and public schools. His initial experience in the professional theater came in 1960 when three of his one-act plays were presented abroad, soon followed by the very successful off-Broadway production in 1963 of *The Typists* and *The Tiger*, starring Anne Jackson and Eli Wallach. This production won for Schisgal considerable recognition with both the Vernon Rice and the Outer Critics Circle Awards, but the next production won for him everlasting fame. In November, 1964, *Luv*, directed by Mike Nichols and starring Anne Jackson, Eli Wallach and Alan Arkin, opened at the Booth Theater on Broadway. His subsequent Broadway productions have been: *Twice Around the Park*, *Jimmy Shine*, (starring Dustin Hoffman), *All Over Town*, *An American Millionaire*, *The Chinese* and *Dr. Fish*.

Mr. Schisgal was nominated for an Academy Award for his screenplay of *Tootsie*, starring Dustin Hoffman. He also wrote the film scenario for *The Tiger Makes Out* (starring Anne Jackson and Eli Wallach) and an original television play, *The Love Song of Barney Kempinski*, starring Alan Arkin. His novel *Days and Nights of a French Horn Player* was published by Little, Brown and will soon be produced as a film. His play *Songs of War* premiered in Los Angeles in 1989; his play *Popkins* was presented in Paris at Théâtre L'Atelier in 1990; and his play *Theatrical Release* will open in Paris during the 1991/92 season. Mr. Schisgal lives with his wife, Reene, and his two children, Jane and Zachary, in New York City and Easthampton.

Characters:

BOB

BETSY

Scene:

A stage.

Center, a round, wooden table and two armless wooden chairs, all brought in from a second-hand furniture store. A black dial wall telephone on a wooden column, left. An old, battered steamer trunk with faded airline and hotel labels on it, right.

Time: Now.

At rise: BOB *and* BETSY *are seated at table, playing gin rummy. They are performers, dressed in their costumes. They have on too much makeup, too much hair pomade: it's as if they have been waiting to go on stage for too long a period of time and have excessively prepared themselves.*

BOB *wears a black, single-breasted, one-button vaudevillian's suit: the jacket is too small, the pants are too short—we see several inches of white sock; he wears a wide, round-collared white shirt and a red, knotted scarf instead of a tie; black, glossy, patent leather shoes; a gray derby.*

BETSY *wears an off-the-shoulder yellow rayon blouse with a short, pleated skirt; white nylon tights and black Mary Jane patent leather shoes with polka-dot bows; a wide ribbon is in her hair; a charm bracelet and birth-stone ring; a Minnie Mouse wristwatch.*

BOB: *(Mournfully)* Betsy?

(No response from BETSY. *In a panic:)*

Betsy!

BETSY: *(Now hears him)* What? What is it?

BOB: Why didn't you answer me the first time? Why do I have to repeat everything twice? Do you get pleasure out of ignoring me? filling me with anxiety? apprehension? insecurity? Is this some kind of new sadistic game you're playing?

BETSY: I didn't hear you, Bob. I was concentrating on the cards. It's as simple as that. Don't complicate things, please. Now what do you want?

BOB: *(Sighs)* What are we gonna do?

BETSY: I don't know what we're gonna do. How am I supposed to know? We have to pass the time; we have to keep busy; we have to be helpful and supportive; we have to be considerate and affectionate. We have to observe the amenities of life. That's all I know.

BOB: Can we do this forever? Aren't there limitations? When do we reach a point where we collapse? suffer an emotional breakdown? fall prey to various nervous disorders? Or worse?

BETSY: Don't ask me. You're asking the wrong person. I don't have the faintest idea. Don't forget, I haven't had this experience before either.

BOB: It's like we dropped out of life.

BETSY: That's what it's like.

BOB: It's like the earth swallowed us up and nobody knows we're still alive.

BETSY: I never thought it would happen, not in a million years.

BOB: Who could have imagined it?

BETSY: No one. Absolutely no one.

BOB: I'm humiliated. I'm embarrassed. I'm ashamed to walk out the door. What if I run into somebody I know? What if he asks me what I've been doing with myself? How do I explain it to him?

BETSY: Don't even try.

BOB: He wouldn't believe me.

BETSY: He wouldn't. Practically speaking, though, the chances of you running into anyone we know is practically nil.

BOB: That's true. They're all gone. Vanished. Disappeared. But we used to know a lot of people.

BETSY: Are you kidding? We used to know thousands of people, literally and actually thousands of people.

(They pronounce each name with great deliberation and enjoyment)

BOB: Do you remember Mr. and Mrs. Françoise De Pre Labouchere?

BETSY: Of course I remember them. They owned a rooming house in Charleston, South Carolina. We used to play badminton with them every afternoon. Do you remember Josiah Burbank Skeffington?

BOB: The juggler with the Canadian circus. He taught me how to catch red snappers in that lake near Toronto. Josiah Burbank Skeffington.

BETSY: There was a Mr. and Mrs. Raymondo Archibald Orlioffski from Mapleville, Indiana.

BOB: Mrs. Heather Courtney Berlinvasser.

BETSY: Sir Cedric Purcell McGilligan.

BOB: Sandy Patricia Hershkowitz.

BETSY: Daniel Montenegro.

BOB: Muhamed Abdul Razak Fayed.

BETSY: We knew thousands of people, thousands of them. We were so popular . . .

BOB: I couldn't walk down the street without bumping into somebody I knew.

BETSY: I couldn't stick my head out the window without someone yelling . . . *(Imitates)* "Hey, Betsy, how you doin', honey?"

BOB: *(Imitates)* "Hey, how's it goin' there, Bobby? How are tricks?" They used to yell at me from their cars, from their stoops . . .

BETSY: "Yoo-hoo, Betsy, remember me from the Players Club in Philadelphia?"

BOB: "How about a drink with us after the show, Bob-old-boy!" They were always trying to buy me drinks.

BETSY: They'd buy me presents. All the time. I'd find flowers and boxes of chocolate-dipped cherries in front of my hotel door every morning.

BOB: You know, when we first started out together . . .

BETSY: Seventeen years ago. The same year we were married.

BOB: We worked nine straight months without a single . . . without one, single, solitary day off!

BETSY: It was amazing.

BOB: So many shows, so many bookings . . . Uptown, downtown, upstate, out-of-state . . .

BETSY: We were always working. We were always in demand.

BOB: We turned down jobs, for cryin'-out-loud!

BETSY: How could we keep up with them? The phone was ringing . . .

(Looks to phone. BOB *looks to phone. A long sad beat)*

From the minute we got up in the morning . . .

BOB: All day, whether we were in or not . . .

BETSY: The phone rang and rang . . .

BOB: *(Mimes imaginary phone conversation)* "Hello, who is this? Why the hell are you calling so damn early in the morning?"

BETSY: *(The same)* "Do you know what time it is?"

BOB: "We worked until four in the A.M., for cryin'-out-loud!"

BETSY: "No, no, out of the question. We're unavailable, Liebling. Get the Cunninghams."

BOB: "How about the Spinas? Use them. We're exhausted!"

BETSY: "It's no use begging. We can't . . . We . . . We . . ." *(It's too depressing for her to continue)*

BOB: Incredible.

BETSY: It's incredible.

BOB: Not to hear from Liebling . . . How long is it?

BETSY: Weeks, months, years . . . I don't know anymore. The last job we got from him was the Resorts Lounge. In Atlantic City.

BOB: Were we bad there?

BETSY: Bad? What are you talking about? We were wonderful; fantastic!

BOB: And before that? In Miami?

BETSY: We got a standing ovation, for God sakes!

BOB: And . . . And . . . Reno? How were we in Reno?

BETSY: Are you losing your mind? The owner himself came over to us and said, "I want you guys back. Tell Liebling to call me."

BOB: "Tell Liebling to call me. I want you guys back."

BETSY: *(A short beat)* Bob? *(No response from him. In a panic)* Bob!

BOB: *(Now hears her)* Yeah?

BETSY: What was that for? Are you trying to get even with me because I didn't hear you before? Are you being spiteful? deliberately cruel? If I call your name, it seems to me a simple act of courtesy to respond without scaring me to death!

BOB: I didn't hear you. I did not hear you. Why are you making such a big thing out of it? Now whatta you want?

BETSY: Why don't we get out of these clothes and get into something more comfortable?

BOB: And if Liebling calls?

BETSY: We'll get dressed.

BOB: But what if he calls and has a job for us and we have to be on a bus or a plane or a train in five minutes? Whatta we do then?

BETSY: The chances of that . . . *("happening" would have followed; she decides not to disagree)* You're right. It doesn't hurt to be ready.

BOB: You never know in this business.

BETSY: You don't know.

BOB: Would you be surprised if you learned that at this very minute Liebling is negotiating a deal for us to play two weeks in Acapulco?

BETSY: Not at all. Why should I be surprised? That's what the man does for a living.

BOB: We still have a reputation.

BETSY: Are you kidding? We walk on the stage now, right now, and there'll be people in the audience who'll stand up on their feet and yell for all they're worth, "Bravo! Bravo! We love you, Betsy and Bob! We love you!"

BOB: And while they're still yelling and applauding, we'll segue into . . . *(He sings "Ain't She Sweet," or some such lilting standard.* BETSY *joins in. And in a moment or two,* BETSY *knocks on the table, three times)*

BETSY: Three points. *(And she lays her cards down on the table.* BOB *stares at her, his mouth hanging open.* BETSY *takes the cards out of his hand, counts the points he's stuck with)* Seven, twelve, fourteen, twenty-one . . .

BOB: Betsy?

(No response from her. She is counting the points, silently, mouthing the numbers. In a panic)

Betsy!

BETSY: *(Now hears him)* Yes?

BOB: Don't do this to me! It's a vicious cycle and there's gonna be no end to it if you don't answer when I call your name!

BETSY: How can I answer when I didn't hear you? I was counting the cards!

BOB: Then there's something wrong with your hearing and you'd better go to an eye-ear-and-throat doctor immediately and get your physical condition straightened out!

BETSY: I will! Now what do you want?

BOB: I wanna know why you're knocking! Why don't you play out your hand? It's stupid to knock with three points after playing this lengthy period of time. If you want to win at this game, you go for gin!

BETSY: May I speak without irritating you?

BOB: I'm not irritated. Irritation is not one of my foibles.

BETSY: I'll accept that, but let me make a personal plea. Let's not fight, sweetheart. I beg you. I beseech you. We're both very wrought up, very anxious. One of us could say the wrong word and before you know it we'll start yelling at one another and we'll be more miserable than we are at present. Besides . . . *(Writes score on pad)* . . . I have sixty-seven points and you have . . . two points. I am winning. You are losing. Need more be said on the subject?

(Offended, tight-lipped, BOB *picks up a second deck of cards and deals out a new hand. They look at their cards.* BETSY *picks up a card from deck, discards it.* BOB *does the same.* BETSY *picks up another card, keeps it, discards another from her hand.* BOB *picks up a card, discards another, quietly says:)*

BOB: Gin. *(And spreads his cards on the table)*

(And now it's BETSY's *turn to be chagrined. She closely examines his cards, not really trusting him.* BOB *plucks the cards out of her hand and counts the points she's stuck with)*

Six, sixteen, twenty-four, twenty-eight, thirty-nine, forty-eight, fifty-six, sixty-eight. *(Writes score on pad)* That gives me sixty-eight and you have sixty-seven.

BETSY: *(Pushes cards on table toward him; angles her chair front; crosses arms)* I'm not playing anymore.

BOB: Why not?

BETSY: Because I'm not playing. Do I have to have a reason?

BOB: I know the reason. You're losing, that's the reason. But when you were winning, you wanted very, very much to play. *(Angles chair front; crosses arms)* You're a baby, do you know that? You're a big, spoiled baby!

BETSY: I'm a big, spoiled baby! What do you call yourself?

BOB: I call myself a decent human being.

BETSY: Ha! Don't make me laugh! Your mother spoiled you so badly . . .

BOB: *(Points finger at her)* Watch it. Watch what you're saying. You are opening up a Pandora's box when you bring my mother into our discussions!

BETSY: I . . . I'm sorry. I apologize. I lost my head. It's just . . . *(In anguish)* Why doesn't the phone ring? Why doesn't Liebling call us? Why doesn't anyone call us?

BOB: It's amazing.

BETSY: We don't even get wrong numbers anymore!

BOB: It's positively amazing. It defies understanding. It . . . Wait a second. Wait . . . one . . . second.

BETSY: What? What is it?

BOB: When was the last time we checked the phone . . . *(Said quickly)* . . . to see if it was working?

BETSY: *(Glances at wristwatch)* Twelve minutes ago.

BOB: Betwixt and between, one doesn't know. A lot could have happened in twelve minutes. I'll check it out.

(He fills his lungs and walks with resolve to the phone, whistling with an attempt at casualness. At phone, he takes another deep breath, then snaps up the phone)

BETSY: Is it working? Do you get a dial tone? Do you hear any voices? Any buzzes or static? Any indication that it's operative?

(No response from BOB. In a panic)

Bob, answer me! For God's sake, why don't you answer me? Why do you persist in torturing me? What pleasure could you possibly . . .

(BOB waves for her to be quiet)

BOB: *(Into phone; in a tremulous voice)* Is there anyone who would like to talk to me? Is there anyone out there who has anything to say to me? My name is Bob Abbott. I'm with Betsy Abbott. I am waiting for a reply. *(A few short beats and he slowly hangs up phone; bows head)*

BETSY: Is it working?

BOB: *(Without moving)* It's working.

BETSY: Someone picked up at the other end?

BOB: No. No one picked up.

BETSY: Who were you talking to?

BOB: The dial tone.

BETSY: Bob, sweetheart, I know we discussed this before, but . . . in view of the prevailing circumstances . . . why don't you let *me* call Liebling? I'm not as superstitious as you are. I'm not.

BOB: *(Now moves from phone)* It's more than being superstitious. It has to do with logic and the laws of probability. In all the years Liebling has been our agent, have we ever called him out of the blue, of our own free choice and volition, and did we ever get a job as a result of that call?

BETSY: Uhhh . . .

BOB: Or has he ever said when we called him, "I'm glad you called. I was just going to call you."

BETSY: Uhhh . . . No. He hasn't.

BOB: What *has* he said when we called him of our own free will and volition?

BETSY: "How did you get my number?"

BOB: After being his client for how long?

BETSY: Seventeen years. The same year we were married.

BOB: Did he ever say anything else to us?

BETSY: Yes. Once he said, "We overpaid you on your last check."

BOB: And?

BETSY: "Send us the difference," he said.

BOB: That's what he said. After seventeen years.

BETSY: Another time he yelled at us.

BOB: That's the point I'm making. You look at the record and you'll see that logically and statistically, we never got a single job when we called him first. *(He works on a hat trick with his derby)*

BETSY: It's true. Unfortunately, it's true. *(A short beat)* Bob? Bob? *(No response from him)* There! You're doing it again! You're deliberately frightening me! You're deliberately causing me unnecessary stress and apprehension and . . .

BOB: All right, all right, don't make a federal case out of it! I didn't hear you. Whatta you want?

BETSY: I agree with you about not calling Liebling. But when it comes to our relatives and what few friends we have left . . . Would it hurt if I gave one of them a ring?

BOB: *(Pacing)* They're quite a bunch, our relatives and so-called friends, including our so-called best friends, George and Maryann Freidkin. When we were working, when we could give them free tickets to shows and pick up their tabs for dinner and hotel rooms, they were there, they were all around us, like flies, like bees, like locusts; we couldn't get rid of them. But now . . . now that we're on a slide, now that we're scrounging for a job, a gig, a walk-on, anything, anything we can get our hands on . . . Not a word. Not a single, solitary word from any of them!

BETSY: It's reprehensible, I know, but, Bob, your mother . . . Don't you think I should call your mother? If only to see if she still hates me?

BOB: There's nothing wrong with my mother. If there was, I would have heard about it. I would have . . . *(Turns to phone; shouts in anguish)* When is it gonna ring? When is somebody gonna call us, for cryin' out loud! I can't stand it anymore!

BETSY: Come on, let's play another game of gin rummy. I bet I can beat you this time.

BOB: Tell me, and be honest, Betsy: was I nasty to Liebling? Was I rude? Did I say anything offensive to him?

BETSY: Never. You always said what was on your mind and he respected you for it. He . . .

(The phone rings. They turn to it, expressions of astonishment)

BETSY: *(Continuing)* It's ringing. *(A beat)* Should I . . . ?

(BOB *nods, eyes on phone. Taking a deep breath,* BETSY *rises, moves to phone; hand trembling, she lifts it from cradle. Into phone, small voice)* Hello? *(A short beat)* Yes, it is. *(Covers mouthpiece)* It's . . . Liebling. Do you . . . ?

(BOB *wags his head and hand)*

(Into phone) Liebling? Is that you, Liebling? Yes. We're . . . fine. We're . . . very well. How . . . How are you? You're very well, too? That's . . . wonderful. Oh, he's very well. Very well.

(BOB *presses his ear to phone)*

(Into phone) What have we been doing? Oh, we've been . . . mostly enjoying ourselves. Yes. We've been having a lot of fun.

(Forces a laugh; gestures: does BOB *want the phone?* BOB *shakes his head)*

What? What was that? Really? That . . . That'd be great! What kind of job is it? Where is it? When do we . . .

(BOB *gestures that she's not to show enthusiasm)*

Weeell, on second thought . . . I don't know. We've been so busy . . .

(BOB *nods approvingly)*

No, he's not in now. He went out. I don't know when . . .

(BOB *gestures that he'll take the phone now)*

He's here. He just walked in. Just this minute he walked in. Here he is. He came in just now.

(Hands phone to BOB)

BOB: *(A breath; into phone)* Liebling? Is it you? What? We heard you were out of business, that you went bankrupt. That's what we heard. You're not out of business? How do you like that.

(He hawks a sarcastic laugh. BETSY *frantically gestures for him not to be rude or offensive)*

(Continuing into phone, after nodding to BETSY) A job? No kidding. What . . . ? A movie? They want Betsy and me for a movie? Columbia Pictures?

(He wags his hand to BETSY, *excitedly.* BETSY *jumps up and down, hand over mouth)*

Ten days. Santa Fe. Twenty-five thousand each.

(More hand wagging to BETSY. *More jumping up and down by* BETSY)

It sounds . . . *(Unenthusiastically)* . . . all right. On the face of it. But because of other commitments, I'm afraid Betsy and I have to pass.

(BETSY *looks about in a state of shock)*

Liebling, I can't get out of it! I promised . . . We have a definite . . . Let me ask you this: what's the per diem?

(BETSY *now looks at* BOB: *she knows what he's doing.* BOB *grins at her)*

Are they flying us out there first-class? Where will we be staying? Do we have a car and chauffeur at our disposal?

(BETSY *pulls at his jacket, trying to get his attention: Don't go too far. Don't blow the deal!* BOB *gestures for her to stay cool: Trust me)*

Flying first-class. Okay. What's the per-diem? What? Eight hundred dollars a week? For the both of us? That . . . *That* is offensive, Liebling. *That* is rude and offensive! You can't get a decent hotel room for less than two hundred a night! How the hell do you expect us to live out there? *(A short beat)* Yes. We'll take eight hundred and ten dollars a week. For the both of us. Okay. You got it. What about a car and chauffeur?

(BETSY *paces, biting on her hand: the tension is unbearable for her)*

What do you mean, they won't give it? Well, if they won't give it then you don't get Bob and Betsy Abbott! It's as simple as that! We're not going out there without proper transportation! *(Suspiciously)* What kind of rental? Mid-size or compact? *(A short beat)* Can we get a Japanese car? With an open roof? *(A short beat)* Sky-blue. No. I insist on the color, Liebling. I want a sky-blue, open roof, mid-size Japanese car! Yes, we'll forego the chauffeur if we can get . . . *(Breaks out in a smile)* You got it, Liebling. Wrap it up. It's a deal. I know. I know. You love doing business with me. *(Laughs)* See you out there, old buddy.

(And he hangs up. He stares at BETSY *before nodding)*

We're going back to work.

BETSY: Ohhh. I am so happy. I am so, so . . .

(The phone rings. They turn to the phone, apprehensively)

Who . . . ?

BOB: I don't know.

BETSY: Should I . . . ?

BOB: I'll get it. *(A breath; picks up phone)* Hello. Bob Abbott speaking. *(A short beat; excitedly)* George Freidkin? Is that . . . ? Where . . . ? *(To BETSY)* It's George Freidkin! *(Into phone)* How are you, George? How have you been? Maryann? The kids? You know, I'm really pissed off at you! Why didn't you . . . Not a lousy word!

(BETSY puts her ear to phone. BOB continues into phone)

No! Not true! I called you and you did not return my . . . During the summer. Last summer. Around the Fourth of July weekend. *(To BETSY)* Didn't we call him?

BETSY: *(Into phone)* Ab-so-lute-ly!

BOB: *(Into phone)* That was Betsy. And she doesn't lie, George. You know she . . . All right. Okay. I accept your apologies. Let's drop it. *(A short beat)* What? How the hell did you find out? This is incredible! *(To BETSY)* He heard we're doing a picture for Columbia. *(Into phone)* George, you have to tell me where . . . I just got off the phone with . . . Liebling told you? You spoke to Liebling? Someone in his office? Whatta you mean, you're not telling me! Will you cut it out! *(Laughing)* It's true. We just made the deal. Thank you. Thank you. We'll do it. Soon. I'll have Betsy call Maryann. Right. Take care, buddy. *(He hangs up)* How do you like that? After so long . . .

BETSY: We can invite them up to have drinks here and I'll make reservations for dinner at a nice . . . *(The phone rings. Eagerly)* I have it. *(Into phone)* Betsy Abbott speaking. Who? *(Hand over mouthpiece)* Do you know a man named Monty Duberman?

BOB: Ask him what he wants.

BETSY: *(Into phone)* What is it about, Mr. Duberman? *(A short beat; to BOB)* Did you put money on the horses yesterday?

BOB: *(Takes phone from her; into phone)* Monty? Bob. What happened? *(A short beat)* You're kidding. How much? *(To BETSY)* I won four hundred and sixty dollars!

BETSY: You're fantastic. Absolutely fantastic!

BOB: *(Into phone)* Thanks, Monty. I'll come by later to pick it up. *(He hangs up)*

(And he starts singing and dancing "We're in the Money," or some such happy song. BETSY *joins in. It would be wonderful if they could tap-dance together. The phone rings)*

BETSY: *(Runs to phone; snaps it up; into phone)* Abbott Entertainment Productions here. *(Solemnly)* Sally? What is it? What's wrong? (BOB *clasps his hands together and listens)* Oh. I'm sorry. I am very . . . Yes. Yes. It's no problem. We'll be there. Do you want to come over? I understand. I'll tell him. *(She hangs up, turns to* BOB)

BOB: My mother?

BETSY: She's in the hospital. They're taking tests. It was a heart attack.

BOB: Did they say . . . ?

BETSY: They don't know how serious. No one can see her until six o'clock. They'll call your sister if there's any change. It could be nothing, sweetheart. It could be . . . *(The phone rings.* BETSY *snaps it up; into phone)* Yes? *(A short beat)* What number did you want? *(A short beat)* You have the wrong number. *(Hangs up. The phone rings again)* What's going on here? This is getting ridiculous! *(Into phone)* Hello. *(A short beat)* We didn't ask for any newspaper delivery. We're not . . . *(A short beat)* No, we're not interested. Thanks, anyway. *(She hangs up)* I can't believe this. It's . . . *(Drops the thought)* Do you want me to call your sister back? Do you wanna speak to her?

BOB: *(Seated; bent over)* She'll call. If there's anything . . . I have to know. We'll go to the hospital.

BETSY: Six o'clock. She said we can . . . *(The phone rings)* Do you believe this? Can you believe it?

BOB: *(Murmurs)* Don't answer it. You don't have to answer it.

(But BETSY *snaps the phone up)*

BETSY: *(Into phone)* Yes, what is it? Who? *(To* BOB) It's Frank Peterson. He says he's a friend of Josiah Burbank Skeffington.

BOB: *(Rises)* I'll talk to him. *(Takes phone from her; into phone)* Mr. Peterson? Bob Abbott here. What can I . . . *(A short beat)* I see. Yes. We did. Years ago. My wife and I were touring Canada . . . He taught me how to catch red snapper. We had . . . some wonderful times together. *(A short beat)* When is the funeral? *(A short beat)* I'll do everything . . . humanly possible to be there. Thank you for calling. *(He hangs up, slowly, apprehensively. The phone rings at once)*

BETSY: Let it ring. It's a joke. Someone's playing a joke on us!

BOB: *(Snaps phone up; barks into it)* Who is it? Who? *(A short beat)* I didn't ask for any weather report. What kind of service? We didn't subscribe to any such . . . *(A short beat)* I don't want it, mister! I don't care if it's gonna rain tomorrow or not! You take our name off that list! Immediately! *(He slams phone into the cradle. The phone rings at once)*

BETSY: *(Shouts in a panic)* Bob, don't . . . !

BOB: *(Snaps phone up; into phone)* Now you listen to me! Enough is . . . *(A short beat)* What? Say that again. *(To* BETSY*)* Did you order a lamp from a department store?

BETSY: Yes. I did. I did. Let me have it. *(Into phone)* Did you get the lamp in? You didn't get the lamp in? Then why did you call? *(A short beat)* To tell me you're not getting the lamp in? That's no reason to call! If you didn't call I would assume you didn't get the lamp in! It did not require a call to tell me . . . No. It did not. People have a right not to be disturbed and not have their phone ringing and ringing and . . .

*(*BOB *gently takes the phone from her and lets it dangle, out of the cradle, on its cord. Shortly we hear the "off-the-hook" tone from the phone. Then silence)*

BOB: That's it. No more. That's all the calls we're taking today. And maybe tomorrow, too. Let's play gin. *(Sits at table; starts dealing out cards)*

BETSY: I agree. A thousand percent. When did Liebling say we go to work? *(She can't take her eyes off the dangling phone)*

BOB: About three weeks. We'll know definitely as soon as he gets the schedule. *(Cards dealt)* Betsy?

*(*BETSY*'s eyes are fixed on the dangling phone)*

Betsy!

BETSY: What? What is it?

BOB: *(Throws cards down on table, angrily)* You're deliberately doing it, aren't you? You are deliberately driving me up the wall! *(Rises; paces)* You wanna frighten me! You wanna make me feel that I'm alone in this world, that I have nobody, nobody, that all these years we've been together has been a sham, a fraud, an exercise in futility, a waste, a . . .

BETSY: No, no, it's not true. I'm here. You're there. We're together. We'll always be together. This is a given. This is a fact of life.

(BOB's *eyes are now fixed on the dangling phone*)

You don't ever, ever have to be insecure about that. We have been wedded in holy matrimony. Until death do us part. And I'm not so sure that death *will* do us part because we are bound as one in so many ways, religiously, socially, emotionally and professionally. Don't you agree? Bob? *(Screams)* Bob!

BOB: Huh?

BETSY: How can you . . . !

BOB: Betsy! Betsy!

(He runs to her; holds her tightly; she wraps her arms around him. They both stare at the dangling phone)

What should we do? The tension is unbearable.

BETSY: It is unbearable.

BOB: Can one live without a telephone?

BETSY: I don't know.

BOB: Should we . . . ?

BETSY: Yes, we should. We're being very adolescent. A little while ago we were complaining that nobody was calling us and now that we're getting calls we're still complaining. *(Moves to return dangling phone to cradle)* What are we afraid of? Who are we hiding from? Why are we cutting ourselves off from everybody? If somebody wants to call us, we should be happy to receive their calls. We don't owe anybody any money!

(The phone rings the instant BETSY *returns it to cradle.* BETSY *looks to* BOB, *nervously, before snapping up phone)*

BETSY: *(Into phone; defiantly)* Yes! Who is it? (BOB *holds his breath)* What stationery store? *(A short beat)* I'm Betsy Abbott. Yes. Yes. I bought a lottery ticket. I have it right here. *(Takes ticket out of pocket)* It's six; eighteen; twenty-three; twenty-nine; thirty; thirty-four. *(A short beat)* Are you serious? *(To* BOB) I'm an alternate lottery winner! *(Into phone)* What did you say your name was?

BOB: How much? How much is it?

BETSY: Shhh! *(Into phone)* Mr. Farkas. Yes, Mr. Farkas. I remember. Your store's on Broadway and Eighty-third Street. How much is it? I mean, how much can I win? *(Repeats what she hears for* BOB's *benefit)* We won't know until all the winners hand in their tickets. But you believe it'll be in the vicinity of . . . how much? A few . . . a few . . . thousand . . . dollars.

(BOB *moves to her, hand outstretched; they shake hands.* BETSY *continues into phone)*

Thank you, Mr. Farkas. There'll be a reward for your efforts after the formalities. Thank you again. *(And she hangs up)*

(They both shout and holler and do a bit of "We're in the Money," or some such tune)

You see! You see! And you think we're unlucky! We are the luckiest people in the world!

BOB: I can't believe it! That's two winners in one day! First the horses and now . . .

(The phone rings. They both turn and stare at it for a beat or two. BOB *raises his hand, indicating that* BETSY *shouldn't pick up the phone. With a show of fearlessness,* BOB *picks it up)*

BOB: *(Into phone)* Bob Abbott of Bob and Betsy here. *(A short beat; to* BETSY) Did you see Doctor Barnes this week?

BETSY: I saw him Monday.

BOB: It's his nurse. Is anything wrong?

BETSY: No. Why should there be anything wrong? Let me . . . *("have it." would have followed)*

BOB: *(Into phone)* Can you tell me what the problem is? *(A short beat)* Yes, I know. She . . . What time is that? Is Doctor Barnes available? I'd like to . . . *(A short beat)* I'll speak to him tomorrow. I'll be there with my wife. *(He hangs up)*

BETSY: What did she say?

BOB: Why didn't you tell me you went to Doctor Barnes?

BETSY: It was just for a check-up. There was nothing . . .

BOB: Did he . . . take the mole off . . . ?

BETSY: Yes, he did. But it's a . . . routine, a procedure . . . He explained it to me. They do a . . . a . . . biopsy . . . Wh at did she say? What did the nurse say?

BOB: We have an appointment with Doctor Barnes. Ten o'clock tomorrow. It's nothing. I know it's nothing. A cell change, she said. What's a cell change? What does that mean?

BETSY: I never heard of it before. If it was serious, wouldn't Doctor Barnes get on the phone? Wouldn't he tell me immediately? Wouldn't he not waste any time about it?

BOB: Absolutely. No doubt about it. Let's not conjecture. Let's not speculate. So, what would you like to . . .

(The phone rings. They both stare at phone; whisper to one another)

BETSY: Who . . . ?

BOB: I don't care.

BETSY: Don't you think . . . ? *("we should answer it?")*

BOB: *(Shakes his head firmly)* No. No.

BETSY: But it could be . . . *("important.")*

BOB: I don't care. I don't wanna know anymore. Betsy.

BETSY: Bob! Bob!

(They come together, embrace, all the while staring at the ringing phone; they hold tightly on to one another)

BOB: I don't wanna know anymore. I don't. I don't. I don't. I don't. I don't.

(And again and again if necessary. As phone continues to ring and lights congeal into a spot on the two of them, huddled together, staring at the ringing phone. Spot fades to black)

THE DEVIL AND BILLY MARKHAM

Shel Silverstein

The Devil and Billy Markham was originally produced by Lincoln Center Theater in 1989.

Shel Silverstein

Shel Silverstein was last represented on the New York stage with his play *The Devil and Billy Markham*, which played a double bill with David Mamet's *Bobby Gould in Hell*, collectively titled *Oh, Hell!*, at the Mitzi Newhouse Theater at Lincoln Center. With Mr. Mamet, he co-wrote the screenplay *Things Change* for Columbia Pictures, which starred Don Ameche and Joe Mantegna. In the spring of 1991, his play *Hamlet* was performed at the Ensemble Studio Theater in New York. He has written and illustrated several children's classics, including *Where the Sidewalk Ends*, *A Light in the Attic*, and *The Giving Tree*. His plays include *The Crate*, *Lady or the Tiger*, *Gorilla* and *Little Feet*. He is also a noted cartoonist and the author of many songs and poems. Most recently, his song "I'm Checking Out of the Heartbreak Hotel," from the film *Postcards From the Edge*, was nominated for an Academy Award.

Character:

STORYTELLER

Scene

The STORYTELLER *enters. He wears a ratty topcoat, baggy pants, unmatching vest, wrinkled shirt and spotted necktie. He carries a mop and a bucket. He sets down the bucket and begins to mop the floor, humming to himself. He looks up—surprised to see the audience. He realizes his opportunity. He smiles. He begins to recite.*

The Devil walked into Linebaugh's on a rainy Nashville night.

While the lost souls sat and sipped their soup in the sickly yellow neon light.

And the Devil he looked around the room, and he got down on one knee.

He says, "Is there one among you scum who'll roll the dice with me?"

Red, he just strums his guitar, pretending not to hear.

And Eddie, he just looks away and takes another sip of beer.

Vince, he says, "Not me, I'll pass. I've had my share of Hell."

And kept scribbling on a napkin some song he was sure would sell.

Ronnie just kept whisperin' low to the snuff queen who clutched at his sleeve.

And somebody coughed—and the Devil scoffed.

And turned on his heel to leave.

"Hold on," says a voice from the back of the room.

" 'Fore you walk out that door.

If you're looking for some action, friend, well I've rolled some dice before."

And there stood Billy Markham, he'd been on the scene for years,

Singing all those raunchy songs that the town didn't want to hear.

He'd been cut and bled a thousand times, and his eyes were wise and sad.

And all his songs were songs of the street, and all of his luck was bad.

"I know you," says Billy Markham, "from many a dark and funky place,

But you always spoke in a different voice and wore a different face.

While me, I've gambled here on Music Row with hustlers, hacks and whores

And my dues are paid I ain't afraid to roll them dice of yours."

"Well then get down," says the Devil, "and put that guitar away,

And take these dice in your luckless hands and I'll tell you how this game is played.

You get one roll—and you bet your soul—and if you roll thirteen you win.

And all the joys of flesh and gold are yours to touch and spend.
But if that thirteen don't come up, then kiss your ass goodbye,
And will your useless bones to God, 'cause your goddamn soul is mine."
"Thirteen?" says Billy Markham. "Hell I've played in tougher games.
I've loved ambitious women and I've rode on wheelless trains.
So gimme room, you stinkin' fiend, and let it all unwind,
Nobody's rolled a thirteen yet, but this just might be the time."
Then Billy Markham, he takes the dice, and the dice feel heavy as stones.
"They should," the Devil says, " 'cause they're carved outa Jesus'
    bones!"
And Billy Markham turns the dice and the dice they have no spots.
"I'm sorry," says the Devil, "but they're the only ones I got."
"Well shit," says Billy Markham. "Now I really don't mean to bitch,
But I never thought I'd stake my roll in a sucker's game like this."
"Well then walk off," says the Devil. "Nobody's tied you down."
"Walk off where?" says Billy. "It's the only game in town.
But I just wanna say 'fore I make my play, that if I should chance to lose,
I will this guitar to some would-be star who'll play some honest blues.
Who ain't afraid to sing the words like damn or shit or fuck,
And who ain't afraid to put his ass on the stage where he makes his
    bucks.
But if he plays this guitar safe, and sings some sugary lies,
I'll haunt him till we meet in Hell—now gimme them fuckin' dice."
And Billy Markham shakes the dice and yells, "C'mon . . . thirteen."
And the dice they roll—and they come up—blank.
"You lose!" the Devil screams.
"But I really must say 'fore we go our way that I really do like your style.
Of all the fools I've played and beat, you're the first one who lost with a
    smile."
"Well I'll tell you somethin'," Billy Markham says.
"Those odds weren't too damn bad. In fourteen years on Music Row,
    that's the best damn chance I've had."
Then the Devil takes Billy under his cloak, and they walk out through
    Linebaugh's door,
Leavin' Billy's old guitar there on the sawdust floor.
And if you go to Linebaugh's now, you can see it there today.
Hangin' . . . from a nail on that wall of peelin' gray . . .
Billy Markham's old guitar . . .
That nobody dares to play.

BILLY MARKHAM AND THE FLY

Billy Markham slowly turns on a white hot spit,
And his skin it crackles like a roasting pig, and his flesh is seared and split,
And sulphur fills his nostrils and he's fed on slime and mud,
By a hairy imp with a pointed stick who bastes him in spider's blood,
And his eyeballs boil up inside his skull and his throat's too charred to scream.
So he sleeps the sleep of the burning dead and he dreams unspeakable dreams.
Then in walks the Devil, puttin' little screaming skulls as the bells of Hell start clangin',
And his last shot rolls right up to Billy Markham's toes
And he says, "Hey Bill, how're they hanging?
I'm sorry we couldn't give you a tomb with a view, but right now this is the best we got.
But as soon as we're done with Attila the Hun, we'll move you right into his spot.
Have you met your neighbors? Have you heard them scream? Do they keep you awake in the fire?
Hey, a little more brimstone on number nine—and hoist up them thumbs a bit higher.
Ah, you can't get good help these days, Bill, and there ain't much profit in Hell.
No, turn that adultress upside down—do I have to do everything myself?
I tell you, Bill, it's a full time job, tending these red hot coals,
And all this shovelin' and stokin', fryin' and smokin', proddin' and pokin',
    stretchin' and chokin', why I hardly got time for collecting new souls.
Which brings me to the subject of my little visit, now you're one of them natural born gamblin' men,
And I'll bet you'd give most anything to get those dice in your hands again.
So instead of swimming in this muck and slime and burning crisp as
    (Tastes him) toast . . .
I'll trade you one roll . . . of the dice for the souls . . . of the ones who love you most."
"Trade the souls of the ones who love me most? Not a chance in Hell I will."
"Spoken like a hero," the Devil says. "Hey a little more fire for Bill."
"You can roast me bake me or boil me," says Billy.
"Go and have your fiendish fun.
A coward dies a thousand times—a brave man dies but once."

"Oh beautiful, sensitive, and poetic too," says the Devil
"But life ain't like no rhyme.
And I know ways to make a brave man die a million times."
"Hey take your shot . . . Throw what you got . . . But I won't trade
  love away."
"That's what they all say," laughs the Devil ". . . but when I turn up the
  fire, they play."
And the flame burns white and Bill's flesh burns black and he smells his
  roasting stink.
And the hell rats nibble upon his nose . . . and Billy begins to think.
He thinks about his sweetheart who loved him through his crazy days.
He thinks of his gray-haired momma, hell, she's gettin' old anyway.
He thinks of his baby daughter—He ain't seen her since last fall.
He thinks about walkin' the Earth again and he thinks of the horrible
  pain he's in, and he thinks of the game that he just might win and he
  yells, "Hey—take 'em all."
And—Zap—He's back again at Linebaugh's, kneeling on that same old
  floor.
And across from him the Devil squats
Ready to play once more.
"I guess my point is still thirteen?" Billy Markham asks.
"The point's the same," the Devil sneers, "But the stakes are your loved
  one's ass."
"Well, one never knows," Billy Markham says, "when lady luck's gonna
  smile on a man.
And if a charcoal corpse from Hell can't roll thirteen, then who the hell
  can?"
And Billy Markham shakes the dice and whispers, "Please, thirteen."
And the dice roll out a . . . six . . . and a . . . six . . . and then, as if
  in a dream . . .
A buzzing fly from a plate nearby, like a messenger sent from heaven,
Shits—right in the middle of one of them sixes—and turns it into a seven.
"Thirteen! Thirteen! Thirteen! Thirteen! I have beat the Devil's play."
"Oh have you now," the Devil says, and WHOOSH he blows that speck
  away.
"Which only proves," the Devil says, "that Hell's too big to buck,
And when you're gambling for your ass, don't count on flyshit luck."
"Well, Luck and Love . . ." sighs Billy Markham, "they never do last for
  long,
But y'know that fly shittin' on that die would have made one hell of a
  song."

"You're a songwriting fool," the Devil grins. "There ain't no doubt about it.

As soon as you go and lose one damn game, you wanna write a song about it.

But there's a whole lot more to life and death than the rhymes and tunes you give 'em.

And any fool can sing the blues, *(Sings)* any fool can sing the blues, any fool can sing the blues, let's see if you can live 'em."

Then—Zap!—Billy wakes up back in Hell, bein' stuffed with white hot coals.

While imps dance on his head and shit in his hair and wipe their asses with his soul . . .

And he hears the screams of his momma as she turns in the purple flame.

And he hears the cries of his baby girl as she pays the price of his game.

He hears the voice of his own true love laugh like a child at play,

As she satisfies the Devil in her own sweet lovin' way.

And buzzin' 'cross Bill's burnin' bones and landing on his starin' eye,

And nibblin' on his roastin' flesh is the grinnin' Linebaugh's fly.

BILLY MARKHAM'S LAST ROLL

"Good morning, Billy Markham, it's time to rise and shine."

The Devil's word come grindin' into Billy's burnin' mind.

And he opens up one bloodshot eye to that world of living death.

And he feels the Devil's bony claw and he smells his rotten breath.

"Wake up Sunshine!" the Devil laughs. "I'm giving you another turn."

"I'm turning now," Billy Markham growls. "Go away and let me burn."

"Well, you sure are a grouch when you wake up, but you wouldn't let a chance go by."

"Another chance to roll thirteen? Hey, stick it where your fire don't shine.

I've played your game, now I feel the shame, as I hear my loved ones' cries,

And I'll piss on your shoe, if ever you come near me again with them flyshit dice."

"Dice? Dice? Who said dice? Anybody hear me say dice?

Hey, imp, pour my buddy here a cool glass of water and throw in a nice big chunk of ice."

"And since when," says Billy, "do you go around handing out gifts,

Except pokes from your burning pitchfork or buckets full of boiling shit?"

"Well, it's Christmas," says the Devil, "and all of us down here below,

We sort of celebrate in our own special way, and this year you're the star
of the show.
Why, just last night I was up on Earth and I seen that lovers' moon,
And I said to myself, 'Hey, I bet ol' Billy could use a little bit of poon.' "
"Poon?" says Billy Markham. "Last thing I need is poon.
Talk about gettin' my ashes hauled, hell, I'll be all ashes soon."
"Damn! Damn! Damn!" cries the Devil, "He's been too long on the fire.
I told you imps to fry him slow, now you gone and burned out his desire.
You gotta leave 'em some hope, leave 'em some dreams, so they know
what Hell is for,
'Cause when a man forgets how sweet love is, well, Hell ain't Hell no
more.
So just to refresh your memory, Billy, we're gonna send you back to
Earth.
And I'll throw in a little Christmas blessing to remind you what life is
worth.
For exactly thirteen hours, you can screw who you want to screw,
And there ain't no creature on God's Green Earth who is gonna say no
to you.
While me and all these burning souls and all my imps and fiends,
We're gonna sit down here and watch you on that big 24-inch color
screen.
And we'll see each hump you're humpin', and we'll hear each grunt you
groan,
And we'll laugh like hell at the look upon your face when it's time to
come back home."
"Well, a chance is a chance is a chance," says Billy, steppin' down off the
sizzlin' coals,
"But what if one won't gimme none, what if one says 'no'?"
"No? What if one says 'no'? Ain't nobody gonna say 'no.'
Nobody quits or calls in sick when the Devil calls the show.
Not man nor woman nor beast!" shouts the Devil. "And no 'laters' or
'maybes' or 'buts,'
And before one soul says 'no' to you I will see these Hell gates rust.
But . . . if any one refuses you, I say, any one you name,
Then you'll be free to stay on Earth, now get out and play the game!"
Then a flash of light . . . and a thunderclap . . . and Billy's back on
Earth once more,
And the asphalt sings beneath his feet as he swings toward Music Row.
First he stops in at the Exit Inn to seduce the blond on the door,
Then the RCA receptionist he takes on the office floor.
He nails the waitress down at Mack's, the one with the pear-shaped

breasts, and four of the girls from B.M.I. right on Frances Preston's desk.

He screws his way from M.C.A. to Vanderbilt's ivy walls,

And he pokes everything that giggles or sings or whimpers or wiggles or crawls.

First Debbie, then Polly, then Dotty, then Dolly, then Jeannie, and Jessie and Jan,

Then Marshall and Sal and that redheaded gal who takes the tickets down at Opryland.

And Brenda and Sammy and Sharon and Sandy, Loretta and Buffy and May,

And Terri and Lynne at the Holiday Inn and Joey and Zoe and Faye.

Then Sherry and Rita and Diane and Anita, Olivia, Emmy and Jean,

And Donna and Kay down at Elliston Place—right there in the Pinto Beans.

Then Hazel and Carla and an ex-wife of Harlan's, then Melva and Marge and Marie,

And three fat gospel singers who all come together in perfect three-part harmony.

He is humpin' the Queen of country music, when he hears the Devil moan.

"Make it sweet, Billy Markham, but make it short, you've got just thirty seconds to go.

And all of us here, we're applauding your show, and we'd say you done right well,

And we just can't wait to hear you moan, when you're fuckless forever in Hell."

"Hold on!" says Billy, with one last thrust. "If I got thirty seconds mo',

Then I got the right to one last hump before it's time to go."

"Well, raise your voice and make your choice but you'd better be quick and strong,

And make it a cum to remember, Bill—it's gotta last you eternity long.

So who will it, who will it, who will it be? Who's gonna be the one?

Starlet or harlot or housewife or hippie or grandma or schoolgirl or black-robed nun?

Or fresh-scented virgin or dope-smokin' groupie or sweet ever-smilin' Stew?"

And Billy Markham, he stops . . . and he looks at them all and he says to the Devil . . . "I think I'll . . . take *you!*"

"Foul!" cries the Devil. "Foul, no fair! The rules don't hold for me."

"You said man or woman or beast," says Billy, "and I guess you're all of the three."

And a roar goes up from the demons of Hell and it shakes the Earth across,

And the imps all squeal and the fiends they scream,

"He's Gonna Fuck the Boss!"

"Why you filthy scum," the Devil snarls to Billy, blushing a fiery red.

"I give you a chance to live again and you bust me in front of my friends."

"Hey, Play or Pay," Billy Markham says, "so set me free at last,

Or raise your tail and hear all Hell wail when I bugger your devilish ass."

"OK, OK, OK, you win. Go on back to your precious Earth.

And plod along and plug your songs, but carry this lifelong curse.

You shall lust for a million women and not one's gonna come your way,

And you shall write ten million songs and not one's ever gonna get played.

And your momma and daughter and your own true love they gonna stay down here with me,

And you'll carry the guilt like a moveable Hell wherever the hell you be."

So back on the streets goes Billy again, eatin' them Linebaugh's beans,

Singin' his songs while nobody listens and tellin' his story that no one believes

And gets no women and he gets no hits but he says just what he thinks,

Hey, buy him a round . . . it won't cost much . . . ice water's all he drinks.

But try not to stare at the burns on his wrists as he wipes the sweat from his head,

As he tells how the Devil burned him black

But he turned the Devil red.

BILLY, SCUZZY, AND GOD

We're at the Purple Peacock Rhinestone Bar, all the low are getting high,

And Billy tells his tale again to anyone who'll buy.

With waving arms and rolling eyes, he screams to the drunken throng,

"I've whipped the Devil and lived through Hell, now who's gonna sing my songs?"

Then from the shadows comes an oily voice. "Hey kid, I like your moves."

And out of the back limps a little wizened cat,

With black-and-white perforated wing-tipped shoes.

"Sleezo's the name," the little man says, "but I'm Scuzzy to my friends.

And I think I got a little business proposition you just might be interested in."

"Scuzzy Sleezo hisself," Billy Markham says. "Man, you're a legend in these woods,

You never cut the Devil down, but you done damn near as good.

Why, since I been old enough to jack, I been hearin' your greasy name,

It's an honor to meet an all-star Scuzz. Where you setting up your game?"

"No more games for me," says Scuzzy, "I'm too old and too slow for the pace,

So I'm the world's greatest hustler's *agent* now and Billy, I been studying your case.

I seen your first match with the Devil, and son, it was a Volkswagen/Mack truck collision.

And your second shot, well, you showed me a lot, but you got burned in a hometown decision.

And I says to myself, 'He can go all the way, with the proper guidance of course.

The kid's got the heart, and with a few more smarts, he'd be an irresistible force.'

Yeah, I can show you the tricks and show you the shticks just like a hustler's training camp.

And I'll bring you on slow—then a prelim or so—then—Powee!—a shot at the Champ."

"The Champ?" says Billy Markham. "Now who in God's name is that?"

"Why God himself," says Scuzzy, "you know anybody more champ than that?"

"Hey, a match with God?" Billy Markham grins.

"And what would be the purse?"

"Why, a seat in Heaven forever, of course, 'stead of livin' this no pussy, no hits, no nuthin' Nashville curse.

But I'll drive you like a wagon, son, and I'll sweat you like a Turk.

All for just fifty percent of the take—now sign here and let's get to work."

Now we find ourselves at the funky pool hall known as the Crystal Cue,

And the time is three months later, and the smoke is thick and blue.

And the pool table cloth is stained with tears and blood and ketchup spots.

As a fat old man with a dirty white beard stands practicin' three cushion shots.

"What are we doin' here?" says Billy to Scuzzy. "I been taught and I been trained.

And I don't need no more prelims, I am primed for the Big Big Game."

"Well son," says the old man, sinkin' the four, "why don't you pick yourself out a cue?"

"Hey, Santa Claus," Billy Markham snaps back, "wasn't nobody talkin' to
you."

"Whoa, whoa," Scuzzy says, pullin' Billy aside . . . "if you look close,
you will notice his cue is a lightning rod.

And he ain't no Santa, and he ain't Fat Daddy . . . you just insulted
God."

"Well, hey, excuse me, Lord," says Bill, "I didn't mean to be uncool,

But it sure can shake a fellah's faith to find God hustling pool."

"Well where you expect to find me," says God, "on a throne with cherubs
around?

Hey, I do that six days and nights a week, but on the seventh day . . . I
get down.

Besides I can't believe you came in here just to bat the breeze around."

"You're right about that, Lord," Billy says, "I come to take your crown."

"Beg pardon, Lord," says Scuzzy Sleezo, "I don't mean no disrespect.

But when you're dealing with my boy, don't speak to him direct.

I'm his agent and representative and this kid is hotter than hot,

In his last match, he whipped the Devil, and now we're lookin' for a title
shot."

"Beat the Devil, you say?" laughs God. "Well, I take my hat off to him.

Let him hang up his mouth and pick out a cue and he'll get the shot
that's due him.

Any game he names—any table he's able—

Any price he can afford."

"Straight pool for heaven," says Billy Markham.

"Straight pool it is," says the Lord.

Crack—Billy Markham wins the break and bust 'em cool and clean.

The five ball falls, he sinks the seven, and then devastates the thirteen.

He makes the nine, and he bags the eleven, and he puts the six away,

Then the three and the eight on a triple combination and he wins the
game on a smooth massé.

He wins the next game, the next, and the next, and when he finally does
miss,

He blows the dust off his hands, and his game score stands at 1376.

"Well, my turn at last," says the Lord chalkin' up.

"Son, you sure shoot a wicked stick.

I'll need some luck to beat a run like that: that is without resorting to
miracles or tricks."

"Hey, trick and be damned," Billy Markham laughs.

"Tonight I'm as hot as flame.

So I laugh at your tricks—and I sneer at your stick—
And I take your name in vain."
"Oooh," goes the crowd that's been gathering around.
"Oooh," goes the rack boy in wonder.
"Oooh," says Scuzzy Sleezo. "I think you just made a slight tactical blunder."
"Oooh," says God, "you shouldn't have said that, son, you shouldn't have said that at all!"
And his cue cracks out like a thunderbolt spittin' a flamin' ball.
It sinks everything on the table, then it zooms up off the green.
Through the dirty window with a crash of glass and into the wind like a woman's scream.
Out of the pool hall, up through the skies,
The cue ball flames and swirls,
Bustin' in and out of every pool game in the world.
It strikes on every table, it crashes every rack.
And every pool ball in creation comes rebounding back!
Back through the window, they tumble and crash,
Down through the ceiling they spin.
A million balls rain down on the table, and every one goes in.
"Now, there," says Scuzzy Sleezo, "is a shot you don't see every day.
Lord, you should have an agent to handle your press, and build up the class of your play.
My partnership with this dirtbag here has come to a termination.
But God and Scuzzy Sleezo? Hey, that would be a combination."
Meanwhile, the cue ball flyin' back last, like a sputterin' fizzlin' rocket.
Goes weaving dizzily down the table
And—plunk! Falls right in the pocket.
"Scratch, you lose," says Billy. "I thought you said you could shoot!"
"Scratch," says Scuzzy Sleezo. "I told you my boy'd come through."
"Scratch!" murmurs the crowd of hangers and hustlers.
"At last we have seen it all."
"Scratch!" mutters the Lord. "I guess I put a little too much English on the ball.
Just another imperfection, I never get it quite on the button.
Tell you what, son, I'll spot you three million balls and play you one more double or nothin'."
"Double what?" says Billy Markham. "I already whipped you like a child.
And I won my seat in Heaven, now I'm gonna set it awhile."
"Hit-and-run chickenshit," sneers God. "You said you was the best.
Turns out you're just a get-lucky-play-it-safe pussy like all the rest."

"Whoa-whoa," says Billy. "There's somethin' in that voice I know quite well."

And he reaches out and yanks off God's white beard—and there stands the Devil himself!

"You said you was God," Billy Markham cries. "You conned me and hustled me, too!"

"I am God—sometimes—and sometimes I'm the Devil, good and bad, just like you.

I'm everything and everyone in perfect combination.

And everyone but you knows that there ain't no separation.

(Sings) I'm everything and everyone in perfect combination. And everyone but you knows . . ."

"Please, please," says Billy Markham. "You ain't that great a singer.

And I would like to get to Heaven before they stop serving dinner."

"OK," says God, scribblin' somethin' down. "Give this note to the angel on the wall.

And you sit up there and plunk your harp . . .

"Hey anybody wanna shoot some eight ball?"

So Billy walks out into the parkin' lot with stardust in his eyes,

(Sings) "I got a seat in Heaven."

And he sees a golden staircase stretchin' up to paradise.

(Sings) "I got a seat in Heaven."

And he grips the glittering balustrade, and he begins his grand ascent.

(Sings) "I got a . . ."

"Just a minute, good buddy," yells Scuzzy Sleezo. "How about my fifty percent?

I helped you win the championship—and you wouldn't do ole Scuzzy Wuzzy wrong,

And since the purse is a seat in Heaven, why, you just gotta take me along."

"Just a minute," says Billy Markham. "There's something weird going on in this game.

All the voices that I'm hearin' start to sound just the same."

And he rips off Scuzzy Sleezo's face and the Devil's standing there.

"Good God," yells Billy Markham, "are you—are you everywhere?"

"Yes, I am," the Devil says. "And don't look so damn surprised.

I thought you could smuggle me into Heaven wearing my Sleezy disguise.

'Course I could've walked in as Jehovah, but it just wouldn't have been the same.

But you and your corny Dick Tracy bit—you had to go and ruin my fantasy game.

Go on, climb your golden staircase, enjoy your paradise.

But don't rip off your own face, Bill—or you might get a shockin' surprise.

But, I'll be damned if I let you get to Heaven climbin' that golden stair-
way."

And he plucks out Billy Markham's soul and tees it up, and *whack*—
drives it up the fairway.

And Billy floats out on a sea of light—on a snow white cloud he sails,
While vestal virgins comb his hair, and cherubs manicure his nails.
And up, up to glory, Billy Markham sails away
And high, high above him,
He hears his own songs being played
While down, down below hear Scuzzy Sleezo curse his name,
To the click-click-click of the pool balls,
As God hustles another game.

BILLY MARKHAM 'S DESCENT

Billy Markham sits on an unwashed cloud, his hair is matted and mussed.

His dusty wings hang limp and grey and his harp strings have gone to
rust.

With tremblin' hands and tear-stained cheeks, and a glazed look in his
eyes,

He chews his nails and grinds his teeth, and stares across the skies.
But his thoughts are down in that nether world, in that burning fiery rain.
His thoughts are with his momma, how he longs to soothe her pain.
His thoughts are with his baby girl, how he'd love to ease her cryin'.
His thoughts are with his own true love, how he'd love to bust her spine.
So late that night, while the heavenly harps play "In the Sweet Bye and
Bye,"

Billy reaches for the silken rope that hangs down from the sky.
He has stripped himself of his crown and robes
He has clutched the silken cord:
As he swings himself down without a sound, so's not to wake the Lord.
Down he winds through the perfumed air, down through the marshmal-
low clouds.

And he hangs for a while o'er the city roofs,
Lookin' down at the scurryin' crowds.
Then down, down, through a manhole, to a stench he knows quite well.
Through the sewers of the street, till he feels his feet touch the shit-
mucked shores of Hell.

Then he scales the crusted rusted gates, and he throws a bone to Cerebus
Hounds.

And he swims the putrid river Styx, still down and further down.

Down past the gluttons, the dealers and pimps, down past the murderers' cage.

Down past the rock stars searching in vain for their names on the *Rolling Stone* page.

Down past the door of The Merchants of War, past the puritans slop-filled bin

Past the Bigot's hive, till at last he arrives, at the pit marked BLAMELESS SINS.

And he finds the vat where his momma boils: and he raises her gently from the deep.

And he finds the grate where his little girl burns: and he lifts her and soothes her and rocks her to sleep.

And he finds the pit where his sweetheart sleeps: and he spits on the fire where she lay.

And he curses her as a whore of Hell:

Curses and turns away.

"From this day on, I place my faith only in mother and child.

And never again shall I seek sweet salvation

In some bitch's scum stained smile."

Then back through the river he swims with them

Back over the gate he climbs,

And over the white hot coals he leaps, with the Hellhounds barking close behind.

Then back up the silken rope he climbs, up through the suffering swarms.

Past the clutching hands and the pitiful screams with his two precious loves in his arms.

Just one more pull, just one more pull—then free forever from Hell.

Just one more pull then—"Hello, Billy!"—and there stands the Devil himself.

And now he's wearing his crimson robes and his horns are buffered bright.

And blood oozes through his white-linen gloves and his skin glows red in the night.

And his tail coils like an oily snake and the hell fires blaze in his eyes.

On those craggy rocks, he stands and blocks the way to paradise.

"Well, my, my, my, what have we here in my domain of sin?

In all my years as Prince of the Dark, it's the first case of anybody breaking in.

And of all the daredevil darin' dudes, well, who should the hero be?

But my old friend Billy Markham—who once made a punk out of me.

I heard you was in Heaven, Billy, humpin' angels all day long,

What's the matter—did God get sick to his stomach listening to your raunchy songs?

You made me the laughing stock of Hell, and the whole world laughed along with you.

Now here you come crashin' my party again:

Now tell me, just who's devilin' who?

Now, I didn't invite you down here, Bill, and nobody twisted your arm.

But you're back down here on my turf now, down here where it's cozy and warm.

So no more dice and no more games and no more jive stories to tell.

Just the Devil and a man with three souls in his hand dangling between Heaven and . . .

But, hey what's this? Only *two*? Only *two* souls you've set free?

You must have forgot and left one behind: now who could that third one be?

Could it be your own true love, the one with the sweet wet smile?

The one you curse with each bitter breath 'cause she played with the Devil awhile?

You call yourself free? Tee hee tee hee. Why you prudish judgmental schmuck.

You'd leave your sweet love burn in Hell for one harmless little suck.

What would you rather she had done, leaped in the boiling manure . . .

So's you could keep your fantasy of someone sweet and pure?

She's a woman, flesh and bone, and they do what they do what they do.

And right or wrong, she needs no curse from a hypocrite like you.

So, she shall rule with me—Billy Markham's love shall rule with me. She shall sit next to me on my throne.

And the whole world shall know—that the Devil's heart has more tenderness than your own.

So get your ass back up that rope, climb back to your promised land.

And hold your illusions of momma and daughter tight in your sweatin' hand.

But you'll see, you'll see, they're as human as she and you'll scream when you find it's true.

But please—stay up there and scream to God—Hell's gates are closed to you."

And Billy Markham, clutching his loves, climbs upward toward the skies.

And is it the sharp night wind that brings the tears to Billy's eyes?

Or is it the swirling sulphur smoke or the bright glare of the sun?

Or is it the sound of the wedding feast that the demons below have begun?

BILLY MARKHAM 'S WEDDING

The trumpets of Hell have sounded the word like a screeching clarion call.

The trumpets of Hell have sounded the word and the word will be heard by all.

The trumpets of Hell have sounded the word and it reaches the heavenly skies.

Come angels, come demons, come dancing dead, the Devil is taking a bride.

And out of the Pearly Gates they come in a file two by two.

For when the Devil takes a bride, there's none that dare refuse.

And Jesus himself, he leads the way down through the starless night.

With the Mother Mary at his left side and Joseph on his right.

And then comes Adam and then comes Eve and the saints move close behind.

And all the gentle and all the good, in an endless column they wind.

Down, down to the pits of Hell, down from the heavens they sift—

Like fallen stars to a blood red sea, each bearing the Devil a gift.

The strong and the brave, the halt and the lame, the deaf and the blind and the dumb.

And last of all comes Billy Markham, cursing the night as he comes.

Hell's halls are decked with ribbons of red and the feast has been prepared.

And the Devil and his bride sit side by side in skull-and-crossbone chairs.

And the Devil grins as his guests file in, for he is master now.

And one-by-one they enter his realm—and one-by-one they bow.

And the Devil whispers, "Thank you, Friends," and he swells his chest with pride.

"Come give me your blessings and place your gifts at the feet of my blushing bride.

Lucrezia Borgia has made the punch of strychnine, wine and gin.

And Judas has set the supper table on hallowed, bloody linen.

The Feast is a human bar-b-cue, and the sauce is berri-berri,

Chopped up by Lizzie Borden and cooked by Typhoid Mary.

Here's some half-eaten apples from the Garden of Eden, *(Offers bucket)*

Here's some tidbits from Donner Pass.

Here's some fine old wine an acquaintance of mine

Made out of water, lemme fill your glass.

So you and you, drink of this crimson brew, we're all brothers and sisters under the skin.

And take off your costumes of virtue and sin, and

Let the revels begin."

And slowly and shyly they strip off their wings, and hide their halos away.
And they shyly touch hands—and begin to dance, as Hell's Band begins
    to play.
There is Nero madly fiddlin' his fiddle, and Gabriel blowin' his horn.
And Idi Amin is beatin' his drum and Caligula's bangin' his gong.
Francis Scott Key plays piano and he is there 'cause he wrote that song.
And the pipes of Pan lead the Devil's band and everybody rocks along.
There's Janis and Elvis and Jimi and Cass, singin' them gimmesome
    blues.
And Adolph Hitler and Joan of Arc start doin' the boogaloo.
Lady Godiva jumps off her horse, and Kate Smith starts shakin' her hips.
And the Marquis de Sade does a promenade laughin' and crackin' his
    whips.
Ghengis Khan got a tutu on, and he's doing a pirouette,
When out of the cake with a wiggle and a shake comes a naked Marie
    Antoinette.
And King Farouk, he moons the crowd, while swingin' from the ceiling,
As Adam and the snake have one more drink just to show there's no
    hard feelings.
Isadora Duncan's gettin' kind of drunk, and
Doin' something filthy with a scarf,
And they bring out the turkey, and Jack the Ripper says
"Hey, I'll be glad to carve."
And there's old Dante dealing three card monte, Harpo Marx is tellin'
    jokes,
While Fatty Arbuckle is trying to collect the deposit on a bottle of Coke.
Elliot Ness shows up in a dress and Dillinger asks him to dance,
While Ivan the Terrible's tryin' to get into Susan B. Anthony's pants.
'N bare-ass naked on the balustrade sits Edgar Allen Poe,
Posin' for a two dollar caricature by Michelangelo.
Abraham Lincoln and John Wilkes Booth they're posin' for publicity
    photos,
While out in the foyer Richard the Third is comparing his hump with
    Quasimodo's.
And Catherine the Great she's makin' a date with the horse of Paul
    Revere,
While Don Juan whispers love and lust into Helen Keller's ear.
And General MacArthur and Tokyo Rose, they're gigglin' behind the
    door,
While the daughters of Lot are yellin' "Hey Pop, let's do it just once
    more."

And then John Wayne and Mary Magdalene announce they're going
    steady,
While Abel and Cain form a daisy chain with Jeannette McDonald and
    Nelson Eddy.
And Doctor Faust and Johann Strauss, Nabokov and Errol Flynn,
They're arguin' over some teenaged girl that they're all interested in.
Lee Harvey Oswald's tryin' to make a phone call, getting in some target
    practice,
And Salome's in the hall playin' volleyball with the head of John the
    Baptist.
And Al Capone gives Eva Braun a big bouquet of roses,
And Gertrude Stein has a little more wine and hits on Grandma Moses.
Delilah she's clippin' and snippin' the snakes out of old Medusa's hair,
While Oscar Wilde says to Billy the Kid, "Can I show you 'round up-
    stairs?"
And the Devil he sips his Boilin' Blood
And glances side to side
From the eyes of Billy Markham
To the eyes of his own sweet Bride.
Then the music stops—and all heads turn—and the revellers freeze
    where they stand.
As Billy Markham approaches the throne and says, "May I have this
    dance?"
"And who be this?" the Devil snorts, "with the balls to think he can
Just walk up to the Devil's throne and ask the Devil's Bride to dance?
Can this . . . can this be Billy Markham, who loves only the chaste and
    the pure?
No, Billy wouldn't bow and kiss the hand of a woman he once called
    whore.
But whoever this poor, lonely wretch may be, it is my wedding whim,
That no man be refused this day—step down, darlin', and dance with
    him."
The Devil grins and waves his tail, the music begins again gentle and
    warm,
As the lady nervously steps from her throne into Billy Markham's arms.
And the guests all snicker and snigger and wait, and they watch the
    dancers' eyes,
As 'round and 'round the floor they swirl 'tween Hell and Paradise.
    (Dances with mop)
"Oh, babydoll," says Billy Markham, "I've done you an awful wrong.
And to show you how rotten bad I feel, I even wrote about it in a song.

I never should have called you a dirty whore, and I never should have spit on your bed.

And I never should have left you to burn here in Hell, 'cause you gave the Devil some head.

But if there's any hellish or heavenly way that I can make things right,
For your sweet sake, whatever it takes, I'll get you away tonight."

And the lady smiles a mysterious smile, as 'round the room they swing,
And she whispers low in Billy's ear: "Well, there is . . . one little thing."

Now the hall is empty, the guests are gone, and there on the rusted throne,
Hand in hand in golden bands, the Devil and bride sit alone.

And the Devil stretches and yawns and grins, "Well, it has been quite a day,

And now it's time to seal our love in the usual mortal way."

And the Devil strips off his crimson cloak, and he casts his pitchfork aside,

And he frees his oily two-pronged tail, and waits to take his bride.

And his true love lifts her wedding dress up over her angel's head.

And hand in hand they make their way to the Devil's fiery bed.

And her upturned breasts glow warm in the fire, and her legs are shapely and slim.

And for the very first time since time began, the Devil feels passion in him.

"Now for the moment of truth," he whispers. "My love, my queen, my choice."

"I love you, too, motherfucker," she laughs—in Billy Markham's voice.

And the Devil leaps up and howls so loud that the fires of Hell blow cold.

"Ain't no big deal," says Billy's voice. "While we was dancing, we swapped souls.

Now she's up in Heaven singin' my songs and wearin' my body, too.

Safe forever in the arms of the Lord, while I'm down here in the arms of you."

"Why you creepin' crud," the Devil cries, "I'll teach you to fuck with my brain.

I'll give you a child who weighs ninety-five pounds, you wanna talk about screamin' pain!"

"Oh no, no, no," says Billy Markham. "I will be your wife only in name—
You come near me with that double-pronged dick, and I'll rip it right off of your frame."

"Shhhh . . ." says the Devil. "Not so loud. If Hell learns what's been done.
They'll laugh me off this golden throne and damn me to kingdom come.
And you—You've given me my true love's body with a hustler's soul inside.
You know more of torture than I've ever dreamed—you're fit to be my bride."
"Well, don't take it so hard," Billy Markham says. "You know things could be worse.
Havin' *her* soul in *my* body—now, that would be a curse.
But you and me, we got lots in common, we both like to shoot the shit.
And we both like to joke, and we both like to smoke, and we both like to gamble a bit.
And that should be the makin's for a happy marriage, and since neither one of us is gonna die,
Well, we might as well start the honeymoon—you wanna cut the cards or should I?"

Now the wedding night is a hundred years past and their garments have rotted to rags.
But face to face they sit in the flames, dealing five-card stud and one-eyed jacks.
And sometimes they play pinochle, sometimes they play gin.
And sometimes the Devil rakes in the pots, and sometimes the lady wins.
And sometimes they just sit and reminisce of the night they first were wed.
From dawn to dawn the game goes on . . .
They *never* go to bed.

STRUCK DUMB

Jean-Claude van Itallie &
Joseph Chaikin

Struck Dumb was originally commissioned and produced at the Mark Taper Forum, Los Angeles, California, Gordon Davidson, Artistic Director.

Jean-Claude van Itallie

Jean-Claude van Itallie was born in Brussels, Belgium, in 1936, raised in Great Neck, Long Island, and graduated from Harvard in 1958. He created an avalanche of praise and anticipation with his trilogy of one-act plays, *America Hurrah*, the watershed off-Broadway play of the sixties, which ran for two years in New York City, played at the Royal Court in London and then continued to have productions all over the world. For that play, van Itallie won the coveted Vernon Rice and Drama Desk Awards. He has subsequently won grants for his playwriting from CAPS, the National Endowment, Rockefeller and Ford Foundations, and was twice a Guggenheim Fellow.

Over the last twenty-five years, his writing career has been devoted to English translations of the major plays of Chekhov; an English translation of Jean Genet's *The Balcony;* monologue plays produced at both the Theater for the New City and Manhattan Theater Club; *The Tibetan Book of the Dead,* a classical but contemporary poetic ensemble version of the text; *Naropa,* a play for puppets and people; *Paradise Ghetto,* a play based on the Nazi detention camp for Czech artists; *The Traveller,* his play about a person recovering from aphasia, inspired by Joe Chaikin, with whom he then collaborated on *Struck Dumb.* Van Itallie has recently completed a musical, *The Odyssey,* in collaboration with Tony Scheitinger, and his latest play, *Ancient Boys,* about a gay artist who contracts AIDS, was presented at the La Mama Annex in 1991.

Especially significant has been van Itallie's work with Joe Chaikin's Open Theater. He was the principal playwright for that group and created with them *The Serpent.* That play, produced in the late sixties, won a *Village Voice* Obie Award and established the contributions of both the Open Theater and van Itallie as a major force in the American theater. All of his translations have been abundantly produced and he continues to be that significant force.

Joseph Chaikin

Joseph Chaikin was born in 1937 in Brooklyn, New York, of Russian parents. He went to college at Drake University in Des Moines, Iowa. After working for several years as the central actor with the Living Theater, where he created a memorable performance of Galy Gay in *Man is*

Man and for which he won the Obie Award, he broke off from that company in 1963 in order to form his own company, the Open Theater. Deliberately non-commercial, the Open Theater, nevertheless, did perform publicly in one- or two-night programs of short plays and improvisations in nearly every off- and off-off Broadway house. Its effect on all phases of American avant-garde theater in the sixties, in the words of the *Village Voice,* "has been seminal."

Chaikin's performances have won him three Obie Awards and his work with the Open Theater won him a Vernon Rice Award for "outstanding contribution to the theater." Among other distinctions are a Lifetime Achievement Obie in 1977, Guggenheim Fellowships in 1969 and 1975, and Honorary Ph.D.'s from Drake and Kent State. He has directed productions of *Electra, The Dybbuk, The Seagull, Rearrangements, Tourists and Refugees* and *Trespassing* (for which he also wrote the script), *The Bald Soprano* and *Waiting for Godot.* As an actor, in recent years, he has starred in Beckett's *Endgame* and *Texts, Uncle Vanya, Woyzeck,* and had a major role in Robert Frank's feature film, *Me and My Brother.*

When *The War in Heaven* and *Struck Dumb* were first presented at the American Place Theater, the following information was included in the program:

> These plays are expressive of a cataclysm in Joseph Chaikin's life when, in May, 1984, he had a stroke during the course of his third heart operation. As a consequence, Chaikin became a member of what he calls his "new family," the one million Americans who suffer from aphasia, a disturbance of the ability to understand and express the spoken word. Sam Shepard and Jean Claude van Itallie each collaborated with Chaikin at different moments of his healing process, resulting in *The War in Heaven* and *Struck Dumb.*

Because of the unrelenting and undefatigable help—generous and gracious—from van Itallie, Shepard, Chaikin's sister Miriam, and William Coco, Joseph Chaikin miraculously fought back to a speaking, theatrical and human life. In 1986 he returned to Israel to create a sequel to his *Imagining the Other,* a work he created with an Arab and Israeli Company. Since his stroke, he has performed with Sam Shepard at the Magic Theater in San Francisco and performed *Struck Dumb* and *The War in Heaven* in New York City. Chaikin has been honored with the Edwin Booth Award for his contribution to the New York City theater. His talents, his achievements, his dedication and his courage have established him as one of the rare artists in the American theater.

Joe Chaikin and I have been close friends and co-workers in the theatre since 1963 when Joe founded and directed the Open Theater, of which I was the principal playwright.

In May of 1984 Joe suffered a stroke during heart surgery to repair a faulty valve. As a result of this stroke, Joe became aphasic. His speech and comprehension of speech became "out of phase."

I wrote a play, *The Traveller,* inspired by experiences around Joe's stroke, which premiered in Los Angeles at the Mark Taper Forum in the spring of 1987. During rehearsals I thought it would be useful for Joe to have a play to perform himself along with the short *War in Heaven* which Joe and Sam Shepard had written before and just after Joe's stroke.

Gordon Davidson and Madeline Puzo at the Taper were kind enough to commission *Struck Dumb,* and we started writing while Joe and I and the dramaturg Bill Coco were living close to where our character, Adnan, lives in Venice, California.

Struck Dumb is a play about an aphasic character, who may be played by an aphasic actor needing to read his lines rather than memorize them. Adnan, in the middle of his life, is newborn to language and to the world.

Struck Dumb is a theatrical metaphor for Adnan's mind. Adnan's written thoughts appear to him from all parts of the stage.

It is Joe's hope and mine that *Struck Dumb* will focus attention on the problems and potentials of persons afflicted with aphasia. There are about a million aphasics in the United States. The very nature of aphasia requires a voice.

It has been said that one does not usually recover from aphasia, but that, by dint of hard work and time, one recovers *with* aphasia.

Jean-Claude van Itallie
Boulder, Colorado
March 14, 1989

Character:
ADNAN

Scene:
Place: *Venice, California. Time: 1988*

Facing the audience, on an old oriental carpet, is a comfortable chair and a wooden desk, with a monitor, a tape deck, and a typewriter. Some of the objects have hand-lettered signs on them saying what they are: "desk," and "tapes."

ADNAN, *who is aphasic, may be played by an aphasic actor who cannot memorize lines but who can read them.* ADNAN *may also be played by a non-aphasic actor who does not ever lapse into speaking memorized lines.*

The production provides a spare functional set as well as a changing environment of text and light which helps ADNAN *from place to place on the stage (as if he were going from home to seashore to Santa Monica mall to sunset on the pier).*

ADNAN *is sometimes surprised by his own thoughts when the text appears suddenly on a placard or is lit on a floor-to-ceiling scroll (giving mosque-like overtones to the set).*

Some music and sound may be used but the principal focus is the actor's voice.

During the course of the play the light changes from dawn to night.

WAKING UP

(ADNAN, *fiftyish, is in his "home" area of the stage, behind his desk. He wears comfortable clothing (with maybe a slight middle-Eastern flavor). He does not look poor or alien. As he leans back, the first text comes down to him suddenly from the ceiling on a placard)*
Waking up: it's a shock.
Sleeping: it's dreaming, it's travelling, it's easy.
But waking,
Waking up on earth,
It's amazing.

Every morning: an event.
Every morning, ordinary.

I look, wanting to find "perfect."
But there is no "perfect."
Except sometimes—
A few seconds—they are perfect.

Every every day, waking:
I wonder, what is this room?
What is this day?
What planet?
Light?
Lights?
Sky?
Only one sun?
How to move this body?
Body: it's universe.

Sometimes feeling—it's tremor—
It's trauma—
Starting small, sometimes from nothing—
Trembling: starting tiny, tiny like tic.
Look at my face, look: tic.
   (He shows a tic on his face)
Then twitch.
   (His tic becomes bigger)
Tic becomes a twitch.
And then quiver.
   (His tic becomes even bigger)
And then shudder. Shudder.
   (His whole body starts to shake)
And tremor. Tremor. Tremor.
   (His body shakes more)
And then shake, and shake, and then—
   (He is still)
And then what?
I have a fear of . . . what?

   (ADNAN listens. He has a few characteristic emblematic movements, such as the way he holds his head as he listens for an earthquake, as he does now)

It's difficult—to hear.
Like a blind person, needing to imagine colors—
Listening in the blindness.
  (He listens again)
Feeling, trembling.
Not once, but maybe twenty-five times.
Every day: earthquake.
Cataclysm . . .
It's crisis in universe, stars, planets . . .
Crisis causing changing, of course.
So what is changing?
Changing, it's "evolving."
Even thinking about changing, it's change.

MY HOUSE

My name is Adnan.
I was born in Beirut, in Lebanon,
In a big house.
Beirut, it's an ancient city.
Lebanon, my country,
Five thousand years ago,
It was called Phoenicia.

Now I am living in Venice, California.
I have a bedroom, and a kitchen.

It's morning: I have coffee, and then breakfast:
Toast or something.
I'm eating something—it's a muffin.
It's "taste." I'm amazed—
Shock.
  (ADNAN *listens*)
Tremor, quake—it's shaking again.
Earth groaning again.
  (ADNAN *listens, then returns to normal*)
This room has only three or four things.
Simple, it's better, it's best.

This is my desk. It's wood.
The desk exists longer than I am human,
Longer than my father, longer than my grandfather.
It's from the Shakers.

These are my tapes.
Music, it's pulse and rhythm and melody.
I see music.
My greatest pleasure, it's music: hearing God.

Then, second, it's colors.
I have pleasure also from shapes—like shells, from the sea.
Music, it might be shapes.
Thinking about shapes, shells.
Bodies—
Like air, like clouds . . .
For example spiders—many legs, many arms.
Spider to galaxy, spinning . . . spiral.
Shapes . . .
   (ADNAN *gestures a spiral shape*)
This is my clock. It's new.
Time—oh, yes—it's important to me now,
It's order.
Without clock, one second or one year—no different.
But when I leave my house,
When I go to the ocean,
When I'm looking at the sea,
I do not want a clock at all.

THE SEA

   (ADNAN *walks toward the "beach" area of the stage*)
Here, it's just an ordinary place, Venice,
But—on the sea,
And you have to be living someplace.

I was living in Paris once.
I was a student, learning about the voice.
And then I was singing.
I sang concerts many times.
And then: cataclysm, expulsion:
I was struck dumb.

   (ADNAN *listens*)
I am obsessed about earthquake.
Some people have obsess about ice cream,
Or drugs, or sex.

With me: it's earthquake.
(ADNAN *listens*)
I am thinking about this and that—
And then, after two minutes, again—
(ADNAN *listens. Then* ADNAN *walks*)
Many refugees come to the beach,
Many refugees come speaking French.
I was speaking French when I was three.
Refuse—refugees—
Coming to the beach like tide, waves . . .

Jean-Paul Sartre, he's my friend.
I never met him really.
He's short.
He's ghost.
Before, I was never thinking about ghost at all.
But now, thinking about ghost a lot.
Thinking myself ghost.
Well, not myself,
But ghost using my voice maybe.
(ADNAN *makes a ghostly sound*)
I don't speak so well now,
So why ghost choosing my voice?
I don't know. It's mysterious.
Ghost, it's funny.
(ADNAN *walks*)
Walking on street to ocean every day.
Going outside, I look back at my house:
It's yellow and gray;
It's thin and small;
It's not perfect.
But it's only two blocks from the sea.
If I could have a different house,
I would live in the sea.
My room, it's small.
The sea, it's enormous.

Every day, walking down the street to the sea,
I pick a leaf from the same bush. Every day.
I don't know why.
Every day I taste the leaf.

The taste is bitter:
It's shock to my body.
Earthquake, it's shock to Mother Earth.
>   (ADNAN *listens*)
Listen.
>   (ADNAN *listens*)
I'm listening all the time.
Someone told me once:
Everything everybody ever said
Is still out there in the universe vibrating.
Listen.
It's ghosts' voices vibrating:
Ghosts shuddering, moving, hovering.
>   (ADNAN *walks*)
Every day, on the street,
I meet a dog.
I'm looking into her eyes.
She's looking at me.
>   (ADNAN *looks as if at a dog*)
She's cute: a thousand curlies, her hair.
It's golden and it's brown,
Like cashew, the nut.
She's not my dog really, but almost.
Her name is Cashew.
Not really, but I love the name "Cashew."
Cashew's happy to see me.
>   (ADNAN *is greeting the dog*)
Hello. Hi, Cashew, hi.
She's jumping, she's happy.
But animals not thinking.
Cashew, she's smart.
And she's graceful
Like a ballet dancer,
But she's not thinking at all.
Animals do not drink tea, or coffee, like humans.
Animals are different.

Thinking, it's humans' . . .
Humans' what?
What is thinking?
No answer.

What is endless . . . endless . . . endless?
Eternity—what is it?
No answer.

When body is finished,
What happens to soul?

No answer.

Is something continuing?
What is it?

No answer.

Does Cashew have a soul also?

No answer.

Before, I didn't know I had a soul.
Now that I know, what to do?
What to do with my soul?

I am like: "Man struck dumb after writing letter to God."
Writing: "Dear God, I'm tired of my life.
Please send me something new."
So God strikes him dumb.

It's dangerous, writing a letter to God.
You sometimes get what you want.

People in Venice don't work much.
Everybody's bum, or retired.

My name is Adnan.
I was born in Beirut, in Lebanon.
Once I was a singer.
Now myself, I could be—what?
Orchestra conductor?
Guide to Zoo?
Prince of Wales?
Astronomer?
Deep sea diver?

Dope dealer?
Weatherman?
Foster father?
Actually, I am now a philosopher.
It does not pay well.
I am a philosopher, but I have no answers.
You must live without answers.
I want to know things clearly.
The questions must be clear.
But I must live without answers.
   (ADNAN *walks*)
Walking on sand,
Just thinking, touching on things:
Where land meets water—it's boundary.

The poor and the rich,
Everybody walks on the beach.

There is more sea than land.
Myself, I'm mostly water, like the ocean.
Myself, I'm a mammal.

If I am slippery in this lifetime—
I could be reborn a whale.
Maybe myself already born many times whale,
Living in ocean, my home.
   (ADNAN *touches the water*)
Water.
This is cold water touching my hand.
It's shock.
   (*A placard comes in quickly on a pulley, accompanied by a loud grinding
      sound*)
Water!
Ocean spilling,
Earth, it's splitting, it's cracking,
Ocean, it's spilling,
Earth's face, it's splitting,
Earth brain, it's cracking open.
   (ADNAN *breathes hard. Then he is back to normal*)
The sea is like mother.
French word "mother," sounds the same as the word for sea:
Mer, it's sea, and mother—

It's deep, the ocean.
Nobody knows exactly what's down there.

PRACTICING WORDS

(ADNAN *goes back to his desk. He turns on the tape machine, leans back
in his chair, listening to classical music. We watch him listen. When the
music is over, he reaches for his word cards on his desk*)
I am practicing words.
"Sugar and salt"—it's flowers and metal.
"Astonishing:" it's a word, an explosion.
"My," it's a funny word:
"My" clock. "My" house. "My" word.
And "meaning."
"Meaning," it's a huge word.
To choose a word—it's a choice.
Turning this way, that.
Repetition, repetition: "life," "living," "live," "SHOCK."
And another word: "conscious."
"Unconscious," and "conscious."
And "mysterious."

Anything to do with speech, it's work.

"Abandon:" it's a word.
I want to abandon it.
And "evolving:"
It's another word for dying.
"Evolving:" it happens.
And word "ghost," it's like "guest," and "goats."
Other words: "extreme," "hate,"
"Jealous," "curse," "vengeance," "anguish,"
"Terror," "mourning," and then: "rapture."
And then "galaxies!" Oh.
So my face is my words.
(ADNAN *looks at the audience*)
Look my face.
Here it is.
(*He shrugs*)

THE LETTER

(ADNAN *holds a letter*)
I have a friend.
Before, I didn't know her well.
But since we are both struck by lightning,
She's family to me.
Her name is Diane.
She's 'phasic, like me.

You know, "aphasia?"
It's another word.
It's Greek.
Tragedy.
And some comic.

I like to laugh.
Laughing, it's "infectious."

Listen.
It's a letter.
It's a letter to me.
  (ADNAN *reads the letter*)
"My dear friend. You ask me to tell you what happened to me twelve
  years ago. It's a long time, twelve years. Since my accident. I remember
  being hit by a car—feeling it bounce off me. Then it was coma. It was
  coma for five weeks. They were not sure I'd wake up. I don't remem-
  ber anything. You know coma, coma—it's nothing—it's just a hole.
  Before I was a model, about pictures. I was a famous model. Isn't that
  strange? One day: an accident, and I woke up part of the aphasia
  family."
  (He stops reading)
It's true.
Diane, she's family.
Rest of world—it's abstract to me, it's chaos.
It's Greek again: "chaos."
Universe starting from chaos.
Beginning everything, it's chaos,
Coming from water,
Coming to civilization.
Greek: it's islands, from earthquake.

Aphasia, it's chaos again.
Chaos, it's changing direction suddenly.
From nowhere, left becoming right,
Right becoming left:
Switching—confusion suddenly.
It's chaos?
It's civilization?
Which?

Listen, my mind, I have a question.
What is real—
Universe or stage?

Now thinking about planets and earth.
And now: especially theatre.

So here we are.
    (ADNAN *looks at the audience)*
I'm listening.
Now I'm going to tell a story about ghosts.
    (At his desk, his face is lit eerily by the monitor from which he reads the
    text)
I'm haunted by ghosts.

Ghost has nothing to do with time.
We have different time from ghost.
Ghost has no substance.
Ghost trembles.
Ghost vibrates fast.
Ghost disappears.
It comes,
It goes.
Maybe it's reborn.
Ghost lives in this world
Because there is only this world.
But maybe ghost goes to other planets.

It's mysterious . . .
Ghosts hovering . . .
A ghost doesn't need to dwell in a house.
A ghost is hovering.

If a ghost speaks inside your head,
Do you obey that ghost?
I am rebellious.
I argue with the ghost.

Jean-Paul Sartre, he says to me:
"Adnan, whooo, whooo,
Keep your mind on the ball.
Stop dreaming, whooo, whooo.
Adnan, stake your life to *some*thing, whooo, whooo.
Commit yourself, Adnan, whooo, whooo."
"To what, Jean-Paul?
To what should I stake my life?"
But Jean-Paul, he just says "Whooo, whooo . . ."
And then, he flies away.
He's funny, Jean-Paul.

One ghost—she's a woman I knew thirty years ago—
—her name is Susan Dye.
She died from a brain tumor.
Surgeons put dye right in her brain.
I don't understand that.
Her brain, it turned red.
She had so much pain.
Sometimes, Susan Dye, the ghost,
Talks to me through the pain in my neck.
I'm thinking about the neck.
When a wolf loses a fight with another wolf,
He exposes his neck.
It's vulnerable, the neck.
   (ADNAN *stretches his neck, approaching it with his hand as if with a knife*)
One touch, and that's it.

THE MALL

   (*Slightly comical, simple music as* ADNAN *walks to the "mall" part of the stage*)
Every afternoon walking Santa Monica, the mall.
What's meaning, the word "mall?"
It's street?
On the street—I'm looking at everyone's face.
   (ADNAN *examines the audience*)

It's incredible, faces.

(ADNAN *sees the violinist*)

One guy, he's playing music.

It's violent—no, it's violin.

—"Violin," and "violent," it's similar.

You see, I can't talk well—

He's wanting money in cup.

He's flat in the key of violin.

But later I find myself walking back,

And giving him two dollars.

I don't know why.

It was Mozart.

(ADNAN *walks*)

California, really, it's funny.

One person is talking, talking, talking,

Babble, babble, babble,

And the other person is answering, always "Hmm."

(*He nods his head, as if responding*)

"Hmm."

"Babble, babble . . ."

"Hmm. Hmm. Great, great."

"Babble, babble."

"Hmm. Hmm. Great, great."

"Babble, babble."

"Hmm. Great, great."

(ADNAN *shrugs*)

It's funny.

(ADNAN *points*)

She her, see her over there?

She's young.

She's not beautiful, but almost: pretty

One day a guy, rich, maybe banker,

Coming sexually to her: "Hello."

And she's smiley, "Hello,"

And puts her hand on his shoulder,

And a hand around his waist:

She's taking his wallet!

It's true.

I saw it.

She's pickpocket!

Sometimes, myself wanting to shout on street,
Like crazy person:
"Earth, it's beautiful,
Earth, it's too beautiful.
Watch out, watch out!
Earth, it's dangerous."
But shouting to whom?
To you, my friends.
Who else?
Through the pastry window, I see the cook.
He's working there at the oven.
The cook and myself
We wave through glass,
But we never talk.

That man and that woman
Do not see me.
They are looking in the window of a store.
He calls her Lisa.
Lisa is talking, talking, talking.
Lisa is a liar. I see lying in her face.
Lisa lies so much
She forgets she is lying.
Meanwhile her friend is daydreaming.
His fantasy: to live in the jungle,
To be Tarzan.
But really he works in an office.

What's a curse?
A curse means you are stuck.
You will never be different,
Never grow,
Never change from right now.
That's a curse.

I love to eat.
I like eating in Ethiopian restaurant
With my friends.
Many people's conversation to me, it's babble, of course,
—Like Tower of Babble—
But I like to listen
By watching faces.

I have a friend.
His name is Fred Graves.
It's a serious name.
It's dark.
He could be Fred Dark,
Fred Coffin,
Fred Catastrophe,
Fred Cataclysm,
Or Fred Earthquake.
But he's very happy, really.
He's coming from satellite—
No—I mean Seattle. Seattle.
But now, Fred, he's living in Venice.
Telling Fred: I'm scared of dying.
Freddy, he says to me:
"Adnan, it's not so bad,
So die, already."
It's good advice.
Fred, he's funny.
   (ADNAN *walks*)

SUNSET

Some days, going home,
Seeing sunset from pier,
And seagulls flying.
   (ADNAN *listens*)
I'm listening.
It's evening.
Light.
Lights.
Stars.
Sky.
And seagulls flying.
   (ADNAN *listens*)
I'm listening.
It's new to me,
Watching stars:
Planets, for instance:
There are no numbers . . . the planets . . . endless . . .
Like atoms in a piece of shell.
Violently born, the stars—they must be.
Earth born violently:

Everything swirling.
Universe born violently.
It's not so sweet—
Not like California hangaround.
I relish some violence in myself.
Maybe planets inside yourself-myself.
Planet, it's like light from inside.
It's Venus, Mercury, Saturn . . .
   (ADNAN *listens*)
Earth ending—it's going to happen when?
Earth, it's five billion years old.
Myself five billion years old.
   (ADNAN *listens*)
Earth, it's happening again.
I'm listening.
She's throbbing.
Can you feel, she's throbbing?
   (ADNAN *shakes*)
Earth the Mother, she's trembling,
And everyone behaving like it's not happening.
But animals, really animals, they know.
Oh, yes.
When earthquake coming—before—
All animals running away.
Running north. It's true.
   (ADNAN *listens*)
I'm listening.
It's mysterious.
I am living in water,
In air,
On earth,
And sun is fire.

Planets, stars . . .
Planets are on and on . . .
Like seagulls flying . . .
On and on . . .
Endless . . .
Stars . . .
Sky . . .
You know, it's really endless . . .
Endless . . .

More than possible to imagining . . .
On and on . . .
On and on . . .
On and on . . .
On and on . . .
On . . .

(Lights out)